# Probation and Parole in Ireland

## Law and Practice

# PROBATION AND PAROLE IN IRELAND
## LAW AND PRACTICE

VIVIAN GEIRAN

*and*

SHANE McCARTHY

CLARUS PRESS

**Published by**
Clarus Press Ltd,
Griffith Campus,
South Circular Road,
Dublin 8.
www.claruspress.ie

**Typeset by**
Gough Typesetting Services,
Dublin

**Printed by**
SprintPrint
Dublin

**ISBN**
978-1-911611-60-8

A catalogue record for this book is available from the British Library

*Vivian Geiran* – to Paula, Karl, Nicole and Lauren.

*Shane McCarthy* – to Sinead, Clodagh, Keelin, Caoimhe and James.

# FOREWORD

There has been little sustained practitioner scholarship which engages with the institutional practices of the Irish criminal justice system. Such scholarship is obviously critical in promoting understanding of our practices and in safeguarding the values of fairness, legitimacy and accountability. Professional practitioner accounts provide an 'insider' view, the 'in action' understanding of our process and practices. These insights have an important currency in any descriptive or normative conception of the administration of justice in Ireland. They both supplement and act as an important check on more remote, desk-top analyses, anchoring discussion in professional experiences of the circuits of practice, on 'what works', and indeed 'who works'.

This book by Vivian Geiran and Shane McCarthy should be welcomed in that context – as an attempt to provide a comprehensive understanding of the operation of parole and probation practices in Ireland. They undoubtedly succeed in that objective. Both Vivian and Shane have extensive professional experience of the Irish criminal justice system. Vivian is a former Director of the Probation Service, an Adjunct Assistant Professor in the School of Social Work & Social Policy at Trinity College, Dublin, and a current member, as well as a past-President of the Council of Europe's Council for Penological Co-operation. He was Director of the Irish Probation Service and member of the Parole Board for seven years. Shane is a Consultant Solicitor and has served continuously as a member of the Interim and Statutory Parole Board for the past thirteen years. He also serves on both the Criminal Law Committee and the Human Rights & Equality Committee of the Law Society of Ireland. We are very fortunate to have captured their knowledge, experience and professional expertise in this fine book, beautifully produced by Clarus Press. Their work marries the best of scholarship and professional practice, connecting both communities, as well as advancing knowledge through the seamless integration of professional wisdom with comprehensive scholarship.

Decision-making in the criminal process is subjected to different demands depending on the point in the journey. At pre-trial and trial stage, it is heavily shaped by the presumption of innocence — a foundational principle — which demands that the State bear the burden of adducing sufficient evidence of all the elements of the offence charged against the accused, and that the guilt of the accused must be established beyond reasonable doubt. The normative legitimacy of this principle is rooted in the notion that a wrongful conviction is a deep injustice and a fundamental moral harm. Such a consideration no longer applies, however, following a determination of guilt. At this point, the accused becomes an offender. This status alteration has significant legal, institutional and personal consequences. Though an offender's rights are not entirely suspended post-guilt determination, there are necessarily less restrictions on how institutions make decisions, and the accuracy requirement is no longer so tightly defined.

This book examines these decision-making processes in relation to probation and parole. In doing so, the authors first locate these practices in a modern understanding of our criminal justice system The ultimate foundations of the modern understanding of resolving a crime conflict rested on a strong State; specialised and professionalised investigation, prosecution and enforcement: a methodological, objective and reasoned mode of inquiry; a weak accused scaffolded by procedural and substantive rights and the lawyerisation of the criminal process; and a corpus of expert knowledge and an array of penal sanctions to support the desire to normalise of the offender. Criminal wrongdoing was increasingly reconstituted as a public matter to be resolved almost exclusively through a dispassionate prosecution process.

Our modern understanding of sentencing and sanctioning also altered significantly in the late nineteenth and early twentieth centuries. The system became a more 'knowledgeable form of regulation' (with an emphasis on individualisation, the distal conditions of crime, and the creation of a plethora of 'non-equivalent' penal disposals). Alongside the 'generous' — and mostly already won — procedural safeguards provided to the accused at investigation and trial stages, a person guilty of a crime became entitled at conviction stage to have their individual mitigating circumstances factored into any decision about penal disposal. The process came to be increasingly socialised, particularly through the development of specialised and professionalised knowledge that began to be constructed around the offender. This expertise has been referred to by Foucault as a 'whole set of assessing, diagnostic, prognostic, normative judgments' which began to be lodged 'in the framework of the penal judgment'. Normalisation, regulation, intervention, individualisation, a 'whole machinery' of 'subsidiary authorities' and experts — probation officers, social workers, educationalists, criminologists, psychiatrists, counsellors, psychologists — began to generate a 'corpus of knowledge, techniques, scientific discourses' around the actions of offenders and the readjustment of their life-courses.

Framing the discussion in this way provides a very good context for their discussion of risk assessment instruments in sentencing, probation and the parole process. A very good examination of probation work is also provided in the book, demonstrating how professional practice has moved on from an 'advise, assist, befriend' *modus operandus* to the more complex array of social work practices inherent in the work today. There is also an excellent chapter on community service orders, introduced in Ireland in 1983. In reading the chapter, I was reminded of Deputy Kelly's comments as the Bill passed through the Dáil. Frustrated at the level of legislative and policy imitation occurring, he noted: '[T]his… is simply one more example in the ignominious parade of legislation masquerading under an Irish title ... which is a British legislative idea taken over here and given a green outfit with silver buttons to make it look native'.* That may be so, but this book is a reminder of the sanction's importance and its value as a rehabilitative intervention for offenders. The authors provide an excellent understanding of the manner in which such punishment in the community is articulated, operationalised, practised and understood.

Procedures of restorative justice seek to halt a cycle of offending by vividly demonstrating the emotional consequences of offending behaviour. Part of their attractiveness is their potential to refocus the problem of crime on to the harms caused to individual victims and local communities. By divesting the State of ownership of the crime problem and through dismantling the 'equality of arms' conflict approach, the restorative justice process is designed to empower victims and local communities to give their accounts in their own terms free from the strictures of formal adversarialism. The authors detail the extension of the provision of restorative justice across various stages of the criminal justice system and consider the extent to which it addresses the needs of victims, offenders and society.

The book also offers an excellent analysis of parole, commencing with an examination of *ad hoc* practices through to more prescribed arrangements under the Parole Act 2019. The granting of parole combines many competing interests — those relating to proportionality, individual liberty and autonomy for the offender; those of bodily integrity and privacy for the victim (where applicable), as well as collective concerns about fairness and public protection. The prospect of release and the possibility of review are also important considerations. As one might expect, relevant criteria will encompass the gravity of the offence, the sentence of imprisonment, the period served, the risks of further offending, potential threats to the safety of members of the public, previous offences, the risk of failing

* Dáil Debates, vol 342, col 169, 3 May 1983.

to return to prison on the expiration of any period of temporary release, the conduct of the person in custody, treatment participation, recommendations from relevant parties, the likelihood that leave might facilitate reintegration, substance abuse, educational attainment, and the presence or absence of various 'stakes in conformity'. Various instruments will be of use in making a determination about parole for an offender subjected to a life sentence. These include expert reports, assessment interviews, review of files, risk assessments, psychometric measures, all of which seek to permit an evidence-based diagnostic judgment. These instruments undoubtedly help to make any decision appear objective, value free, rational and fair. The rules, principles, criteria and assessment instruments are very well documented in the book, offering an excellent repository for scholars, practitioners and stakeholders. There is also a very good discussion of other types of conditional release and post-release supervision including supervised early/conditional release, post-release supervision, supervised part-suspended sentence and electronic monitoring.

This book will be an excellent contribution to criminal justice knowledge in Ireland. It will be of interest to a very broad audience, including scholars and practitioners working in criminal justice related areas. It is meticulously researched, and very well written. Both Vivian and Shane are to be congratulated for providing us with a very comprehensive account of the operation of parole and probation practices in Ireland. I am certain that it will be a very welcome addition to the body of scholarship in the field in Ireland.

Professor Shane Kilcommins
Executive Dean,
Faculty of Arts, Humanities and Social Sciences
University of Limerick
21 March 2022

# PREFACE

Probation and parole are two vital components of our criminal justice system. In a quantitative sense, these two parts of our penal system deal every year with thousands of people who have offended, as well as many others affected by or involved in addressing the impact of that offending. Those citizens labelled by society as 'offenders' are frequently defined by their past. It is often said that past behaviour is a significant predictor of future behaviour. Nevertheless, the point has also been made, by Abraham Lincoln among others, that the best way to predict your future is to create it. The reality is that many of us need help along the way to do that — including professional assistance and interventions — and creating new futures can be even more daunting for those bearing the stigma of 'offender.' Practitioners working in probation and parole are facilitators of such change. They are responsible for the assessment and supervision of those members of society who have committed criminal offences and who will be or have been sentenced and subject to court-ordered penal sanctions. The sanctions in question may involve supervision in the community, or custodial sentences, or a combination of both custodial sanction and post-release supervision. Because virtually all probation and parole 'cases' originate in a court and have a legal basis, the boundaries of practice in these cases are set to a significant extent by statute and case law.

Those working in probation and parole bring a range of values, knowledge and skills to bear in their daily work: promoting public safety and community justice, facilitating offender reintegration and seeking to reduce offending and making good the harm it causes. Their work is based on improving public safety and community justice through implementing court orders, holding offenders to account and enabling positive change, while also recognising the rights and autonomy of the individual and their inherent potential. Probation and parole practice is underpinned by established principles of human rights and democracy, professional standards, and the rule of law. This professional practice is also informed by research findings regarding 'what works' and indeed 'who works,' in maximising professional effectiveness. In addition, those working in probation and parole appreciate the significance of the multi-disciplinary aspects of what they do and the overlap of relevant professional disciplines, including those of social work, psychology and the law, for example, and they must learn to negotiate and navigate these professional interconnections to be effective.

Between us, we have over half a century of experience working in the criminal justice system, specifically in probation and parole. Over the course of our time working together, we realised that while there has been a growing body of relevant research and related publications reflecting the evolution of probation and parole in Ireland, there was no single publication or reference work for those studying or practising in probation and parole in Ireland that dealt comprehensively with the Irish probation and parole systems and in which one could find key aspects of relevant law and practice described. In fact, the reality has been that various professionals — including lawyers, members of the judiciary, probation officers, criminologists and others — have had to carry out their own research in order to access even basic facts regarding the practice and legal provisions of probation and parole. In mid-2020 therefore, with this gap in mind and with the needs of the probation and parole practitioner and student to the fore, we made the decision to seek to address the deficit and drafted a proposal for the present book and sent it to Clarus Press. Clarus also recognised the need described and agreed to run with our proposal.

This resulting volume is the first to comprehensively describe and explain the underpinnings and workings of these two key parts of our penal system — probation and parole — in Ireland, for the professional reader, practitioner or student. It should serve as a practical handbook and reference guide for anyone professionally involved in, researching or studying probation and parole in Ireland. Drawing on the authors' extensive experience of working in the criminal justice and penal systems, the book presents a clear description and analysis of the stages and components of probation and parole work. It summarises the relevant legislation, international standards, points to key case law and explores the development of related research and practice and will be a key handbook and essential reading for all practitioners and students of probation, parole, criminology, law, social work, forensic psychology and penal policy.

When we set out on this project, we had yet to fully quantify how extensive the various strands of law and practice literature on probation and parole in Ireland were. That landscape turned out to be even more extensive and disparate than we realised. As a result, it has been both a challenge and a pleasure to bring these various strands together in one volume. That said, we are also conscious that the fields of probation and parole work are continuously developing, as well as being influenced by an ever-expanding range of subject disciplines, legislation, case law and policies. For example, many of the policies of the recently established statutory Parole Board are still being formulated and accordingly that area of practice will require further study in due course. So we are aware that we may not — or in some instances, could not — have anticipated or referenced some important or evolving legal or practice considerations. We look forward therefore to updating this volume, to reflect relevant changes, in due course and would also welcome any feedback or suggestions in that regard from readers.

The authors would like to acknowledge the influence and input of all those who contributed to the production of this book in any way, and specifically all of the colleagues, including probation and parole practitioners who preceded us and those with whom we worked directly or indirectly; all those service users and others impacted by offending who have influenced our practice and thinking; and all those who supplied documentation or pointed us in helpful directions and encouraged us in our research and writing endeavours, both for this book and other related work. From the point where we made our original 'pitch' to write this book, Clarus Press and specifically David McCartney, have been nothing but helpful, encouraging and supportive. Last, but by no means least, we appreciate the patience and understanding of our families, who have endured all that producing this volume has involved for them.

Shane McCarthy and Vivian Geiran
24 March 2022

# TABLE OF CONTENTS

# TABLE OF CASES

# TABLE OF LEGISLATION

**Treaties**



**Other Jurisdictions**

Chapter 1

# INTRODUCTION

## Introduction

The practice of probation and parole in Ireland is over a century old. Many commentators have noted that while all aspects of criminal justice systems and their agencies receive research attention, the field of probation and parole tends to receive less academic scrutiny and exploration. This is probably particularly so in the Irish context. Although other books have included chapters on aspects of probation or parole, and individual journal articles have addressed specific themes or issues in these fields of practice, no single volume to date has attempted to draw together a comprehensive overview of the law and practice in relation to these two important areas of criminal justice work. There has thus been a significant lack in the literature on probation and parole in Ireland, which the present volume seeks to address.

Probation officers and fellow professionals engage with those under their supervision, and motivate them to be accountable in respect of their supervision conditions, progressing on the path to long-term desistance from offending, reintegrating in their communities and making good the harm that crime does. Collectively, those involved in providing, delivering, and managing probation and parole services need, and deserve, the tools to do their jobs to the best of their ability and to maximum effect — in the interests of service users, including victims of crime and wider society. This book is aimed at providing a collection of those vital tools for probation and parole professionals, as well as for those who study in these and related fields.

For the first half-century of probation and parole's existence in Ireland, changes in relevant policy and practice, as well as in their legislative basis, were quite slow — and even stagnant — for long periods of time. The most recent half-century, on the other hand, has been marked with more accelerated developments. A range of new statutes have been enacted, informing probation and parole work, both directly and indirectly. Internationally, practice has developed, with a much-increased focus on community safety and on 'what works' in reducing reoffending and promoting community well-being. From the development of the Risk-Needs-

Responsivity (RNR) model beginning in the 1990s, through the focus on the desistance process, the Good Lives Model (GLM) of practice and the influence of developments in restorative practice, and generally towards implementation of 'what works', 'who works' and evidence-informed practice focused on the 'core correctional practices' (CCPs) required to maximise offender rehabilitation, these recent years have been exciting ones in the evolution of probation and parole practice.

## Who the Book Is Aimed At

This book will be of interest to the general body of probation, parole and legal practitioners, managers and policy makers in Ireland, as well as those studying and researching in those fields, in addition to practitioners and students of criminology, social work, social care, social policy, psychology and related subjects. It will also be of interest to anyone who has an interest in the criminal justice system, and particularly the probation and parole elements of the penal system.

## The Structure of the Book

This book begins with a history of the development of probation and parole in Ireland. It is then structured and sequenced in such a way as to broadly map the journey of the service user — and specifically those who have been accused or convicted of criminal offending — through the probation, parole and related processes, from their first point of contact with the court and penal system, through assessment and supervision, to completion of that journey, whether at the end of a direct, court-ordered supervised community sanction or some form of post-custody supervision period. The chapter headings in the book represent distinct themes and phases of the above journey.

While probation and parole legislation and policy in Ireland is not renowned for rapid change, developments of one sort or another — in law, policy or practice — do occur from time to time on an ongoing basis. Every attempt has been made to ensure that the content is as up to date as possible. Every effort has also been made to 'future-proof' the content, insofar as possible. In addition, the areas of law and practice covered are more detailed than might first appear to be the case. While the authors have sought to include all relevant aspects, priority has been given to describing and discussing the areas of law and practice that generate the higher volumes of activity and practice. Nevertheless, attempts have been made to address all relevant areas, including those where less 'activity' may take place on a day-to-day basis. Summaries of the individual chapters in the book are as follows:

*Chapter 2 – History of Probation and Parole in Ireland* sets out the history of the development of probation and parole in Ireland, beginning as separate but connected humanitarian initiatives and alternatives to the worst excesses of the penal system at the time of their beginning. The chapter includes comparative links to parallel developments internationally, setting the scene for the following chapters.

*Chapter 3 – Offender Assessment* describes the place and importance of assessment of offenders in the criminal justice system, and specifically the assessment of those who are being considered for probation supervision or parole. In particular, the role of structured risk assessment instruments used by probation officers, and their implications for practice, is considered, as are some of the narratives and social constructions around assessment of risk and what that can imply.

*Chapter 4 – Probation Work* explores the meaning, law and practice of probation as the term is understood in three ways: as a specific and immediate form of court-ordered supervision, as an organisational system, and as a wider area of (probation) practice, covering the various elements of the complex array of social work that probation officers do, falling under their general role of helping offenders to become ex-offenders and promoting community safety and social justice. As well as the specific probation laws and programmes in Ireland, relevant international research and practice developments, as well as their implications for probation in Ireland, are summarised and discussed.

*Chapter 5 – Community Service* sets out the 1983 law on community service as a direct alternative to imprisonment, and includes subsequent legislative amendments, and the practice framework that has been developed and managed as a result. Research on the impact of community service in Ireland, suggestions for a possible re-focusing of the measure as a sanction in its own right, as well as creative practice developments are also discussed. In particular, the incorporation of community service work into the innovative Community Return – supervised early release – scheme, and the introduction of Integrated Community Service, among other developments, are explored.

*Chapter 6 – Restorative Justice and Victims* reflects on the increased level of attention paid to the rights and needs of those who have been victims of crime, as well as on the growing popularity and usage of restorative justice and restorative practices more generally in probation practice. Still in its relatively early stage of development in Ireland, restorative justice approaches offer promising opportunities for all those involved in, or impacted by, offending to take part in the processes to address and make good the harm offending causes.

*Chapter 7 – Parole* describes the long history of parole internationally, as well as the establishment of an initially *ad hoc* system of parole in Ireland, up to and including the enactment and commencement of the Parole Act 2019 and what that means for current and future parole practice in Ireland. The changing parole processes, many of which are still being put in place at the time of writing, are also discussed, with the likely future way forward being processed and mapped for the reader.

*Chapter 8 – Other Types of Conditional Release and Post-Release Supervision* deals with the various forms of supervised early/conditional release, post-release supervision, and supervised part-suspended sentences provided for in law and practice. While in the past, sentencing may frequently have appeared to involve a somewhat binary decision between either community or custodial sanctions, in more recent decades there has been a move to increasing the range and use of options for more 'hybrid' sentences, incorporating custodial and community-based elements. This chapter addresses those options collectively.

*Chapter 9 – Children and Young People* addresses the specific legislative and practice provisions for children who have offended. This involves detailed exploration of the relevant provisions of the Children Act 2001, as amended. In terms of practice, approaches to work with children and young people have increasingly been set in the context of the child's or young person's unique phase on the lifecycle and their particular needs related to that stage of development.

*Chapter 10 – Electronic Monitoring* considers the cautious development of legal provision for the electronic monitoring (EM) of offenders in Ireland. Policies and legislation in relation to this measure have considered a number of possible options for the use of EM in offender supervision. To date, just one such context for the use of EM, that of early/conditional release from prison has been used in practice. This and other future possibilities are considered in this chapter.

*Chapter 11 – Other Issues and Challenges* covers a number of issues that impact significantly on probation and parole practice, but which do not otherwise fit neatly under any other chapter heading. The range of issues reflect the complexity of probation and parole work, as well as the importance of engaging the commitment of all of government and of wider civil society in the important work of community well-being, public safety and specifically offender rehabilitation and reintegration.

Where relevant, as well as legal provisions and practice developments, policy statements and positions are also referenced as appropriate. So-called 'soft law' in the form of United Nations and Council of Europe standards documents and similar instruments and their implications for law and practice in probation and parole are also included. Similarly, where specific international connections or developments in probation or parole are relevant, these are referenced and highlighted through the text.

While the book is structured in the context or layout of a pathway or journey through the criminal justice process, each of the following chapters stands alone insofar as it covers a reasonably discrete area of law and practice. That said, as referenced through the publication, many of the topics covered in individual chapters overlap with those in other chapters and where this is the case, readers are pointed to relevant other chapters and indeed other sources, for more information on the topic in question.

## Terminology – Probation Organisation

There can be differences between jurisdictions in the terminology used to describe what we in Ireland may know as *probation* and *parole*. The term parole is probably less problematic, as described and defined in Chapter 7 of this book. The term probation can have a number of different meanings, as outlined in Chapter 4. These complexities are relatively manageable in the present context however, particularly as the relevant organisation is called simply *The Probation Service*. Nevertheless, there have been changes from time to time in what the probation agency in Ireland has been titled, ranging from Probation and Aftercare, through Welfare Service, to Probation and Welfare Service, and finally to Probation Service. Generally, the term Probation Service is used throughout the book, except in places where historical references are quoted and may use earlier terminology. Similarly, the *penal system* is a term sometimes used to describe the prison apparatus alone. The present authors hold the view that the penal system comprehends the entire system of criminal punishment or penality. In the context of this book, the penal system includes the probation and parole organisations, structures and services, as well as the prison system, of course.

## Terminology – The People and the Processes

In a similar way, the terminology we use to refer to various actors in the justice system has evolved and changed over time. There is increasing recognition that the terms and terminology we may have used in the past can contribute to prolonging and even creating stigmatisation and discrimination towards those affected. For example, it was previously routine to call those in custody *prisoners* or *convicts*. Other terms are often used nowadays, including for example: *those in the care of the prison service*. In the probation and parole contexts, commentators historically used a number of terms, including *probationers* and *parolees*. As social workers, probation officers frequently refer in day-to-day practice to *clients*. In some contexts, the same individuals may be referred to as service users, customers or stakeholders.

In general, there is a tendency to move away from labels that carry a descriptor in themselves, such as *offender*, or *victim*. It is more common and accepted now to use terms such as person with a criminal conviction, or person on probation, or person who has been victimised, or a survivor of a crime. Throughout this book, an approach incorporating some flexibility has been adopted in this regard. This is partly to use terminology that appropriately reflects what is being quoted or cited, such as the name of organisations, agencies, persons etc at a particular point in time. More generally, every attempt has been made to use terminology and language that is non-labelling and non-discriminatory as far as possible, while also making reading the current text as easy as possible. Specifically, terms such as *offender* and *prisoner* are used in places where it is easier to do so and where the term accurately describes the person's current context or location. There are also issues in relation to terminology such as *rehabilitation* versus *desistance*, for example. Such issues can arise in the context of concerns about who owns the processes in question. While the term rehabilitation may be clear and understandable to relevant practitioners for example, it can also imply an expert-object relationship. The term desistance on the other hand, implies more ownership by the person being supervised, of the process in question. In all this, the authors are happy to contribute to the relevant debate on these issues, while asking for readers' forbearance in relation to the present text and also apologise for any difficulties arising.

# CHAPTER TWO

# HISTORY OF PROBATION AND PAROLE IN IRELAND

## Introduction

The practices and policies in relation to probation and parole have intersected and developed in tandem for many years, with many of the developments in each area having common geographical and historical roots. Any examination of probation and parole must take due account of their place in the criminal justice and sentencing system, and the rationales pertaining to the latter. To understand contemporary developments in this area, it is essential to provide a historical context to the development of probation and parole, as many of the modern developments in this area are rooted in the theories of the eighteenth and nineteenth centuries.[1] Prior to studying the history of probation and parole it is, however, necessary to examine the rationales underpinning modern systems of punishment.

## Rationales Behind Modern Systems of Punishment

From the seventeenth to the mid-eighteenth century, crime across most of Europe was seen as an offence against the monarch,[2] with punishment based around retribution and deterrence, reflecting the seriousness of the crime, whilst largely ignoring the circumstances of the individual offender.[3] Punishment based on the Biblical notion of retribution being 'an eye for an eye' was consistent with Kant's principle that offenders get what they deserve.[4] However, such punishment was often disproportionate to the actual criminal acts, with public humiliation, torture and death being the most common penalties for offending.[5] Criminal behaviour was essentially seen

1 Andre Normandeau, 'Pioneers in Criminology: Arnould Bonneville De Marsangy (1802 – 1894)' (1969) 60(1) J Crim L, Criminology & Police Science 31.

2 David Garland, *The Culture of Control* (OUP 2001) 30.

3 Shane Kilcommins and others, *Punishment and the Search for Order in Ireland* (Institute of Public Administration 2004) 6.

4 Immanuel Kant, *Metaphysical Elements of Justice – Part I of the Metaphysics of Morals* (Hackett Publishing 1999) xxxvi, 36 and 137.

5 Michel Foucault, *Discipline and Punish: The Birth of the Prison* (Vintage Books 1977) 3-32.

as the product of free will and rational choice.[6] The criminal justice system in this era was largely indifferent to the specific characteristics of offenders, with punishment meted out in precisely the same manner to all offenders.[7]

By the end of the nineteenth century, following the Prison Act 1865[8] which applied to the United Kingdom (including, at the time, Ireland), and the development of penal codes in the UK and the USA, there was a shift towards individualisation of crime and punishment, with the focus changing from the crime to the individual criminal.[9] Punishment shifted from a focus on harsh deterrence towards offender correction, culminating in a rehabilitative model, which was to prove influential for much of the twentieth century. This rehabilitative model, with an emphasis on individualisation, became the dominant criminal justice ideology from the late 1890s to at least the 1970s. This system considered treatment, as opposed to punishment, as being the most appropriate response to criminal activity.[10] The associated ideology was based on the belief that human behaviour is the product of antecedent causes, and that once those causes of behaviour had been identified, they could be treated.[11] Exponents of the "Rehabilitative Ideal"[12] also believed that the punishment of imprisonment should be geared towards the reformation of the offender, not only through fear of being punished again but by a change in the offender's character and habits.[13] Advocates of this theory further believed that the period of incarceration should be used to train the prisoner for a life free of crime, with educational and vocational training and psychological techniques being directed to this end.[14] It should, however, be noted that even though the concept of rehabilitation became widely accepted, what constituted rehabilitation was sometimes variable and the methods employed in attempts to

---

6 Thomas O'Malley, *Sentencing Law and Practice* (Thomson Round Hall 2006) 27.

7 Shane Kilcommins, *The Introduction of Community Service Orders – an Historical Interpretation* (Barry Rose Law Publishers 2002) 142.

8 *Prison Act 1865*, 28 and 29 Vict C 126.

9 Andre Normandeau, 'Pioneers in Criminology: Charles Lucas – Opponent of Capital Punishment' (1970) 61(2) J Crim L, Criminology & Police Science 221.

10 Kilcommins (n 3) 7.

11 Francis A Allen, 'Criminal Justice, Legal Values and the Rehabilitative Ideal' (1959) 50(3) J Crim L & Criminology 226.

12 A Keith Bottomley, 'Parole in Transition: A Comparative Study of Origins, Developments and Prospects for the 1990s' (1990) 12 Crime & Justice 319.

13 Allen (n 11) 227.

14 See David Garland, *Punishment and Welfare; A History of Penal Strategies* (Aldershot 1985). Garland sets out that with the emergence of the 'penal-welfare' complex in the early 20th century came the notion that the offender should be rehabilitated not just in the interests of his own welfare but also in the interests of society as a whole.

encourage rehabilitation also changed considerably over the course of this period. On occasion, academic opinion was critical of confinement in prison as a means of aiding rehabilitation and as early as the 1930s it was stated that 'it is impossible to train men for freedom in a condition of captivity'.[15] Similarly, there was no structured system for the identification of what kind of rehabilitative work would be effective, with early approaches based on a moralistic view of criminality addressed through education and hard work, but failing to appreciate the causes of criminal behaviour.[16] These problems with identifying effective means of rehabilitation led to the rehabilitative ideal being subject to a full scale attack in the 1960s and 1970s, led by a series of technical articles maintaining that 'nothing works'.[17] The 'nothing works' ideology stated that rehabilitative purposes are fine in principle but fail to deliver in practice. The 'nothing works' school supported this view with research showing that, with few exceptions, penal sanctions with rehabilitative elements were no more successful than others in terms of preventing recidivism.[18] This issue will be discussed subsequently in this chapter. However, it should be noted that the rehabilitative model remains a principal ideology in the Irish criminal justice system.

The rehabilitative model developed in a parallel fashion to the emergence of the positivist paradigm,[19] which argued that certain physical, psychological, sociological and environmental factors could weaken an individual's ability to desist from crime.[20] The rehabilitative model allowed judges to choose from an extended array of penal disposals, which facilitated them to select a sanction appropriate both to the offence and the offender — with treatment as opposed to punishment being the 'rehabilitative ideal'.[21] Such approaches also reflect the utilitarian view that punishment has consequences for both society and offenders, and so should not exceed the severity of the crime. As the notable Russian author,

---

15 Alexander Paterson (1884-1947), penologist as quoted in Andrew Ashworth, *Sentencing and Criminal Justice*. (Cambridge Univ Press 2010) 288.

16 Gresham M Sykes, *The Society of Captives – A Study of a Maximum Security Prison* (Princeton University Press 2007) 11. See also Richard SE Hinde, 'Sir Walter Crofton and The Reform of the Irish Convict System 1854-1861 — II' (1977) 12(2) Irish Jurist 333.

17 Douglas Lipton, Robert Martinson, and Judith Wilks, *Effectiveness of Correctional Treatment: A Survey of Treatment Evaluation Studies* (Praeger Publishers 1975).

18 O'Malley (n 6) 39.

19 For a general discussion of these historical developments see Michel Foucault, *Abnormal: Lectures at the College de France 1974-1975* (Verso 2003).

20 O'Malley (n 6) 28.

21 Allen (n 11). For an Irish perspective see Kilcommins (n 3) 7.

Dostoyevsky, said following his own incarceration, 'the degree of civilisation in a society can be judged by entering its prisons'.[22]

The most recent phase or form of the punishment narrative is the 'late-modern' variety, which is based upon the management and control of offenders rather than their rehabilitation.[23] This represents what some view as the death of rehabilitation, with a shift in the aims of punishment away from individualised treatment towards the aggregate control or incapacitation of criminals.[24] These policies, which focus on protecting the public from risk, and which promote incapacitation as a solution to crime problems, can fairly be viewed as being at odds with the politics of solidarity that underpinned the welfare state and the 'rehabilitative ideal'.[25] This concept of the 'rehabilitative ideal' will be explored subsequently in this chapter and throughout this book.

## The Purpose of Punishment

It has been suggested that punishment must serve a number of core goals, but we must also question what purpose punishment serves in meeting the needs of both society and victims on the one hand, and the individual offender, on the other.[26] The preference for one theory of punishment over another is often the product of a personal value system or a prevailing political ideology.[27] Punishment, in the criminal justice context, thus involves a consideration of the following potential objectives, singly or in combination:

(a) **Retribution**: Retribution rests on the theory of just deserts and that the guilty should be punished;[28] punishment under this approach should be proportional to the offence. Retribution resides in the community's desire 'to express its repudiation of the crime committed, and to establish and assert the welfare of the community against

---

22 Fyodor Mikhailovich Dostoyevsky, *The House of the Dead* (Penguin Classics 1985). See also Parole Board. Annual Report (2017) 3, where the Parole Board quotes Nelson Mandela as stating '[a] Nation should not be judged by how it treats its highest citizens, but its lowest ones.'

23 Gwen Robinson, 'Late-Modern Rehabilitation: The Evolution of a Penal Strategy', (2008) 10(4) Punishment & Society 430.

24 David Garland (n 2) 75-102.

25 ibid 127. See also Allen (n 11).

26 Stanley A Cohen, 'An Introduction to the Theory, Justifications and Modern Manifestations of Criminal Punishment', (1981) 27(73) McGill LJ 73.

27 Thomas O'Malley, *Sentencing Law and Practice* (Thomson Round Hall 2016) 28.

28 Kevin M Carlsmith, John Darley, and Paul H Robinson, 'Why do we punish? Deterrence and just deserts as motives for punishment' (2002) 83(2) J Personality & Social Psychology 284.

the evil in its midst' as opposed to being 'revenge'.[29] Retribution and deterrence are difficult to defend as drivers of punishment unless it is accepted that the commission of crime is invariably, or mostly, an exercise in free will.[30]

(b) **Deterrence**: Deterrence involves the belief that the imposition of sanctions helps prevent the occurrence of the forbidden act; this form of punishment can act as both an individual and general deterrence. Individual deterrence is based on the assumption that the imposition of a sufficiently severe punishment will deter the particular offender from repeating the same offence or any other offence whatsoever. General deterrence involves the attempt, through a sentence handed out to a particular offender, to deter others from engaging in similar conduct. However, critics have indicated that deterrence is only effective if the offender views the sanction as severe and justified, if they are concerned about apprehension and if the punishment is inevitable.[31]

(c) **Rehabilitation**: This view of punishment considers the penal sanction as a means to correct aberrant behaviour through education or therapeutic adjustment, having evolved from the concept whereby rehabilitation was a religious and spiritual process ('redemptive rehabilitation') to one which has become a highly medicalised and rationalised process ('reformative rehabilitation').[32] It assumes that offenders can be corrected and that rehabilitation is the best way to protect the individual criminal from themselves, and to protect society from the incidence of crime.

(d) **Incapacitation (and protection of the community)**: According to its traditional meaning, 'the protection of the community' means the safeguarding of society through the removal of the offender from the community, either temporarily or permanently. Society is only truly protected in the longer term when there is near certainty of apprehension and conviction upon the commission of an offence, although that has never been the case in reality.

---

29 Jeremy Bentham, *The Rationale of Punishment* (Kessinger 2008), as quoted in Cohen, 'An Introduction to the Theory' (n 26) 74.

30 O'Malley (n 6) 28.

31 Cohen (n 26) 73.

32 James J II Beha, 'Redemption To Reform; The Intellectual Origins Of the Prison Reform Movement' (2008) 63 NYU Annual Survey of American Law 774.

The development of modern theories and practice of punishment represents a history of how society progressed from the barbarism of 'gallows and the lash,' to penal transportation to the colonies and, thereafter, to incarceration as the primary method of punishment. Such developments may be seen in terms of a humanitarian progression from a system based upon retribution to one that eventually came to value offender rehabilitation as an important element of broader criminal justice. One problem that arose in the context of the introduction of rehabilitative efforts in managing offenders was a lack of understanding of crime and its associated processes and *milieu*, which hampered efforts to reduce the incidence of offending. Although re-education and moral adjustment formed core tenets of Victorian reform ideals, it became apparent over time that such models did little to engage with — or even to acknowledge — the various social, psychological and economic factors that foster and contribute to criminal behaviour. This detachment between attending to those who had engaged in criminal behaviour on the one hand without inquiring *why* certain individuals or groups might be more prone to such behaviour on the other, hindered the development of effective rehabilitation. This myopic approach eventually gave rise to the 'nothing works' movement, based on the rather shaky premise that because the strategies adopted did not work for every offender, then rehabilitation itself was not effective and did not work. The 'nothing works' movement appears to be in retreat over recent decades, with an ongoing revival in rehabilitation, including an attendant and much greater focus on a 'what works' perspective.[33]

No one of the four purposes of punishment listed above is pre-eminent or paramount. In fact, any one, or a combination, of the four can be cited as an objective in sentencing in individual cases. Unlike some other jurisdictions, neither the Irish legislature nor the judiciary has ever stipulated that one purpose of punishment must be preferred over the others.[34] On the one hand, this presents rather a muddled arrangement. On the other, it provides the judiciary

---

33 Robert Martinson, 'What Works? – Questions and Answers about Prison Reform' (1974) 35 Public Interest 22. It should however be noted that Martinson subsequently re-evaluated this position in a later less well-publicised article, 'New findings, new views: A note of caution regarding sentencing reform' (1979) 7 Hofstra L R 243. For further discussion see Thomas H Williams, 'What Works? Evidence-Based Practices in Parole and Probation' (2007) J Community Corrections 5-23.

34 O'Malley (n 27) 29. It should however be noted that in 2014 the Strategic Review Group on Penal Policy highlighted that the 'dual purposes of punishment and rehabilitation should be the primary considerations in the imposition and management of criminal sanctions as being in the interests of best serving society, protecting victims of crime and deterring future offending. See

with a good deal of flexibility, which enables the individual circumstances of each case to be taken into account. To be just and effective, the sentencing judge must accommodate these competing demands and also pay attention to not only the interests and need of the collective, but to the offender and victim as well.[35] Having considered the rationale underpinning modern punishment, it is now necessary to examine the process by which an appropriate sentence is imposed in an individual case within the Irish criminal justice system.

**Sentencing in Ireland**

Sentencing in the Irish Court system is grounded in the concept of proportionality. In the case of *People (Attorney General) v O'Driscoll*[36] it was stated that the courts had a duty to pass appropriate sentences in each case having regard to the particular circumstances of that case — not only in regard to the particular crime but in regard to the particular offender.[37] This method of deciding a penalty is focused on the long established notions of culpability, intent and damage done, and is commonly referred to as 'just deserts' sentencing.[38] 'Just deserts' in the Irish context, involves an application of the doctrine through the lens of the principles of proportionality, which allows for greater focus on the circumstances of the offender, whereas 'just deserts', in its purer and cruder form at least, insists that the gravity of the offence should be the dominant consideration, if not the only one, when selecting punishment.[39] This consideration of the personal circumstances of the offender avoids accusations of unfairness which would arise from the application of 'just deserts in an unjust society'.[40] The fact that in Ireland almost all offences carry maximum rather than mandatory sentences means that a sentencing court must calibrate a proportionate punishment according to the gravity of the specific offence and the personal circumstances of the offender.[41] This position was subsequently re-affirmed in later cases such as *People (DPP) v M.*[42]

It is clear that the sentencing policy adopted by the Irish courts

Penal Policy Review Group, Strategic Review of Penal Policy: Final Report (Department of Justice 2014) 8.

35 Cohen (n 26) 75-77.

36 (1972) 1 Frewen 351.

37 ibid (359 per Walsh J).

38 O'Malley (n 27) 33.

39 O'Malley (n 6) 19.

40 ibid 33.

41 O'Malley (n 27) 137.

42 [1994] 3 IR 306.

attempts to balance a number of different aims. The proscribed activity impacts the offender, the victim, the police and the wider community, together with the accompanying phenomena of any injury, loss or damage caused. In theory, the penal sanction comprehends concern for all of these components. As a practical matter, the penal sanction can never completely fulfil its mandate, since the ideals it seeks to serve are fundamentally contradictory.[43] The courts balance, inter alia, the gravity of the offence, the circumstances of the offender and the offender's treatment needs as well as the effect of the crime on the victim. However, that some of these aims may conflict with each other does not appear to have been generally acknowledged by the courts.[44] Balancing these aims may also create conflicts, not only between individual sentencing aims, but may further conflict with the aim of public protection. In addition, sentencing judges should not take account of the possibility of remission or early release when selecting a sentence, as early release is an executive function in Ireland.[45] Having examined the imposition of modern punishment and sentencing practices in Ireland, it is now necessary to examine the evolution and development of the related concepts of probation and parole.

## Historical Development of Probation and Parole

As discussed above, from the seventeenth to the mid-eighteenth century, the dominant form of punishment for a crime was directed at the body, with the gallows, whip, branding tools and stocks being the most common methods of punishment.[46] Although the practice of placing people in custody has a very long history, imprisonment in its early manifestation was mainly a period in 'limbo' where all the suspected offender had to look forward to was the hangman's noose or the lash.[47] Prisons and gaols were also places where someone might be incarcerated pending their payment of a debt. Prisons at this time were generally squalid places where one's detention could be indefinite or at the whim of a lord or king. With the growth of humanitarian ideals, alternatives were sought to the executions, floggings, burnings and mutilations which society had

---

43 Cohen (n 26) 73.

44 Ashworth (n 15) 73.

45 See the cases of *Murray v Ireland* [1991] ILRM 465, *Ryan v Governor of Limerick Prison* [1988] IR 198 and *Dowling v Minister for Justice Equality and Law Reform* [2003] 2 IR 535 for further discussion on this area.

46 Kilcommins (n 3) 3.

47 Sykes (n 16) xxix. See also Normandeau. "Pioneers in Criminology: Charles Lucas" (n 9) 219 where it is stated that as late as 1771, the French jurist Jousse claimed that imprisonment was simply a method of holding the suspected criminal before trial and was not a method of punishment.

used as its response to crime,[48] and it was recognised that such cruel and brutal punishments debased not only the victim but also the society which deployed them.[49]

A frequent alternative to the hangman's noose was transportation. Transportation of convicts from Great Britain and Ireland, initially to America, as a punishment was a feature of the criminal justice system between 1718 and 1775. Between 1788 and 1853, large numbers of convicts were transported from Great Britain and Ireland to Australia, before the practice was discontinued in 1868. Following the discontinuation of transportation, with its attendant replacement by imprisonment of offenders for short or extended periods of time, in their own communities, as well as their eventual release back into those same communities, custodial sentences became, in many cases, the default penal sanction. Over time, the role of prison also evolved to becoming a sanction in which reform and rehabilitation of the offender, through this punishment, became paramount. This focus on rehabilitation of prisoners gave rise to the concept of parole, in the first instance, and in turn to probation, the latter evolving initially out of a wish to offer a community-based rehabilitative alternative to the prison itself.

Parole was not formally established within the prison system until the 19th Century,[50] at which stage it became embedded within legal frameworks both in France[51] and Great Britain, and subsequently in Ireland due to its connection with Britain.[52] Amongst the numerous administrators and pioneers who were responsible for driving the development of what was to become our modern concept of parole, two individuals feature prominently; Alexander Maconochie, appointed Governor of Norfolk Island Prison in 1840 and Sir Walter Crofton, appointed Chairman of the Board of Directors of the Irish Convict Prisons in 1854.[53] Captain Maconochie was appointed

---

48 Sykes (n 16) xxix.

49 See John Vincent Barry, 'Pioneers in Criminology – Alexander Maconochie (1787 -1860)' (1956) 47(2) J Crim Law, Criminology & Police Science 146, where the developing social unacceptability of vindictive justice is discussed.

50 The word 'Parole' was first used when the system was introduced in America in the 19th century. Up until that point the system had been known by the various names of 'probation-pass', 'ticket of leave' and 'license' with the term 'parole' subsequently being adopted. See Helen Leland Witmer, 'The History, Theory and Results of Parole' (1927) 18(1) J Crim Law & Criminology 24.

51 See Normandeau (n 1) 28, which clearly sets out the strikingly similar developments in criminal law in France at this time.

52 See Arthur Taft, 'Parole: Principles and Practice of a Prison Release Procedure' (1941) NYU PhD Thesis 1, where he traces the history of the word 'parole'.

53 See Sean Aylward and Jim Mitchell, 'Irish Prisons: Past, Present and Future Challenges' (2003) 65(7) Corrections Today 98. See also Mary Carpenter,

Prison Governor of Norfolk Island Prison, an island prison off the coast of Australia. As Prison Governor, he introduced a number of reforms and was the first to propose a system of remission based on the principle that prisoners' liberation should be dependent on their own efforts, not solely upon the lapse of time, and that prison sentences should be reformative in order to prepare prisoners to re-enter and adapt into society.[54] Notwithstanding that Maconochie's system was tremendously successful, with very low rates of recidivism,[55] his reforms were abandoned in early course. However, his ideas for reform were widely publicised and were most favourably received in Ireland by Sir Walter Crofton who proceeded to refine and improve the implementation of the rehabilitative principles espoused by Maconochie.

In 1854, Sir William Crofton was appointed as chairperson of the board of the Irish Convict Prisons.[56] The Board designed a system based on three principles to attempt to improve the functioning of the penal system in Ireland.[57] Their first principle was that convicts are better and more properly trained in small numbers, with advancement depending on themselves; secondly, that the exhibition of their training and labour in the community, would induce the public to accept them into communities on their subsequent release; and finally that supervision of released convicts when in the community, involving co-operation between the police and prison governors and utilising technologies such as photography, would act as a deterrent to released prisoners returning to a life of crime.[58] This system effectively represented a penal-welfare system based around individualisation rather than uniform punishment, accompanied by a semi-determinate sentence to accommodate the unpredictable progress of individual prisoners.[59] In addition to the reforms within the prison system, new kinds of institutions also emerged, such as inebriate reformatories for those whose drinking led them to break the law and borstals designed to cut criminality off at its source by treating young adult males.[60]

---

*Reformatory Prison Discipline as Developed by The Rt Hon Sir Walter Crofton in the Irish Convict Prisons* (Longmans, Green, Reader and Dyer 1872) 3.

54 Tim Carey, *Mountjoy–The Story of a Prison* (Collins Press 2000) 74.

55 ibid 3. See also John Clay, *Maconochie's Experiment* (John Murray 2001) 249- 252.

56 Elizabeth Eileen Dooley, 'Sir Walter Crofton and the Irish or Intermediate System of Prison Discipline' in Ian O'Donnell and Finbarr McAuley (eds), *Criminal Justice History, Themes and Controversies from pre-Independence Ireland* (Four Courts Press 2003) 196. See also Aylward and Mitchell (n 53) 1.

57 Hinde (n 16) 135.

58 Hinde (n 16) 135.

59 Kilcommins (n 3) 21.

60 ibid.

Crofton's system was designed to allow prisoners to gradually and progressively earn greater freedoms, prior to an eventual release. This stage was most relevant to the development of the modern systems of parole and probation and was unique to the Irish system, being a testing ground for the self-discipline of convicts before their release.[61] The testing ground provided by this system also had the added advantage of assessing whether or not prisoners had indeed been reformed by their experiences in custody,[62] with this testing taking place in quasi-open prison conditions.[63] As offenders progressed through their sentences, they were granted ever greater freedoms. The moral control of this system, based on trust, was described as 'more powerful than bolts and bars'.[64] Crofton was adamant that the prisoner's progression to a position of less restraint and greater temptation needed to be very carefully graduated.[65] It has been noted that at the latter stages of their sentences, the prison officers worked actively with the convicts to encourage their progression and were not solely custodians.[66]

'Individualisation' was a key component of the later stages of Crofton's system and he considered it key that the institutions where these principles were being implemented should be small and should not exceed a capacity of one hundred prisoners.[67] The role of James Organ in the developments of this system will be considered subsequently in this chapter, however it is clear that he also was fully committed to individualisation and the reformative effect it had on prisoners.[68] The central emphasis of Crofton's system, and the like-minded thinkers of the time, was reform. This reform was not only aimed at the convict but it also targeted the prejudices the general public held about convicts.[69] Crofton stated that, in his opinion, obtaining employment and gaining acceptance by society greatly reduced the likelihood that released prisoners might reoffend. *A contrario,* in the absence of employment, such prisoners would likely be drawn back to their old haunts, their former associates and, by degrees, resume their original 'career of crime.'[70] From the beginning, Crofton emphasised the importance

---

61 Aylward and Mitchell (n 53) 3.

62 Carpenter (n 53) 296.

63 ibid 35.

64 Carpenter (n 53) 35.

65 Edward Wheatley Balme and others, *Observations on the Treatment of Convicts in Ireland* (Simkin Marshall & Co 1862) 35.

66 Gerry McNally, 'James P Organ, the 'Irish System' and the Origins of Parole' (2019) 16 Irish Probation J 42, 46.

67 Hinde (n 16) 333.

68 McNally (n 66) 51.

69 Carey. Mountjoy (n 54) 76.

70 Hinde (n 16) 143.

of education in reformation of the offender and ensured the engagement of capable school-teachers within the prisons.[71]

In Crofton's system, if prisoners were released on licence, they were subject to strict rules and supervision arrangements until the remaining portion of their sentence – which was to be served on licence — had expired.[72] This was similar to practices in other European jurisdictions where the benefits of supervising prisoners on release were also recognised.[73] This post-release supervision in Ireland involved each released prisoner being visited fortnightly by his supervisor, and detailed reports of each of these supervisory visits were furnished to Sir Walter Crofton. In Dublin, these parolees were supervised by James Organ, the lecturer at Smithfield Prison. Outside of Dublin, local police supervised the conditional release.[74] Where the released prisoner secured employment, it is recorded that employers were generally happy with such supervision.[75] It was noted that the employers providing offers of employment for these released prisoners exceeded the prisons' availability to provide people, such was the acceptance of, and confidence in, the reformative effect of Crofton's system.[76] It is worth noting that, in Ireland, extra care was always taken to ensure that the supervision did not cause the conditionally released prisoner to be recognised in the community as a former convict, though steps were always taken to ensure their employers were aware of that fact.[77]

In Ireland, Crofton considered these post release visits and supervision to be a vital element of his system.[78] In the event of the convict breaching any of the conditions attached to his discharge, or being uncooperative in terms of supervision, the police were immediately asked to intervene.[79] This close supervision encouraged

---

71 Patrick Carroll-Burke, *Colonial Discipline, The Making of the Irish Convict System* (Four Courts Press 2000) 161.

72 ibid 125.

73 Normandeau (n 1) 28 which describes the supervisory system in France in the 1840s and states the advantages of testing prisoners in the community for a certain period of time and at the ordinary tempo of life. For contemporaneous developments in Germany see Hoefer, Friedrich, 'Georg Michael Von Obermaier – A Pioneer in Reformatory Procedures' (1937) 28(1) J Crim Law & Criminology 13. For further discussion of Von Obermaier's system see Eriksson, Torsten. *The Reformer: An Historical Survey of Pioneer Experiments in the Treatment of Criminals* (Elsevier Scientific Publishing 1976) 92.

74 McNally (n 66) 47.

75 Dooley (n 56) 208.

76 Wheatley Balme (n 65) 98.

77 ibid 106, where it is stated steps were always taken to ensure that 'Their origin was unknown to all but their master.'

78 Hinde (n 16) 143.

79 ibid 316.

public confidence in the operation of this system in Ireland, and indeed its success in Ireland was deemed to be as a result of general confidence that the penal system was likely to produce a reformatory effect on those subjected to it. The system was based on the notion that before release, a prisoner should be placed in conditions of comparative liberty and after discharge, he should be in a state of conditional liberty. If the prisoner proved by his conduct that he was not reformed, then he was sent back to prison. Finally, during this period of conditional liberty, the prisoner was subjected to a system of supervision designed to aid rather than hinder them in their honest efforts to do right.[80] Crofton's system was seen as highly successful, which is all the more remarkable when it is considered that approximately 75% of the Irish prison population at the time engaged in Crofton's system,[81] including those who were identified as highly recidivist in their behaviour.[82] Crofton retired in 1862 and 'by the 1890s the last vestiges of his system had disappeared' in Ireland.[83] Despite the disappearance of much of Crofton's system in Ireland, it is acknowledged that he had a great impact on the development of penal philosophy internationally and his ideology was subsequently developed further in other jurisdictions.

Prior to considering the development and evolution of probation and parole in other jurisdictions, as well as in Ireland, it is worth re-visiting the role of James Organ in the genesis of parole and probation in Ireland. In one of his very early reports he set out his role, notionally as the prison teacher, and as someone 'who should act as the parent and the friend as well as the teacher'.[84] He further stated that 'the prison teacher must not only teach — he must convince… Advice, accompanied by sympathy, has a great effect even on the incorrigible prisoner, if prudently and wisely given.'[85] Crofton's commitment to individualisation of prisoners has already been referenced, however it is recorded that Organ sought, in his own words, to 'observe the ways of the prisoners, hear their tales, listen to their grievances and become acquainted with their hopes and fears', to obtain an intimate knowledge of them and to use this to assist and support them.[86] In providing concrete guidance and practical support in the reformation, supervision and settlement of ex-convicts in the community, Organ led the way and provided

80 See Carpenter (n 53) 48. See also Wheatley Balme (n 65) 23.
81 Wheatley Balme (n 65) 40.
82 ibid 40.
83 Carey (n 54) 112.
84 McNally (n 66) 49.
85 ibid 50.
86 ibid 51.

the model for the development of parole and probation and his work is acknowledged as being effectively the forerunner of the Probation Service and its work.[87] His work was also the basis of the subsequent development of parole and probation in America, including the establishment of the Elmira Reformatory, in New York in 1869. The system implemented at Elmira provided for the supervised release of selected, young prisoners, whose time in custody was dependent on their response to training and their behaviour in the institution.[88]

## Early Developments in Parole in the USA

Subsequent developments in parole in America included the establishment, around 1916, of the proposition that there was a need for a close relationship between institutional treatment and parole. In this regard, the belief was established that, from the moment an offender entered an institution, parole should be his objective and the institution should plan to prepare them for it. This preparation for parole included the prison making arrangements for gathering a full and complete set of information about every offender including their personal history before his or her coming to the institution, a history of court appearances and offending behaviour, a study of the offender's family relationships, together with the reports emanating from within the prison system, such as reports from the prison doctor, psychologist, education director, psychiatrist and others.[89] The information gathered was utilised to plan the institutional life of each individual offender within the particular institution where they were serving their sentence.

In 1930, an entirely new system of parole was established in New York, in which the release decision was taken by a single Parole Board, independent of the prison.[90] This newly established Parole Board was also charged with the task of supervising persons on parole. The advantage of this consolidation was that it allowed for greater efficiencies and consistency in the decision-making process. This Parole Board informed its release decision-making process with research and mathematical computations to determine what factors would bear the closest relation to success or failure on parole.[91] Having selected the most important factors, they

87 ibid 57.
88 Bottomley (n 12) 321.
89 Winthrop D Lane, 'A New Day Opens for Parole' (1933) 24(1) J Crim Law & Criminology 89, 99.
90 Taft (n 52) 23.
91 ibid 56, which lists some of the relevant factors as criminal record, family

constructed 'predictability tables' (also known as 'experience tables' or 'expectancy tables')[92] by which an offender's chances of success or failure on parole could be determined and stated in terms of percentages — in other words 'risk assessment'.[93] This risk assessment was also utilised upon release, with the offender being under the supervision of a parole officer and the frequency of contact between the offender and the officer could range from every few days to once a month, depending upon the perceived risk posed by the offender.[94]

The decision as to whether sufficient progress to release the offender had been made did not depend on progress within the institution alone, and the parole board was also furnished with information about the offender, such as his or her habits, activities, associations, reputation, the offence he or she had committed, previous offence history, academic progress and plans and preparation for the future. These factors were considered relevant in determining the perceived risk of recidivism.[95] The subsequent development of more sophisticated risk assessment tools is discussed later in this book.

The practice of parole in America developed further in the 1950s with the introduction of a 'clinical model', which stressed the professional capacity of parole agents to craft treatment programmes responsive to the individual needs of the parolee. A review of these developments in parole illustrates that a significant shift in the manner in which parole operates occurred during the twentieth century. The system evolved from an *ad hoc* local consideration of a prisoner's progress in the prison setting to a more structured process. The latter included consideration of an individual offender's therapeutic needs as well as focussing on the risks each particular offender represented. This process also incorporated a greater focus on the supervision of the offender in the community. Having reviewed international developments in the area of parole in the 20th Century, it is now necessary to examine the developments in probation in Ireland during that period.

---

relationships, kind of neighbourhood in which offender was brought up, work habits, mentality, disciplinary record in the institution, etc.

92 Ernest W Burgess 'Is Prediction Feasible in Social Work – An Inquiry Based upon a Sociological Study of Parole Records' (1928) 7(4) Social Forces 533, where the calculation of the risk for parolees was considered analogous to insurance premium calculations: 'The practical value of an expectancy table should be as useful in parole administration as similar rates have proved to be in insurance.'

93 Lane (n 89) 105. See also Taft (n 52) 56.

94 Thomas G Blomberg and Karol Lucken, *American Penology – A History of Control* (Aldine Transaction 2010) 14.

95 ibid 75.

## Historical Development of Probation in Ireland

Following James Organ's untimely death in 1869 at the age of 46, parole and probation officer duties were discharged, on a voluntary and strictly denominational basis by charitable bodies acting as informal court missionaries. The passing of the Probation of Offenders Act 1907 ended this practice in name only, with the church and voluntary agencies continuing in a personal and visible manner in courts in Ireland until the 1970s, in partnership with a small professional Probation Service, established in the early twentieth century and maintained in the years following Independence. One advantage of the enactment of the 1907 legislation was that it defined the duties of the probation officer, subject to the directions of the court, as being:

> To visit or receive reports from the probationer, to see that he [sic] observes the conditions of the order, to report to the Court as to his behaviour, and to advise, assist and befriend him, and, where necessary to try and find him employment.[96]

The Probation of Offenders Act 1907 remains the principal legislation in the work of the Probation Service up to current times. This is not to say, however, that there have not been changes in practice.

Probation practice in Ireland changed little in form and content from the earliest years of the service until the 1960s.[97] Up to the 1960s the service was limited in size, capacity and operations.[98] In 1964, Charles Haughey, then Minister for Justice, announced the appointment of two prison welfare officers to be 'responsible for advising ordinary prisoners on personal and domestic problems, for helping them to secure employment and for the giving of after-discharge counsel and advice'.[99] In 1969, a report was commissioned to examine the Probation and After-Care Service and also being tasked with making recommendations for feasible and necessary improvements to the service. Even though this report remains unpublished it is seen as having had a pivotal and critically important role in kick-starting the development of the Probation

96 Probation of Offenders Act 1907, s 4.

97 Gerry McNally, 'Probation in Ireland: A Brief History of the Early Years' (2007) 4(1) Irish Probation Journal 5, 17.

98 Gerry McNally, 'Probation in Ireland, Part 2: The Modern Age, 1960s to 2000' (2009) 6 Irish Probation Journal 187.

99 Martin Mansergh, *The Spirit of the Nation: The Speeches of Charles J Haughey* (Mercier Press 1986) 40.

Service to what it has become.[100] This report outlined an expansive vision and detailed plan for a nationwide service working with adult and juvenile offenders. It proposed a national service based on a regional structure, and outlined the tasks and duties of officers in relation to courts and prison releases.[101] The old Service had been run on an *ad hoc* basis with little direct management, few changes in practices or tasks, little developed policy or practice guidelines and an apparent disregard for, and lack of interest in, the operation or practice of probation elsewhere.[102] The new service that emerged in the 1970s and beyond represented a major break with the past, with the first evidence of a new planned and structured approach.[103] This approach towards a more professionalised service resulted in a very rapid expansion of the service through the late 1970s and the mid-1980s. However, it must be emphasised that the service has not yet been established on a statutory footing, although it does operate largely independently of the Department of Justice on a day-to-day basis.[104]

Over the years the service would be known at different times as the 'Welfare Service of the Department of Justice' and the 'Welfare and Aftercare Service' before changing to the 'Probation and Welfare Service' in 1979,[105] before being formally settled as the 'Probation Service' in 2011.[106] Despite these changes in nomenclature, and new legislation and new responsibilities arising over the years, the Probation of Offenders Act 1907 remained, and still remains, the core mandate of the service. The 1907 Act laid down a primary function of the probation officer as being to 'advise, assist and befriend' the offender.[107] This definition reflected the original charitable ethos of the role, however over time it has been acknowledged that 'the practice of social work has become more scientific'[108] and the growth in the complexity of the probation system has resulted in a need for

100 McNally (n 97) 190.

101 ibid 191.

102 ibid 196.

103 ibid 196.

104 Vivian Geiran, 'The Development of Social Work in Probation', in Noreen Kearney and Caroline Skehill (eds), *Social Work in Ireland: Historical Perspectives* (Institute of Public Administration 2005) 77, 78.

105 McNally (n 97) 20.

106 See Criminal Justice (Community Service) (Amendment) Act 2011, s 13 which states that 'officers of the Minister assigned to perform functions in the part of the Department of State for which the Minister is responsible commonly known as the Probation and Welfare Service before the coming into operation of this section shall, on and after that date, be known as the Probation Service and, references in any enactment to the Probation and Welfare Service of that Department of State shall be construed accordingly.'

107 Geiran (n 104) 84.

108 Report of the Departmental Committee on the Social Services in the Courts of

much greater formal training and education. Although the work of the probation officer has been extended in various ways over time, the role as defined in the 1907 Act remains the founding and enduring definition of probation work in Ireland.

The 1907 Act, reflecting the social, political and judicial values of the late nineteenth and early twentieth centuries, was however increasingly interpreted in its broadest terms to facilitate innovation and developing practice as well as to accommodate and support evolving government and service priorities.[109] The role of the probation officer has historically involved providing offender assessment reports to courts and supervising those placed on supervision orders. Historically, supervision was more often than not carried out in a manner based on the probation officer's own individual skills and experience, as opposed to in any structured, or organisationally consistent fashion. Over time, this role developed to include the assisting of offenders in custody and also the supervision of offenders nearing the end of their sentences on temporary release in the community, under the provisions of the Criminal Justice (Temporary Release) Act 1960.[110] The 1960 Act will be discussed in greater detail later in this book, as it is core to the operation of early release and resettlement of prisoners and specifically to the operation of the parole system in Ireland. With increased requirements for probation officers to have professional qualifications at recruitment, allied to provision of in-service training programmes, and the development of evidence-based research internationally, over more recent decades in particular, approaches to the delivery of probation supervision in Ireland have evolved to reflect these enhanced and evolving professional approaches.

The absence of fundamental legislative reform has not prevented the Probation Service from continuing to evolve and develop new practices and programmes, including those informed by family therapy, systems theory, community development approaches, 'what works' theory and cognitive behaviour programmes, needs and risk assessment and restorative justice schemes.[111] Many of these developments arose from the restructuring following the 1969 report and the increasing public and political interest in criminal justice and social policy issues. In the 1960s, 1970s and into the

Summary Jurisdiction (1936) as quoted in Ken Pease, 'The Probation Career of Al Truism' (1999) 38(1) Howard J Crim Justice 2, 3.

[109] McNally (n 97) 22.

[110] McNally (n 98) 204.

[111] ibid 205.

1980s, the focus in penal reform was the pursuit of alternatives to custody, reflecting the centrality of imprisonment and prisons in sentencing and penal policy narratives. It was to be some years later before community sanctions would earn acknowledgement and positive recognition as preferred first options in penality, and before custody was, in principle at least, to be considered only as a last resort.

It must be remembered that, as with social work generally, probation in Ireland and Britain has its shared roots in charitable voluntary work, which became professionalised over time. The Probation Service has a long tradition of community engagement in service delivery, rooted in the principles of community-based voluntarism. Many programmes for offenders which have been supported and funded through the Probation Service have been done in partnership with local communities with management committees including voluntary and community representation.[112] The work of probation officers has evolved and the supervision of offenders with addictions, incorporating practical partnerships with appropriate treatment services and engagement with communities, have proved to be a major area of work for the Probation Service. Prior to the 1960s, serious alcohol abuse and related behaviour and impoverishment were acknowledged and persistent social problems in Ireland. These were everyday social problems and challenges for the probation officers in dealing with courts, communities and families from the earliest establishment of probation systems and legislation in these islands. The explosive development of wider drug misuse from the 1970s onwards and its impact on offending and the criminal justice system, proved a significant challenge for the Probation Service and served as a further catalyst for change and development in this area.[113]

Since the 1970s there have been various reports highlighting the central role that probation should play in the criminal justice system by providing alternatives to custody. These reports have generally strongly supported the work of the Probation Service, however the recommendations contained in these reports have often been delayed in implementation and there has frequently been a failure to provide proper resourcing to implement the recommendations.[114] In one of these reports, 'the Whitaker Report',[115] the Committee of

[112] Geiran (n 104) 81.
[113] McNally (n 98) 213.
[114] ibid 210.
[115] Committee of Inquiry into the Penal System Report (The Stationery Office 1985).

Inquiry into the Penal System provided a comprehensive review of the penal system and established a wide-ranging outline of principles and recommendations to direct and govern penal policy and practice. The Report stated that '[a] progressive strengthening of the Probation and Welfare Service is essential for more effective and extensive use of alternatives to custody.'[116] This report also illustrated the symbiotic relationship between the work of the Probation and Welfare Service and the functioning of a parole system with the Report recommending the establishment of a Sentence Review Group (SRG), which will be discussed later in this chapter.[117] Before further examining the overlap between parole and probation in Ireland it is necessary to first examine the specific development of parole in Ireland.

## Parole in an Independent Ireland

Ireland's independence from the United Kingdom under the 1922 Anglo-Irish Treaty had little material effect, initially, on the management of prisons in Ireland.[118] Within the prisons, the regime for ordinary prisoners was little different from that which went before under British rule, being governed by prison regulations promulgated by the General Prisons Board in 1895, 1902 and 1915. This situation continued until the introduction of the Prison Rules in 1947, a development which merely consolidated the existing rules dating back to the Prisons Act of 1826 in a conservative and unimaginative fashion.[119] There were, however, some changes of personality in certain key positions.[120]

In the thirty years from the 1930s to the 1950s, Ireland had virtually the lowest crime levels in the developed world and the only development of note in the operation of the prison system throughout these decades was the abolition, in 1949, of the 'ticket of

[116] ibid para 5.12.

[117] Dáil Debates Vol 401, 12 July 1990, Written Answer of Ray Burke, Minister for Justice to Tony Gregory TD, Question 151.

[118] Aylward and Mitchell (n 53) 4. See also Mary Rogan, *Prison Policy in Ireland; Politics, Penal-Welfarism and Political Imprisonment* (Routledge 2011) 22, where the author Brendan Behan is quoted as stating that when the Free State took over control of the prisons the only change was 'to the badges on the warders' caps.'

[119] Rogan (n 118) 34.

[120] Sean Aylward, 'The Irish Prisons Service, Past, Present and Future – A Personal Perspective,' in Paul O'Mahony (ed), *Criminal Justice in Ireland* (Institute of Public Administration 2002) 574, which gives the example of the position of the Governor of Mountjoy where Sean Kavanagh, the Mountjoy Governor from 1928 to 1962 was an inmate there during the War of Independence 1918 -1921.

leave' system which had prevailed for prisoners who were granted release before the expiration of their sentences on the condition that they had to report to the police on a regular basis. From 1949 on, these individuals were to be released unconditionally.[121] The Criminal Justice Act 1951 provided that the power to remit a sentence could be exercised by the President in all cases and on 'other authorities'.[122] In non-capital cases, this power was delegated to the Minister for Justice, granting him or her the power to remit sentences on conditions as he or she saw fit; a provision which further attempted to humanise prison life by allowing for full or partial remission of sentences when the occasion arose.[123]

By the mid-1950s, a static Irish demography — resulting from a combination of low birth rates, high emigration[124] and very low levels of reported crime — left only three Irish prisons in operation with an average daily custody level of less than 400 prisoners.[125] It is further worth noting that in 1954, only one prisoner in the entire system was serving a sentence for over ten years, with the majority of sentences being for three months or less.[126] In 1958, the lowest average daily population in the prison system in the history of the state was recorded, being 369 prisoners.[127] When the Criminal Justice Act 1960 (which created the mechanism for Temporary Release) was introduced, there were fewer than 400 prisoners in jail with 40% of those serving sentences of less than three months.[128] This low prison population was cited as a constraint against acting boldly in terms of penal policy, as the limited number of prisoners, combined with the preponderance of short sentences, did not provide sufficient opportunity to enable 'any training or rehabilitation measures to take effect'.[129] However, this rate of imprisonment hid the realities of the large number of people detained, in most cases inappropriately, against their will in psychiatric hospitals as well as industrial and reformatory

---

121 Rogan (n 118) 76.
122 Criminal Justice Act 1951, s 23.
123 Rogan (n 118) 81.
124 Aylward (n 120) 574 in which he partially attributes the low crime rate to perhaps 'being as a result of the high rate of emigration at this time which removed from the State the young men who would constitute the bulk of the prison population in every country.'
125 Aylward and Mitchell (n 53) 4.
126 Rogan, *Prison Policy in Ireland*, *supra* n 118 at 80.
127 ibid 83.
128 Thomas O'Malley, 'The Ends of Sentence: Imprisonment and Early Release Decisions in Ireland.' Paper delivered at Fitzwilliam College, Cambridge, June 2008. The paper was later published in Nicola Padfield, Dirk Van Zyl Smit, and Frieder Dünkel (eds), *Release from Prison: European Policy and Practice* (Willan Publishing 2010) 246.
129 Rogan (n 118) 84. See also 26 March 1957, Dáil Debate, Vol 161, Col 233.

schools,[130] which housed sixty times more inmates than the entire prison system during this era.[131] The closure of many of these industrial and reformatory schools,[132] and the complete overhaul of many of the psychiatric hospitals, led to a dramatic reduction in the total number of people involuntarily detained in Ireland.[133]

Section 2 of the Criminal Justice Act 1960 gave the Minister for Justice power to make rules allowing for the temporary release of prisoners from all penal institutions, for whatever period he or she saw fit.[134] The Act permitted the granting of 'temporary release' rather than 'early release', and it was envisaged that the prisoner would be released for a defined period with the expectation that they would return to prison thereafter, unless granted a further extension. Whilst originally introduced to allow for temporary release on compassionate grounds, such temporary leaves of absence were also advocated as a benefit for long-term prisoners to prepare them for release and possible employment.[135] On occasion, particularly when the prison system has come under pressure with capacity, temporary release has frequently been employed to manage prison overcrowding,[136] however it is proposed in this book to look at temporary release primarily in the context of a flexible, humanitarian and reforming mechanism as it was intended to be under the Criminal Justice Act 1960[137] as opposed to being utilised as a prison numbers management tool.

Section 2 of the Criminal Justice Act 1960 was for many years the sole legislative basis for the entire parole system in Ireland. Section 2, as noted earlier, provides for prisoners to be granted temporary release pursuant to that section, as opposed to being granted 'early release' or 'conditional release'. The Parole Act 2019 refers to prisoners being 'released from custody subject to conditions' and seems more akin to a conditional release as opposed to a temporary release. Following the introduction of the Criminal

---

130 Kilcommins and others (n 3) Ch 3.

131 O'Malley (n 27) 3.

132 The only detention schools for children in Ireland, catering for both boys and girls, are located at the Oberstown Campus, Lusk, Co. Dublin. This represents a reduction from the fifty industrial schools which previously operated in Ireland.

133 Kilcommins and others (n 3) 76.

134 Rogan (n 118) 93.

135 Rogan (n 118) 93.

136 Diarmuid Griffin, 'The Release and Recall of Life Sentence Prisoners: Policy, Practice and Politics', Irish Jurist 53 (2015) 11.

137 O'Malley (n 128) 246, which points out that at the time that temporary release was introduced in Ireland there were only 400 prisoners in custody, 60% of whom were serving sentences of three months or less.

Justice Act 1960, there were no substantial developments in relation to the Irish parole system until 1985, when the Committee of Inquiry into the Penal System published its report ('the Whitaker Report'). As mentioned earlier, this report dealt with the very wide ranging issues facing the prison service at the time and included recommendations for the management of offenders, including some in relation to the Probation Service. One of the recommendations of this report was the establishment of a Sentence Review Group (SRG), which had the purpose of advising the Minister for Justice in relation to the administration of long duration prison sentences.[138] The SRG was established in 1989 as a non-statutory body and all offenders who had served a term of seven years[139] or more of their sentence, were entitled to apply to have their cases considered by the group.[140] This included life sentences but excluded prisoners serving sentences for capital murder. The stated role of the SRG was to provide the Minister for Justice with independent advice on the administration of both long term and life sentences.[141] Prior to the establishment of the SRG, there was no systematic review process for all long term offenders, although some individual cases were considered on an *ad hoc* basis.[142] The SRG acted in an advisory manner only, on a non-statutory basis;[143] with decisions relating to early release remaining within the remit of the Minister for Justice.[144]

A further report published in February 1997, 'Towards an Independent Prison Agency', made a range of recommendations, amongst which was the establishment of a Parole Board on a statutory basis to advise the Minister for Justice in relation to long-

---

138 Dáil Debates Vol 401, 12 July 1990 – Written Answer of Ray Burke TD, Minister for Justice, to Tony Gregory TD, Question 151.

139 Dáil Debates Vol 430, 13 May 1993 – Temporary Release of Prisoners–Written Answer of Máire Geoghegan-Quinn TD, Minister for Justice, to Michael McDowell TD and Jim O'Keeffe TD. The criteria operated by the Sentence Review Group are also set out in *The Management of Offenders – A Five Year Plan* (Department of Justice, 1994) Appendix IV.

140 Seanad Debates Vol 155, 29 April 1998 – Written Answer of John O'Donoghue TD, Minister for Justice, Equality and Law Reform to Senator Kathleen O'Meara.

141 Seanad Debates Vol 125, 13 June 1990, Private Business, Prison Policy, Motion–Speech of Seamus Kirk TD, Minister of State at the Department of Agriculture and Food.

142 Seanad Debates Vol 128, 16 May 1991, Prison Services, Statements–Speech of Noel Treacy TD, Minister of State at the Department of Justice.

143 Seanad Debates Vol 125, 13 of June 1990, Private Business – Prison Policy: Motion where Senator Joe Costello criticised the fact that the Sentence Review Group was not established on a statutory basis, as recommended by the Whitaker Committee of Inquiry.

144 Dáil Éireann, Written Answers of Michael McDowell TD, Minister for Justice, Equality and Law Reform, Prison Sentence Management, 9 October 2002.

term prisoners.[145] This recommendation matched developments in many other jurisdictions, where parole was being transformed from a political, discretionary and informal process to an increasingly formalised and judicial one.[146] Further encouragement to establish a Parole Board came from the High Court in the case of *People (DPP) v Finn*[147] where Keane CJ suggested that the Government might consider setting up a statutory Parole Board.[148] The Minister for Justice subsequently announced his intention to establish a statutory Parole Board, establishing same in the first instance on an administrative basis.[149] On 6 December 2000, the Taoiseach informed Dáil Éireann of the Government's intention to bring forward legislation to establish an Interim Parole Board and on 7 December 2000, the Minister for Justice confirmed that it was intended to firstly establish the Interim Parole Board on an interim administrative basis, to draw on its operational experience prior to proceeding to place same on a statutory footing.[150] For over twenty years from its establishment, the Interim Parole Board was not placed on a statutory footing and continued to act in that 'interim' capacity. Following the passing of the Parole Act 2019, a statutory Parole Board was established in 2021. The operation of this statutory Parole Board will be considered in subsequent chapters. Having reviewed the development of both parole and probation in Ireland it is now necessary to briefly examine the overlap between parole and probation in Ireland.

## The Overlap between Parole and Probation in Ireland

In recent times the work undertaken by the Probation Service has included a commitment to utilising an increased range of approaches in working with challenging and higher tariff (including life sentenced) prisoners, as well as with prisoners on intensive supervision schemes that were introduced in the late 1970s and early 1980s. In these schemes, groups of offenders participated in programmes as conditions of their temporary release, under the supervision of a probation and welfare officer.[151] The purpose of these schemes was, through planned and programmed intensive

---

[145] Towards an Independent Prisons Agency: Report of Expert Group (Expert Group on the Prison Service 1997) 7.3.

[146] Griffin (n 136) 2.

[147] [2001] 2 IR 25.

[148] ibid 46-48.

[149] Dáil Debates Vol 528, 12 December 2000, Written Answer of John O'Donoghue TD, Minister for Justice, Equality and Law Reform to Paul Connaughton TD.

[150] Dáil Debates, 6 November 2001, Vol 543(2), Col 700, John O Donoghue TD, Minister for Justice, Equality and Law Reform.

[151] McNally (n 98) 214.

contact, to initiate and support positive behaviour change and enable participants to establish a law-abiding career in their communities. A further task increasingly undertaken by the Probation Service has been providing pre-sentence reports and supervision in cases of higher tariff and higher risk offenders. This role involves delivering effective and accountable reports and supervision.[152] Both of these roles are linked to, and are directly comparable with, the supervision of prisoners who are granted temporary release by the Minister for Justice as well as those who have been granted a parole order by the Parole Board. This type of supervision will be examined in greater detail later in this book, as will the Probation Service involvement in various schemes provided for higher tariff and higher risk (of reoffending and of causing harm) offenders, including for example a range of intensive supervision programmes such as those at the Bridge Project and comparable programmes, as well as more recently via the Joint Agency Response to Crime initiatives, among others.

The increasing role of the Probation Service in managing offenders in the community was envisaged in 'The Management of Offenders: A Five-Year Plan'.[153] This report proposed an expanded role for the management of higher tariff offenders by the Probation Service in the community and other supervised sanctions. This report stated:

> It is essential ... to provide... the development of a system by which suitable offenders at an appropriate stage of their sentence may be released back into the community, under the supervision of the Probation and Welfare Service.[154]

It must be noted, however, that legislative change has not kept pace with the expanding role of the Probation Service in practice and service delivery. Notwithstanding all of the modern developments in the role and function of the Probation Service, it is worth reiterating that the Probation of Offenders Act 1907 remains fundamentally unchanged in Ireland. The enduring nature of the Probation Act 1907 has created other difficulties. An example of a lacuna in this area, when considering the current role and function of the Probation Service, is that whilst the 1907 Act allowed for the supervision of offenders, it did not make formal provision for pre-sanction reports, nor indeed is there formal provision for risk assessment reports for the Parole Board (save that the Parole Act 2019 gives the Parole Board the power 'to direct that a report in

---

152 ibid 215.
153 Department of Justice, *The Management of Offenders – A Five Year Plan* (1994).
154 ibid para 5.6

writing in respect of the relevant person be prepared and furnished to it by or on behalf of … the Probation Service').[155]

This legislative development once again illustrates the overlap and interconnection between the Probation Service and the Parole Board in the discharge of their respective functions. The main overlap between the respective functions of these two bodies will however be in the area of supervision of parolees in the community. The Probation of Offenders Act 1907 gave Probation Officers a supervisory role in relation to certain offenders and one of their duties was to bring the offender before the court for punishment if the offender 'showed themselves undeserving of the leniency that had been shown him.'[156] The Parole Act 2019 places similar duties on parolees, who would be supervised by probation officers and provides that the Parole Board can revoke a parole order where it is satisfied certain conditions attached to their parole have been breached or the parolee is posing an undue risk to the safety and security of the public. These applications to revoke parole can be made by certain categories of persons/bodies including the Probation Service. These applications will clearly show a need for a balance to be struck between the caring side of social work and its controlling one and it is envisaged that further policies and procedures will need to be developed by the Probation Service detailing the manner in which it will exercise its powers in this regard.

This, however, is merely one of the balancing exercises undertaken by probation officers in their dealings with probationers and parolees. Another example of a choice is deciding where to allocate resources — should there be an emphasis on those deserving of leniency, such as young offenders or less serious offenders, or should the emphasis be placed on the need to manage those perceived as dangerous and at risk of causing harm through reoffending? This debate will undoubtedly be influenced by the role envisaged for the Probation Service in the Parole Act 2019, as well as through the provisions of the Community Sanctions Bill 2014, when enacted.[157]

---

[155] Parole Act 2019, s 13(2)(c).

[156] Memorandum Issued by the Secretary of State for the Home Department with Reference to the Probation of Offenders Act 1907 (Cd 3981) (1908).

[157] A Criminal Justice (Community Sanctions) Bill with revised Heads was included in the Legislation Programme–Autumn Session 2021 (Office of the Government Chief Whip, 28 September 2021).

## Conclusion

This chapter charted the development and evolution of probation and parole in the modern criminal justice landscape. This mapping of the origins and developments in parole and probation allowed a clear understanding of the dimensions and scope of parole and probation and detailed why and how they developed. This chapter also conducted an examination of the history and development of modern punishment in the criminal justice system. This examination of the development of modern punishment allowed for a contextual understanding of the positions of parole and probation within the criminal justice system. In studying the development of modern punishment, it was examined how society moved forward from the barbarism of 'gallows and the lash,' as the primary modes of punishment, to the eventual adoption of incarceration as the primary method of punishment. These developments represented a social humanitarian shift from sanctions heavily weighted to retribution, to a system which eventually came to value the rehabilitation of offenders as an important element of the criminal justice system. Effective rehabilitation was also shown to require an understanding of the social, psychological and economic factors that promote criminality and this chapter engaged with the 'nothing works' and subsequent 'what works' debates in this area, issues which will be discussed in greater detail in subsequent chapters. This chapter also examined the manner in which sentences are imposed in Ireland, with particular emphasis on the principle of proportionality when deciding on the appropriate sentence for an individual offender.

This chapter also examined the history and the evolution of the concepts of parole and probation. In this regard, early pioneers in the development of parole and probation, such as Alexander Maconochie, Sir William Crofton and James Organ were highly influential. Their systems, where prisoners were required to demonstrate an ability to resist temptation and were afforded the ability to earn ever increasing trust and freedom, were a clear component in the early development of the rehabilitative model. These systems were designed to give prisoners hope, as well as an opportunity to change, and encouraged prisoners to adopt co-operative behaviour and to engage fully in the rehabilitative opportunities available to them in the custodial setting. These aims of parole and probation remain as relevant today as they were in the times of Maconochie, Crofton, Organ and similar pioneers in this field. The modern systems of parole and probation are clearly recognisable from the systems developed by those pioneers, albeit in a more refined form, and with a greater emphasis on the concept of risk and its management and with a primary focus on reducing risk of reoffending, as well as on offender reintegration in society.

This chapter examined the non-statutory nature of both the Irish Parole Board (in its 'interim' form) and of the Probation Service and the early frameworks out of which the role and purpose of both the Parole Board and the Probation Service evolved. This chapter also briefly examined the recent placing of the Parole Board on a statutory basis, an issue which will be considered further in later chapters in this book. It is worth emphasising that many of the recent developments in penology, parole and probation mirror much of the early thinking that was set out in this chapter. It is also noteworthy that many of the suggested recommendations for reform in this area also mirror some of the historical discourse in relation to parole and probation. For example, making prisoners aware of the rules of the parole and probation systems as a means of inducing them to co-operate was a central tenet of Crofton's model. Additionally, Crofton's opinion that obtaining employment and gaining acceptance by society greatly reduced the likelihood that released prisoners might reoffend is an insight which resonates with much recent thinking and will be examined further in later chapters. Furthermore, the manner in which Crofton publicly promoted the rehabilitation of offenders was shown to have greatly contributed to the success of his system in Ireland and fostered a general confidence that the penal system was likely to produce a reformatory effect on those subjected to it. This illustrated that Crofton's reforms were not only aimed at the convict, but also targeted the prejudices the general public held about those with criminal convictions.

Further features of modern parole and probation systems, introduced by Crofton, include the imposition upon the prisoner of strict rules and supervision arrangements until the remaining portion of their sentence — which was to be served on licence — had expired. The issue of the imposition of conditions and the monitoring thereof will also be dealt with in depth in subsequent chapters. It is clear from the foregoing brief review of this chapter that many of the current themes and proposed solutions in probation and parole were also present in earlier, including Victorian times, thus rendering the insights garnered via historical analysis, of additional importance and value.

CHAPTER THREE

# OFFENDER ASSESSMENT

## Introduction

Offender assessment has become a central feature of probation and parole work in Ireland and internationally. These assessments help to inform sentencing and offender case management decisions. While initially contemplated as mainly providing background information on the person being assessed, offender assessments now focus more on estimating risk of reoffending, identifying the factors or issues that may have contributed to their offending, their suitability for a community sanction or parole, as well as the subject's individual and social needs and their likelihood of cooperation with supervision in the community and specifically avoiding further offending. Although assessment reports were not originally contemplated in the foundational Probation of Offenders Act 1907, they soon came to be sought in practice by judges, who identified the value of such assessments in arriving at sentencing and related decisions. Pre-sanction or pre-sentence assessment reports have long since become established parts of sentencing in many cases and even though they are legislated for in other jurisdictions, the majority of such assessments carried out by probation officers in Ireland are not so provided for in statute law, although they have featured in a number of relevant case law decisions.[1]

Offender assessment as conducted by the Probation Service is generally focused on an assessment of risk of reoffending. These assessments are usually conducted as either pre-sentence reports to the courts or are provided to the Parole Board as sentence-management reports. It is now a matter of established Probation Service policy and practice that all 'cases' commence with an assessment, which informs the management of that case. The specific type of assessment used in any case is dictated by the nature of the individual referral, the requirements of the specific assessment and the type of supervision being considered. Such assessments are also provided in cases involving early release or post-release supervision, particularly having regard to the supervision in the community of higher tariff and higher risk offenders, including

[1] For example, *DPP v Linda Mulhall* [2008] IECCA 13, per Macken J.

those granted temporary release following advancement through the parole process. The Parole Act 2019 provides that a parole order can be revoked 'where the parolee poses an undue risk to the safety and security of the public'[2] and where 'the revocation of the order is justified by the gravity of the risk.'[3] It is accordingly necessary to examine what risk is, with particular reference to risk in relation to the probation and parole processes. This will be done later in the chapter. As risk assessment is such a fundamental consideration in probation and parole, this chapter will concentrate specifically on risk assessments in that regard, however the principles enunciated in this chapter are equally applicable to risk assessments conducted in other contexts. While it is necessary to consider critical questions — such as 'what is risk?' — relevant international standards will be outlined in the first instance.

## International Standards

The importance of offender assessment in the context of deciding on and managing community sanctions, has been recognised by both the United Nations (UN) and the Council of Europe (CoE). Although not addressing the theme in great detail, the UN's 'Tokyo Rules'[4] state that:

> 3.2 The selection of a non-custodial measure shall be based on an assessment of established criteria in respect of both the nature and gravity of the offence and the personality, background of the offender, the purposes of sentencing and the rights of victims.

As long ago as 1999, the CoE's Recommendation on prison overcrowding[5] stated that:

> 22. In order to make community sanctions and measures credible alternatives to short terms of imprisonment, their effective implementation should be ensured, in particular through:

2 Parole Act 2019, s 33(1)(a)(i).

3 Parole Act 2019, s 33(1)(b).

4 United Nations Standard Minimum Rules for Non-Custodial Measures (The Tokyo Rules), adopted by General Assembly resolution 45/110 of 14 December 1990.

5 Council of Europe, Recommendation N° R (99) 22 of the Committee of Ministers to member States concerning Prison Overcrowding and Prison Population Inflation.

- the provision of the [appropriate] infrastructure...; and
- the development and use of reliable risk-prediction and risk-assessment techniques as well as supervision strategies, with a view to identifying the offender's risk to relapse and to ensuring public protection and safety.

A decade later, the Appendix to the CoE's European Probation Rules defined offender assessment as follows:

> Assessment means the process of estimating the risks, needs and strengths of an offender before planning an intervention and/or providing advice to judicial or other competent authorities. In addition, assessment seeks to identify the causes of offending, and whether measures can be taken to reduce the likelihood of its reoccurrence.

The European Rules on Community Sanctions and Measures[6] require that the imposition and implementation of community sanctions must be non-discriminatory, while 'account shall be taken of the diversity and of the distinct individual needs of suspects and offenders' (r 6). In addition:

> Rule 22: The nature and duration of a community sanction or measure shall be in proportion to the seriousness of the offence and the harm done to victims, and shall take into account any risks assessed as well as the individual's needs and circumstances.

> Rule 34: Controlling activities shall only be undertaken to the extent that they are necessary for the proper implementation of the sanction or measure imposed. They shall be in proportion to the offence committed or alleged, shall take into consideration the individual circumstances of the suspect or the offender, including risk and needs factors and the rights and interests of the victim. Such activities shall be limited by the aims of the sanction or measure imposed.

> Rule 60: Any conditions or obligations specified in a community sanction or measure shall be determined taking into account the individual's needs and circumstances, and

6 Council of Europe, Recommendation CM/Rec (2017) 3 of the Committee of Ministers to member States on the European Rules on community sanctions and measures.

their risks of reoffending (and in particular of causing serious harm).

The European Probation Rules include a full section on offender assessment, commencing with the point that:

> [Rule] 66. When required before and during supervision, an assessment of offenders shall be made involving a systematic and thorough consideration of the individual case, including risks, positive factors and needs, the interventions required to assess these needs and the offenders' responsiveness to these interventions.

The Probation Rules also require (r 67) that assessments take the offender's 'views and personal aspirations, as well as their own personal strengths and responsibility for avoiding further offending' into account and (r 68) that 'the offenders shall be made aware of the process and outcomes of the assessment. In terms of when assessments should be carried out, the Rules (70) specify that they should be undertaken:

a. at the time of determining the appropriate sanction or measure or when diversion from formal criminal proceedings is being considered;
b. at the beginning of a period of supervision;
c. whenever there are significant changes in the offender's life; when consideration is being given to a change in the nature or the level of supervision;
d. at the end of the supervision measure.

Relevant staff should be trained in offender assessment (r 71), and where standardised assessment instruments are used [see below for more on this, in the Irish context], 'staff shall be trained to understand their potential value and limitations and to use these in support of their professional judgement.' It is important to emphasise, as stated above, that offender assessments, carried out by probation officers and others, have a number of functions and purposes, including informing initial decision-making and also in planning and managing implementation, evaluation and enforcement of community-based sanctions on an ongoing basis. These latter functions are reflected in rr 72 to 87 of the Probation Rules. Such assessments must also be recorded as part of the relevant agency case records (r 88).

## The Council of Europe on Assessment of Dangerous Offenders

Risk assessment and management is covered extensively in the CoE Recommendation on dangerous offenders.[7] This Recommendation provides a number of useful definitions, in Part I (1):

a. A dangerous offender is a person who has been convicted of a very serious sexual or very serious violent crime against persons and who presents a high likelihood of re-offending with further very serious sexual or very serious violent crimes against persons.
b. Violence may be defined as the intentional use of physical force, either threatened or actual, against persons, that either results in, or has a high likelihood of resulting in, injury, psychological harm or death. This definition identifies four means by which violence may be inflicted: physical, sexual and psychological attack and deprivation of liberty.
c. Risk is defined as the high likelihood of a further very serious sexual or very serious violent offence against persons.
d. Risk assessment is the process by which risk is understood: it examines the nature, seriousness and pattern of offences; it identifies the characteristics of the offenders and the circumstances that contribute to it; it informs appropriate decision making and action with the aim of reducing risk.
e. Risk management is the process of selecting and applying a range of intervention measures in custodial and community settings and in the post-release period or in the context of preventive supervision, with the aim of reducing the risk of very serious sexual or very serious violent crime against persons.

The CoE recommendation on dangerous offenders had quite a lot to say about risk assessments and their implications and use in decision making and sentence management, including that (r 13): 'Risk assessment should be commissioned by the judicial authority', and that (r 15): 'The judicial authorities should, where possible, be provided with pre-sentence reports about the personal circumstances of the offender whose dangerousness is being evaluated.' In a specific section (Part III) dealing with risk

7 Council of Europe Recommendation CM/Rec (2014) 3 of the Committee of Ministers to member States concerning dangerous offenders.

assessment principles, the CoE Rules on dangerous offenders provide that:

> 26. The depth of assessment should be determined by the level of risk and be proportionate to the gravity of the potential outcome.
>
> 27. Risk assessments should involve a detailed analysis of previous behaviours and the historical, personal and situational factors that led to and contributed to it. They should be based on the best reliable information.
>
> 28. Risk assessment should be conducted in an evidence-based, structured manner, incorporating appropriate validated tools and professional decision making. Those persons undertaking risk assessments should be aware of and state clearly the limitations of assessing violence risk and of predicting future behaviour, particularly in the long term.
>
> 29. Such risk assessment instruments should be used to develop the most constructive and least restrictive interpretation of a measure or sanction, as well as to an individualised implementation of a sentence. They are not designed to determine the sentence although their findings may be used constructively to indicate the need for interventions.
>
> 30. Assessments undertaken during the implementation of a sentence should be seen as progressive, and be periodically reviewed to allow for a dynamic re-assessment of the offender's risk:
>
> a. Risk assessments should be repeated on a regular basis by appropriately trained staff to meet the requirements of sentence planning or when otherwise necessary, allowing for a revision of the circumstances that change during the execution of the sentence.
>
> b. Assessment practices should be responsive to the fact that the risk posed by an individual's offending changes over time: such change may be gradual or sudden.
>
> 31: Assessments should be coupled with opportunities for offenders to address their special risk-related needs and change their attitudes and behaviour.
>
> 32. Offenders should be involved in assessment, and have

information about the process and access to the conclusions of the assessment.

The Rules on dangerous offenders go on to differentiate between risk management in custody and in the community, the need to balance rehabilitative with restrictive provisions to reduce reoffending, and to incorporate structures to facilitate appropriate multi-disciplinary and interagency working, as well as for assessments and resulting case management plans to be flexible, responsive and subject to regular review.

## Other Council of Europe Standards on Assessment

The issue of risk assessment is also covered in a number of other CoE Recommendations, including those in relation to juveniles,[8] conditional release / parole[9] and restorative justice. The Recommendation on Electronic Monitoring[10] addresses the subject as follows:

> Rule 4: The type and modalities of execution of electronic monitoring shall be proportionate in terms of duration and intrusiveness to the seriousness of the offence alleged or committed, shall take into account the individual circumstances of the suspect or offender and shall be regularly reviewed.
>
> Rule 16: The modalities of execution and level of intrusiveness of electronic monitoring at the pre-trial stage shall be proportionate to the alleged offence and shall be based on the properly assessed risk of the person absconding, interfering with the course of justice, posing a serious threat to public order or committing a new crime.

Risk assessment is also referenced in the standards document in relation to restorative justice (RJ),[11] which requires sufficient time to be given to RJ facilitators in criminal matters to carry out such assessments. The above section illustrates the importance

---

8 Particularly r39.1 and 48.2 of Recommendation CM / Rec (2008) 11 of the Committee of Ministers to member States on the European Rules for juvenile offenders subject to sanctions or measures.

9 Particularly r 7 and r 37 Recommendation Rec (2003) 22 of the Committee of Ministers to member States on conditional release (parole).

10 Council of Europe, Recommendation CM/Rec (2014) 4 of the Committee of Ministers to member States on electronic monitoring.

11 Council of Europe, Recommendation CM/Rec(2018)8 of the Committee of Ministers to member States concerning restorative justice in criminal matters.

attached to offender assessment and particularly assessment of an individual's risk of reoffending, as reflected through the relevant international standards on the subject, all of which point to the centrality of such assessment processes in probation and parole work and structures.

## The Law in Ireland and Offender Assessment

With some notable exceptions, there is a relative lack of specific legislation in relation to offender assessment in Ireland. The Probation of Offenders Act 1907, neither envisaged nor provided for such assessment reports to court.[12] The 1907 Act did however provide that a probation order could be imposed where a Court '... is of opinion that, having regard to the character, antecedents, age, health, or mental condition of the person charged... it is expedient to release the offender on probation...' The Act thus provided solely for the imposition of a probation order, to be supervised – if and as decided by the Court – by a probation officer. The duties of a probation officer, as set out in section 4 of the Act, primarily deals with the offender supervision process. It does, however, include provision (s 4(c)) 'to report to the court as to his[13] [*sic*] behaviour', clearly in a context of updating the court on progress — or otherwise — of the supervisee. That said, the provision of pre-sanction assessments evolved over time, both in the United Kingdom and in Ireland, as their value in assisting sentencing decisions was identified by judges in practice and the latter's requests for such assessments grew, at the same time as probation officers' ability and willingness to provide them developed in parallel. In the British context, such evolution has been analysed and described by McWilliams,[14] and referenced in the Irish context by commentators such as Geiran[15] and Quigley.[16] In the previous chapter, it was pointed out that the Parole Act 2019 gives the Parole Board the power 'to direct that a report in writing in respect of the relevant person be prepared and furnished to it by or on behalf of

---

12 See separate chapter on Probation.

13 That is, the probationer's or supervisee's behaviour.

14 William McWilliams, 'The Mission Transformed: Professionalisation of Probation Between the Wars' (1985) 24(4) Howard J Crim Justice 257-274 and William McWilliams, 'The English Probation System and The Diagnostic Ideal' (1986) 25(4) Howard J Crim Justice 241-260.

15 Vivian Geiran, 'The Development of Social Work in Probation', in Noreen Kearney and Caroline Skehill (eds), *Social Work in Ireland: Historical Perspectives* (Irish Association of Social Workers/Department of Health and Children/ Institute of Public Administration 2005).

16 Etain Quigley, 'Pre-sentence Reports in the Irish Youth Justice System: A Shift to Risk-Oriented Practice' (2014) 11 Irish Probation J 63.

... the Probation Service.'[17] While the majority of assessment reports completed by probation officers are undertaken for the courts, this obligation to furnish assessments to the Parole Board is another important assessment function of the Probation Service.

## Community Service and Children

The Criminal Justice (Community Service) Act 1983 requires a Court considering the imposition of a community service order, in lieu of a prison sentence, to request a probation officer's report as to suitability of the person for community service and the availability of appropriate unpaid work.[18] These community service assessment reports are not required to address issues of risk of reoffending or offender rehabilitation. Section 99 of the Children Act 2001[19] was the first piece of primary legislation specifically dealing with the provision of probation officers' reports to courts. This section of the Children Act requires a court considering the imposition of a supervised community sanction, a sentence to detention, or a detention and supervision order, to 'adjourn the proceedings, remand the child and request a probation and welfare officer to prepare a report in writing,' to assist the court in sentencing and to provide '...information on such matters as may be prescribed, including any information specifically requested by the court.' Such reports must be prepared by the probation officer and presented to the court within 28 days in the first instance, with the possibility of 'one extension of not more than 14 days... on application by the person preparing the report.'[20]

## Assessment of Those Convicted of a Sexual Offence

Section 28 of the Sex Offenders Act 2001 requires a court sentencing an offender for a scheduled sexual offence to consider '...whether to impose a sentence involving post-release supervision' (s 28(2)), and in so doing have regard to:

(a) the need for a period, after the offender has been released into the community, during which his or her conduct is supervised by a responsible person,

(b) the need to protect the public from serious harm from the offender,

---

17 Parole Act 2019, s 13(2)(c).

18 See separate chapter on Community Service.

19 See separate chapter on Children and Young People.

20 Children Act 2001, s 100.

(c) the need to prevent the commission by the offender of further sexual offences, and

(d) the need to rehabilitate or further rehabilitate the offender.

[and that]

(3) For the purposes of this section, the court may, if it thinks it is necessary to do so, receive evidence or submissions from any person concerned.

In sentencing in respect of sexual offences, scheduled under the Sex Offenders Act 2001, 'submissions' as provided for under s 28(3) above might involve reports from professionals involved in the delivery of treatment programmes or similar interventions with the offender at that time. In many cases, they include pre-sanction assessment reports specifically requested by the court from the Probation Service. Outside of the examples above, there is no statutory provision in respect of pre-sanction assessment reports prepared for courts by probation officers. The Community Sanctions Bill 2014 does, however, envisage a clarified role for such assessment reports. At the time of writing, such Bill is yet to be enacted.

## Defining 'Risk'

Risk can be defined as the probability that a harmful event will occur or alternatively, can be understood as a calculation under conditions of uncertainty as to whether a loss, damage or harm will occur.[21] Accordingly, risk is understood in criminal justice as a solely negative phenomenon that is a calculation of the likelihood of potential negative outcomes.[22] Criminal justice is concerned with recidivism risks, the rate and prevalence of offending and reoffending, the seriousness of offending and the harms suffered by individual victims and the public. In general terms the criminal justice system has defined risk as:

- The *risk of reoffending* – will an offender reoffend and what is the probability of this within a particular time scale?
- The *risk of reconviction* – will an offender offend, be arrested and reconvicted within a particular time scale

[21] Hazel Kemshall and Jacki Pritchard, *Good Practice in Risk Assessment and Risk Management 2 – Protection, Rights and Responsibilities* (Jessica Kingsley Publishers 1997) 235.

[22] Anthony Giddens, 'Risk and Responsibility', (1999) ModLRev 62(1) 1-10.

(eg one or two years). This is not the same as reoffending risk as the offender may reoffend but not be apprehended or convicted.[23]

- The *risk of harm* – will the offender commit a harmful (violent) offence, and in particular an offence of 'serious harm'?[24]

Risk is a multidimensional construct, its most common dimensions being its nature, its probability, its severity, its imminence and its frequency.[25] Risk is the probability or possibility that harm will occur; it is not the harm itself. Harm is the impact or consequence of the risk having occurred or the manifestation of the negative outcome which is feared. The term 'danger' describes the actual or potential exposure to harm, and when used about offenders/prisoners it is about the propensity of these individuals to present a risk of harm to others.[26] In essence, the dangerous behaviour and the probability that it will occur are assessments of two different things; the first is about the type of behaviour of concern, the second is about the risk or likelihood that it will take place.[27] The assessment of risk is considered in terms of likelihood (imminence) and impact (seriousness of harm). It is important to understand these two dimensions of risk; some crimes (like shoplifting for example) have relatively little impact or harm but, statistically, are the ones most likely to be repeated. Other offences (for example murder) are unlikely to be repeated but cause serious harm when they are committed.

## Risk and the Criminal Justice System

The assessment of risk has become ever more central to modern criminal justice systems. Risk assessment, in this context, has been defined as: '...the assessment of the likelihood and impact of or harm of (re)offending' and risk management as '...the reduction of the likelihood and/or impact of the risk of offending.'[28] The

---

23 See Ernest W Burgess, 'Is Prediction Feasible in Social Work – An Inquiry Based upon a Sociological Study of Parole Records' (1928) *Social Force* 7(4) 536, where this was identified as an issue as early as 1929.

24 Hazel Kemshall, Bernadette Wilkinson, and Gill Mackenzie, Risk of Harm Guidance and Training Resources. Version 4.36 (De Montfort University) 2011.

25 Ashimesh Roychowdhury and Gwen Adshead, 'Violence risk assessment as a medical intervention: ethical tensions.' (2014) Psychiatric Bulletin 38(2) 75, 77.

26 Kemshall and Pritchard (n 21) 236.

27 Kemshall and Pritchard (n 21) 236.

28 Rob Canton and David Hancock, *Dictionary of Probation and Offender Management* (Willan Publishing 2007) 274.

bifurcation theory, a term coined by Anthony Bottoms[29] which will be discussed in greater depth later in this chapter, is a type of penal policy in which punishments are simultaneously increased for serious offenders and decreased for less serious offenders.[30] This theory has had an increasing influence in the Irish and English criminal justice systems, and involves resources being tailored to the level of risk identified in the offender being supervised. When dealing with offenders in the community and the possible release of some back into society, it is necessary to examine not only the probability of the person reoffending but also the risk of harm or potential impact, arising out of that conduct. Of course, there is also the risk, for example, of not releasing a prisoner at the most appropriate time – with the consequent waste of resources and possible institutionalisation of the prisoner – which illustrates that release decisions are almost never between certainty and risk but rather a balancing exercise between two risks.

Recidivism in the context of probation and parole has been defined as those who have been subject to a supervised community sanction, or released from a custodial prison sentence, and were subsequently convicted of a further offence within a defined period, for example of three years.[31] All measures of recidivism have their limitations and as political and social values change, rates of reporting, detection, prosecution, conviction and sentence for crimes vary. This in turn will impact on recidivism whatever indicators or measures are used.[32]

## Dangerousness, Harm and Progression of Risk

In assessing the dangerousness of an offender, for example in probation and parole release decision-making, the notion of harm must be at its core.[33] Any assessment of dangerousness should include consideration of the following: the nature of the harm involved; its magnitude; its imminence; its frequency; the likelihood or unlikelihood that it will occur (risk); situational circumstances and conditions that affect the likelihood of harm occurring; balancing between the alleged harm on the one hand

29 Anthony E Bottoms, 'Reflections on the renaissance of dangerousness' (1977) 16 Howard J Crim Justice 70-96.

30 Canton and Hancock (n 28).

31 Probation Service, *Recidivism Study 2008-2013* (Probation Service Research Report 4) 2013, 4.

32 ibid.

33 Nigel Walker, *Aggravation, Mitigation and Mercy in English Criminal Justice* (Blackstone Press 1999).

and the nature of society's intervention on the other.[34] In assessing dangerousness we have to bear in mind that it is an ascribed quality based to a large extent on what a person has done. It is transient and situationally specific. When assessing risk it is the assessment of the future likelihood of an event happening.

When examining risk it is necessary to consider the notion of progression, such as set out in Walker's theory of this, which involves differentiating between the offender who harms others only if sheer bad luck brings him/her into a situation of provocation or 'temptation' and the offender who gets into such situations not by chance but following inclinations, and also those individuals who do more, and who create opportunities to offend.[35] There are multiple typologies for every kind of offender reflecting motivations and behaviours or situational determinants. A typology such as Walker's assists in identifying those who are a 'chance, one off' offender, those who have an initial predisposition, those who are actively grooming, and those for whom committing the dangerous act is their sole *raison d'être*.[36] This can aid in determining the likelihood of repetition, escalation, and amenability to intervention.[37] There is no finite definition of risk as we have seen from the above, rather there are a range of factors which impact and determine the scale and complexity of risk.

Now that a definition of risk has been considered, it is necessary to examine how risk can be assessed for particular categories of offenders.

## Defining Risk Assessment

A key element of the probation and parole processes is seeking to carry out a risk assessment/evaluation of each case at 'intake', including referrals by the courts and those coming before the Parole Board. Consequently there is a risk assessment incorporated into most if not all probation supervision cases[38] and into the review

---

34 Kemshall and Pritchard (n 21) 240.

35 See Nigel Walker, 'Dangerousness and Mental Disorder' (1994) 37 *Royal Institute of Philosophy Supplements* 181.

36 Kemshall and Pritchard (n 21) 243.

37 ibid.

38 While risk of reoffending assessments are carried out in all probation supervision cases, they are generally not carried out in relation to persons being considered for community service. This is because of the specific statutory requirements of community service assessments (see separate Chapter on Community Service). Sometimes, an assessment of reoffending or of causing harm may be specifically indicated. This may be related for example to concerns

dossier in each parole case. Internationally, and to a lesser extent in Ireland, this concentration on risk has seen major changes in the management of offenders with a shift from purely traditional social work and rehabilitation (managing and responding to the past) to more of a prioritisation of the management, containment and controlling of categories of risk (managing the future); from working with what people have already done, and their own individual and social needs, to managing and influencing what they might do in the future.[39]

The history of formal risk assessment in criminal justice can be largely traced through 'four generations of risk assessment'.[40] The first generation of risk assessment were clinical risk assessments. A clinical risk assessment is a subjective judgement often conducted by psychologists, psychiatrists or social workers who evaluate an individual based on their interactions with the offender and their experience as a professional.[41] These clinical risk assessments are largely based on the clinical judgment and intuition of the professional doing the assessment, however, the use of such unstructured clinical approaches has on occasion led to inconsistency, bias and poor transparency in the decision-making process.[42] The second generation risk assessment tools involved more standardised assessments that made use of actuarial methods over subjective judgement and were generally based on static factors.[43] (These static factors used included, for example, age at first offence or number of previous convictions; ie factors that are 'fixed' and also have an established bearing on future behaviour). These second generation risk assessments can comprise structured actuarial models. These models are generally based on research and mathematical computations to determine what factors were most significant in influencing reoffending. These factors historically allowed 'predictability tables'[44] to be constructed by which an offender's chances of success or failure on probation and parole

in relation to the appropriate management of such person on a community service work placement.

39 Philip Whitehead, *Modernising Probation and Criminal Justice – Getting the Measure of Cultural Change*. (Shaw & Sons 2007) 47.

40 Donald A Andrews and James Bonta, *The Psychology of Criminal Conduct* (Matthew Bender & Co 2010) 310.

41 James Bonta and Donald A Andrews, 'Risk-need-responsivity model for offender assessment and rehabilitation' (2007) 6(1) Rehabilitation 1-22.

42 Siobhan Young, *Literature Review – Risk Assessment Tools for Children in Conflict with the Law* (Irish Youth Justice Services 2009) 5.

43 ibid.

44 See Burgess (n 23) 534.

could be determined and stated this in terms of percentages, or risk levels — in other words 'risk assessment'.[45]

The third generation of risk assessment tools incorporated both clinical and actuarial methods and aimed to also include assessment of dynamic risk factors, to enable an individualised risk assessment.[46] (These dynamic risk factors are factors associated with risk of reoffending but which are also potentially changeable, such as attitudes, peer group, substance misuse, employment etc.). The newer, fourth generation of risk assessment tools, rather than simply predicting offending, aim to systematically bring together information about an offender's history and needs to develop a treatment plan, with this approach being known as structured clinical judgement.[47] The focus on 'needs' in this type of risk assessment involves the identification of the areas in an offender's life that should be targeted for intervention/supervision in order to decrease their likelihood of future criminal behaviour. It has, however, been noted that some research has found the predictive value of second generation assessment tools to be at least equivalent to, if not superior to that of third and fourth generation tools and it has also been questioned whether fourth generation tools merely create additional complications and unnecessary challenges.[48] Some of these issues are related to how risk assessment instruments and processes are used, and by whom.[49]

## Modern Theories and Risk Levels

In its modern usage, risk assessment is the assessment of the likelihood of reoffending and the impact or harm caused by this reoffending. Risk assessment aims to judge, as accurately as the available information allows, the likelihood or probability that an offender who has been convicted of an offence will go on to commit further offences, and the potential harm that might arise from such offending.[50] This question is most commonly posed

---

45 See Arthur Taft, 'Parole; Principles and Practice of a Prison Release Procedure' (1941) NYU PhD Thesis 56, which quotes the Burgess method of parole prediction as published in 1928 which studied risk under 22 listed headings.

46 Young (n 42) 5.

47 ibid.

48 James Hess and Susan Turner, *Risk Assessment Accuracy in Corrections Population Management: Testing the Promise of Tree Based Ensemble Predictions* (Irvine Centre for Evidence-Based Corrections) 2.

49 The so-called 'Who Works' element of probation and parole work, in addition to the longer recognised aspect of 'What Works' – see separate chapter on Probation Work.

50 Probation Service, *General Information on Risk Assessment Instruments used by*

when an individual has recently been found guilty of a crime, as authorities need to know how to appropriately deal with the individual.[51] Research has consistently shown that assessing each individual's risk of reoffending, matching supervision and treatment to an offender's risk level, and targeting his or her unique criminal risk factors and needs with proven programmes, significantly improves offender outcomes, reduces reoffending and enhances public safety.[52] In the Irish context, probation officers and psychologists generally conduct these assessments and they form an important part of decisions regarding what kind of sanction is most appropriate for an offender, whether to release an offender on parole, what factors need to be targeted by interventions and what supports the offender may need, to support rehabilitation and reintegration in the community.

Risk assessment is therefore about assessing the likelihood that something bad will happen, which would cause distress and harm to others.[53] These calculations can either be expressed as statistical probabilities of outcome based upon actuarial data, that is data derived from large groups of persons of a similar type, or as clinical judgments based upon clinical assessment techniques of interviewing, observation and the examination of social histories, or a combination of these approaches. Risk assessment instruments are developed from knowledge and information that differentiate between those offenders who (statistically) most often reoffend and those who rarely do so. Risk assessments, by analysing the statistical correlations between factors and adverse outcomes, estimate the probability that a convicted offender, as a member of a particular group, will commit a further offence and is not intended to predict the actual future behaviour of that individual offender. These assessments assign the individual to a risk category based on the characteristics he or she shares with other offenders and knowledge of the actual reoffending rates for large groups of offenders with those characteristics. These risk assessments generally assess the offender for the presence or absence of various criminogenic factors and are based on the results of the total 'score'. International research, in the medical field, suggests that risk

---

*the Probation Service in work with different categories of offenders* (2014) 7.

51 Mark Wilson, 'Assessing Risk', presented to seminar entitled 'Law on Risk' at Dublin City University where it is stated that of the 10,593 Risk Assessment Reports conducted by the Probation Service in 2010, 10,501 were for pre-sanction reports for the Courts, 74 were for the Parole Board and 18 were for repatriation reports.

52 Pew Centre on the States, 'Risk/Needs Assessment 101: Science Reveals New Tools to Manage Offenders' (September 2011) 4.

53 Roychowdhury and Adshead (n 25) 77.

assessments usually lead to one of four conclusions; firstly, patients assessed for the first time are assessed as low, medium, high or very high risk;[54] secondly, patients being reassessed are deemed to be the same risk as in the previous assessment, or, are deemed higher or lower risk than their previous assessment.[55] A similar methodology is employed by probation officers and psychologists in assessing and monitoring risk in the criminal justice sphere.

Recent years have witnessed an increased interest in the development of flexible, actuarial risk predictors for offending. These predictors use factors identified in research studies and then devise ways of applying those to arrive at a score for an individual which gives a probability of reconviction for a further offence within a specified follow-up period.[56] The actuarial assessment involves an examination of both static and dynamic factors, with such static factors including matters such as previous behaviour (including age at first arrest and prior convictions),[57] gender[58] and age.[59] Statistical calculations are used to predict the likelihood that an offender will be reconvicted based on the reconviction rates for offenders with similar characteristics in similar situations. Actuarial risk predictors have gained currency in the difficult decision-making of probation, as well as parole release.[60] Whilst generating higher rates of accuracy than clinical assessment alone, the application of any actuarial scale involving the transferability of statistical information about groups to the probable behaviour of a specific individual is problematic. A risk assessment tool will only indicate that a particular offender belongs to a cohort of potential offenders that has this arithmetic likelihood of being reconvicted. It could be that this individual might offend more or might not offend at all. It is purely a prediction based upon prior recorded scenarios. These actuarial risk assessments provide guidance as to the general band of risk that an offender falls into, be it low, medium, high or very high. It is important to understand what such a categorisation means,[61] and it is also important that there is a consistency in the use

54 Young (n 42) 7.
55 Roychowdhury and Adshead (n 25) 77.
56 Anthony Beech, Dawn D Fisher, and David Thornton, 'Risk Assessment of Sex Offenders' (2003) 34(4) Prof Psychol Res Pr 340.
57 Pew Centre on the States (n 52) 3.
58 Kemshall, Wilkinson and Mackenzie (n 24) where it is stated that women are less likely to seek violent solutions to their problems.
59 ibid, where it is stated that young men are more likely to reoffend and most violent offending is committed by young men.
60 Dirk Van Zyl Smit and Alessandro Corda, 'American Exceptionalism in Parole Release and Supervision', Kevin R Reitz (ed), *American Exceptionalism in Crime and Punishment* (OUP 2018) 19.
61 See Louise Scott, 'Assessing Risk: A Report on the Family Justice Council

of such stock phrases as 'low risk' and 'high risk'[62] as research, both internationally and in Ireland cautions that professionals operating in this sector may have different understandings of risk and risk 'levels.'[63] After all, it does not imply that an individual assessed as very high risk will inevitably reoffend, just that they are much more likely to do so than an offender assessed in a lower risk bracket.[64]

## Static and Dynamic Risk Factors

Risk assessment instruments generally measure *static* or unchanging risk factors, such as number of previous convictions, *dynamic* or changeable risk factors, such as peer relationships or substance misuse, and/or a combination of static and dynamic factors so as to estimate the likelihood of further offending.[65] Static Risk Assessment Instruments focus on a relatively small numbers of unchangeable, yet highly predictive factors, such as the number of arrests, the number of prior probation or parole violations and age at date of first arrest or conviction. On the other hand, Dynamic Risk Assessment Instruments measure characteristics, circumstances, and attitudes that can change throughout one's life. Research studies have revealed that there are at least seven dynamic risk factors closely associated with criminal conduct that can be assessed and altered through effective interventions, namely antisocial personality, pro-criminal attitudes, social supports for crime, substance abuse, poor family/marital relationships, school/ work failure and lack of pro-social recreational activities.[66] In addition, risk assessment tools can use a combination of static and dynamic factors, with a balancing exercise between the factors which cannot be changed against those which can change and/or which have changed.[67] When utilising risk assessment tools which incorporate dynamic factors, cognisance must be taken of the fact that the offender's risk and need factors will change over time and the offender would have to be reassessed periodically to ensure accurate ongoing classification.[68] The need to re-assess regularly is to consider the effects of setting and situational factors and how

---

Annual Seminar' Family Law Week (8 May 2014) www.familylawweek.co.uk/ site.aspx?i=ed12653.

62 Jay P Singh and others, 'Rates of Violence in patients classified as high risk by structured risk assessment instruments' (2014) 204(3) Brit J Psych 180-7.

63 Young (n 42) 2.

64 Probation Service (n 50) 7.

65 ibid 1.

66 Pew Centre on the States (n 52) 3.

67 Jo Dobry, 'Dealing with Dangerousness: The Parole Board Perspective' (2003) 51(5) CJM 12.

68 Pew Centre on the States (n 52) 5.

these factors change over time as well as the interactions between these changing factors and the attitudes, behaviour and other characteristics of the individual.[69]

## Risk Assessment in Ireland

Research utilised by the Irish Probation Service has revealed that, compared to using clinical judgement alone, structured assessment tools are much more effective at predicting offenders' risk of failure in the community.[70] Unstructured clinical judgement refers to a purely clinical opinion on risk, without necessarily following a set structure.[71] 'Unstructured' in this regard can be a misleading term, in that there may be structure imposed on the evaluation but it will vary from practitioner to practitioner, and perhaps even from one offender to another assessed by the same practitioner. This approach has the advantage of being flexible, quick and person-centred, and it was the traditional way of assessing risk for many years. Research indicates that when professionals rely on their judgement alone in assessing the risk of reoffending they are accurate only 50% of the time. However, when the same professionals use an actuarial instrument as utilised by the Irish Probation Service their predictive accuracy increases to between 67% and 76%.[72]

There are two approaches to using risk assessment tools, the first of which is to use them in a manner similar to the insurance industry where measurable predictor and outcome variables are inputted and the assessment is determined by fixed and explicit rules. The second manner in which these tools are utilised is as part of a 'structured professional judgement' where comprehensive background information is collated and various items are rated for their absence, partial absence or presence. These factors are then utilised in multiple relevant scenarios with the risk then generally being summarised as low, moderate, high or very high.[73]

The fourth generation risk assessment tools, which combine attention to criminogenic risk factors with the main statistically based predictors of reconviction, are regularly used to calculate risk assessments in Ireland. These risk assessments combine actuarial

---

69 Saleem Shah, 'Dangerousness; A Paradigm for Exploring Some Issues in Law and Psychology' (1978) 33(3) Am Psychol J 226.

70 Probation Service (n 50) 8.

71 ibid.

72 ibid.

73 Roychowdhury and Adshead (n 25) 78.

and clinical assessments. Clinical assessment methods are used to predict both the risk of reoffending with the likelihood and nature of potential harm. However it must be stressed that these tools cannot be used to make individual predictions and the individual circumstances of the offender must always be considered. The clinical assessments involve one–to-one, in-depth interviewing and observation of the offender, helping the practitioner to understand risky behaviour by establishing:

> ...the significant personality traits predisposing persons to be risky, the particular situational factors which may trigger or exacerbate those traits, how significant factors interact over time and how motivations to commit certain acts are played out and in what circumstances.[74]

From the above it can be seen how vitally important that the personal, social and environmental dynamic factors are also considered in these risk assessments, with particular emphasis on the specific circumstances of the particular individual being assessed. It should be noted however that according to meta-analyses, actuarial tools generally outperform structured clinical judgement, which in turn outperforms unstructured clinical judgement.[75] Over time, these actuarial clinical tools have become more sophisticated and their predictive ability has improved considerably. Additionally, assessment tools specific to particular types of crimes (eg violent crimes) and offenders (eg sex offenders) are now available and are used in the daily practice of probation and psychology staff in their work with offenders in Ireland.[76]

## Cautions in Relation to Offender Risk Assessment

There are four potential outcomes of a risk of harm assessment. Offenders assessed as being at high risk of violence may actually be violent ('true positive' outcome) or may desist from future violent behaviour ('false positive'). Similarly offenders assessed as being at low risk of future violence may actually be violent ('false negative') or may desist from future violence ('true negative'). Clearly the aim

---

74 Hazel Kemshall, Reviewing Risk: implications for policy and practice in the Probation Service. A review of research on the assessment and management of risk and dangerousness (Home Office, Research and Statistics Directorate, 1996) as quoted in Kemshall, Wilkinson and Mackenzie (n 23).

75 Jay Singh and Seena Fazel, 'Forensic Risk Assessment- A Metareview' (2010) 37(9) CJB 965-988.

76 USA Department of Justice, *Core Competencies – A Resource for Parole Board Chairs, Members and Executive Staff* (NICIC 2010).

of accurate risk assessment, and the task of the Probation Service and the Parole Board, is to maximise the frequency of true positive and true negative predictions.[77]

In relation to the two inaccuracies which can occur: false-positives can result in harsher sanctions including longer than necessary custodial sentences being served with the consequent infringement of liberty or the probationer/parolee being subject to restrictions and intrusive supervision in the community, giving rise to a waste of resources. Conversely, false-negatives can put members of the community in grave danger. Both sets of errors can be very costly.[78] It has however been shown that efforts to reduce the numbers of 'false positives' increases the number of 'false negatives'.[79] It must be remembered that the Irish Interim Parole Board for example dealt with offenders who had received custodial sentences in excess of eight years in duration and who hence had been convicted of very serious crimes. The consequences of such persons reoffending (though small in number) could be extremely dire and the Interim Parole Board for example was accordingly at pains to ensure that 'false negatives' did not occur. The statutory Parole Board will be in a similar situation due to the existence of strong social and political pressures which demand a 'better safe than sorry' outlook. Whilst there are strong negative reactions by the community to errors associated with the release of dangerous prisoners, there appears to be relatively little public concern about errors leading to unnecessary confinement[80] — false positives are tolerable, false negatives are not.[81]

In this regard it has been noted that the risk of harm which would justify continued detention would be harm which would have a marked and lasting effect, unlikely to be remediable, on a person's quality of life.[82] The Interim Parole Board appears to have been remarkably successful at ensuring false negatives did not occur.[83] Despite the relative rarity of 'false negatives' in the Irish parole system, an example of a 'false negative' case having an extremely detrimental effect on the credibility of the criminal justice system, prior to the establishment of the Interim Parole Board, occurred

---

77 Roychowdhury and Adshead (n 25) 79.
78 Kemshall and Pritchard (n 21) 237.
79 See Walker (n 35) 182.
80 Shah (n 69) 228.
81 Diarmuid Griffin, *Killing Time: Life Imprisonment and Parole in Ireland* (Palgrave Macmillan 2018) 114.
82 See Walker (n 35) 184.
83 Diarmuid Griffin, 'The Release and Recall of Life Sentence Prisoners: Policy, Practice and Politics' (2015) 53 Irish Jurist (ns) 34.

in the notorious case of Thomas Murray who proceeded to commit murder whilst on temporary release.[84] One of the effects of this crime being committed by a parolee was the immediate suspension of programmes of temporary release for all prisoners in Ireland for a period of time.[85] The lack of 'false negatives' in cases where temporary release was recommended by the Interim Parole Board however gives rise to the concern that the Interim Parole Board may have been very risk adverse and were only recommending 'sure things' for release.[86] This scenario gives rise to the question as to whether the Interim Parole Board were engaged in 'risk management' or 'risk control'. With risk management the intent is not to eliminate risk but to manage it and mitigate the risk of violence posed by the offender. Risk management will be accompanied by a realisation that there will be failures but that there is a recognition of the cost both of false negatives and false positives and the aim is to reduce the joint costs of these errors. Risk management generally includes strategies of monitoring, treating and supervising the offender together with victim safety planning. Risk control on the other hand is a strategy to prevent the recurrence of a new crime with the strategy being to eliminate the offender's ability to participate in further crimes.[87] As we have seen, there are significant issues associated with so called risk assessment and this chapter will now look at how the Irish authorities assess such risk.

## Particular Influences on Risk Assessment in Ireland

The *Murray*[88] case (referred to above) and the attendant Olden Report,[89] were the catalyst for the introduction of more robust and formal risk assessments in Ireland, particularly in relation to the parole process.[90] In the course of the investigation into the circumstances surrounding this case, in 2001, the Department of Justice confirmed that the use of formal risk assessment tools in Ireland was 'not commonplace'.[91] This situation evolved to the

84 John Olden, *Report of Mr John Olden on the Management of the Sentences of Thomas Murray, Life Sentenced Prisoner* (2 April 2001).

85 ibid.

86 Probation Service (n 31) 6, which discloses that the overall recidivism among the full prison population after two years was 32.9% and 41% after three years.

87 Barbara Hudson, *Justice in the Risk Society* (Sage Publications 2003) 50.

88 See Olden (n 84).

89 ibid.

90 Dáil Éireann. Written Answers, Michael McDowell TD, Minister for Justice, Equality and Law Reform – Prison Sentence Management, 9 October 2002.

91 Observations on Olden Report by Director General of the Irish Prisons Service contained within the Olden Report (n 84). See also Griffin (n 81) 109, where the former Chairman of the Sentence Review Group, TK Whitaker is quoted as

extent that the Interim Parole Board frequently required risk assessments of prisoners before making any recommendation. The Interim Parole Board also stated that a risk assessment would often be a fundamental requirement before any suggestion of temporary release could arise.[92] On occasion they went even further by stating that these risk assessment reports must indicate that the prisoner has reduced their risk of reoffending before the Board would recommend periods of temporary release or time in an open prison prior to possible release into the community.[93] Whilst it is acknowledged that there is certainly evidence that the Interim Parole Board adjusted towards a more risk-oriented approach,[94] and that risk assessment will be fundamental in the work of the statutory Parole Board, it must also be stressed that such risk assessment instruments can never be relied upon *exclusively* in release decision-making.[95] A Parole Board, in discharging their function, must look at the past, the present and the future to assess the readiness of the offender to be gradually reintegrated into a community, with a manageable degree of risk.[96] The 'past' factors frequently examined by the Interim Parole Board included information from the Gardaí, the courts, criminal history, family, education, employment, details contained within victims' submissions as well as whether the offender has been subject to previous periods of community supervision.[97] The consideration of these factors by the Interim Parole Board was important in the context that 'Nothing predicts future behaviour like past behaviour' and 'previous conduct is the least unsatisfactory of predictors'.[98] 'Present' factors can include drugs/alcohol dependency, behaviour, violence, benefits from programmes such as anger management, education upgrading, sex offender treatment and institutional behaviour.[99] 'Future' factors can, amongst other considerations, include a Parole Board conducting an assessment of the release

---

stating that risk assessments were not provided to the SRG who were instead left to 'appraise matters with our judgement.'

92 Parole Board, Annual Report (2003) 3.

93 ibid.

94 Griffin (n 81) 109.

95 See Observations on Olden Report by Director General of the Irish Prisons Service (n 91).

96 See Renee Collette, 'Protecting the Community Through the Structured Reintegration of Offenders' (Unpublished speech delivered at the Association of Paroling Authorities International Annual Conference (APAI) November 2011) 31.

97 ibid 33.

98 See Walker (n 35) 186, where it is stated that so far as sane violence is concerned the more often an offender has been convicted of it the higher the probability that he will be convicted again.

99 See Collette (n 96) 34.

plan, predictions of compliance with supervision, availability of accommodation and the availability of family and community support for the offender on release.[100]

## Risk Assessment Instruments Used by Probation in Ireland

The Irish Probation Service currently uses several structured risk assessment instruments, with separate instruments for adult offenders,[101] youth offenders,[102] sex offenders[103] and domestic violence offenders.[104] In addition to these risk assessment instruments the Irish Probation Service also uses a separate structured professional assessment framework to assess the risk of an offender causing serious harm. Serious harm is defined as personal, physical or psychological harm which is life threatening and/or traumatic and from which recovery is usually difficult or incomplete.[105] The nature of the cases considered by the Irish Parole Board is such that risk of serious harm is frequently a consideration in release decisions. The Probation Service Risk of Serious Harm (or PS/ROSH) is not a statistically validated risk assessment instrument as such, but rather a structured mechanism to inform and supplement the professional judgement of the assessing probation officers and is used in conjunction with other relevant actuarial risk assessment instruments.[106]

When assessing typical adult offenders in Ireland the appropriate general risk of reoffending assessment tool[107] combines seventeen static (or unchanging) and thirty seven dynamic (or changeable) risk factors to estimate the likelihood of reoffending by a convicted offender over the following twelve months, if in the community.[108] When considering the depth of information required to complete these risk assessments it becomes apparent that there is a possibility that an information deficit could arise from only using clinical

---

100 ibid.

101 Probation Service (n 50) 2. Level of Service Inventory Revised (LSI-R) for male and female offenders aged over 18.

102 ibid 3. Youth Level of Service and Case Management Inventory (YLS/CMI) for male and female offenders aged 12 to 17 years.

103 ibid 4. Risk Matrix 2000 (RM2000) and Stable and Acute 2007 (SA2007) for sex offenders.

104 ibid 5. Spousal Assault Risk Assessment (SARA) for domestic violence offenders.

105 ibid 6.

106 ibid 2.

107 ibid.

108 ibid.

judgement. The use of an assessment tool highlights the need for the assessor to collect far more detailed information about the background, social relationships and behaviour of the particular offender.[109] The dynamic risk factors take account of individual circumstances and identify the most appropriate targets for intervention during a period of imprisonment and/or supervision with the expectation that if these issues are effectively addressed it will result in a reduced chance of reoffending.[110]

## Risk Assessment for Early Release, Including Parole

Integrated Sentence Management in the Irish prison system involves prisoners taking greater personal responsibility for their own development through active engagement, goal setting and periodic review to measure progress.[111] This system will also be of benefit when evaluating participation in available programmes which could impact on risk. As these risk assessments have such a dynamic nature they are required to be re-applied at regular intervals and also following specific interventions or changes in circumstances.[112] Risk assessments are conducted in prisons on behalf of the Parole Board and are incorporated into the reports of all prisoners eligible for consideration by the Parole Board. These reports are prepared by either the Probation Service or by the IPS Psychology Service (whichever is deemed the lead agency in relation to a particular prisoner). As these reports are prepared for every parole eligible prisoner, these reports will include those for whom release is imminent, prisoners with a likely date of release many years into the future and prisoners whose release date is entirely unknown. In those cases where the release date from prison is unknown or is many years into the future it is difficult to use a risk assessment tool containing predominantly dynamic or changeable risk factors, to give an accurate estimate of risk level for reoffending following release. In this situation the offender's circumstances on release cannot be realistically anticipated and therefore dynamic items are scored based on behaviour or attitudes demonstrated prior to and in custody.[113] In the absence of factual information about the circumstances and potential timescale for

---

109 Geraldine O'Dwyer, 'A Risk Assessment and Risk Management Approach to Sexual Offending in the Irish Probation Service' (2007) UCD MSocSc (Social Work) 75.

110 Probation Service (n 50) 2.

111 See Dáil Debates, Written Answer by Alan Shatter TD, Minister for Justice, Equality and Defence (Alan Shatter) to Terence Flanagan TD, 24 April 2012.

112 Probation Service (n 50) 3.

113 Probation Service (n 50) 3.

release the overall risk level assigned is essentially hypothetical and less reliable as an estimate of reoffending upon release. In these circumstances the on-going risk assessments conducted in the custodial setting are predominantly utilised to determine and measure a prisoner's progress in the custodial setting and to identify appropriate targets for intervention during the next part of the prisoner's sentence.

One problem with the use of risk assessment tools in the context of deciding whether or not to immediately grant parole is that the risk assessment tests are conducted in a prison setting and the dynamic elements of the assessments are by necessity scored on the best evidence available regarding the offender's attitudes and behaviours prior to and during custody and the anticipated circumstances on release.[114] However, it must be considered that factors which were present at the time of prior offending may re-emerge in some cases following release and gains in prison may be undone. For some offenders, such as domestic violence or sexual offenders, very specific circumstances in the community, such as victim access may create a very sudden escalation of risk.[115] This will necessitate a reassessment of risk and review of the case management of this offender leading to either no further action, additional conditions or a recall to prison. A further example is if an offender is returning to live in a family situation characterised by substance misuse, this will have to be considered alongside any progress with substance abuse made in custody. Consideration of a dynamic risk factor such as substance abuse gives rise to such considerations as to whether the prisoner was not using the substance solely because of barriers to availability in custody or because of a determination to recover from their previous addiction?[116] In such circumstances the risk assessment tool is used both to estimate the risk of reoffending after release but also to identify the targets for intervention and risk management during supervision, post release.[117] Accordingly it is important that these dynamic factors would be reflected in ongoing, regular risk assessments.[118] As has been stated already, the ongoing consideration of risk is an important facet of the role of a probation officer in monitoring and supervising parolees and probationers in the community.[119]

---

114 ibid.

115 ibid 10.

116 Probation Service, *Incorporating the Risk Assessments into Parole Reports: Guide for Probation Officers* (2014) 3.

117 ibid 3.

118 ibid 2.

119 Parole Act 2019, s 33(1)(a)(i) and s 33(1) b).

## Assessing Risk of Sexual Reoffending

When assessing the risk of reoffending relating to sexual offenders in Ireland, the risk assessment tools generally used are the Risk Matrix 2000 and the Stable and Acute 2007. Risk Matrix 2000 (or RM-2000) is a two-staged process which utilises an examination of three static risk factors, namely age at commencement of offending, number of appearances in court on sexual offences and total number of appearances in court. Points are awarded in relation to each factor and the offender is placed in one of four categories (low, medium, high or very high). The second stage of the RM-2000 details four aggravating factors which are: whether the victim was male, whether any or all of the victims of sexual offending was a stranger, non-contact sexual offences and a lack of a long term intimate relationship. If two aggravating factors are present the risk category is raised one level and if all four aggravating factors are present the risk is raised two levels.[120] As described by Scotland's Risk Management Authority,[121] the Stable and Acute 2007 (or SA-07) instrument:

- ...is a two-part actuarial risk assessment instrument designed to assist with the community supervision of individuals who have committed sexual offences [where]
- The Stable-2007 measures 'stable dynamic' risk factors which are potentially changeable but may endure for months or years... [covering] 13 major risk areas... [and]
- The Acute-2007 measures 'acute dynamic' risk factors defined as highly transient conditions which can change over a period of weeks, days or even hours. The instrument assesses 7 areas of risk.

It should however be noted that other considerations are applied in alternate sexual offending risk assessment tools.[122]

In relation to sex offenders in the community, the Probation Service frequently co-ordinates a multi-agency approach in order to ensure risks of reoffending are effectively monitored and managed through the Sex Offender Risk Assessment and Management (SORAM) model which co-ordinates the efforts of the Probation Service,

---

120 Beech, Fisher and Thornton (n 56) 344. See also Georgia D Barnett, Helen C Wakeling, and Philip D Howard, 'An Examination of the Predictive Validity of the Risk Matrix 2000 in England and Wales' (2010) 22 Sex Abuse 443.

121 Scotland Risk Management Authority (2019) *Stable and Acute 2007 (2007)* available at: https://www.rma.scot/wp-content/uploads/2019/09/RATED_SA07_August-2019_Hyperlink-Version.pdf .

122 ibid 345.

the Child and Family Agency, the Irish Prison Service, An Garda Síochána, the local authorities and others.[123] Having considered how risk assessments are conducted in Ireland it is necessary to examine how the Parole Board utilise these assessments and what level of risk they consider acceptable.

## Other Issues in Assessing Risk for Parole

In most jurisdictions, other than Ireland, the sentencing judge is concerned with risk, but must also satisfy society's need for the demonstration of punishment, deterrence and community outrage.[124] With the exception of risk, none of these factors are relevant in considering the granting of parole, save and in so far as it is necessary for the Parole Board not to undermine confidence in, and public acceptance of, the criminal justice process.[125] This point was particularly re-iterated in the Irish context by the Minister for Justice, who when commenting on the parole system as operated by the Interim Parole Board stated the importance of 'ensuring public confidence is retained in the criminal justice system'.[126] The Parole Act 2019 stipulates that the Parole Board when making decisions must have regard to whether 'it is appropriate in all the circumstances that the parole applicant be released on parole'[127] and one of the factors which is relevant to that consideration is maintaining confidence in the criminal justice system. In Ireland there is a clear distinction between how trial judges deliberate on sentencing and the factors that the Interim Parole Board considered when making sentence management recommendations to the Minister for Justice and the factors which are to be considered by the Parole Board when deciding on parole applications. There is a substantial body of Irish case law which clearly states that the sentence to be imposed by the sentencing Judge at the conclusion of a criminal trial must be based on the principle of proportionality, with the actual sentence being proportionate not only to the gravity of the offence committed, but also to the personal circumstances of the particular offender.[128] The dominance of the proportionality principle in the Irish criminal justice system would appear to

---

[123] Probation Service, Annual Report (2013) 9.

[124] Hon Justice JW Gendall 'International Perspectives on Parole: Transition from Defence to Prosecution Counsel to Judge to Parole Board Chair and Handling Public Criticism' delivered at Association of Paroling Authorities International Annual Conference, Providence, Rhode Island (21 May 2013) 15.

[125] ibid.

[126] See Alan Shatter TD, Minister of Justice and Equality, Speech at the 'Parole in Ireland' Conference (25 October 2013).

[127] Parole Act 2019, s 27(1)(b).

[128] *People (Attorney General) v O'Driscoll* (1972) 1 Frewen 351.

preclude the imposition of preventative sentences along the lines practiced in the United Kingdom.[129]

Notwithstanding constitutional considerations which a preventative detention approach would raise in the Irish context,[130] such an approach appears to run counter to intuitive notions of justice in that it punishes people for crimes they have not yet committed.[131] In addition, when we decide to exercise the right to detain someone not because they deserve it, or for longer than they deserve, but solely for the sake of other people's safety, this is in a sense a type of human sacrifice.[132] This issue of preventative detention has been considered by the Irish Courts on a number of occasions. The case of *People (Attorney General) v O'Driscoll*[133] established the principle that the sentencing process in Ireland should not be concerned with the potential for future reoffending by that offender at an unspecified date. In the case of *People (Attorney General) v O'Callaghan,*[134] which involved a consideration of the rules applicable to bail, the Court ruled that a person should not be deprived of their liberty based on an apprehension that they might commit a further offence. This judgment was based on the broader right to personal liberty and the presumption of innocence and even though this principle has been reversed by way of constitutional amendment insofar as it relates to bail, there is every reason to believe the principle remains secure in relation to sentencing.[135]

## Public Safety and Preventative Detention

As it has been shown that there appears to be no role for preventative detention in Irish sentencing law,[136] it is important to examine the disparities between what is considered at sentencing stage and

---

129 To study the position in the United Kingdom see Criminal Justice Act 2003, which introduced the concept of imprisonment for public protection, which is an indeterminate sentence.

130 Thomas O'Malley, *Sentencing Law and Practice* (Thomson Round Hall 2006) 86, where the case of *State (Healy) v Donoghue* [1976] IR 325 is discussed, and it is noted that the Court located proportionality in sentencing within a constitutional, as opposed to legal, context.

131 ibid 43.

132 See Nigel Walker, *Sentencing Theory, Law and Practice* (Butterworths 1985) 190.

133 See n 128.

134 [1966] IR 501.

135 O'Malley (n 130) 42.

136 See *Lynch & Whelan v Minister of Justice* [2010] IESC 34; [2012] 1 IR 1, Murray CJ. The Irish Courts have consistently maintained that there is no role for preventative detention in sentencing law – *Carmody v Minister for Justice, Equality and Law Reform* [1998] ILRM 370; *People (DPP) v Bambrick* [1996] 1 IR 265.

parole decision stage. Whilst the courts appear prohibited from including preventative considerations in their deliberations,[137] the Interim Parole Board clearly regarded incapacitation to protect the public from dangerous offenders as one of their primary considerations when formulating their recommendations to the Minister on any particular case. It is worth reminding ourselves that the Interim Parole Board has stated that:

> ... public safety is of paramount importance and is the key factor when the Board is reviewing a case.[138]

In the absence of consideration of the risk of future offending by the sentencing courts, it can be seen that the role of both the Interim Parole Board and the statutory Parole Board and their examination of the risk of possible future offending is all the more vital in terms of public safety. This position was repeatedly acknowledged by the Interim Parole Board in various annual reports.[139] As risk to public safety was indicated as the key factor of concern of the Interim Parole Board and is also core to the decision-making of the statutory Parole Board it is important to examine the role risk plays in the parole process.

By examining the published annual reports of the Interim Parole Board and various public pronouncements of the Chairmen of the Interim Parole Board and the Ministers for Justice it can be seen that the Interim Parole Board in making recommendations to grant temporary release to individual offenders was in effect involved in a balancing exercise. The Interim Parole Board in recommending who was to be released was balancing between the following: the benefits of releasing a prisoner for a substantial period of supervision during which his or her behaviour can be monitored and influenced; the risk of reoffending during that period; the possibility that the longer period of supervision will help an offender avoid reoffending during the period of parole supervision; as well as the financial benefit of reducing the need for prison places.[140] In Ireland, however, as the Parole Board is

---

137 Hugh O'Flaherty, 'Punishment and the Popular Mind: How Much is Enough?', Speech delivered at First World-wide Common Law Judiciary Conference at Washington DC, 23 May 1995 (subsequently published in Hugh O'Flaherty, *Justice, Liberty and the Courts* (Round Hall Sweet and Maxwell 1999) and also reproduced in Paul O'Mahony (ed), *Criminal Justice in Ireland* (Institute of Public Administration 2002) where, at 376-7 O'Flaherty lists the considerations applied by a sentencing judge in imposing sentence.

138 See Parole Board, Annual Report (2013) 6.

139 See Parole Board, Annual Report (2003) 3 and 6.

140 See Tom Ellis and Peter Marshall, 'Does Parole Work? A Post-Release

independent of the Irish Prison Service it pays only limited regard, if any, to the administrative issue of the prison population. It simply concentrates on what is the minimum level of intervention necessary to support the safe release of the individual offender into the community. Moreover, it has been held that whilst considerations of general deterrence are relevant at the sentencing stage, they are not relevant to parole decision-making.[141]

Internationally, it is accepted that a Parole Board should be principally concerned with risk and the safety of the community.[142] Risk to the community, however, cannot be the only criterion applied as this might lead to some prisoners, such as an offender in a 'historical' sexual abuse case, who may no longer present a risk being released almost immediately after committal, irrespective of the nature or the gravity of the offence.[143] The immediate release of such an offender, irrespective of risk or the lack of it, would not be publicly acceptable unless there were exceptional mitigating factors such as extreme infirmity or ill health.[144] It is clear from such scenarios that in some instances it does not matter whether the offender will be a danger in the future or not – in some cases the decision is about a notion of justice and not just about safety.[145] The Parole Act 2019 addresses these concerns by making it mandatory that the Parole Board would consider the nature and gravity of the offence to which the sentence of imprisonment being served by the parole applicant relates and the sentence of imprisonment concerned and any recommendation of the court that imposed that sentence.[146]

A particularly acute dilemma occurs in the sentencing and parole process when offenders are deemed dangerous and when the perceived likelihood of reoffending derives from a mental disorder suffered by the offender. In sentencing, these offenders are entitled to proportionate sentences based on the gravity of their offending conduct and personal circumstances. The presence of a medical condition, which diminishes the offender's subjective culpability, should logically provide a ground for reducing the sentence the Judge would otherwise deem appropriate. However, the Parole

---

Comparison of Reconviction Rates for Paroled and Non-Paroled Prisoners' (2000) 33(3) Aust NZ J Criminol 302 for further discussion of this issue.

141 *Reid v New Zealand Parole Board* [2006] NZCA 232 as quoted in Thomas O'Malley, *Sentencing: Towards a Coherent System* (Thomson Round Hall 2011) 223.

142 Gendall (n 124) 15.

143 O'Malley (n 141) 222.

144 ibid. See also Griffin (n 81) 155.

145 Dan Gardner, Risk – The Science and Politics of Fear (Virgin Books 2009) 237.

146 Parole Act 2019, s 27(2)(a) and (b).

Board's stated aim, of protecting the public to the greatest extent possible may point to an extended period of custody in such circumstances as in weighing up risk to the public the Parole Board does not concern itself with whether the crime was committed as a result of negligence, recklessness, mistake or delusion, it instead looks to future risk of serious harm.[147] It appears that in such cases the same factor, such as a mental disorder, could end up being treated as a mitigating factor in sentencing and an aggravating factor when the case is being considered by the Parole Board.[148] This is of particular concern as the Interim Parole Board has highlighted the fact that many of the life sentence prisoners that they were involved with have serious psychological/mental health issues.[149]

## Legal Consideration of Risk in Parole Decisions

When the Parole Board made recommendations to the Minister for Justice these recommendations included assessments of the risk of harm posed by the offender and also an assessment of the offender's risk of reoffending. Section 2(2)(d) of the Criminal Justice Act 1960[150] states that the Minister must take account of:

> the potential threat to the safety and security of members of the public (including the victim of the offence to which the sentence of imprisonment being served by the person relates) should the person be released from prison.

The Parole Act 2019 places a similar onus on the Parole Board and directs that prior to granting a parole order the Parole Board must be satisfied that:

> (a) the parole applicant—
>
> (i) would not, upon being released, present an undue risk to the safety and security of members of the public (including the relevant victim), and

---

147 See Walker (n 35) 187.

148 Thomas O'Malley, 'Recent Developments in Sentencing,' Paper delivered at the 13th Annual National Prosecutors' Conference (19 May 2012) 7. See also Walker (n 35)184, where he sets out the difficulties in obtaining evidence of the risk profile of people with a mental disorder as so many disordered people are in secure institutions or insecure but supervised ones.

149 See Parole Board, Annual Report (2014) 4. For further discussion see Harry Kennedy and others, *Mental Illness in Irish Prisons – Psychiatric Morbidity in Sentenced, Remanded and Newly Committed Prisoners*. (National Forensic Mental Health Service 2005).

150 As inserted by the Criminal Justice (Temporary Release of Prisoners) Act 2003

(ii) has been rehabilitated and would, upon being released, be capable of reintegrating into society,

Assessing which prisoners to grant parole to is a task which clearly requires the careful allocation of scarce resources calibrated according to the risk that is manifested. It must of course be acknowledged that the risks to be considered should not merely be the risk of violation of social norms, but instead involve risks where significant physical or psychological injury to persons or substantial destruction of property.[151] The Parole Act 2019 (quoted above) specifies that the relevant consideration is 'an undue risk to the safety and security of members of the public'.

## Matching Supervision and Service Provision to Risk Level

Research has shown that correctly matching offenders to programmes based on their risk levels is one of the keys to reducing recidivism.[152] The appropriate matching of offenders to programmes is vital as research has shown that certain intensive programmes work very well with high risk offenders but actually can increase recidivism rates among low-risk offenders. This finding occurs because mixing risk groups exposes the lower risk offenders to the more destructive behaviours of higher risk offenders and jeopardises the pro-social relationships and productive community engagement they may have.[153] Further, risk classifications help criminal justice officials maximise use of limited resources. Targeting higher risk offenders with proven programmes ensures that resources are concentrated on offenders with whom they can have the greatest impact. This concept has developed hand in hand with the concept of 'bifurcation'.

Bifurcation, a term coined by Anthony Bottoms,[154] is also known as the twin track approach and is defined as a type of penal policy in which punishments are simultaneously increased for serious offenders and decreased for less serious offenders.[155] In practise this often means that incarceration is reserved for those who have committed the most serious offences or pose the greatest risk. Less serious offenders are sent along an alternative track and dealt with

151 Shah (n 69) 226.

152 See Tim Chapman and Mike Hough, *Evidence Based Practice: A Guide to Effective Practice* (HM Inspectorate of Probation 1998).

153 Pew Centre on the States (n 52) 3.

154 Bottoms (n 29) 70-96.

155 Canton and Hancock (n 28).

in the community.[156] This system allows resources to be tailored to the level of risk identified in relation to the offender being supervised. There is evidence that this bifurcation approach is now being utilised in Ireland as illustrated firstly, by the recent growth in restorative justice schemes in Ireland and also by the introduction in 2011 by the Minister for Justice of a scheme whereby the courts are obliged to consider community service as an alternative to prison terms of less than 12 months.[157]

The introduction of these schemes in recent years has had the effect of removing more minor matters from the criminal justice system.[158] This progressive thinking is not replicated in the processing of more serious cases, and in this regard it can be seen that the average term of imprisonment served by prisoners convicted of murder has increased significantly. This policy of bifurcation allows the criminal justice system to appear simultaneously hard and soft, showing compassion and understanding to those convicted of minor offences whilst reserving incarceration for those who present the greatest risk.[159] David Garland has also argued that developments in international penal systems have been characterised by increasing bifurcation[160] with longer sentences being served by more serious offenders, based on risk assessments, whilst less serious offenders are given non-custodial sentences or granted temporary release because of resource constraints on the prison system.[161] Prison sentences and levels and intensity of probation and parole supervision are more and more coming to be distributed through methods of risk assessment,[162] with risk assessment being utilised to 'sort' offenders into groups according to 'the degree of control warranted by their risk profiles'.[163] One matter worthy of consideration when examining such an approach is that calibrating resources to the risks identified in risk assessments can lead to very limited resources being made available to those who pose little or no risk of committing serious crimes but who could still benefit from increased support. This approach often leaves offenders who do

156 ibid.
157 Criminal Justice (Community Service) (Amendment) Act 2011.
158 Alan Shatter TD, Minister of Justice and Equality, 'Repairing the Harm: A Victim Sensitive Response to Offending', Speech at launch of the Probation Service Restorative Justice Strategy (18 November 2013).
159 Shane Kilcommins and others, *Crime, Punishment and the Search for Order in Ireland* (Institute of Public Administration 2004) 259.
160 David Garland, *The Culture of Control* (OUP 2001) 8.
161 Roger Matthews and Jock Young (eds), *The New Politics of Crime and Punishment* (Willan Publishing 2003) 27.
162 Hudson (n 87) 58.
163 Gwen Robinson, 'Late-Modern Rehabilitation: The Evolution of a Penal Strategy' (2008) 10(4) Punishm Soc 434.

not pose a high risk at the point of sentencing, or upon their release from prison, with limited access to support while their needs in relation to accommodation, training and employment, addiction services and other support may be equal to, if not greater than, those of higher risk offenders.[164]

## The Impact of Risk Assessments

When considering risk, the sentencing Court, and certainly the Parole Board are evaluating the risk to the public of the person committing a serious offence at a time when they might otherwise be in prison.[165] This in turn is balanced against the benefit to both the offender and the public of the offender being allowed to remain, or being released from prison back into the community under a degree of supervision which might assist their rehabilitation and thereby lessen the risk of their reoffending in the future, thus balancing public safety and offender rehabilitation.[166] In addition there is another balancing exercise; the risk to the public of being victimised must be balanced against the risk to offenders (actual and potential) of undeserved restriction of liberty or other forms of deprivation.[167] As the operative part of each of these tests is clearly 'risk', it leads to the question – what level of risk, in sentencing or in granting parole, should be considered acceptable? Whilst it can be stated that every such decision regarding an offender carries an inherent degree of risk, the statistics which would have enabled for example the Interim Parole Board's 'tolerance' for risk to be calculated are simply not available and accordingly it is impossible to gauge what level of risk the Interim Parole Board found acceptable when making their release recommendations to the Minister for Justice.

## Criticisms of Risk Assessment Instruments

Although statistical prediction commonly outperforms intuitive or clinical judgement it is important to note that it does have a number of limitations.[168] Firstly, actuarial scales yield a probability

---

164 Agnieszka Martynowicz and Martin Quigley, *'It's like stepping on a landmine...' Reintegration of Prisoners in Ireland* (Irish Penal Reform Trust 2010) 35.

165 Review Committee Cm 352, The Parole System in England and Wales: Report (Her Majesty Stationary Office 1988) (the Carlisle Report).

166 O'Malley (n 141) 217.

167 Hudson (n 87) 46.

168 O'Dwyer (n 109) 74 in which she compared the use of clinical judgement alone and the use of risk assessment tools. Her study found that when clinical judgement was solely used the respondents tended to overestimate the risk.

of future recidivism for a group sharing similar characteristics of the offender and not a certainty in relation to the particular offender; they only answer the question 'In a group with these characteristics how likely is it that a member of the group will commit the outcome in question within the specified time frame?' They cannot answer the question of whether this person will commit another crime that is different from the first.[169] An actuarial based risk assessment can only state a probability score of risk, it cannot identify individual exceptions to the rule, nor can it offer risk minimisation interventions and cannot determine or measure whether the impact of treatment or rehabilitation ameliorates the risk.[170] This renders risk infuriatingly passive for some offenders, leaving them with the view that risk assessment is something that is done to you and not with you.[171] To the extent that the parole release decisions are made by consideration of risk assessments it can be argued that the period of imprisonment is no longer about the punishment fitting the crime, nor even about being appropriate to the characteristics of the offender but is instead decided by the offender's categorisation within a particular group.[172]

In addition, because all existing instruments have been developed around official recidivism rates, which are themselves based on reconviction rates, the probabilities associated with each risk category inevitably underestimate true re-offence rates.[173] In addition, recidivism rates are influenced by legislation, sentencing practice, resource levels of criminal justice agencies as well as volumes of crime committed and rates of detection and resolution.[174] It has also been suggested that the selection of variables, the choice of modelling techniques and the methods of calculation employed to identify and reduce risk are often unreliable, an unreliability which is compounded by different forms of bias. Specific issues regarding bias and related matters in risk assessments carried out in the probation context have been identified and discussed by a number of practitioners, researchers and other commentators.[175]

---

169 Roychowdhury and Adshead (n 25) 80.

170 Kemshall and Pritchard (n 21) 239.

171 Ioan Durnescu, 'Experiencing Supervision; From 'Sparing the First Offenders' to 'Punishment in the Community' and Repairing the Harm Done' in Fergus McNeill, Ioan Durnescu, René Butter (eds) *Probation; 12 Essential Questions* (Palgrave Macmillan 2016) 202.

172 Hudson (n 87) 48.

173 Beech, Fisher and Thornton (n 56) 345.

174 Probation Service (n 31) 17.

175 Geraldine O'Dwyer, 'A Risk Assessment and Risk Management Approach to Sexual Offending for the Probation Service' (2008) 5 Irish Probation J 84-90; Wendy Fitzgibbon, Claire Hamilton and Michelle Richardson, 'A risky business: An examination of Irish probation officers' attitudes towards risk assessment'

In terms of bias, it has been noted that almost all criminological prediction studies use some form of official record of offending as the criterion variable, usually arrest, conviction or incarceration. This has significant theoretical implications, as one can never disentangle the extent to which official measures confound actual criminal behaviour with the labelling of criminality in the justice system. Thus, if arrest is the criterion measure and police agencies are biased or selective in their arrest procedures — by race or social status, for example — then the study will likely identify those factors associated with police selection procedures as 'predictors' of criminality.[176] An example of the unreliability of such risk assessment tools is illustrated by examining the Risk Matrix 2000 tool which despite its widespread and officially sanctioned use has not been subject to any form of rigorous evaluation, and according to validation studies carried out in England and Wales, its accuracy is in the 'moderate' range.[177]

Similarly, the American Psychiatric Association, in a communication to the US Supreme Court, stated that its 'best estimate is that two out of three predictions of long term future violence made by psychiatrists are wrong'.[178] Nevertheless the US Supreme Court has ruled repeatedly that such testimony is legally admissible as evidence as the mental health professionals' predictions were 'not always wrong ... only most of the time'.[179] In this regard research conducted in England found very high 'false positive' rates in prediction attempts with nine out of ten serious sexual offenders thought by the Parole Board to be high risk not being reconvicted of a sexual offence within four years of their release.[180] It must however

---

(2010) 57(2) Probation J 163-174; Etain Quigley, 'Pre-sentence Reports in the Irish Youth Justice System: A Shift to Risk-Oriented Practice?' (2014) 11 Irish Probation J 63-86; Denis Bracken, 'Probation Practice with Non-Irish National Offenders in the Republic of Ireland' (2015) 12 Irish Probation J 95-112; Nicola Carr and Niamh Maguire, 'Pre-sentence Reports and Individualised Justice: Consistency, Temporality and Contingency' (2017) 14 Irish Probation J 52-71; Annie McAnallen, 'From the High, Hard Ground of Theory to the Swampy Lowlands of Risk Assessment in Practice: The Real-Life Challenges of Decision-Making' (2018) 15 Irish Probation J, 70-83

176 Matthews and Young (n 161) 236 which quotes Peter Jones, 'Risk Prediction in Criminal Justice' in Alan Harland (ed) *Choosing Correctional Options that Work: Defining the Demand and Evaluating the Supply* (Thousand Oaks Sage Publications 1996).

177 Don Grubin, 'Validation of Risk Matrix 2000 for Use in Scotland – Report Prepared for the Risk Management Agency' (2008). See also Walker (n 35) 182.

178 Gerd Gigerenzer, *Reckoning with Risk: Learning to live with Uncertainty* (Penguin Books 2002)186.

179 ibid.

180 Lucia Zedner, *Criminal Justice* (OUP 2004) 100.

be recognised that there are considerable technical difficulties in attempting to predict events with very low base rates.[181]

It has also been shown that there can be substantial variations between the results of one risk assessment tool and another, when the same information is inputted in relation to a particular offender.[182] Furthermore, it is very important that the manner in which the results of risk assessments are communicated, understood and applied is very important. Sentencers and parole decision-makers may well have little training on risk assessment[183] and accordingly there is potential for such decision makers, untrained in risk assessment, to draw inferences from the data in an individual case at hand which might not be appropriate or accurate.[184] The fact that parole and other decision-makers may have little training in this area places an even greater onus on probation officers and others preparing risk assessments for them to ensure that such reports are clear, accessible and comprehensible.

## Consistency and Flexibility in Risk Assessment

A further area of concern is that if clinicians rely totally on actuarial instruments they may ignore unusual factors, and circumstances, that are present in a particular case. After all, potentially dangerous offenders do not necessarily have anything in common except the likelihood that they may seriously harm somebody else.[185] Also, actuarial risk assessment is based on static factors that cannot change, which often creates difficulties in a therapeutic setting, where positive change is often the aim of the treatment being provided by the services conducting the risk assessment, yet the nature of the assessment means that there is little that either the clinician or the offender can do to reduce risk.[186] Another problem is that the actuarial risk assessment may be misleading for unusual

---

181 Shah (n 69) 227.

182 See Singh and others (n 62) 180-7.

183 Griffin (n 81) 82, where it is noted that Interim Parole Members on appointment did not receive in-service training regarding the role of the Interim Parole Board in the context of the criminal justice system or their individual role in the decision-making process.

184 ibid 113.

185 Susan Easton and Christine Piper, *Sentencing and Punishment – The Quest for Justice* (OUP 2005) 293.

186 Roychowdhury and Adshead (n 25) 80. See also Amanda Matravers, *Sex Offenders in the Community – Managing and Reducing the Risks* (Willan Publishing 2003) xv, where it is stated 'at a time when we know more than ever about sex offender characteristics and responses to treatment, the focus on risk assessment overshadows the range of strategies currently available to policy-makers and practitioners.'

individuals with characteristics that were not well represented in the samples used to construct or test the actuarial instruments.[187] In addition the risk assessment is dependent on the information about the offender collected through clinical interview and observation and file review and accordingly the quality of information of the judgment yielded depends on the quality of the information available and the accuracy with which it is processed – the assessment tool is only as good as the person administering it.[188] There are concerns that the base rates of violence (ie the known prevalence of a specified type of violent behaviour within a given population over a period of time) are so low that even a highly accurate risk assessment instrument would result in significant errors.[189]

## Other Potential Impacts of Risk Assessment

There is an inherent tendency that decisions made using risk assessments will lead to expansionist policies of incapacitation, if mistakes are made in predicting high risk offenders then the public's response may well be to demand that the range of offenders within the net be broadened.[190] There is also a very real danger of those administering the risk assessment applying 'precautionary logic'.[191] Whilst it is acknowledged that an actuarial risk assessment will be more predictive than chance in approximately 70% of cases it must be recognised that this only measures relative risk of the participants and gives no statistical basis for the allocation of offenders to the categories of very high, high, medium or low risk.[192] There are also further questions as to the accuracy of these tests and accordingly it is difficult to confidently justify the restrictions placed on individual offenders as being proportionate to the risk assessed.[193] Similarly, in an Irish context, it has been queried as to whether reliance on such a statistically inaccurate tool would be

187 Beech, Fisher and Thornton (n 56) 345.

188 Young (n 42) 8.

189 Olden (n 84). See also Kemshall and Pritchard (n 21) 241.

190 Easton and Piper (n 185) 133.

191 Paddy Richardson, Employment on Release–Presentation to the Association for Criminal Justice Research and Development, Penal Policy Reform Conference at Wheatfield Prison Dublin (20 September 2014) 8, where 'precautionary logic' is described as 'a concept best described as "you are always on the safe side if you give a negative prognosis."'

192 Singh and others (n 62) 180-7.

193 Roychowdhury and Adshead (n 25) 79. See also the Australian case of *Fardon v AG* [2004] HCA 46, Kirby J (dissenting).

compatible with the Irish constitution and the administration of justice.[194]

It has also been shown that most risk assessment instruments may not incorporate all of the variables identified as predictive, one notable example being that the offender's current age is not taken into account in most actuarial classification schemes.[195] This is despite the fact that research has shown that age can have a striking effect on recidivism with a general decline in recidivism after the age of 35, with a further decline from the age of 60, when sexual recidivism rates for many may reduce considerably. Slightly different effects have been observed for those previously convicted for rape of adults and those guilty of child sexual abuse, with the rate of sexual recidivism declining more sharply for rapists, although it should be borne in mind that these refer to statistical cohort findings and that not all individuals represented by such categorisations necessarily match the statistical trends in their own individual behaviours.[196]

The absence of attention being placed on the offender's age as a consideration in many of the assessments of risk in Ireland is all the more unfortunate as national research studies have clearly shown that there is a generally progressive reduction in recidivism through different age groups.[197] Furthermore, even where the age of the person is taken into account, it may not be taken into account in the most informative manner, with the RM2000/s for example scoring all offenders aged 35 or above in the lowest risk age band despite the fact that evidence suggests that people aged above 50 may differ in risk profile from those in their 30s and 40s.[198] Also, the group-based nature of prediction methods often conflict with popular notions of justice, with members of particular groups being deemed to be a risk despite the fact that they may never have committed a crime. Such effects of risk assessment can accordingly promote the continued marginalisation of populations already on

---

194 For comments particular to an Irish setting see O'Flaherty, 'Punishment and the Popular Mind' in O'Mahony (n 137) 381.

195 Raymond A Knight and David Thornton, Evaluating and Improving Risk Assessment Schemes for Sexual Recidivism; A Long Term Follow Up of Convicted Sexual Offenders, research report submitted to US Department of Justice (2007). See also Probation Service (n 31) 8.

196 ibid. See also Probation Service (n 31) 8.

197 Probation Service (n 31) 8, which found a progressive reduction in recidivism through the different age groups studied.

198 Barnett, Wakeling and Howard (n 120) 443. It should however be noted that more recent tools such as the SARN or START do consider more factors for sex offenders and increasingly all risk assessments are beginning to incorporate protective factors that mitigate risk.

the fringe of the economic and political mainstream.[199] Such caveats in relation to offender risk assessment do not negate the use of such assessments but rather serve to point up the need for those professionals using such instruments in their assessments to be trained and skilled not only in the application of the instruments, but to also be able to explain their interpretation and usage in comprehensive assessment processes.

## Further Potential Dangers in Risk Assessments

There is a danger that the use of risk assessment instruments can affect the ethos of those dealing with offenders, with a potential change in focus from individual assessment and treatment to 'techniques to identify, classify and manage groupings sorted by dangerousness'.[200] Some argue that the emphasis on risk assessments has accordingly caused the focus to move decisively from reintegration of the offender to prioritising considerations of public safety, perhaps to the exclusion of other important issues, including the need to 'do justice.'[201] This can render the system no longer about reforming, remoulding or improving the lives of those who have offended, including prisoners, but instead about administering and managing criminality in an efficient and extensive manner.[202] It must be remembered in this context that the Probation of Offenders Act 1907 remains the core mandate of the Probation Service and it lays down the primary function of the probation officer as being to 'advise, assist and befriend' the offender.[203] The modern emphasis on risk assessments raises the legitimate query as to whether or not this core mandate is still being fulfilled to the maximum appropriate extent.

Research has also found that some practitioners can often view the completion of the risk assessment as an isolated piece of work, to the detriment of other tasks relevant to the management of the offender such as report writing and intervention planning. Furthermore, an over-reliance on risk assessments may be seen as ethically flawed — it presumes the individual offender will follow a course of action in the future and punishes them accordingly, for a choice not yet made.[204] In effect, this runs counter to the very ethos

---

199 Matthews and Young (n 161) 237.
200 Whitehead (n 39) 46.
201 Van Zyl Smit and Corda (n 60) 19.
202 David Garland, *Punishment and Welfare; A History of Penal Strategies* (Aldershot 1985) 260.
203 Geiran (n 15) 84.
204 Easton and Piper (n 185) 134.

of probation and parole and the rehabilitative ideal upon which they rest.[205] It must always be remembered that actuarial methods of prediction do not address the causes of criminal behaviour, and are therefore unlikely to be able to effectively change the conditions which encourage offending — after all you cannot help, support and engage with offenders in a process of change, sitting in front of a machine.[206] Thus, practically and politically, they are a poor tool – in isolation – for reducing crime and protecting the public.[207] However, it must be acknowledged that whilst they will not cure the sociological causes of crime, they can be effective at identifying specific treatment needs in offenders and accordingly in focusing attention on these needs.

It must at all stages be remembered that whilst risk assessments can help inform and guide sentencing and parole decisions, they should not be dispositive or determinate, instead they should serve as an anchor for decision-making, with professional — including judicial — discretion remaining a crucial component in decisions.[208] It must also be remembered that there is no one-size-fits-all risk assessment tool — great care must be taken to ensure that the appropriate risk assessment tool or tools are utilised in each particular case.[209]

Notwithstanding the many criticisms listed in relation to the predictive and practical value of risk assessment tools, these criticisms are all predicated in the position that the results of the risk assessment are properly understood and utilised. Research has however disclosed that members of the Irish Interim Parole Board when interviewed demonstrated a limited understanding of the rudiments of risk and its technologies. They did not receive appropriate training and were not comfortable with the language of risk and actuarialism.[210] Furthermore, this research revealed that at times members of the Interim Parole Board expressed scepticism towards formal risk assessments and instead placed significant weight on their 'common sense' approach and identified risk factors which they deemed relevant to their own deliberations in individual cases. This research suggests that training in relation to the manner in which risk assessments are utilised by all involved in the parole process is vital.[211]

---

205 Young (n 42) 21.
206 Whitehead (n 39) 53.
207 Matthews and Young (n 161) 237.
208 Pew Centre on the States (n 52) 5.
209 ibid.
210 Griffin (n 81) 19.
211 ibid.

## Conclusion

This chapter analysed and explored risk, with particular emphasis on the study of risk as it relates to the criminal justice system. This examination involved an elemental study of the history and development of the notion of risk assessment and the manner and methods utilised to conduct same. This study of risk assessment was particularly focussed on the manner in which risk assessments have been used in Ireland and have evolved over recent decades. This examination of the use of risk assessment instruments in Ireland naturally led to a study of the manner in which risk assessment instruments are utilised in the sentencing, probation and parole process in Ireland.

This review of risk assessment instruments led to a consideration of some of the most oft quoted criticisms of risk assessment tools and the dangers presented by the over-reliance on such instruments was examined. Regardless of the criticisms directed towards these tools and the dangers posed by an over reliance on same it appears these instruments are now a permanent part of the Irish criminal justice landscape and it is vital for all key stakeholders to understand not only the role and purpose of these instruments, but also their limitations.

CHAPTER FOUR

# PROBATION WORK

## Introduction

This chapter will deal with what is known as *probation*, as conceptualised in the present context in the following three ways:

1. The specific court-imposed sanction of a probation bond under the Probation of Offenders Act 1907, as well as;
2. Generic probation practice, encompassing the broad scope of what may be summarised as *what probation officers do*, including but not confined to what is encompassed in 1 above; and
3. The phenomenon of what we know as the organisational probation system.

Therefore, in relation to generic probation (assessment and supervision) practice *per se*, this chapter will discuss not only the sanction of immediate, court-imposed probation supervision under the 1907 Act (more on this below), but also other forms of offender supervision and related work carried out by probation officers, whether the requirement for such supervision is imposed directly and immediately by a court, or in the context of post-custody supervision,[1] as many if not all of the same principles and practices apply to these latter, and more generalised, definitions of probation practice. In this context, and from the point of view of practice in Ireland, the following sections will deal with probation supervision beyond that imposed in a formal, legislatively-based court-mandated probation order as we know it, but also include probation *supervision during deferment of penalty* and supervision as a condition of a fully suspended sentence.

In addition, although other chapters in this book discuss different categories of probation supervisee,[2] and types of probation

1 Including supervision on *parole*. Please see Chapter 7 for more information on the Irish system of parole. Chapter 8 deals with other forms of conditional release from custody and post-release supervision of offenders, incorporating supervision by a probation officer.

2 For example, Children and Young People in Chapter 9, or other categories of persons discussed in Chapter 11.

interventions and supervision itself,[3] the overarching principles and practices outlined in this chapter are considered collectively in the generic sense, whatever the nature or source of the referral for supervision and the characteristics of the person being supervised, or the type of offence/s they have committed. Finally, while similar generically-based approaches to supervision are taken by probation officers using restorative justice interventions, specifically with those who have offended, interventions with victims of crime,[4] although adopting similar social work principles, skills and methods, would differ qualitatively compared to those interventions used with offenders.

Also included under the present chapter heading is the provision of care, support and other relevant interventions provided in the absence of formal legal orders. These latter examples of probation work include various types of social work engagement with individuals in the community or in custody, where there is no direct statutory responsibility or requirement to be involved. Such cases are often encompassed under the heading of *voluntary supervision*. It will be argued that all interventions and programmes implemented by probation officers, with the aims of offender rehabilitation and reintegration, reducing victimisation and promoting community justice, whether imposed by a court as a direct and immediate community sanction, or provided in the context of any early release from prison or detention with a condition of probation supervision, including any form of post-release supervision or parole, as well as in other (eg 'voluntary') contexts, represents what may be described collectively as *probation work*. While a formal probation order made under the Probation of Offenders Act 1907, as a court-imposed community sanction, in some respects is the only such provision or measure that strictly fits the bill of probation *per se*, the services and programmes provided by probation officers in response to the other types of supervision referenced above are broadly if not completely the same in practice and can therefore be described as coming under that broad heading of *probation work*. That said, where subjects discussed in this chapter overlap with those covered in other chapters, the subjects or issues referenced here will include pointers to the further detail addressed in the other relevant parts of this book.

---

3 Chapter 5 on Community Service, Chapter 6 on Restorative Justice and Victims, Chapter 7 on Parole, Chapter 8 on Conditional Release and Other Post-Release Supervision and Chapter 10 on Electronic Monitoring.

4 For example, the completion of a Victim Impact Report requested by a court, under the Criminal Justice Act 1993, s 5.

## Defining 'Probation' and 'Probation Officers'

The origin of the meaning of the word *probation* is rooted in the Latin verb *probare* — to test, whereby it is the person subject to probation who is being tested, usually to be of good behaviour. According to Canton and Hancock:[5]

> The term 'probation' derived from the Latin noun *probatio*, meaning a period of proving or testing – is both the name of a court disposal… and of services which administer such orders. Offenders who are placed on probation are given an alternative to harsher sentences, allowing them to remain in the community under supervision, subject to specified conditions. The concept has symbolic significance because of its association with certain principles and values.

In its early twentieth century manifestation, probation was the term applied in cases where criminal courts bound defendants over to be of good behaviour for a specific period of time, during which they could be returned to court to face the original charge if they did not 'prove themselves' through good behaviour. The term probation in modern times has a number of different, but not necessarily mutually exclusive, meanings. Probation can be understood as a system and as a type of supervision of those who have offended, in the community. More recently, in a range of jurisdictions, probation work has come to mean the full range of work and tasks undertaken by probation agencies and by probation officers.

Defining probation has preoccupied researchers and practitioners in the field since the earliest days of its history. Trought,[6] citing Robinson, described:

> …probation as being a function of education rather than of justice…. that probation is, strictly speaking, an educational service so far as it refers to the reformation of the offender. The problem of the offender is 'how to live better', and the purpose of probation is to teach him [sic] just that and to get him to do it now in the imperfect world in which he finds himself.

Any definition of probation *per se* is inevitably linked to defining the purpose and role of the probation officer. Just a few years after

---

5 Rob Canton and David Hancock (eds), *Dictionary of Probation and Offender Management* (Willan 2007) 220.

6 TW Trought, *Probation in Europe* (Basil Blackwell 1927) 186-187.

Trought's description of probation in Europe, Le Mesurier,[7] writing about the British probation system, warned that:

> The wisest laws, even when they are used with the utmost care and intelligence by the Courts, can only bring forth the full fruits of which they are capable if they are administered by officers who understand their nature, and carry them out, not merely in the dead letter, but in the living spirit. The importance of the probation officer as an official of the Court who is also a social worker dealing directly with the vital problem of turning asocial and anti-social persons into good citizens of the State, can hardly be overrated. His [sic] calling is not easy, and the qualifications needed for success are many and various.

More recently, and in the international, and specifically European, context the European Probation Rules[8] define probation as follows:

> Probation relates to the implementation in the community of sanctions and measures, defined by law and imposed on an offender. It includes a range of activities and interventions, which involve supervision, guidance and assistance aiming at the social inclusion of an offender, as well as contributing to community safety.

In some jurisdictions (eg in Scotland), what is commonly referred to elsewhere as probation is called, for historical and other reasons, 'criminal justice social work' instead. In yet other jurisdictions, the same work may be described as 'community corrections'. In others still, the overall range of probation tasks may be undertaken by a number of different actors. For example, it is the case in much of North America that probation and parole are organised and delivered by two completely separate organisations and systems. In many, if not most countries, probation and parole services are delivered by government/public services. This is the case in Ireland, where probation, as well as parole supervision, are delivered by the Probation Service. In other jurisdictions, probation services, or part thereof, may be delivered by or in cooperation with commercial entities.[9] In Britain, for a number of years, probation

---

7 L Le Mesurier, *A Handbook of Probation and Social Work of the Courts* (National Association of Probation Officers 1935) 52.

8 Council of Europe (2010) Recommendation CM / REC (2010) 1 of the Committee of Ministers to member States on the Council of Europe Probation Rules, Appendix II.

9 This is particularly the case where there are supervision programmes incorporating 'electronic monitoring' (EM) of offenders. In such instances, the

was delivered by a kind of 'hybrid' – incorporating a public service and commercial – model of service delivery.[10] In Austria, the Netherlands and Catalunya for example,[11] probation services have been fully managed and delivered for many years by State-funded non-governmental organisations. While the Probation Service in Ireland is a separate and stand-alone agency of the Department of Justice (see below for more on this), in some other jurisdictions probation and prison systems form part of a joined-up 'Prisons and Probation Service,' or 'Department of Corrections' or such agency with a similar organisational title.

For the purposes of the present publication, the term 'probation' strictly speaking is applied to the work undertaken under the legal framework of the Probation of Offenders Act 1907, as well as the relevant provisions of the Children Act 2001. At the same time, the general term 'probation work' is intended to refer to the broad range of work undertaken by the Probation Service, aimed at offender rehabilitation and reintegration in society. In this context, probation work represents the work undertaken by probation officers supervising people on statute-based court orders for probation, as well as the work undertaken with those subject to the full range of community-based supervision by the service, including those on community service,[12] supervision during deferment of penalty,[13] and post-release supervision and supervised conditional release, as well as fully or part-suspended custodial sentences incorporating supervision. The term also covers work undertaken by probation staff in custodial settings, including

---

EM is very often provided through commercial partners who work closely with the probation and prison organisations. In some EM programmes, the monitoring is provided and managed fully by the commercial company. See separate chapter on EM for more.

10 From Summer 2021, that 'hybrid' model has been replaced by a return to public service delivery of probation services, as part of HM Prison and Probation Service.

11 Autonomous community – and jurisdiction – in the North-East of Spain.

12 While community service, strictly speaking, comes within the definition of 'probation work' set out here, community service in Ireland (see separate Chapter 5 on Community Service) is legally framed primarily as a punishment, a direct alternative to imprisonment and a standalone sanction. Consequently, in what might be termed 'straightforward' community service cases, the individual subject to such an order frequently completes the order with minimal involvement or intervention by the relevant probation officer. That said, as described in Chapter 5, practice in Ireland has moved increasingly to acknowledge the reality that many of those undertaking community service face other life challenges that warrant the input of probation officers and others, with a view to enhancing the individual's rehabilitation and reintegration in the community.

13 See more on this particular and unique form of court-ordered supervision later in the chapter.

but not only work on behalf of the Parole Board, as well as more general assessment, rehabilitative and reintegrative work done with those in custody.

This use of terminology is not unique to Ireland, but rather reflects similarities with the relevant terminology used in other jurisdictions as well. That said, in Britain for example, there was a drift in recent decades away from the use of the terms probation, probation work and probation supervision, to terminology such as offender management, reflecting the parallel trend towards an increasingly punitive focus on risk assessment and risk management (see Chapter 3). In some jurisdictions, such as Spain, there does not exist a directly comparable word or term for what we call probation, which type of provision comes instead under a broader heading of 'alternative measures.' Nevertheless, even in such jurisdictions, the approach to the management of offenders that is known in Ireland and elsewhere as probation is understood as incorporating particular features, including specific legislative and organisational provisions, and can be discussed comparatively. In spite of the exceptions described above, the term probation generally maintains its virtually universal understanding and 'currency' as a court disposal and system of related services. In that context, as pointed out by Burnett[14] the term: 'Probation is symbolically loaded. It is a brand name that has international recognition.'

## Probation Officers

Those designated as probation officers have traditionally been those individuals appointed to carry out the functions associated with the supervision of probation orders and related work. The Probation of Offenders Act 1907, which will be considered in more detail below, described 'probation officers' and their duties as follows:

> 3(1) – There may be appointed as probation officer or officers for a petty sessional division such person or persons of either sex as the authority having power to appoint a clerk to the justices of that division may determine, and a probation officer when acting under a probation order shall be subject to the control of petty sessional courts for the division for which he [sic] is so appointed…

[14] Ros Burnett, 'Probation,' in Robert Canton and David Hancock, *Dictionary of Probation and Offender Management* (Willan 2007) 221.

4 – It shall be the duty of a probation officer, subject to the directions of the court –

(a) to visit or receive reports from the person under supervision at such reasonable intervals as may be specified in the probation order or, subject thereto, as the probation officer may think fit;

(b) to see that he observes the conditions of his recognizance;

(c) to report to the court as to his behaviour;

(d) to advise, assist and befriend him, and, when necessary, to endeavour to find him suitable employment.

These early descriptions of a probation officer's statutory responsibilities did not define the activities of the role *per se*. Part of the original vision was that in fact anyone possessing the appropriate background, attitude, character, values and moral authority could be a probation officer, although it became apparent that such individuals should possess certain attributes and skills if they were to fulfil the probation officer role well. In addition, during the early years of probation as a system and a legal sanction, there really did exist only probation officers — without any real supporting administrative or organisational structure — as the mainstay of that system. It was only years later that organisational management and related structures evolved and became part of the fabric of probation systems as we have come to know them.

More modern legal definitions of the probation officer role and their duties are contained in the Children Act 2001 and the Criminal Justice (Community Service) Act 2011. The Children Act describes the '[d]uties of probation officers',[15] insofar as children supervisees are concerned, thus:

259 – While a child remains under the supervision of a probation and welfare officer pursuant to this Act, whether in accordance with an order of a court or otherwise, the officer shall, subject to the directions of the court, where appropriate, and in addition to the terms of and any conditions attaching to any particular placement –

a) visit, assist, advise and befriend the child and, where feasible, the child's parents or guardian or other adult in whose residence the child may be residing,

b) see that the child observes the terms and any conditions attaching to the supervision, and

[15] See separate Chapter 9, on Children and Young People, for more on this aspect of the probation officer role.

c) where necessary and appropriate, endeavour to find the child suitable employment and accommodation.

The 2011 community service statute[16] updated the general legal definition of a probation officer in that regard and states:

> 13(1) – The officers of the Minister assigned to perform functions in the part of the Department of State for which the Minister is responsible commonly known as the Probation and Welfare Service before the coming into operation of this section shall, on and after that date, be known as the Probation Service and, references in any enactment to the Probation and Welfare Service of that Department of State shall be construed accordingly.
>
> (2) A person appointed by the Minister who was before the coming into operation of this section referred to as –
> (a) a probation officer,
> (b) a welfare officer, or
> (c) a probation and welfare officer,
>
> shall, on or after that date, be referred to as a probation officer and, references in any enactment to an officer referred to in paragraph (a), (b) or (c) shall be construed accordingly.

The role and duties of a probation officer in modern times tend to be more clearly defined in job descriptions and strategic policy statements for example. Nevertheless, that description is still firmly rooted in the legal and related responsibilities associated with the position, rather than a summary job description providing a detailed role definition, as such. These present-day responsibilities are listed as including:[17]

- Preparation of assessment reports on offenders;
- Managing the supervision of offenders subject to a range of court orders including probation orders, community service orders and post custody supervision;
- Delivery of young persons probation programmes under the Children Act 2001;
- Ensuring offenders' compliance with court orders and other orders.

---

16 Criminal Justice (Community Service) Act 2011.

17 See Probation Service website – March 2021 advertisement for the recruitment of locum probation officers, at: http://www.probation.ie/EN/PB/0/EF09819C46EAD0E38025867E0045BB57/$File/Update%20Locum%20Competition%20Booklet%202021%20(003).pdf accessed on 2 June 2021.

- Delivery of interventions with offenders to reduce offending, establish pro-social behaviour and reduce victimisation.

As probation practice over many years has become more developed and professionalised, and increasingly located in, as well as delivered through, managerial organisational structures, specific additional roles and new grades of staff have been created, to add value to and rationalise the probation supervision role, traditionally carried out by probation officers alone. Many probation organisations — including the Irish Probation Service — employ psychologists and specialist community service supervisors, for example.

Such psychologists may provide different assessment and specialised intervention inputs,[18] for example. Community service supervisors[19] are recruited on the basis of people-management and technical skills and relevant work background. They are employed to supervise groups of offenders undertaking physical and either unskilled or semi-skilled work on community service group work programmes.[20] Other specialist roles and staff grades, including for example probation assistants and probation service officers, among others, have also been added to modern probation service structures in some jurisdictions, to further develop organisational efficiency and effectiveness. This is based on the rationale that those trained and skilled in the assessment, supervision and case management of offenders[21] for example, are allowed, through appropriate organisational structures, to focus as much as possible on the core roles and functions for which they are best-qualified. Other specialist grades of worker employed in probation services include various professional administrative grades, specialists in finance, governance, human resources, estate management, procurement and accounting, among others. All of these may be employed by a probation service, yet the probation officer is still the person whose unique role tends to include the assessment of offenders and for holding the legal responsibility for the supervision of offenders on supervision orders, including holding the person being supervised to account for any breaches of their supervision conditions. In Ireland, there is not a separate staff grade

---

18 For example, in relation to issues associated with psychological functioning, mental illness, mental disorder or emotional distress.

19 In Ireland, community service supervisors are designated as technical civil servants.

20 See Chapter 5 for more on Community Service.

21 Particularly those assessed as presenting a higher level of risk of reoffending and/or of causing harm.

of parole officer, this supervision function also being carried out by probation officers.

## The History and Development of Probation Internationally

The history of probation, particularly in the British and wider Anglophone context, has been described and summarised by a number of authors.[22] Comparable commentary on the early history of the development of probation in Ireland has also been described elsewhere.[23] That early history and evolution, especially in these islands and more specifically in Ireland, is also elaborated and discussed in Chapter 2 of this book, dealing with the historical development of both probation and parole. As described by Vanstone, the overall development of probation, in terms of its organisation and practice, may be said to have evolved from '…a Christian model premised on the notion that offenders could be changed by homilies and exhortation…' moving through the 'rehabilitative model' and the so-called 'new rehabilitation' of the early and late twentieth century, to more recent focus on:

> …the effective improvement of the problem-solving skills of individual offenders in order to reduce the risk that they pose to others in the community is now the dominant objective of practice, but that still leaves room for a focus on the wider context of people's offending.[24]

While international developments in relation to probation practice, as well as wider criminal justice policy trends have undoubtedly influenced the evolution of policy and practice in Ireland, some of the more recent and relevant developments, especially those related

---

22 For example: William McWilliams, 'The Mission to the English Police Courts 1876-1936' (1983) 22(3) Howard J Crim Justice 129-147; William McWilliams, 'The Mission Transformed: Professionalisation of Probation between the Wars' (1985) 24(4) Howard J Crim Justice 257-274; William McWilliams, 'The English Probation System and the Diagnostic Ideal' (1986) 25(4) Howard J Crim Justice 241-260.

23 For example: Nicola Carr, 'Community sanctions and measures,' in Deirdre Healy, Claire Hamilton, Yvonne Daly and Michelle Butler (eds) *The Routledge Handbook of Irish Criminology* (Routledge 2016) 319-336; Vivian Geiran, 'The Development of Social Work in Probation' in Noreen Kearney and Caroline Skehill (eds), *Social Work in Ireland: Historical Perspectives* (Institute of Public Administration 2005); Gerry McNally, 'Probation in Ireland: A Brief History of the Early Years' (2007) 4 Irish Probation J 5-24; Gerry McNally, 'Probation in Ireland, Part 2: The Modern Age' (2009) 6 Irish Probation J 187-228.

24 Maurice Vanstone, *Supervising Offenders in the Community: A History of Probation Theory and Practice* (Ashgate 2004) 159.

to the organisation and practice of probation work in Ireland, will be considered here now.

## Evolution of the Probation Service and Probation Practice in Ireland

Two particular landmark reviews and policy developments in Ireland, influencing the evolution of probation practice and the use of community sanctions more generally as key components of penal policy, were the so-called 'Whitaker Report'[25] review of penal policy and the review and two reports by the Expert Group on the Probation and Welfare Service.[26] According to the 1998 Report of the Expert Group[27] on the Probation and Welfare Service:

> The Probation and Welfare Service has been in existence since the early 1960s when it was established following a recommendation of an Interdepartmental Committee set up to examine vandalism. At the time, the Service was confined to the Dublin Metropolitan Courts and the Prisons in the Dublin area. In 1969, a Departmental review of the Service was undertaken, following a significant increase in the demands of the Service from a number of District Court areas and the number of young persons being committed to custody. A further review of the Service in 1979, saw it restructured to its present form.

As well as the 1985 Whitaker Report on the Penal System and the subsequent Expert Review of the Probation and Welfare Service and the Group's two reports (referenced above), the Comptroller and Auditor General published a value for money review of the Probation Service in 2004.[28] While the Whitaker Report was a general review of the penal system, it did include significant discussion and recommendations regarding the Probation Service, including advocating greater use, as well as 'extension and strengthening,' of community sanctions such as probation. The Report also recommended the introduction of:

---

25 Committee of Inquiry into the Penal System Report (1985).

26 Probation Service, *Expert Group on the Probation and Welfare Service: First Report* (1998) and Probation Service, *Expert Group on the Probation and Welfare Service: Final Report* (1999).

27 Probation Service (1998) (n 26) 14.

28 Comptroller and Auditor General, *The Probation and Welfare Service: Report on Value for Money Examination* (2004).

- More effective sanctions for those offences not warranting the use of imprisonment,
- Alternatives to be available where either the circumstances of the offence or the characteristics of the offender make prison an unsuitable punishment,
- Other sentencing options likely to reduce reoffending to be used, and
- Specialised programmes to be introduced for 'habitual offenders.'[29]

The Expert Group Review, established in November 1997 by John O'Donoghue TD, Minister for Justice, following a Government decision, was a major organisational review and, by its nature, focused on the Probation Service. The Group, through its two reports, assessed what needed to be done to modernise the Service and ensure its continuing relevance in the criminal justice system, on behalf of Irish society. The terms of reference of the Expert Group, which was chaired by Brian McCarthy, chairman of the Fexco company, were to examine:

1) the role of the Probation and Welfare Service having regard to recent and current developments,
2) the needs of the Service, in the context of its proper role, to deliver an effective and efficient service, and
3) the organisational status of the Service,

and make recommendations and report back to Government within 4 months.

The Expert Group made two reports, the first in 1998,[30] followed by its final report in 1999.[31] The Group made its first, interim, report on the basis that '...before addressing the future needs [of the Service]... certain measures must be taken immediately in order that the Service can carry out its present responsibilities more effectively' and made specific recommendations that should be taken as a matter of urgency, while the work of the Group continued. In this interim report, the Expert Group identified '[p]roblems within the Probation and Welfare Service.'[32] These included issues with the Service's high levels of work demands, organisational structure, resourcing, staffing, recruitment, finance, research and statistics, ICT and staff training and development.

29 Committee of Inquiry (n 25) 44.
30 Probation Service (1998) (n 26).
31 Probation Service (1999) (n 26).
32 Probation Service (1998) (n 26) 16-24.

This report made six recommendations, described as 'immediate priorities', as follows:

1. That the number of staff serving be brought up to levels previously approved by government decisions and that the system for recruitment of staff be streamlined.
2. Investment in a comprehensive public information and awareness programme in relation to the Probation Service.
3. That an invitation to tender for a new IT system should issue immediately.
4. That a comprehensive staff training needs analysis be undertaken.
5. That resources be allocated to the development of data and research in the service.
6. That the regulations in relation to insurance for community service should be amended, to remove difficulties presenting for voluntary groups involved in providing community service placements.[33]

The Group's final report was issued in 1999 and made thirty recommendations,[34] regarding improvements, as summarised under the following three headings:

1. *Policy and legislative framework:* greater range of non-custodial sanctions; need for updated probation legislation; community sanctions to be established as sanctions in their own right, rather than as 'alternatives to custody'; greater interagency coordination; expansion of probation and bail hostels; expansion of sex offender treatment programmes; development of research and evaluation to inform practice; and establishment of relevant research priorities.
2. *Structures and Staffing:* establishment of a statutory Probation Agency; clarification of the service's role; a Service Director to be appointed as Chief Executive Officer; development of a number of specific functions and areas of responsibility within the service; appropriate regional structures to be developed; staff numbers, grades and salaries to be determined; two distinct service sections to be established — one for criminal law, the other for family law; establishment of an advisory forum for the service; appointment of an Inspector of Probation;

---

33 Probation Service (1998) (n 26) 25-26.
34 Probation Service (1999) (n 26) 8-13.

relationships with other agencies to be developed through negotiated agreements; and that provision be made for staff mobility throughout the service.

3. *Role of the Service:* The expansion and development of the Probation Service role in the court, as well as in prisons and places of detention; that the Service be adequately resourced to fulfill its functions in the family courts; the probation officer role of providing independent objective assessments to the courts to be maintained, including in the family law courts; any drug court established to have the benefit of probation officer input; that the role of probation officers be enhanced in areas such as addictions and other relevant behaviors; that the service clarify for the courts the nature and range of programmes provided for those under supervision, including for those with drug and alcohol problems; structures and resources to be provided to allow for the provision of comprehensive aftercare services for prisoners; staff from the Probation Service no longer to be seconded to the Adoption Board; and that the role of the service in the special schools for young people to be discontinued.

While a number of the recommendations of the Expert Group were not actioned, many of the key ones were, including some of those in relation to the appointment of a director and establishment of appropriate organisational structures. Others — such as the modernising of the Probation Act 1907 legislative provisions — remain aspirational, yet not accomplished at the time of writing. Either way, the two reports and their recommendations have set the benchmark and foundation for the present-day Probation Service as things stand.

The 2014 Strategic Review of Penal Policy[35] subsequently described some of the functions of probation supervision as follows:

> In terms of community sanctions, probation supervision, community service orders and suspended sentences with supervision conditions are the main penalties available. Sanctions implemented by the Probation Service aim to reduce risk of harm and re-offending, make good the harm done by crime and ensure that court orders are implemented in the community. Probation Service staff work with offenders to help them become ex-offenders.

---

35 Department of Justice and Equality, *Strategic Review of Penal Policy: Final Report* (2014) 46.

That review concluded[36] that '...the overarching purpose of criminal and penal policy should be to make Ireland a safer and fairer place' and recommended that:

- A multi-agency approach to the development of appropriate, alternative non-custodial sanctions is required...;
- Community sanctions should be developed so as to be capable of addressing the higher risk offender and address the underlying causes of offending. Targeted supervisory sanctions tailored to the individual needs of a particular offender may provide an appropriate solution but requires the collaborative effort of those responsible for the supervision of the offender and those responsible for service provision...;
- The unnecessary use of imprisonment, such as for the non-payment of fines, must be seriously reduced... while other alternatives to imprisonment such as community service.... should be pursued and the use of restorative justice promoted...[37]

as well as recommending that:

- ...imprisonment be regarded <u>as a sanction of last resort</u> [emphasis in original], and that this principle be incorporated in statute.
- ...that non-custodial sanctions should become the default position in dealing with less serious offenders, and
- ...that, in all cases where a custodial sentence is imposed by a court, the Court should set out its reasons in writing for so doing... [and] that this requirement be incorporated in statute. [38]

Among other proposals, the Report recommended:

- ...increased focus on and promotion of community service as an alternative to imprisonment... [including] that the Probation Service examine the feasibility of introducing, on a pilot basis, an integrated community service where community service would be imposed with conditions, such as a mandatory restriction on movement order or addiction treatment, where appropriate; [39]

---

36 Department of Justice and Equality (n 35) 8.
37 ibid 9.
38 ibid 91-94.
39 Department of Justice and Equality (n 36) 49. See Chapter 5 for more on this.

- ...greater use of structured temporary release...[40]
- ...the continuation and the expansion of the Community Return and Community Support Scheme.[41]

The Report also recommended 'the extension of the restorative justice programmes.'[42] The Strategic Review Report, which was accepted and published by the Minister for Justice, became and still is, up to the time of writing, Government policy in this area. In that respect, the Report gives considerable weight to the future development of community sanctions, including probation supervision, community service and the various types of supervised early-release and post-custodial supervision programmes referred to.

## The Irish Probation Service More Recently

Since at least the 1970s, when staff numbers increased relatively significantly and with the introduction of more Senior Probation Officers, the primary collective organisational unit of service delivery in the Service has been the team, headed up by a Senior Probation Officer, who generally manages and supports a small number of probation officers, community service supervisors and perhaps one clerical officer. While there have been a series of major milestones in the organisational and practice developments in Irish probation over the course of the past half-century, developments in the early decades of the current millennium have been particularly significant for a number of reasons. The relative significance of these has arisen not just because of their recentness, but also arising from their relatively radical nature in terms of change, and because of this as a result their direct impact on current practice. The appointment of Michael Donnellan as the first director[43] of the Probation Service, in 2005, gave effect to some of the most significant recommendations of the Expert Group that had reported some six years earlier. That appointment was followed by the reorganisation of the service, placing it on a solid foundation for ongoing development.

One of the early initiatives taken by the newly-appointed director was to carry out an internal review — or audit — of various aspects of the organisation, structure and practice in the

---

[40] ibid 84.

[41] ibid 87. For more on Community Return and Community Support programmes, see Chapter 5.

[42] ibid 52.

[43] Previous Heads of Service had been designated as the Principal Probation and Welfare Officer.

agency. External consultants, working with Probation Service staff, examined all facets of probation structures, operations and policies and reported accordingly.[44] Some of the report's thirty-one findings and recommendations included suggestions regarding changes in: strategy, leadership and management, structure and the implementation of policies and practice, as well as caseload management, and proposed developments in HRM, ICT, and relationships with partner bodies in the community and voluntary sector. Two key actions arising from the findings of the as-is audit were the establishment of two groups, to further review: (a) the organisational structure of the Probation Service and (b) to review existing policies and operating procedures and to make recommendations accordingly. As a result, the service was reorganised into five geographical regions, organised on a county boundary basis, within existing resources, and headed up by a regional manager, as follows:

**Figure 1: Regional Organisation of the Probation Service**

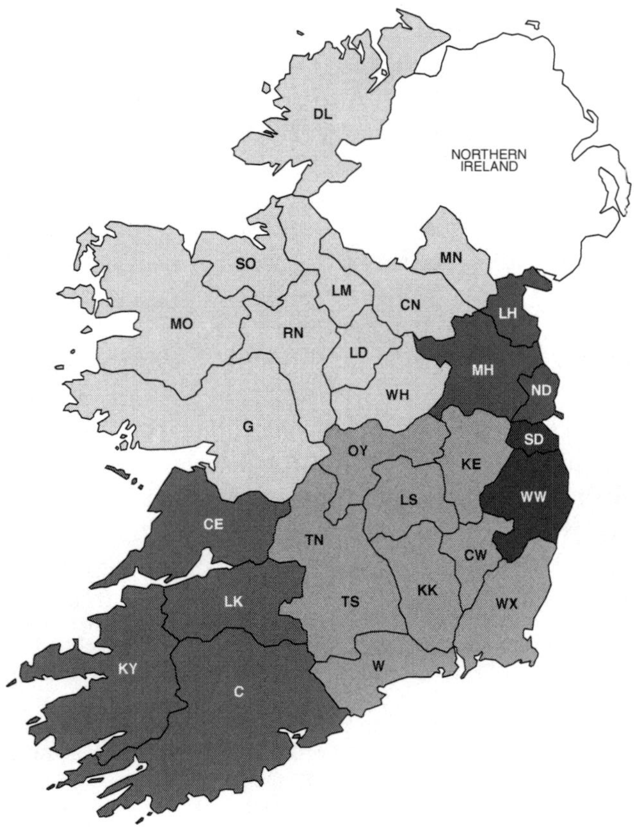


[44] Probation Service (2007) *An 'As Is' Audit of Probation Operations in Ireland, July – October 2006.*

It was also decided to introduce two 'national' regions: one in respect of 'young persons probation', the other for 'prisoners, risk and resettlement'. These latter two regions were established for a number of reasons, including to bring a greater level of coherence and consistency to the organisational structure, to provide greater clarity in relation to the agency's interface and cooperation with external partners, to facilitate staff working in these areas to have a greater sense of collective identity, and ensure a greater degree of consistency in practice and service delivery. Two key criteria for the drawing of the five geographical boundaries were that regional boundaries should be contiguous with county boundaries[45] and that each region should have a similar level of population as the others.[46] Each region is comprised of a number of teams, generally headed up by a senior probation officer.

## Probation Work — Overview

In a statement to an Oireachtas Committee in November 2018,[47] then Director of the Probation Service, Vivian Geiran, summarised the work of the Service as follows:

> The Probation Service in Ireland is an agency of the Department of Justice. The two primary areas of work undertaken by the Probation Service are:
> (1) offender assessment and
> (2) offender supervision.

As outlined by Geiran,[48] probation practice in Ireland is strongly linked to and based in social work values, principles and practice methods. As is the case in other branches of social work, in probation practice, every client case should start with a clear referral (request for service). This is followed in turn by completion at an early stage of a comprehensive assessment of the individual, which should in turn inform the case management plan, incorporating the specific actions and interventions and so on, aimed at addressing

---

45 One anomaly in this was the division of Dublin into a 'North' and 'South' side, on the basis of simple clarity, rather than a division on the basis of aligning with the four local authorities in Dublin (pp 93–110).

46 Each region had a population, on this basis, of between 800-900,000.

47 Probation Service, Briefing to the Oireachtas Joint Committee on Justice and Equality, Meeting in Relation to (a) Pre-legislative Scrutiny of the General Scheme of the Sex Offenders (Amendment) Bill 2018, and (b) Detailed Scrutiny of the Sex Offenders (Amendment) Bill 2018 [PMB] (28 November 2018).

48 Vivian Geiran, 'The Relationship between Probation Practice and Social Work in Ireland: Time to Tie the Knot Once and For All?' (2021) Winter, Irish Social Worker Journal.

the individual's needs and especially those assessed as most likely to be linked to risk of future reoffending. The overall process map, outlining the journey of an individual, through referral, assessment and supervision, from starting to ending, is represented in the following figure.

**Figure 2: Representation of Probation Case Workflow**

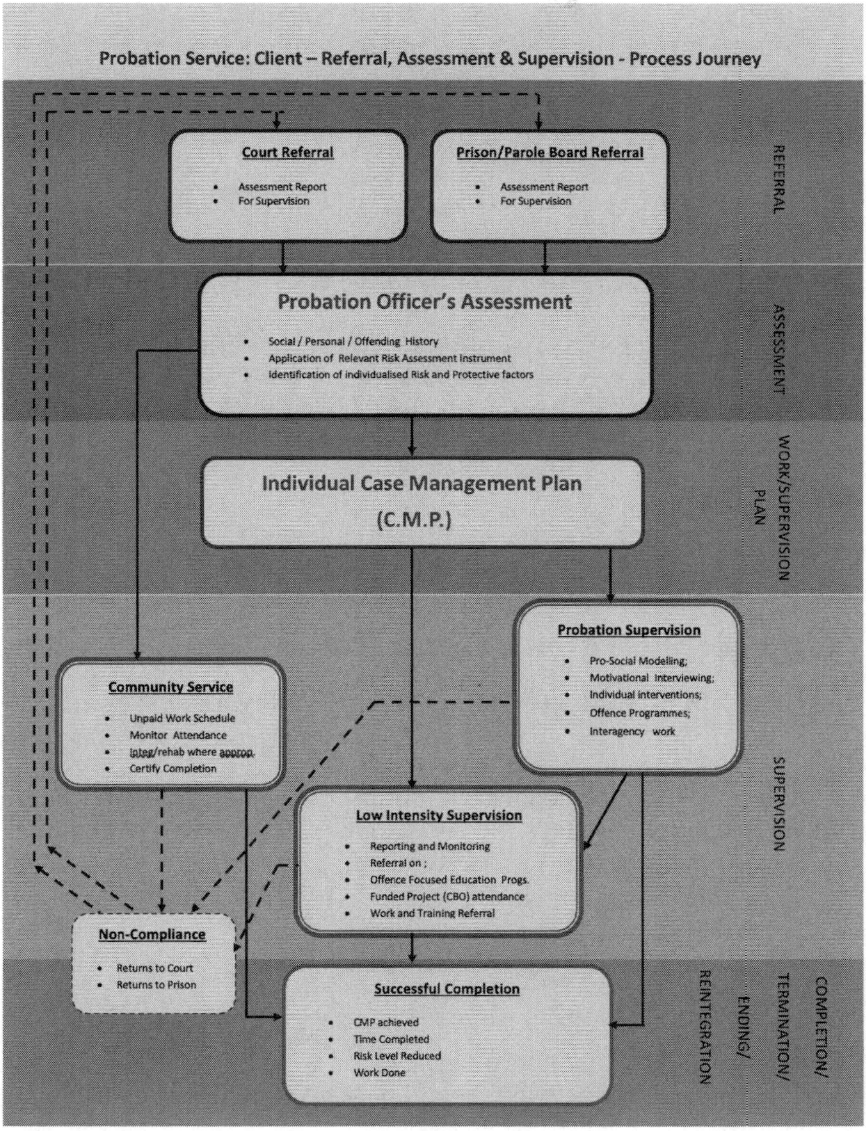

## Offender Assessment

Assessment, in general health, social work, and social care, as well as forensic and criminal justice settings, can be defined[49] as:

> the collection and processing of data to provide information for use in making decisions about the nature of the problem and what is to be done about it (Ivry, 1992)[50] – [and] is a cognitive, thinking process; it involves thinking about data that have been collected. The outcome of assessment is a service plan, which provides a definition of the problem for work, objectives or solutions to be achieved, and an action plan to accomplish the objectives.

The matter of criminal justice, probation and parole assessments, is addressed in more detail in Chapter 3. In general terms, as described by Geiran,[51] in his statement to the Oireachtas Committee:

> Most assessments are undertaken by probation officers at the request of the courts, to assist in sentencing decisions, and to identify what factors need to be addressed in order to reduce an individual's likelihood of reoffending. Other individual offender assessments are undertaken by probation officers on behalf of the Parole Board and the Irish Prison Service, for example.

## Offender Supervision – Overview

On the subject of supervision, Geiran[52] summarised that:

> Probation supervision includes a range of interventions undertaken with offenders, mainly in the community, aimed at helping them to reduce their risk of reoffending and make good the harm caused by their offending. Specifically, these interventions, which are based on the probation officer's initial risk and needs assessment, enlist the co-operation of the offender and those around them (eg family, other positive supports) to address any dynamic (ie open to possible change) issues or factors which may have contributed to their offending. These factors can include: anti-social attitudes,

49 Beulah Roberts Compton and Burt Galaway, *Social Work Processes* (Brooks/Cole Publishing 1999) 253.
50 J Ivry, 'Teaching geriatric assessment' in Joanna Mellor and Renee Solomon (eds), *Geriatric social work education* (Haworth 1992) 3-22.
51 Probation Service (n 47).
52 ibid.

> pro-criminal associates, substance misuse or addiction, homelessness, mental health issues, lack of positive role-models, poor problem-solving and self-management, and unemployment, among others. What we term 'probation type supervision' also includes work with those in custody, helping them prepare for reintegration in the community, again with a focus on helping to reduce their risk of reoffending. Community service is a direct alternative to prison, available to the courts, for those sixteen years of age and over, who are guilty of an offence that would otherwise attract a custodial sentence, and who can then be ordered to perform unpaid work in the community as an alternative sanction.

And added that:

> At the core of what Probation staff do across all our programmes is to: motivate offenders to change, to help them increase both their ability to change, and facilitate improved opportunities for change. Probation officers do this through the development of positive professional relationships, within clear role boundaries, and using skills and interventions based on those shown by research to be effective. These in turn are founded on social work training, and national and international standards of good practice, including for example the Council of Europe Probation Rules (2010). While those we work with are, in the main, those who have committed criminal offences, a central focus for probation work is the impact of offending on victims, and the needs, rights and position, of victims of crime. Our work would be one-dimensional if we only focused on the offender. In doing what we do, we need to be conscious of, and seek to repair where possible, the broken relationship between offender, victim and the wider community. We do this in a number of ways. When preparing a pre-sanction assessment on an offender, we assess, as part of that, the impact on the particular victim or victims, the offender's understanding of that impact, and how we can help that offender to avoid creating more victims again in the future. We also provide opportunities to offenders to make good the harm they have caused. This includes performance of community service, as well as a number of reparative and restorative interventions and programmes that we run, many of these in conjunction with partner agencies.

## Probation Practice as Social Work – Principles, Values and Practice

Geiran[53] has argued elsewhere that probation practice shares most if not all of the features of social work. The approaches, practice models, skills, methods and interventions in probation work overlap with social work to such a significant extent as to be indistinguishable from each other. Social work in general, as well as probation practice as one branch of such work, increasingly calls upon the probation officer to employ a diverse 'toolkit' of skills and methods. There has been a movement in recent times to consolidate the probation 'toolkit' of skills, methods and practice into a comprehensive professional practice framework, based on key principles, using a firm evidence base, combined with methods that are proven to be effective, in order to achieve the best outcomes. One such model, or framework, is what is known as the ASPIRE — Assessment, Planning, Implementation, Review and Evaluation — model, described in detail by Canton and Dominey, who summarise ASPIRE as:

> Roughly, *assessment* works out what the problems are; *planning* specifies what needs to be done and how this will take place; *implementation* involves putting the plan into effect; *review* and *evaluation* consider what has taken place – and may set the scene for a further assessment. [54]

At a more 'granular' level, one particularly key element, or part of the 'toolkit' of probation social work is, as referenced above, the worker's skill and ability at motivating clients to make positive and lasting change in their lives. In landmark papers, Prochaska and DiClemente (1982, 1983 and 1992)[55] set out a model of change that has had widespread application in social work and related professions. As referenced by Loughran (2019),[56] the '…concept of the wheel of change is well-known in social work' and 'there is a direct connection between motivation and outcomes.' For this reason, it is worth pointing to the value of the wheel of change as a model of the behavioural change process.

---

53 Geiran (n 48).

54 Rob Canton and Jane Dominey *Probation* (2nd edn, Routledge 2018) 177-200.

55 James O Prochaska and Carlo C DiClemente, 'Transtheoretical therapy: Toward a more integrative model of change,' (1982) 19(3) Psychol Psychother 276-288; James O Prochaska and Carlo C DiClemente , 'Stages and processes of self-change of smoking: Toward an integrative model of change,' (1983) 51(3) J Consult Clin Psychol 390-395; James O Prochaska and Carlo C DiClemente, 'In search of how people change: Applications to addictive behaviours' (1992) 47(9) Am Psychol 1102-1114.

56 Hilda Loughran, *Counselling Skills for Social Workers* (Routledge 2019) 187-188.

The following is diagrammatic representation of the wheel of change.

**Figure 3: The Wheel of Change**

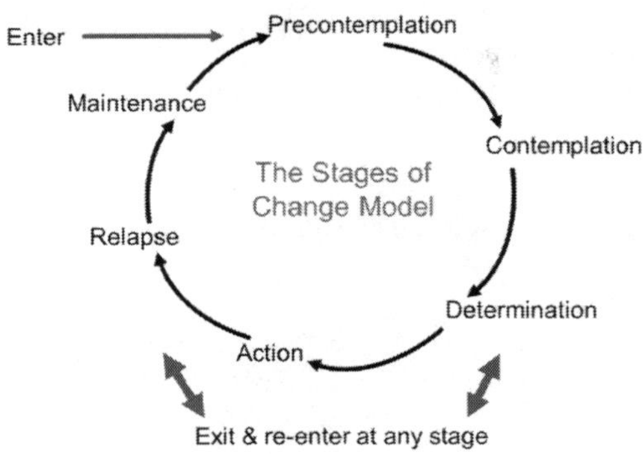


As Loughran also pointed out, such a model of change is useful in helping us understand the stepped process involved, the nature of the change journey and appreciating the relevant steps and their significance for service users, including that '...motivation to change is increased by previous success in changing' (the need to find and build on strengths) and that, in turn, 'success builds a repertoire of skills for change.'[57] A summary of specifically useful skills and methods for probation officers, and especially how such a framework and 'toolkit' for practice is being developed and applied in the Irish context, will be considered further under *Core Correctional Practices* below.

## The Community and Community Based Organisations

It is also important to note the valuable role a range of partner organisations, including a number in the community and voluntary sector, as well as wider civil society, play in offender rehabilitation and reintegration. Since the earliest days of probation in Ireland, the community and voluntary sector has played a key role. With the enactment of the Criminal Justice Administration Act 1914 (see more below), the part played by community organisations on probation work has been recognised, acknowledged and resourced. Indeed, in Ireland, a relatively high percentage of the Probation Service's annual budget goes to funding community based organisations that provide relevant services to those individuals under Probation

---

57 ibid at 188-189.

Service supervision.[58] The community and voluntary organisations in question provide a range of services, including those related to: mentoring; accommodation; education, training and employment; substance misuse; citizenship, community development and pro-social activities; positive use of leisure time; family programmes; offending behaviour programmes; mental health initiatives; youth services and social enterprise, among others. See also Chapter 11 for more on the involvement of wider civil society in the rehabilitation and reintegration of offenders.

## Key Developments in Probation Practice — RNR and What Works

The history of changes in perceptions regarding offender rehabilitation are discussed in Chapter 2. That discussion covers the evolution, following many years of rehabilitative optimism, to an emerging view incorporating a 'nothing works' perspective on offender rehabilitation, following Martinson's article, through to a renewed exploration of and focus on 'what works,' recalibrating and re-prioritising the goals and practice of probation. Since the 1990s at least, there has been a growth in the development of what is known as 'what works,' focused on ensuring the implementation of practices, interventions, and programmes that have been demonstrated through research findings to be effective in reducing one's risk of reoffending. The central principles of what works are those of Risk, Need and Responsivity, which have been summarised by Canton and Dominey as follows:

- The *risk principle* states that the higher the risk of reoffending, the more intensive and extended the supervision programme should be. The principle can accordingly be used to determine who should be worked with and to what level. As well as a principle of effective practice, it is a reasonable device for targeting resources on those who are most likely to offend again.
- The *need principle* insists that the focus of intervention must be on those needs or factors associated with their offending. These are known as crimongenic needs… some well-established factors are known to be associated with offending, notably: pro-criminal attitudes, antisocial personality, pro-criminal associates, social achievement

[58] See Probation Service, Annual Report 2020 (Probation Service 2021) 78-79, for a full list of the sixty-two organisations so funded.

(education, employment), family/marital status, substance abuse, and recreation issues.

- *Responsivity* (defined by Dominey)[59] as 'ensuring that all interventions, programmes and activities with offenders are run in a way which is engaging, encourages full participation and takes account of issues of identity and diversity.'

Other 'what works' principles identified and summarised by Canton and Dominey (2018)[60] include the following:

- *Respect for the person* (importance of values, including practice that is just, humane, decent and professional),
- *Community based programmes* (are more effective than ones run in custodial settings),
- *Multimodal approaches* (a diverse repertoire of interventions will be required for those with multiple problems or issues to be addressed),
- *Structured assessment* (interventions based on structured and validated assessment methods), and
- *Programme integrity* (that is, the programme is delivered in the manner intended).

The 'critical importance of relationships' is also recently being reasserted in probation practice, as described by Canton and Dominey (2018)[61] including through:

- The firm, fair and clear use of authority,
- Modeling pro-social and anti-criminal attitudes, cognition and behaviors, teaching concrete problem-solving skills,
- Using community resources (brokerage), and
- Forming and working through warm, open and enthusiastic relationships (arguably the most important component).

The above developments in relation to what works have been summarised and discussed in further detail by Andrews and Bonta (2010);[62] Burnett and Roberts, 2004;[63] Canton and Dominey, 2018;[64]

---

59 Canton and Dominey (n 54) 122.

60 ibid 122-123.

61 Canton and Dominey (n 54) 124.

62 Donald Andrews and James Bonta, 'Rehabilitating criminal justice policy and practice' (2010) 16(1) Psychol Pub Pol & Law 39-55.

63 Ros Burnett and Colin Roberts (eds), *What Works in Probation and Youth Justice: Developing evidence-based practice* (Willan 2004).

64 Canton and Dominey (n 54).

Bonta and Andrews (2017),[65] among others. The principles of 'risk, need and responsivity' (or RNR) have come to predominate much of the thinking in relation to offender assessment and management, in probation work in Ireland and internationally, to this day.

## Desistance and the Good Lives Model

More recently still, the emergence (although it may be more appropriate to say *re-emergence*) of a focus on the desistance paradigm, in terms of understanding offending behaviour patterns and how to change them for the better, has and continues to have a significant impact on probation and parole practice. While acknowledging that '[t]here is no single accepted definition of desistance' from crime, Canton and Hancock[66] defined the phenomenon as: 'The process by which people come to cease and sustain cessation of offending behaviour, with or without intervention by criminal justice agencies.' According to Healy:

> Desistance was first 'discovered' in the nineteenth century by Adolphe Quetelet who was the first to describe the relationship between age and crime. The age-crime curve shows that offending tends to increase during the teenage years but declines steeply from the mid-20s onwards, eventually reaching a point where offending is at or close to zero. Although there is some inter-country variation in the timing and shape of a criminal career, the existence of desistance has been confirmed by numerous studies in diverse cultural and social contexts... This has led to desistence after a criminal career being described as the norm rather than the exception...[67]

Gelsthorpe and Morgan,[68] citing Maruna and Farrall,[69] concur with the latter on the point that: 'the verb "to desist" means to abstain from doing something' and '[l]ikewise, in criminology, desistance is almost always used to mean "the continued state of non-offending" rather than factors that lead to it.' Gelsthorpe and Morgan also

---

65 Donald Andrews and James Bonta, *The Psychology of Criminal Conduct* (6th edn Routledge 2017).

66 Canton and Hancock (n 54) 90.

67 Deirdre Healy, 'Desistance-focused practice,' in Philip Birch and Louise Sicard (eds), *Prisons and Community Corrections*, Routledge Innovations in Corrections (Routledge 2020) 260.

68 Loraine Gelsthorpe and Rod Morgan (eds), *Handbook of Probation* (Willan 2007) 360.

69 Shadd Maruna and Stephen Farrall, 'Desistance from crime: a theoretical reformulation' (2004) 43 Köln Z Soziol Sozialpsychol 171-194.

reference Lemert in highlighting the two phases of 'primary' and 'secondary' desistance. Differentiating between these two, albeit closely related concepts, Gelsthorpe and Morgan[70] reference Lemert's[71] theorising on primary and secondary deviation, which included the statement that: 'Primary deviation involved the initial flirtation and experimentation with deviant behaviours', while 'secondary deviation on the other hand, is deviance that becomes "incorporated as part of the 'me' of the individual".' Transferring these (*primary* and *secondary*) categorisations of patterns of deviant behaviours to desistance, Gelsthorpe and Morgan[72] state that:

> Primary desistance, Maruna and Farrall argue, represents desistance at its most basic and literal level: any lull or crime-free gap... in the course of a criminal career. Because we are interested – at both the theoretical levels and in terms of practice – most with desistance that results in the total ending of the criminal career, the focus of desistance research would be on secondary desistance. In other words, with the movement from the behaviour of non-offending to the assumption of a role or identity of a non-offender or 'changed person.' In secondary desistance, crime not only stops, but 'existing roles become disrupted' and a 'reorganization based upon a new role or roles will occur'[73] [and that there is] compelling evidence that long-term desistance does involve identifiable and measurable changes at the level of personal identity or 'the "me" of the individual'.[74]

Nevertheless, Gelsthorpe and Morgan,[75] citing Foote and Frank,[76] note also that 'desistance is no end state where one can be; rather, it is a perpetual process of arrival.'

## Who Works

As referenced above, there has been much focus in community sanctions research and practice over the past three decades or so on *what* works in reducing one's risk of reoffending. This has

70 Gelsthorpe and Morgan (n 68) 360.
71 Edwin M Lemert, *Social Pathology: Systematic Approaches to the Study of Sociopathic Behaviour* (McGraw-Hill 1951) 76.
72 Gelsthorpe and Morgan (n 68) 360-361.
73 Lemert (n 71) 76.
74 ibid.
75 Gelsthorpe and Morgan (n 68) 361.
76 CE Foote and AW Frank, 'Foucault and therapy: the disciplining of grief,' in Adrienne S Chambon, Allan Irving and Laura Epstein (eds), *Reading Foucault for Social Work* (Columbia University Press (1999).

been reflected in the identification and organised application of those interventions and programmes proven to be more effective at achieving the goal of reduced recidivism, as described above. More recently, an increasing level of attention has been focused on what qualities the individual probation or parole worker brings to their work and how those qualities and skills can be enhanced and applied to greatest positive effect. This has come to be conceptualised as *who* works, often seen as complementary to the implementation of *what* works, in terms of effective interventions and programmes, delivered by skilled staff using evidence-informed practice, in a self-reflective way and where every effort is made to maximise client *engagement*.[77] As described by Geiran and Durnescu:

> Both theoretical models – RNR and Desistance – argue that although the content of an intervention is critical, the way it is delivered is equally important. This idea was developed further in the so-called 'who works' literature that describes the skills and the characteristics needed for staff to work effectively for reducing the risk of reoffending and supporting desistance.[78]

These authors go on to describe some of the specific skills that probation and parole officers need to be most effective. These are frequently referred to now as *core correctional skills* or *core correctional practices*, which will now be considered.

## Core Correctional Practices

As described by Haas and Smith,[79] those involved directly in providing probation and parole services and interventions are concerned, *inter alia*, with reducing rates of recidivism and risk of reoffending among their respective client populations, asserting — as described above — that:

> Research evidence on what works in the rehabilitation of offenders has continued to grow over the past several decades. This has led to the discovery of many evidence-based practices

---

77 See Canton and Dominey (n 54) 188-189, for more on engagement.

78 Vivian Geiran and Ioan Durnescu, *Implementing Community Sanctions and Measures: Guidelines* (Council of Europe 2019) 26-34.

79 Stephen M Haas and Jaclyn Smith (2020) 'Core Correctional Practice: The role of the working alliance in offender rehabilitation,' in Pamela Ugwudike and others (eds), *The Routledge Companion to Rehabilitative Work in Criminal Justice* (Routledge 2019) 340.

> and principles of effective correctional intervention that – when properly adhered to – have been shown to improve reductions in recidivism (Andrews and Bonta 2010; [80] Bonta *et al*,[81] 2013; Duwe, 2017;[82] Haas, 2013[83]).

The collectivity of skills and methods proven to be effective in achieving the above goals have come to be described by a range of commentators as core correctional practices, that is the methods which, if applied by skilled practitioners, in the context of a professional relationship that maximises engagement with the supervisee, will be most likely to have a positive effect. Pioneers like Trotter[84] and Miller,[85] among others, have introduced and developed social work and probation practice methods that have been proven to be effective with 'involuntary clients', including but not necessarily confined to probationers. According to Ugwudike, this wider collection of core correctional practices were:

> First identified by Andrews and Kiessling (1980)[86]... [and] initially comprised five dimensions: positive relationship with the client; effective use of authority; prosocial modelling and reinforcement; problem-solving; and the effective use of community resources. The skills have since been expanded to include cognitive restructuring and motivational interviewing.[87]

Haas and Smith[88] cite Dowden and Andrews (2004)[89] as asserting that: 'Core Correctional Practices (CCPs) are designed to 'increase the therapeutic potential of rehabilitation programs for offenders,'

---

80 Donald Andrews and James Bonta, *Psychology of Criminal Conduct* (5th edn, Matthew Bender 2010).

81 James Bonta and others, 'Taking a leap: From pilot project to wide-scale implementation of the strategic training initiative in community supervision (STICS)' (2013) 15(1) Justice Research and Policy 17-35.

82 Grant Duwe, *The Use and Impact of Correctional Programming for Inmates on Pre- and Post-Release Outcomes* (National Institute of Corrections 2017)

83 Stephen Haas, 'Current practice and challenges in in evidence-based community corrections' (2013) 1(15) Justice Research and Policy 1-15.

84 Chris Trotter, *Working with Involuntary Clients: A guide to practice* (Sage 1999)

85 William R Miller and others, *Motivational Interviewing: Helping People Change* (3rd edn, Guilford Press 2013)

86 D Andrews and J Kiessling, 'Program structure and effective correctional practices: a summary of the CaVIC research,' in Robert Ross and Paul Gendreau (eds), *Effective Correctional Treatment* (Butterworth 1983).

87 Pamela Ugwudike, Peter Raynor and Jill Annison, 'Conclusion,' in Ugwudike (n 81) 424.

88 Haas and Smith (n 79) 340.

89 Craig Dowden and DA Andrews, 'The importance of staff practice in delivering effective correctional treatment: A meta-analytic review of core correctional practice' (2004) 48(2) Int J Offender Ther Comp Criminol 203-214.

recognising that 'an offender is more apt to engage in treatment, and services are more likely to be effective, if a good therapeutic alliance is created.'

Haas and Smith (2020)[90] have correctly identified that demonstrating that evidence-based practices '(including CCPs) can be implemented with fidelity in large-scale correctional settings remains a challenge for the field.' These organisational and practice delivery issues have been discussed by Bourgon[91] and O'Connor[92] among others. The Probation Service in Ireland[93] has similarly identified both the value and the organisational challenges in implementing effective practices on a consistent basis nationally and have embarked on a process to systematically do just that, building on established probation practice and adapting the international research findings and the relevant approaches, methods and programmes for Irish legal and cultural needs. The outline framework, or what might be described as the relevant Irish probation practice 'scaffolding,' for the consolidated practice model is also described by Durnescu *et al*.

## International Standards

While the United Nations' 'Tokyo Rules' on community sanctions[94] do, as their titles suggest, cover a range of community sanctions, probation supervision in general runs though many of the sanctions described and on which standards are enunciated. What we describe as probation supervision (see above) is provided for in the Tokyo Rules[95] under the heading of 'Sentencing dispositions,' where it is envisaged or implied — in the context of court-ordered supervision of an offender by a probation agency — under the following sub-headings: (b) *Conditional discharge*, and specifically under (h) *Probation and judicial supervision*. Other forms of probation supervision – in the context of post-release management of offenders – are outlined under the heading of measures 'to

[90] Haas and Smith (n 79) 345.

[91] Guy Bourgon, Leticia Gutierrez and Jennifer Ashton, 'The Evolution of Community Supervision Practice: The Transformation from Case Manager to Change Agent' (2011) 8 Irish Probation Journal 28-48.

[92] Thomas P O'Connor, Bradford Bogue, Samantha Collins and Sorcha O'Connor, 'Staff Development and Practice Models: When We Get Better Our Clients Get Better' (2019) 8 Advancing Corrections 10-29.

[93] Ioan Durnescu, Margaret Griffin and John Scott, 'Developing an Irish Offender Supervision Framework: A Whole System Approach' (2020) 17 Irish Probation Journal 24-42.

[94] United Nations (1990) United Nations Standard Minimum Rules for Non-Custodial Measures (The Tokyo Rules), Adopted by General Assembly resolution 45/110 of 14 December 1990, 3.

[95] Tokyo Rules, r 8.2, 3.

avoid institutionalisation and to assist offenders in their early reintegration into society,' and including programmes such as parole as well as half-way houses for example.[96] As with court-ordered sanctions, the ones we are concerned with here are those involving or incorporating supervision by a probation officer and which usage the UN Rules recommend, as follows:

- At trial and sentencing stage [with]:
- Social inquiry reports being encouraged, as well as
- A range of sentencing dispositions being available.
- The purpose of supervision being: To reduce reoffending and assist offender's integration into society – to reduce likelihood of reoffending.
- Supervision to be carried out by competent authority, prescribed by law.
- Apply most suitable type of supervision in each case.
- Provide offender with appropriate care and assistance to promote reintegration.

For over four decades, the Council of Europe has had a Working Group dedicated to the development of standards in probation and prison systems across the Council's 47 member States. This Working Group — the Council for Penological Cooperation (PC-CP), has generated a range of standards documents, covering various aspects of the work undertaken by probation and prison services, including the Council of Europe's (CoE) European Probation Rules (CoE, 2010),[97] which provide the following useful definitions:

- *Probation:* relates to the implementation in the community of sanctions and measures, defined by law and imposed on an offender. It includes a range of activities and interventions, which involve supervision, guidance and assistance aiming at the social inclusion of an offender, as well as contributing to community safety.
- *Probation agency:* means any body designated by law to implement the above tasks and responsibilities... may also include providing information and advice to judicial and other deciding authorities to help them reach informed and just decisions... guidance and support to offenders while in custody to prepare their release and resettlement... restorative justice... and assistance to victims of crime.

---

[96] Tokyo Rules, r 9, 4.

[97] Council of Europe (n 8).

[and, in *Basic Principles*]

> 1. Probation agencies shall aim to reduce reoffending by establishing positive relationships with offenders in order to supervise (including control where necessary), guide and assist them and to promote their successful social inclusion. Probation thus contributes to community safety and the fair administration of justice.

## The Law on Probation

The Probation of Offenders Act 1907[98] has been the foundational legislation providing for supervised community sanctions in Ireland for over a century. As described by a Probation Service policy document[99] on the subject:

> 1.1 The Probation of Offenders Act 1907 (as amended by the Criminal Justice Administration Act 1914 and Criminal Law Amendment Act 1935) is the primary legislation governing adult offenders on probation. The Act gives the criminal courts the means to sanction offenders by requiring them to observe conditions set by the court while they remain at liberty in the community or to dismiss a charge with no further penalty.
>
> **1.2 Scope of the Act**
> 1.2.1 Section 1 of the Act sets out the persons to whom it applies, the circumstances in which it may be used and the orders a court may make.
>
> 1.2.2 A court may make an order where *any person* is charged with a summary offence and that charge is proven. A District Court may make an order without proceeding to convict the person (1907.1(1)). A higher court may also make an order (but not an order to dismiss a charge) where *any person* has been convicted on indictment with an imprisonable offence (1907.1(2)).
>
> 1.2.3 The Act gives a court a very wide range of criteria to rely on in making an order. Some of these relate to characteristics of the person charged (character, antecedents, age, health, or mental condition) and some to the offence itself (trivial nature

---

98 Full reference for the 1907 Act: The Probation of Offenders Act 1907 (7 Edw 7 c17).

99 Probation Service (2008) Supervising the Probation Order: Policy and Procedures (Probation Service 2008) 7-10.

or extenuating circumstances). The court may also do what it considers expedient.

1.2.4 A court may make two types of order. The first is to dismiss the information or charge where there has not been a conviction for the offence. The effect of a dismissal is that there is no penalty imposed by the court and the person leaves court without any further obligations to it. The second type of order is to discharge the offender conditionally. The conditions of the order are that the person will enter into a recognisance, will be of good behaviour and will appear if called upon during a specified period not exceeding three years. The court may also require sureties or guarantors to enter into the recognisance (1907.1(1)(ii)).

1.2.5 A court may order the offender to pay damages for injury, compensation for loss and costs of the proceedings where either type of order is made (1907.1.3).

**1.3 Recognisances**

1.3.1 When a recognisance contains conditions relating to or concerning arrangements for the supervision of the offender by a named person then that order is referred to as a probation order.

1.3.2 A recognisance may contain any conditions which the court considers necessary to prevent the repetition of the same offence or the commission of other offences. Two specific examples of such conditions are provided; place of residence and abstention from alcohol (CJA Act, 1914.8). The 1907 Act had three groups of conditions to which courts were restricted. These conditions were concerned with (a) personal associates and frequenting places; (b) abstention from alcohol when the offence was alcohol-related and (c) lifestyle. The restriction on using these groups of conditions only were removed by the 1914 Act but they are still in use in probation orders currently and validly because of the considerable power of the court to impose conditions.

1.3.3 The court must give the offender a written notice stating in simple terms the conditions to be observed (1907.2(3)).

**1.4 Probation Officer Duties**

1.4.1 Probation officers are given the responsibility of supervising offenders placed on probation orders. Four particular duties are described in the 1907 Act including the famous injunction 'to advise, assist and befriend the offender' (1907.4(d)). The other duties refer to personal contact with the offender, ensuring the offender observes the conditions of the recognisance and reporting to court...

**1.5 Power to Vary and Discharge**

1.5.1 A court may, following an application from a probation officer, vary the period of the order by reducing or extending it (to a maximum of three years). It may vary the conditions of the order also by altering them (including deleting) or inserting additional conditions (1914.s9(a)). The offender has a right to be heard in relation to such applications.

1.5.2 A court may discharge a recognisance if it is satisfied upon application from a probation officer that supervision is no longer necessary (1914.s9(b)). The offender does not have a right of audience before the court.

**1.6 Failure to Observe Conditions**

1.6.1 A court may have an offender failing to observe the conditions of the recognisance brought before it. There are two mechanisms for this: a warrant for arrest following a sworn information or a summons requiring attendance at a specified time and date by the offender and his/her sureties (1907.6(1)).

1.6.2 An offender when arrested may be brought before any District Court. If that court is not the court before which he/she is bound by the recognisance to appear the offender may be remanded in custody or on bail to the binding court.

1.6.3 The court before which the person is bound by the recognisance may convict and sentence the offender for the original offence. It may do so forthwith and without further proof of guilt on being satisfied that the person has failed to observe any condition of the recognisance (1907.s6(5)). The failure to observe any condition of the recognisance is not an offence in itself.

**1.7 Power to Make Rules**

1.7.1 Rules may be made for carrying into effect and administration of the Act (1907 ss7 & 9). These powers are now vested in the Minister for Justice, Equality and Law Reform and the various court committees whose rules become statutory instruments.

> 1.7.2 Practice in the District Court is guided by the District Court Rules 1997. They prescribe the practice and procedures to be followed and the forms to be used in the District Court proceedings to which they relate on and from the operative date of 1 May 1997. The Rules are established by the District Court Rules Committee, in exercise of the powers conferred by section 91 of the Courts of Justice Act 1924, section 72 of the Courts of Justice Act 1936, section 34 of the Courts (Supplemental Provisions) Act 1961 and section 24 of the Interpretation Act 2005 with the concurrence of the Minister for Justice, Equality and Law Reform.[100]

The 1907 Act was subsequently updated with the passing of the Criminal Justice Administration Act 2014, which provided, *inter alia*, for the inclusion of a range of specific, as well as flexible, supervision conditions in a probation order (s 8). Section 7 of the 1914 Act also provided for the government recognition and funding of so-called 'societies' — which might now be comprehended as NGO/community and voluntary sector bodies — and which have as their goal the rehabilitation of offenders.

## Other Legislation

In addition to the core probation legislation described above, a number of other statutes address probation-related issues and directly influence aspects of probation work in various respects. Some of these other pieces of legislation are described and discussed in other relevant chapters. Others still, while relevant, have a relatively small impact on the day-to-day work of probation officers, sometimes because they are used in small numbers of cases. It is not possible to cover all of these in detail here. Nevertheless, the main pieces of legislation relevant to probation work are listed as follows:

| **Subject Heading / Legislation** | Notes / Summary |
|---|---|
| **Probation**<br>• Probation of Offenders Act 1907<br>• Criminal Justice (Administration) Act 1914 | Foundational probation legislation. See present chapter for more. |

[100] Now the Minister for Justice.

| **Subject Heading / Legislation** | Notes / Summary |
|---|---|
| **Community Service**<br>• Criminal Justice (Community Service) Act 1983<br>• Criminal Justice (Community Service) (Amendment) Act 2011 | Established community service as a direct alternative to imprisonment. The 2011 Act requires judges to consider community service in lieu of custodial sentences of under twelve months. |
| **Supervised Release and Parole**<br>• Criminal Justice Act 1960 (as amended)<br>• Criminal Justice (Temporary Release of Prisoners) Act 2003<br>• The Parole Act 2019 | Allows, *inter alia,* early release of a person serving a prison sentence, whether on temporary release or on a parole order under probation supervision. |
| **Transfer of Prisoners**<br>• Transfer of Sentenced Persons Act 1995<br>• Transfer of Sentenced Persons (Amendment) Act 1997 | Assessment and transfer of persons serving a custodial sentence from one country to another. |
| **International Transfer of Probation Orders**<br>• Criminal Justice (Mutual Recognition of Probation Judgments and Decisions) Act 2019 | Provides for supervised community sanctions, such as probation or community service, imposed in one country to be legally transferred and served in another country. |
| **Supervised Suspended Sentences**<br>• Criminal Justice Act 2006<br>• Criminal Justice (Suspended Sentences of Imprisonment) Act 2017 | Covers both fully and part-suspended sentences, with supervision conditions. See the present chapter (below) and Chapter 8 for more. |
| **Electronic Monitoring**<br>• Criminal Justice Act 2006 | Provides for electronic monitoring of persons on probation (not commenced) and on early release from prison (commenced – see Chapter 10 for more on this). |
| **Children**<br>• Children Act 2001 (as amended) | Comprehensive piece of legislation, modernising the approach to children in the criminal justice system (see Chapter 9 for more). |
| **Sex Offenders**<br>• Sex Offenders Act 2001<br>• Criminal Law (Sexual Offences) Act 2017 | Legislation covering the management, including assessment and post-release supervision of those convicted of a scheduled sexual offence. |
| **Victims and Restorative Justice**<br>i. Criminal Justice Act 1993<br>ii. Criminal Justice (Victims of Crime) Act 2017 | Provides (i) for Victim Impact Reports and (ii) for general victim rights, including access to restorative justice programmes (see Chapter 6 for more). |

| Subject Heading / Legislation | Notes / Summary |
|---|---|
| **Misuse of Drugs**<br>• Misuse of Drugs Acts 1977 and 1984 (as amended) | Provides for pre-sanction assessment reports in certain cases, as well as for imposition of supervised recognizances – similar to probation order, including appropriate treatment – under the Act. |
| **Fine Default**<br>• Fines (Payment and Recovery) Act 2014 | Allows for imposition of a community service order in default of a fine. |

In addition, the Criminal Justice (Spent Convictions and Certain Disclosures) Act 2016, as well as the Children Act 2001, s 258, deal with the issue of when one's criminal convictions can, in certain circumstances, be considered 'spent' and would no longer count as a 'criminal record.' They are, as such, relevant to the overall context of aspects of probation work, including to probation's concern for advancing human rights and social justice, although they do not necessarily impact in terms of providing for particular probation programmes or interventions.

## Supervision During Deferment of Penalty

The use of *supervision during deferment of penalty* has evolved as a practice by the courts in Ireland. This practice is also sometimes referred to colloquially as *adjourned supervision*. There is not a formal name for this practice, in the context that legislatively it does not exist at all,[101] although it does exist in practice. *Supervision during deferment of penalty* is probably a technically more correct representation, in terms of describing what the measure is: a period of supervision (by a probation officer), while the decision on eventual penalty is deferred. *Adjourned supervision* would seem to imply that it is the *supervision* itself that is adjourned, which is completely not the case, although this term probably gained popularity in practice because it is shorter and perhaps easier to use than the more appropriate term. The deferral of penalty in such cases is generally to give the offender time to comply with supervision and any conditions imposed, aimed at reducing their risk of reoffending or for some other related reason, such as giving them time to make good the harm they have caused.

The duration of the deferment of penalty with probation supervision, as well as the number of such successive adjournments

[101] Except in limited circumstances, in cases involving children, as outlined in the Children Act 2001, s 144. See Chapter 9 for more in relation to probation work with children.

in one case, can vary considerably from one court to another, and indeed from one case to another. Court decisions following such periods of adjournment can similarly vary. Decisions might, in different circumstances, comprise dismissal of the matter on the merits and without further penalty, imposition of a formal supervised community sanction (such as a probation order); substitution with a fine, suspended custodial sentence, or indeed a custodial sentence itself (the latter being more likely where the defendant might have been deemed to be non-compliant with the supervision conditions during the adjournment).

The use of supervision during deferment of penalty clearly has a number of potentially positive uses and benefits. These include allowing a time of real testing of the defendant's motivation and maintaining the court's 'Sword of Damocles' more visibly held over the defendant and in turn increasing the possibility that that will increase client motivation to comply with supervision. Indeed, it is possible that much positive work can be completed with the client during this period of time. As well as being a time of strong motivation for service users and those around them, as the period of 'crisis' brought about by the court appearance is extended and brought into focus, this in turn can be a powerful and enduring motivator for positive change and help to achieve positive behaviour change and provide a good foundation for building a better lifestyle. Not all features of supervision during deferment are positive or straightforward however. Some of the problematic aspects arising relate to unregulated use of the measure, as well as the length of some adjournments and the number of repeated adjournments in some cases.

In the context of probation organisational management, the practice of supervision during deferment is discouraged as far as possible, as it gives rise to a number of challenges. These include a concern, especially in the absence of a firm legislative basis for the measure, regarding whether it should be used at all. There are also concerns around issues of appropriate procedural justice and the right of a defendant to have a decision made in their case, at an appropriate point and in a timely way, as well as the right of the Probation Service — having carried out an initial assessment and pre-sanction report — to 'get on with' the work they are best-placed to do. There has also been a concern that because supervision during deferment of penalty is completely at the discretion of the court in any individual case, its use could give rise to concerns about increased subjectivity in sentencing decisions. Finally, from an organisational point of view, the number of update assessment reports requested in such cases can put undue and perhaps unnecessary demands on the Probation Service and others, such as treatment providers and that the level of resources allocated annually to this area of work might go unacknowledged, in terms of budgetary allocations and related considerations.

## Suspended Sentences with Probation Supervision and Other Measures

A number of other legislative measures and sanctions, incorporating probation supervision in certain cases, are used by courts. Section 99 of the Criminal Justice Act 2006 makes provision for the imposition by a court of fully-suspended and part-suspended sentences. Such sentences may be imposed with or without supervision. Since the introduction of the 2006 legislation, both fully and partly-suspended sentences with probation supervision have been used frequently by the courts. Various types of supervised early release from custodial sentences and post-release supervision orders are also available and in use.[102] Supervised recognizances under the Misuse of Drugs Acts, although still available to the courts, are used rarely — if at all — nowadays.[103]

Most, if not all probation and parole organisations, deal with the reality that individuals under supervision move to other jurisdictions, either on a temporary or permanent basis, for various reasons. This is especially true in the context of borderless travel on the island of Ireland, as well as generally unrestricted movement between EU member states. A number of legislative measures have been introduced (see list above) to provide for transfer of prisoners between co-operating jurisdictions. Similarly, the (EU-based) international transfer and mutual recognition of probation decisions and court orders has been a significant development.[104] The numbers involved annually in both of these programmes are quite low and it is beyond the scope of the present publication to go into the practice implications in detail here.

In addition to the above statutory measures, there have also been organisational arrangements possible for structured transfer of

---

[102] More information on these various orders are included, where appropriate, in Chapters 8 (Conditional Release and Other Post-Release Supervision), 9 (Children and Young People) and 10 (Electronic Monitoring).

[103] For example, the Probation Service, *2020 Annual Report* (2021) 52-64 – reports no such orders made in the years 2018 to 2020.

[104] David O'Donovan, 'Transfer of Probation Supervision between Member States: An EU Initiative' (2009) 6 Irish Probation Journal 77-90.

case management from one jurisdiction to another on a voluntary, bilateral and reciprocal basis. This type of administrative arrangement has historically been most commonly used with criminal justice counterparts in Northern Ireland and the rest of the United Kingdom, although it has also arisen from time to time in relation to individuals travelling back to Ireland from third countries.[105] One of the challenges of the latter ('voluntary') type of case in particular is the general absence of legal powers for the 'receiving' country and its probation officers to take action in the event of behaviours that give cause for concern arising in any case. The voluntary nature of such arrangements, in cases where there is an absence of legislative provisions, means that probation assistance can be provided on the basis of an agreed case management plan, however compliance with the agreed plan cannot generally be enforced. The 2019 legislation (see above) enabling the mutual recognition of probation judgments and decisions, where applied, does provide a legislative basis for the management and enforcement of such transferred supervision orders.

As mentioned earlier in this chapter, the fundamental approach to the case management and supervision of the individuals subject to all the different types of supervision order is generally reasonably standardised in terms of basic approach. This means that the work involved is based on the same probation work model, framework of practice and using appropriate methods and interventions from the established probation practice 'toolkit,' adapted and individualised depending on the individual circumstances, needs and risks presented.

## Low Intensity Supervision

The Probation Service has made provision for some categories of individual to be supervised at a less intrusive level than usual if certain criteria are met. The features of such supervision, known as low intensity supervision, would include less frequent attendance for meetings with the probation officer by the supervisee, minimal if any formal programme participation requirement, and periodic monitoring and checking of adherence to supervision conditions, including staying out of further trouble. This is used, in the first instance, on the basis that, according to RNR principles, the level

[105] Of course, since their exit from the EU, the UK has effectively now also become a third country for these purposes. At the time of writing, a number of the issues arising have yet to be resolved.

of service provided should be commensurate with the level of assessed risk of reoffending and risk of causing future harm. If someone is assessed from the outset as presenting a low level of risk of reoffending, then they may be assigned to low intensity supervision from the beginning. Otherwise, if they have been under probation supervision for some time, during which they have cooperated with their supervision programme to such an extent that their assessed level of risk of reoffending has reduced, they may similarly be moved from standard to a low intensity supervision regime.

So, in summary, there is 'standard' supervision as the default, with 'intensive' and 'low intensity' supervision above and below that standard respectively and utilised for those at higher or lower risk levels as the case may be. Risk assessment and management are both viewed as dynamic and interconnected, and there is a clear need to constantly re-evaluate risk of reoffending and related factors. Critically, someone under low intensity supervision should always be in a position to escalate issues of concern that may arise to their supervising officer, so that such issues may be addressed and more intense interventions — whether directly by the probation officer or their team, or someone else — be applied, or matters arising being addressed by referral to another appropriate service for example, if and as needs be. In the same way, the supervising probation officer must be in a position to escalate the level of supervision applied in cases where issues of concern and which might indicate an increase in risk of reoffending (eg someone's return to drug use, or losing their employment or accommodation) come to their attention.

## Other Forms of Non-Mandated, including 'Voluntary' Supervision

The Probation Service has generally prioritised referrals for which it is mandated legislatively or otherwise, particularly referrals from courts, prisons and the Parole Board. At the same time, there is a longstanding tradition of providing 'voluntary' supervision[106] in some instances, even where there is no legal or other formal requirement to do so. Over the past two decades or so, Probation Service management has moved to clarify what areas

106 Some practitioners and commentators would take issue with the use of the term 'supervision,' combined with 'voluntary' in such instances. This is because the very essence of 'supervision' in the probation work context would generally imply mandatory requirements on the person being supervised, with potential legal consequences in the event of non-compliance.

of work should be prioritised. This has been especially crystallised following the 2006 Audit of services and the consequent review and realignment of Probation Service structures and boundaries and a review of organisational practice policies and procedures. This in turn has resulted in a clear and ordered list of cases to be prioritised by probation teams in the context of limited resources that have to be managed. Two of the criteria influencing this prioritisation have included (a) legal mandate for the work, and (b) assessed level of risk of reoffending and of causing harm (based on the RNR model of resource allocation and case management, already described).

That said, and in the context of supporting those with previous convictions and at risk of further offending, Probation Service guidelines do allow for probation officer involvement with individuals, on a case-by-case basis, where there is no statutory mandate but where there is either a request from the individual to have support provided by their probation officer for an ongoing, but generally limited, period of time or else where the probation officer is in a position to maintain an 'open door' to the possibility of future contact should the need arise for the client. That could be the case where their circumstances might change and because the probation officer knows them well, has their trust, and may for example be well-placed to advocate appropriately on their behalf at a time of need. It is important to reiterate though, that the option or space for such voluntary 'supervision' is generally limited, particularly where individual probation officer or team resources are pressurised and priority must be given to those for whom there is a legal obligation to be supervised and where these present at a higher risk of reoffending.

## Discussion and Conclusions

This chapter has considered the history, evolution and different conceptualisations of what *probation* is and how it is understood, as a 'brand' or concept, as much as a response to those who have offended, and as a specific supervised community sanction aimed at holding those who have offended to account and helping them to avoid reoffending and to reintegrate in their community. The wider applications of the term, encompassing the many and varied aspects of the work that probation officers do have also been discussed. Probation work, as we know it in Ireland, has a history stretching back for over a century, with its roots in when Ireland was part of the United Kingdom. This work, and the range of sanctions and other interventions provided, are now a well-established part of the criminal justice system and available for the use of the courts and other stakeholders — pre-conviction, at sentencing, as immediate court-ordered sanctions and post-custody. The provisions of various pieces of legislation relevant to probation work have been outlined and when appropriate, the reader has been provided with pointers to other chapters, where there have been overlapping themes and issues covered in more detail in those other parts of the book, or indeed elsewhere. In addition, the more recent developments in probation practice, particularly in the context of its basis in social work and the development of more effective probation practice, have also been considered and described in outline. McNeill and others suggest that, as well as everything else, probation is also '...a lived experience... an evolving institution and... a historical artefact.'[107] Notwithstanding its various challenges over the years, as McKnight pointed out: 'The Probation Service, as a title, embodies the values of a service and a profession that is internationally recognised and respected.'[108] In Ireland, probation as a 'set' of supervised sanctions, as a professional practice and as an organisation, seems to be well-established and well positioned to continue to contribute to the wider work of the criminal justice system, in enhancing community justice and wellbeing.

---

107 Fergus McNeill, Ioan Durnescu, and René Butter, *Probation: 12 Essential Questions* (Palgrave Macmillan 2016) 264.

108 J McKnight, *NOMS – the Vision, the Blueprint and an Alternative: Napo's Response* (Napo 2005) 4.

CHAPTER FIVE

# COMMUNITY SERVICE

## Introduction

It has been acknowledged that 'the relationship between work and punishment is highly complex', community service — in this context, unpaid work as part of a penal sanction — is now well-established as one of the most popular community sanctions, in Ireland as well as internationally.[1] In Ireland, between 2,000 and 3,000 such orders are made by the criminal courts each year.[2] The general popularity of community service internationally, with sentencers and the public, has been attributed to the fact that '… it serves numerous purposes and aims — such as diversion from custody, reduced costs to the criminal justice system, reparation and rehabilitation — and because it can be seen to provide tangible benefits for the community.'[3]

## International Definitions and Use of Community Service

The Council of Europe has defined the sanction itself in the following terms:

> Community service is a community sanction or measure which involves organising and supervising by the probation agencies of unpaid labour for the benefit of the community as real or symbolic reparation for the harm caused by the offender. Community service shall not be of a stigmatising nature and probation agencies shall seek to identify and use working tasks which support the development of skills and the social inclusion of offenders.[4]

1 Anne Worrall and Clare Hoy, *Punishment in the Community: Managing offenders, making choices* (Willan 2005) 131.

2 See, for example: Probation Service, *Annual Report 2019* (Probation Service, 2020) 55.

3 Gill McIvor, 'What is the Impact of Community Service?' in Fergus McNeill, Ioan Durnescu and René Butter (eds), *Probation: 12 Essential Questions* (Macmillan 2016) 107.

4 Council of Europe, Recommendation CM/Rec (2010) 1 of the Committee of Ministers to member States on the Council of Europe Probation Rules (Adopted

In Ireland, as will be described below, community service is a direct alternative to imprisonment. In some jurisdictions it can be used as a stand-alone sanction or as part of a wider community-based sanction 'package,' imposed on an offender at one time. Both of these 'variants' reflect court-ordered sanctions, where community service is specifically mandated, either as a single, stand-alone sanction, or as part of a combination of measures. There can be other variations on this theme: in Norway, for example, community service had been available as a sanction to the courts since 1994, however following its low level of usage over time, the Execution of Sentences Act 2001 in that country changed the legislative basis for community sentences, enabling a court to make a generic community sentence of a specific length, of between 30 and 240 hours. Within this framework, the correctional (probation) service has significant operational discretion in deciding — based on the probation officer's assessment — the component contents of any sanction, including whether, as well as if and how and to what extent, community service should be incorporated into the community sentence.[5] The preference, in practice in Norway, appears to be that most if not all community sentences there incorporate some community service component.

Although community service has been primarily manifested, wherever it has been introduced, as an immediate, court-ordered sanction, it has also come to be used in some jurisdictions as part of post-release supervision of offenders, released early for example on 'parole' or similar type programmes. In Ireland, there are a number of different legislative and other provisions in relation to post-release supervision of offenders (see chapters 7 and 8, which address these different provisions). Nevertheless, although it has not been used to date as part of either court-ordered post-release supervision of offenders in Ireland, nor of the parole process *per se*, community service work has been a central component of the Community Return programme, since that scheme of early release from prison, for eligible prisoners serving custodial sentences of between one and eight years, was introduced in 2011.[6]

---

by the Committee of Ministers on 20 January 2010, at the 1075th meeting of the Ministers' Deputies).

5 Gerhard Ploeg, 'Chapter 24 – Norway,' *Probation in Europe* (Confederation of European Probation (CEP) 2008) 15-18. Available online at: https://www.cep-probation.org/wp-content/uploads/2018/10/2008Norway.pdf.

6 While some more about this use of community service is discussed further below, see separate chapter on post-release supervision (Chapter 8) for more specific information on the use of community service programmes as part of the Community Return scheme in Ireland.

## The History and Development of Community Service Internationally: Its Growth and Uses

The origins of community service historically and internationally have been debated by a number of commentators over the years. Guilfoyle pointed out that some researchers have argued that the origins of the community service order (CSO) could be traced back through various work-based penal sanctions including slavery, transportation, penal servitude and impressment.[7] Guilfoyle, however, points out that Kilcommins disputed such a link, claiming that 'tracing continuities and affinities in this way is ahistorical and "distorts the contemporary significance and character of CSOs whilst also obscuring the contextual usage of past penal practices".' For the purposes of the present publication, the point made by Guilfoyle: '…that when exploring the origins of the CSO, one need not look beyond the jurisdiction that first introduced a community service sanction within its formal criminal justice system…. [whereby] two jurisdictions come to the forefront: Tasmania and England and Wales',[8] with both passing relevant legislation in 1972, is a reasonable historical starting point.

Looking briefly to the earliest manifestations of community service in modern times, McIvor points out that:

> While examples of criminal sanctioning with an emphasis on the performance of socially useful work can be identified historically, the first modern community service work programme was developed in Alameda County, California in 1966 and involved those convicted of certain road traffic offences performing unpaid work for the community as a requirement by the municipal court.[9]

McIvor[10] goes on to describe the international evolution and development of community service, from its first *ad hoc* use as referenced above, through its early official funding and development in the USA, beginning in the 1970s, to its introduction by legislation in Britain in 1973 — a significant historical point of departure, as adverted to by Guilfoyle, referenced above. The then new community service order was — and still is — administered and managed by the Probation Service in Britain,[11] where the

7 Eoin Guilfoyle, 'What Exactly is a Community Service Order in Ireland?' (2017) 14 Irish Probation Journal 189.

8 ibid 190.

9 McIvor (n 3) 108.

10 McIvor (n 3) 108-110.

11 Up to June 2014, probation services in England and Wales were delivered by

Criminal Justice Act 1972 provided for the possibility of community service orders of between 40 and 240 hours unpaid work being imposed by courts on offenders aged seventeen years and over. Following the success of initial pilot schemes,[12] community service was introduced throughout England and Wales in 1974 and in Northern Ireland[13] and Scotland in 1979.[14]

Some commentators have argued that the introduction of sanctions such as community service, in the 1970s and 1980s for example, reflected the growing view at that time that rehabilitation did not work (see chapter 2 on the history of the development of community sanctions) and the stance, in Britain for example, that '…rehabilitation was soft and that what offenders needed was greater control and surveillance,': which in turn 'appealed to 'common sense' arguments that if offenders were to be kept out of prison, then the alternatives had to be tough and demanding.'[15] As noted by Worrall and Hay (2005), community service, against this backdrop, 'proved a popular sentence with courts and resulted in a dramatic decline in the use of probation orders,' as the numbers of community service orders grew.[16] Others have contextualised the emergence of the CSO in England and Wales … 'at a time when there was disillusionment with imprisonment' itself, in the wider context of a rising prison population in Britain at that time.[17] As a result, the Advisory Council on the Penal System (ACPS) was tasked 'to consider what changes and additions could be made to the existing range of non-custodial penalties'.[18] The 1970 report[19] of the ACPS sub-committee, chaired by Lady Barbara Wootton, 'recommended the development of a new sanction that would require offenders, in appropriate cases, to engage in some form

thirty-five individual Probation Trusts. Since June 2014, the Trusts have been replaced by a National Probation Service (NPS) managing high risk offenders and twenty-one Community Rehabilitation Companies (CRCs), across the country, which manage low and medium risk offenders. At the time of writing, further changes have been initiated, effectively involving the absorption of the CRCs into the NPS.

12 K Pease and others, *Community service orders* (Home Office Research Study No 29) (Her Majesty's Stationary Office 1975).

13 John Bourke, 'Community Service in Northern Ireland' (2007) 4(1) Irish Probation Journal 77-84.

14 Gill McIvor, *Sentenced to serve: The operation and impact of community service by offenders in Scotland* (Avebury 1992).

15 Such as Worrall and Hoy (n 1) 24.

16 ibid.

17 See Guilfoyle (n 7) 191.

18 ibid.

19 Non-Custodial and Semi-Custodial Penalties, Report of the Advisory Council on the Penal System (Home Office, 1970).

of part-time service to the community'.[20] Within two years, the Criminal Justice Act 1972, which provided for the introduction of the CSO, was enacted in Britain.

## Aims and Objectives of Community Service

There have been debates, throughout the history of its development and implementation, as to the aims, objectives and purposes of community service as a community-based sanction. Robinson[21] for example, argued that, in a context of 'vulnerability of rehabilitative CSM [community sanctions and measures] to their own instrumentalist logic suggests a need to look in other directions for more durable or secure sources of legitimacy.'[22] In this context, it was argued, that '...a reparative approach could retain the proportionality central to the justice model but eschew damaging forms of punishment in favour of more constructive options.' Thus, community service can be viewed as offering a *reparative* option, which can involve reparation or payback to the wider community, if not to individual victims of crime. Robinson went on to point out though, that 'community service, in many jurisdictions has not been 'marketed' solely or even principally as a reparative sanction.'[23] Citing McIvor, writing about the experience in Scotland for example, Robinson describes the 'multifarious purposes' of community service, as being:

> ...intended to fulfil a number of sentencing aims including *punishment* (through the deprivation of the offender's free time), *rehabilitation* (through the positive effects of helping others) and *reparation* (by undertaking work of benefit to usually disadvantaged sections of the community). The *reintegrative* potential of community service was to be achieved through the offender being enabled to remain in the community, retaining employment and family ties, and, through coming into contact with others while carrying out unpaid work, avoiding social isolation.[24]

---

20 See Guilfoyle (n 7) 191.

21 Gwen Robinson, Fergus McNeill and Shadd Maruna, 'Punishment *in* Society: The Improbable Persistence of Probation and Other Community Sanctions' in Jonathan Simon and Richard Sparks (eds), *The SAGE Handbook of Punishment and Society* (Sage 2013) 332.

22 For example, suggesting the efficacy of CSMs in terms of public protection or rehabilitation of offenders.

23 Robinson, McNeill and Maruna (n 21) 332.

24 Gill McIvor, 'Paying back: 30 years of unpaid work by offenders in Scotland' (2010) 2(1) European Journal of Probation 41-61.

Referring to the fact that '...community service... at different times has had quite different legal meanings and functions – as a standalone sanction or as an adjunct to probation supervision, as a direct alternative to custody, or as an autonomous sanction in its own right', Robinson points to this phenomenon as a probable factor in the '...popularisation of community service as "all things to all people"...'[25] – citing examples of how it has come to be used in the United Kingdom jurisdictions, elsewhere in Europe, and in different parts of Africa, where community service has been adopted differently in different countries. For example, they describe how, in some parts of Africa, '...community sentencing tends to focus almost entirely on community service...' where, it has been suggested that such an approach 'fits well with cultural traditions of making amends as a response to wrong-doing.'[26]

While community service has been held out, when introduced in various jurisdictions including Ireland, as a replacement for, or outright alternative to, the imposition of custodial sanctions, this intended promise of significantly reducing the numbers in prison has largely not been fulfilled, or at least not to the hoped-for extent. In Britain for example, it has been suggested that:

> community service made little impact on the use of imprisonment by courts, encouraged net-widening and may even have 'enabled a smoother transition towards the "justice" model... with the emphasis in future likely to be on creating more punitively interventive proposals.'[27]

In this context, it was also argued, community service became '... an accompaniment to imprisonment, not an alternative to it.'[28]

## International Standards for Community Service

The matter of community service is addressed in the United Nations' 'Tokyo Rules' on community sanctions.[29] This is in the wider context of the availability, decision-making and application of non-custodial sanctions and measures, as well as the principles

---

25 Robinson, McNeill and Maruna (n 21) 332.

26 L Ehlers, 'Probation in Africa,' in Rob Canton and David Hancock (eds), *Dictionary of Probation and Offender Management* (Willan 2007) 228-229.

27 Worrall and Hoy (n 1) 132.

28 ibid.

29 United Nations, Standard Minimum Rules for Non-Custodial Measures (The Tokyo Rules), adopted by General Assembly resolution 45/110 of 14 December 1990, 3.

that should apply to the application and management of community sanctions in practice. There is limited reference to community service itself in the UN Rules beyond simply referencing the community service order as one of the community sentencing dispositions that a judicial authority should have at its disposal, placing community service in the context of a wider range of non-custodial measures, all of which should take into consideration 'the rehabilitative needs of the offender, the protection of society and the interests of the victim...'[30] The Tokyo Rules also comment on the value of public participation in the management and delivery of community sanctions, which should 'complement the efforts of the criminal justice administration.'[31] In addition, 'public participation should be regarded as an opportunity for members of the community to contribute to the protection of their society.'[32] This latter principle has particular and direct relevance for the application of community service in the context that management of CSOs, by their nature, tend to incorporate the involvement of individuals or local organisations and bodies in local communities, who enable or support the offender to undertake their CSO through the provision of appropriate unpaid work. This tends in turn to involve members of local communities, or at least those running community and voluntary organisations, in direct contact with individual offenders, in contexts whereby such direct and targeted contact with those identified as having offended, would otherwise probably not occur. Such offender-community contacts, facilitated and supported by probation staff and partner bodies, in and of themselves are seen as facilitating positive steps towards reintegration of the offender in the community, as well as enabling the direct 'making good' or reparation for harm done – to the local community – by the person who has been ordered to complete the CSO.

The Council of Europe (CoE) standards in relation to community service are contained in a number of CoE instruments, including in the European Probation Rules and the European Rules on Community Sanctions and Measures. The (2017) European Rules on Community Sanctions and Measures[33] are more specific in relation to the standards they set out for the implementation of community service, in the wider context of implementing the range

---

30 United Nations (1990) 8.1, 3.

31 ibid 17.1, 6.

32 ibid.

33 Council of Europe, Recommendation CM/Rec (2017) 3 of the Committee of Ministers to member States on the European Rules on community sanctions and measures, adopted by the Committee of Ministers on 22 March 2017, at the 1282nd meeting of the Ministers' Deputies, Strasbourg, France.

of community sanctions and measures that may be available in a CoE member State. Rules in the 2017 Recommendation[34] relating directly to community service include the following:

> (Rule) 39. Tasks assigned to offenders doing community service shall be socially useful and meaningful and make use of and/or enhance the offender's skills as much as possible.
>
> 40. Community service shall not be undertaken for the purpose of making profit for the implementing authorities, for their staff, or for commercial profit.
>
> 41. Working and occupational conditions of offenders carrying out community service shall be in accordance with all current health and safety regulations. Offenders shall be insured against accident, injury and public liability arising as a result of implementation.
>
> 49. The kind and amount of information about individuals given to agencies which provide community service work placements or personal and social assistance of any kind shall be defined by, and be restricted to, the purpose of the particular action under consideration. In particular, it shall normally exclude information about the offence.

In addition, Rule 37 also states that 'Community sanctions and measures shall always work to support desistance from crime even where they involve high levels of surveillance and control.' This rule raises the issue that community service, as in the case of any supervised community sanction, should aim to be rehabilitative, as well as punitive, reparative or restorative.

Community service had also been addressed in the earlier Council of Europe instrument – the European Probation Rules of 2010,[35] which in addition to the subsequent (2017) basic definition referenced above, includes the following:

> (Rule) 48. Community service shall not be undertaken for the profit of probation agencies, their staff or for commercial profit.
>
> 49. In identifying suitable tasks, the probation agencies shall

---

34 ibid.

35 ibid.

take into account the safety of the community and of the direct beneficiaries of the work.

50. Health and safety precautions shall adequately protect offenders assigned to community service and shall be no less rigorous than those applied to other workers.

51. Probation agencies shall develop community service schemes that encompass a range of tasks suitable to the different skills and diverse needs of offenders. In particular, there must be appropriate work available for women offenders, offenders with disabilities, young adult offenders and elderly offenders.

52. Offenders shall be consulted about the type of work they could undertake.

An earlier Council of Europe Recommendation,[36] on the subject of responding to the issue of prison overcrowding, had also referenced community service as a potential measure to be considered at various stages, to help reduce the prison population, as follows:

(Rule) 14. Efforts should be made to reduce recourse to sentences involving long imprisonment, which place a heavy burden on the prison system, and to substitute community sanctions and measures for short custodial sentences.

15. In providing for community sanctions and measures which could be used instead of deprivation of liberty, consideration should be given to the following [followed by a list of various supervised community sanctions, suspended sentences and restrictions of liberty of movement, including]:

- community service (ie unpaid work on behalf of the community),

17. Combinations of custodial and non-custodial sanctions and measures should be introduced into legislation and practice, such as unsuspended custodial sentences, followed by community service, (intensive) supervision in the community, electronically monitored house arrest or, in appropriate cases, by an obligation to undergo treatment.

[36] Council of Europe (1999) Recommendation No R (99) 22 of the Committee of Ministers to member States concerning Prison Overcrowding and Prison Population Inflation (adopted by the Committee of Ministers on 30 September 1999, at the 681st meeting of the Ministers' Deputies).

As summarised by Geiran and Durnescu, on behalf of the Council of Europe: 'The constructive potential of community service has led to its increased favour with and use by courts in many countries,' and to the positive rehabilitative and reintegrative potential of the measure being explored by many implementing agencies.[37]

## The Law in Ireland on Community Service

The basic or introductory law on community service in Ireland is set down in the Criminal Justice (Community Service) Act 1983, as amended.[38] In the context where the 1907 Probation of Offenders Act was (and still is) the foundational legislation providing for supervised community sanctions in Ireland, the 1983 Act was a major development in this legislative framework, governing the work of the Probation Service in managing community sanctions and measures.

The 1983 Act provided, *inter alia*, that:

> s 3. – (1) Subject to section 4, the court by or before which an offender is convicted may, instead of dealing with him [sic] in any other way, make, in respect of the offence of which he is convicted, an order (in this Act referred to as a "community service order") under this section.
>
> (2) A community service order shall require the offender to perform, in accordance with this Act, unpaid work for such number of hours as are specified in the order and are not less than 40 and not more than 240.

The Act (s 2) went on to specify that its provisions apply to offenders over the age of sixteen years:

> convicted of an offence for which, in the opinion of the court, the appropriate sentence would but for this Act be one of penal servitude, of imprisonment or of detention… but does not apply to where any such sentence is fixed by law.

As described by the Law Reform Commission: 'A CSO may be made by any court (other than the Special Criminal Court) in respect of an offender who has been convicted of an offence which, in the court's opinion, the appropriate sentence would have been one of

---

37 Vivian Geiran and Ioan Durnescu, Implementing Community Sanctions and Measures: Guidelines (Council of Europe 2019) 54.

38 Criminal Justice (Community Service) Act 1983.

imprisonment.'[39] In the above (s 2) provision, the 1983 legislation clearly sets the community service order as a direct alternative to a custodial sentence.[40] In a very real sense, the sentencing Judge is required, having found the defendant guilty, and then decided — having taken all the relevant factors into account — that a specific custodial sentence is appropriate, to further decide then that it is appropriate, taking all relevant factors into account, that it would be appropriate to consider substituting a specific community service order of 'not less than 40 and not more than 240 hours' of 'unpaid work', in lieu of the custodial sentence.

## Assessment of Suitability for Community Service

Before formalising the decision to actually impose a community service order, the sentencing judge is required, under the 1983 Act,[41] to ensure that a number of conditions are met, specifically that:

> 4.-(1)(b) the court is satisfied, after considering the offender's circumstances and a report about him [sic] by a probation and welfare officer (including, if the court thinks it necessary, hearing evidence from such an officer), that the offender is a suitable person to perform work under such an order and that arrangements can be made for him to perform such work, and
>
> (b) the offender has consented.

The three key elements therefore, to be included in the probation officer's assessment of the candidate for community service, on behalf of the court, are:

1. that the offender is suitable to perform community service,
2. that appropriate work is available in the community to be performed, and
3. that the offender has agreed to undertake that work and complete the community service order.

In practice, the question of the offender's suitability as prescribed under the legislation, can and does cover a range of issues. These include the person's physical and mental health, their attitude to the current offence and previous offences and their previous

39 Law Reform Commission (2020) *Report: Suspended Sentences* [LRC 123-2020] 32.

40 Criminal Justice (Community Service) Act 1983, s 3.

41 Criminal Justice Act 1983, s 4.

cooperation or non-cooperation with supervised community sanctions, among other issues. The second point regarding the requirement that appropriate work be available in the community is also important. 'Appropriate' covers the requirement that the work be carried out for the benefit of the local community, is unpaid and is work that can readily be undertaken by the individual offender, having regard to their abilities, skills and availability, and to the accessibility of the work itself. The work to be undertaken must also be work that would otherwise not be done and by having the work undertaken as community service, must not replace or displace someone else's paid work.

The third element of an assessment of suitability for community service, as listed above — that of the offender's consent — is equally important. At a basic level, there is little point or value in the probation officer carrying out an assessment of an offender recommending them as suitable for community service, if in fact they have not agreed to carry out any order that might be made. In this regard, it is critical that the probation officer makes clear to the offender at the assessment stage what specific 'terms and conditions' will be involved if they are subject to a community service order, including what will be expected of them in terms of times and pattern of attendance and the likely work that will be involved, as well as what will be seen as constituting compliance and non-compliance with any community service order made. Ideally, such requirements and planned practical arrangements, including the timeline for attendance and completion of the CSO, should be negotiated and agreed in advance with the offender.

In addition, issues such as the person's home and family circumstances, including any caring responsibilities, travel or mobility issues etc, need to be taken into account. The probation officer will also seek to assess the factors that are likely to support or militate against the person successfully undertaking community service. As well as one's individual circumstances and context, these can include factors outside the individual themselves. For example, care may need to be taken to establish if the person in question is under threat from other individuals or criminal groups. The presence of such threat would influence when and where someone might be placed to undertake CSO work, in order not to further expose the individual in question to such threat. It may also be the case, from time to time and in certain localities, that the demand for community service work placements, vis-à-vis the number of offenders to be placed at any one particular time, may exceed the number and range of community service work placement opportunities available at that time in that particular area. This can lead to challenges, including delays, in placing people on CSO work programmes. Other relevant elements of the 1983 legislation provide for: situations where more than one order is in force at the same time (s 5), the service of copies of orders (s 6), offender's change of residence (s 10), the issue of jurisdiction and the operation of the Act in the Circuit Court (s 12), the making of regulations (s 14) and other related details.

## Other Legal Issues in Relation to Community Service

In terms of the issue of making a community service order at the same time as imposing another criminal sanction, the Law Reform Commission has suggested that: 'A CSO may be combined with other orders, but the legislative framework prohibits the imposition of a sentence of imprisonment, whether suspended or not, in combination with a CSO.'[42] The Commission goes on to suggest that the CSO and the suspended sentence '...share some common features' and that:

> Neither penalty may be imposed unless a court is satisfied that a sentence of imprisonment would otherwise be appropriate ie the custody threshold must be deemed to have been passed. The legislation governing both penalties also provides for potentially similar consequences in the event of a breach of conditions. Both penalties can also be said to cater for broadly similar sentencing aims.

The 1983 act was followed by two statutory regulations in 1984 which set out a number of specific legal requirements in relation to the imposition or serving of a community service order.[43] These include (SI No 325): definitions of relevant terms, including designated relevant [probation and welfare] officers for the purposes of the Act, requirements that relevant probation officers ensure that a 'sponsoring' body in the community, which provides CSO work placements must be adequately insured, that work performed 'is of benefit to the community or to an individual or group of individuals in need' and that relevant officers 'carry out any general or special direction issued by or on behalf of the Minister.' This regulation also sets out requirements for offenders to give signed acknowledgement of receipt of a CSO; that the 'offender

---

[42] Law Reform Commission (n 39) 33.

[43] SI No 325 of 1984: Criminal Justice (Community Service) Regulations 1984; and SI No 327 of 1984: District Court [Criminal Justice (Community Service) Act 1983] Rules 1984.

shall obey all instructions given to him [sic] under the Act by or on behalf of a relevant officer', that 'an offender shall not be required to perform work under a community service order for more than eight hours in any day without the approval of a relevant officer.'

In addition, this Regulation provides that a relevant officer may excuse an offender for non-attendance for community service work on any day where the absence 'is due to illness or to any other unavoidable cause' and that any such period of absence 'shall not be reckoned as time spent in performing such work.' Regarding time worked per day, the Regulation allows that this may include: 'time taken by the offender to travel to the place' of work and 'any time during which work is interrupted by weather or by any other unavoidable cause', with the proviso that 'any such period shall not exceed one hour without the approval of a relevant officer.' Finally, the Regulation provides for the possibility of an offender being paid 'such travelling and other expenses as may be necessary to enable the offender to perform the work', where they would otherwise be unable to do so, 'by reason of his [*sic*] lack of means'; and also that where an offender completes a CSO, the relevant officer shall inform the relevant (sentencing) court of that compliance with the order. Statutory Instrument No 327 of 1984[44] provided for the making of the relevant District Court [Criminal Justice (Community Service) Act 1983] Rules 1984, and for the form of CSOs themselves, how and in what format a relevant (probation) officer should take action in relation to proceedings for non-compliance with a CSO, including applying to court for issuing a summons, service of summons by An Garda Síochána, applications to court by an offender, lodging of papers with the court, managing situations where the judge making a CSO is not the judge normally assigned to the district of residence, and procedures where a CSO is subsequently amended in court.

## The Community Service Legislation Updated

The 1983 community service legislation was subsequently updated through the passage of the Criminal Justice (Community Service) Amendment Act 2011. As pointed out by Carr (2016), the new legislation 'required the court to consider the imposition of a CSO as an alternative to custody for sentences of 12 months or less.'[45] Although the court could still impose community service orders in respect of longer sentences, sentencing courts were not *required*

---

[44] SI No 327 of 1984 came into effect on 10 December 1984.

[45] Nicola Carr, 'Community sanctions and measures,' in Deirdre Healy and others, *The Routledge Handbook of Criminology* (Routledge 2016) 323.

to always consider the alternative community service option in all such cases. According to Carr: 'The evident intention of the 2011 Act was to encourage a greater use of community service by the judiciary and consequently to reduce the resort to short prison sentences.'[46] In theory at least, a community service order can only be imposed within the terms of the 1983 Community Service Act, as amended. Nevertheless, the Law Reform Commission has pointed out that while 'there is no specific provision under section 99 of the Criminal Justice Act 2006[47] for a condition of unpaid work [as part of a suspended or part-suspended custodial sentence]' that nevertheless:

> ...given the broad discretion afforded to sentencing courts in respect of the conditions of suspension that it may impose, it is possible for sentencing courts to impose community-based conditions of suspension, including that the offender perform unpaid work in the community. [48]

Two further legislative changes, impacting the use of community service in Ireland, have been incorporated in the introduction of the Fines Act 2010 and the Fines (Payment and Recovery) Act 2014, among which provisions the legislature sought to modernise the way in which 'fine defaulters' are dealt with by the courts and including through the provision of alternative sanctions for those in default of fine payment. Historically, the only alternative for non-payment of a court-ordered fine was a custodial sentence. These were often very short sentences, resulting in a fine-defaulting individual being committed to prison for a matter of a few weeks at most, more often for some days, or even hours, before being released. Nevertheless, at times, a significant percentage of all committals to prison were in respect of fine default. For example, in 2012, 48.8% of all committals[49] to prison that year were in respect of custodial sentences imposed for fine default.[50] The 2014 statute in relation to payment and recovery of fines was commenced in January 2016 and provides for payment of fines by instalment, as well as a range of alternative measures where someone defaults on payment of a fine, including a community service order in lieu, as well as attachment orders and recovery orders; with imprisonment only being applicable where another order is not appropriate or where an alternative community service order is made but

---

[46] ibid 323-324.

[47] Criminal Justice Act 2006 ss 99 (3) and (4).

[48] Law Reform Commission (n 39) 300.

[49] That is, 8,304 committals for fine default, out of a total of 17,026 committals to prison in 2012.

[50] Irish Prison Service, *Annual Report 2012* (Irish Prison Service 2013).

not completed.[51] The 2014 Act provides for the substitution of community service orders of between 40 and 240 hours work where a fine has been imposed following conviction on indictment, with 30 to 100 hours work being deemed the appropriate penalty where the fine is imposed following summary conviction (in the District Court). After initial technical/legal difficulties, there have been on-going challenges in the implementation of the above fines legislation, including with operationalising the steps in relation to assessment for, and imposition of, community service orders in default of fine payment. Since 2018, the Probation Service has recorded statistics on the numbers of court referrals for assessments of offenders for community service in lieu of payment of a fine. These statistics show that there were 384 such referrals by the courts in 2018 and 626 in 2019.[52] An interagency working group was established to review the operation of the fines legislation in practice and to make recommendations for any change. At the time of writing, this work had not been concluded.

## Management, Enforcement and Non-Compliance

Management of CSOs and dealing with non-compliance, are covered by a number of legislative provisions in the 1983 Act. Sections 7, 8, 9, 11 and 13 of the Act of 1983 deal with issues arising from management of an order in practice and in particular where there has been alleged non-compliance with a community service order and follow-up action is to be taken.

The legislation requires the Probation Service to return to Court an offender if he/she:

- Fails to report to a Probation Officer as directed from time to time
- Fails without reasonable excuse, to comply with the requirement to perform satisfactorily the number of hours specified in the order
- Fails to notify the Probation Officer to whom he/she is required to report of any change of address.[53]

This can be progressed through the probation officer applying for a summons under the Criminal Justice (Community Service) Act 1983, s 7(4) for alleged non-compliance. The Community

---

[51] Available at: http://www.irishstatutebook.ie/eli/2014/act/7/enacted/en/html .
[52] Probation Service, Annual Report 2019 (Probation Service 2020).
[53] Criminal Justice (Community Service) Act 1983, s 7.

Service Order remains in existence until any outstanding element of it is completed by the offender or the matter is finalised by the court. Steps taken to ensure compliance with an order and to take enforcement action must be reasonable, proportionate and timely.

Offenders are liable to be returned to court under ss 7(4) or 11(1) if they fail to perform work to a satisfactory standard or fail to behave appropriately on site. Where an offender fails to comply with an order, efforts are generally made, as far as possible, to encourage compliance such that it is possible to either complete the order or at least demonstrate to the court that all reasonable opportunities have been given to the offender to comply with the order prior to any enforcement measures. If the community service order is returned to the District Court in the offender's district of residence, the community service order can be revoked by the Court or finalised in an alternative manner.[54] Only the District Court in the area the community service order was made or the Judge who made the original order has authority to revoke it.[55]

When a probation officer decides to return to court an offender who fails to report for community service as directed, to comply with the requirement to perform satisfactorily the number of hours specified, or to notify the probation officer of a change of addresss, the probation officer can make an application for a summons for non-compliance under the Criminal Justice (Community Service) Act 1983, s 7(4). This will usually follow a series of clear and identifiable failures on the part of the offender, including for exampe: missed induction or other appointments or scheduled day/s on site, with appropriate warning letters issued and providing an opportunity for the offender to provide an acceptable excuse for non-attendance.

Where the offender does not provide an acceptable excuse within an appropriate period of time, the relevant Probation Officer takes steps to ensure that the CSO is suspended and the offender in question has 'crossed the rubicon' in terms of non-compliance and therefore resolution of the matter — one way or another, must await the return of the case to court and a judicial decision. That said, where an offender in such a situation makes contact and expresses a desire to re-engage this will generally be given consideration on the basis of the relevant facts and wider context. If the decision is made to give the individual another opportunity, they will normally be advised that one more failure to attend as instructed will result in the matter being returned to the attention of the court.

---

54 Criminal Justice (Community Service) Act 1983, s 6.

55 Criminal Justice (Community Service) Act 1983, s 8 and the 2011 Act, s 7.

## Evolution of Practice in Ireland

Regarding the origins of the CSO in Ireland, as Guilfoyle (2017) has pointed out, '[the original relevant legislation of] England and Wales is… the most logical and beneficial starting point, as the Irish CSO has undeniably strong roots in the English and Welsh CSO.'[56] According to Carr (2016): 'The most significant expansion in the role of the [Irish Probation] service to date came with the passage of the Criminal Justice (Community Service) Act 1983.'[57] Following the commencement of the 1983 legislation, the first community service order came into effect in 1985. Since then, use of the sanction has waxed and waned over the intervening years, in terms of the numbers of orders made by the Courts annually. There were 698 Orders made in 1985, after which annual numbers rose, year on year, to an initial peak of 1,759 in 1993. After that, annual numbers of CSOs made fell, more or less stabilising between 1997 (1,167) and 1999 (1,342), before declining again to a new low of 756 in 2001. Following another three years (2002-2004) of relative stasis, annual numbers rose again, to a new high of 2,738 in 2011, before falling yet again, followed in turn by an increase in more recent years. Throughout however, the CSO has maintained its general attractiveness to sentencers, policymakers, commentators on criminal justice matters and the wider public, as a just and appropriate sanction in a wide range of cases.

Guilfoyle, having described the development of this sanction, summarised that, at its core, the CSO introduced in Ireland was three things:

1. *It was an alternative to imprisonment.* A CSO could be imposed only on offenders who would otherwise have been sentenced to imprisonment.
2. *It was a punishment.* It punished offenders by requiring offenders to carry out unpaid work in their spare time.
3. *It was reparative.* It allowed offenders to make general reparation by carrying out work that would otherwise not have been done.[58]

In terms of probation practice, McCarthy (2014)[59] stated that: 'Community Service is one of the penal community sanctions administered by the Probation Service in Ireland', with the role

---

56 Guilfoyle (n 7) 190-191.

57 Carr (n 45) 323.

58 Guilfoyle (n 7) 197.

59 Justin McCarthy, 'Community Service at the Crossroads in Ireland' (2014) 11 Irish Probation Journal 125.

of the probation officer incorporating a range of relevant tasks, including (1) assessment of offenders' suitability for a CSO, (2) inducting programme participants, (3) managing attendance compliance and (4) returning non-compliant cases to court. In terms of day-to-day organisation:

> Community service is most often performed by participants at a group project, supervised by a Community Service Supervisor and facilitated through a network of host agencies that includes schools, voluntary sector agencies, community organisations, charitable organisations and local authorities.[60]

According to the Probation Service,

> The range of work generally carried out by offenders undertaking Community Service includes painting, decorating, landscaping, clearing/maintenance of community facilities (indoor and outdoor), graffiti removal and site clearance, restoration or enhancement of community facilities and centres, school garden project development, grass cutting, and work with voluntary and community groups.[61]

In April 1998, the Department of Justice, Equality and Law Reform published an invitation to tender for an evaluation of the operation of the Criminal Justice (Community Service) Act, 1983. The evaluation was to critically assess the operation of the CSO scheme in Ireland, with the following objectives:

- to provide comprehensive data on CSOs including: incidence, duration, nature of work, associated offence, sentencing court, offender profile, factors influencing decision on imposition of CSO, completion rate, recidivism rate, supervision, public response, benefits and costs;
- to assess the factors and procedure applicable to the court's decision on the CSO issue; to assess the manner in which a CSO sanction is implemented and supervised;
- to ascertain the extent to which the CSOs are imposed and implemented uniformly in rural and urban areas;
- to assess how, and to what extent, CSOs are diverting offenders away from prison;
- to assess the costs/benefits of CSOs (including factors

---

60 ibid.

61 Probation Service, *Standard Operating Procedure Manual for Staff* (internal document, unpublished 2014).

such as recidivism, comparison with prison, and the community response);
- to make a critical comparison of the operation of the CSO legislation with its operation in other countries (particularly in other member states of the European Union). This will include an assessment of the extent to which Ireland complies with its obligations in this area under Council of Europe recommendations; and
- to assess the scope for an enhanced role for CSOs within the Irish criminal justice system.

The resulting research report, carried out by the Centre for Criminal Justice at the University of Limerick, was published in 1999.[62] It made a range of findings and drew conclusions as follows:[63]

- **Offender profile:** The 'standard recipient' of a CSO was described as being typically a young, single, unemployed or under-employed male, with poor educational qualifications and vocational skills, living in the parental home. Just over half had a previous criminal record – 40% of these for 'minor' offences, while a 'significant proportion had served a previous prison sentence. There were variations between different parts of the country, particularly between Dublin as compared to other areas: in Dublin, for example two-fifths of the individuals concerned were found to have 'suffered from drug or alcohol dependency in the past and four-fifths had a previous criminal record.'
- **Offences:** The most common offences for which CSOs were made, were: property offences (41%), road traffic and vehicle offences (24%), offences against the person (23%), public order offences (9%) and others (3%). The report also found considerable variation in the spread of offences across different District Court areas, as well as noting variations in such trends between urban and rural areas. In one area, all but one of the CSOs imposed, for example, were in respect of driving offences.
- **Orders (imposition):** The report found that 'generally, CSOs are used in accordance with the legislation' although there were findings of CSOs being used in conjunction with other punishments, and at least one case in which less than the statutory minimum number

62 Dermot Walsh and Paul Sexton, *An Empirical Study of Community Service Orders in Ireland* (Department of Justice, Equality and Law Reform 1999).
63 ibid 97-101.

of hours CSO was imposed. The report also found significant variations in the range of alternative prison sentences imposed (for which CSOs were substituted – the average length being 5.1 months), as well as in the length of CSOs (the average length being 141 hours), and differences between 'urban' and 'rural courts in relation to these disparities.

- **Orders (management):** In almost one in three cases, 'the community service work was not commenced until more than two months after the CSO was imposed', with Dublin faring better on this front, compared to other parts of the country. More than four fifths of CSOs were worked through to completion, although almost 40% of offenders were served with one or more warning letters for breaches of their obligations. Around a quarter of CSOs were completed within two months, with 'well over one third' talking more than six months to complete.
- **Work projects** consisted in the main of 'environmental work, painting and decorating, gardening and helping out at old people's homes, youth clubs and charities' with evidence that 'the nature of the work is such that it would not normally be done if it had to be paid for' and that 'offenders generally adopt a positive attitude to their community service work.' Some problems with 'host' organisations having appropriate insurance cover were identified.
- **Courts and court procedures:** The District Courts were found to use CSOs extensively, but with clear variations between court areas and depending on individual Judges. The study found little usage outside District Courts, with no apparent reason for this. Sentencing hearings involving CSOs tended to be very brief, with probation officers' assessment reports being identified as either: (a) detailed (over 50% of all reports), (b) concise (33% of reports), or (c) very brief (10% of reports). Judges were said 'for the most part to act on the basis of the community service report when deciding to impose a CSO.'[64]

The report also found that there was 'evidence to suggest that CSOs are being used in some instances for offences which might not have attracted a custodial sentence if the CSO option had not been available.'[65] Similarly, some judges and others expressed the

---

[64] Walsh and Sexton (n 62) 100.

[65] ibid 97.

view that 'the legislation was too restrictive in confining CSOs as a substitute for a prison term.'[66] Almost half of all offenders involved did not have a previous conviction and the 'most frequent offences committed by these offenders are road traffic offences, public order offences and less serious assaults.'[67] The research recorded that: 'The relationship between the number of CSO hours and length of alternative prison term varies substantially and randomly across court areas.'[68] The national average of this 'equivalence' was found to be that one month of imprisonment was equivalent to a CSO of 27 hours, while in individual areas, this could vary from 63 to 11 hours. The researchers pointed to a perceived 'considerable uncertainty about the number of CSO hours which should be imposed relative to the length of the prison term' and that 'this uncertainty is exaggerated, at least in some areas, by a tendency to resort to CSOs in cases where a prison term would not normally have been imposed had CSOs not being available'.[69]

## Value for Money Review of Community Service

A Value for Money (VFM) and Policy Review of community service was subsequently completed by external consultants, on behalf of the Department, in 2009.[70] The Review set out to:

1. identify the aims and objectives of community service,
2. examine the continued validity of those objectives and their compatibility with the overall strategy of the Department and the Probation Service,
3. identify the associated outputs of the scheme,
4. establish the level of Probation Service staff time used in the supervision of the scheme,
5. consider its effectiveness, and
6. evaluate the relevant data and information resources.[71]

The review found that the Community Service scheme represented 3.8% (€2.295 million) of total Probation Service voted expenditure, and 11% of Probation Service expenditure when staff time and indirect costs are factored in. In addition, the review found variations in how community service was organised and managed

---

66 ibid.
67 ibid 98.
68 ibid.
69 ibid.
70 Value for Money and Policy Review of the Community Service Scheme (Department of Justice, Equality and Law Reform 2009).
71 ibid 84.

across the country and made a series of recommendations for change, including:

| Finding | Recommendation | Action/s |
|---|---|---|
| 1. Community service (CS) is cost-effective but usage by courts has been declining. | Encourage greater use of CS as alternative to custody. | Analyse sentencing patterns, identify locations where more offenders can be identified for CS. |
| 2. Use of CS by courts is low in large parts of the country. | Develop CS in a more targeted way, on a regional basis. | Review deployment of CS supervisors; document steps to make CS a more attractive option for the Courts; identify alternative work placements where necessary. |
| 3. Wide disparities in the average length of CS orders and of alternative sentences.[72] | Circulate statistical data on imposition of CS orders to the judiciary and others. | Circulate annual or quarterly information with analysis of statistics. |
| 4. Successful completion rate of CS is around 80-85% | Ensure a speedy process is in place to deal with non-compliance. | Commence CS orders within 14 days of imposition; establish rapid revocation process; monitor completion rate on a quarterly basis. |
| 5. Ongoing capacity utilisation[73] on CS work projects, on aggregate, is approximately 33%. | Increase capacity utilisation on supervised projects and include such utilisation as a performance indicator for community service reported at local, regional and national basis on a regular basis. | Examine location of CS supervisors compared to originating CSOs. Include capacity utilisation as key performance indicator. Aim to increase capacity usage – in stages, over two years – from 33% to 70%. |

[72] This type of inconsistency had been found previously by Walsh and Sexton (n 62); and would be again, in Kate O'Hara and Mary Rogan, 'Examining the Use of Community Service Orders' (2015)' 12 Irish Probation Journal, for example.

[73] *Capacity utilisation* refers to the extent to which a community service work project or 'site' is utilised per day, or over another time interval. This is significant because, from an organisational resource point of view, it is in the interests of efficiency that the relevant capacity utilisation is maximised; otherwise human and other resources are not being employed to greatest impact, which can in turn result in community service work projects being unduly delayed and extended waiting times in the placement of offenders onto these work sites.

| Finding | Recommendation | Action/s |
|---|---|---|
| 6. Supervisors identified that site selection is key to improving efficiency and effectiveness. | Review all existing CS sites for suitability and effectiveness, and introduce a strategy for future site selection. | All sites and strategy to be in place by end 2009. |
| 7. Data currently available to manage CS is of limited value. | Upgrade IT infrastructure to accommodate more robust CS data reporting strategy. | Implement upgrades and practice enhancements required, in 2009. |
| 8. Cost and management information in relation to community service is weak. | A costing system is needed, to enable the Probation Service track all relevant direct and indirect costs and provide operational information on a site and regional basis. | Appropriate systems to be put in place. |
| 9. The management of CS involves a disproportionate amount of some Senior Probation Officers' (SPO) time. | Review the role and functions of SPOs and other Probation Service staff; propose the more effective use of these resources; consider a revised staffing structure for delivery of CS. | Carry out the review by end of 2009. |
| 10. Need for evidence based national research to assess the impact of CS on the level of reparation and added value to the community and how additional value may be achieved in terms of positive change in offender behaviour and reintegration. | The proposed White Paper on Crime to incorporate this issue in examining the range of non-custodial sanctions. | Commence consideration of this by end 2009. |
| 11. Key performance metrics not in place for CS operation and management. | Build performance framework and implement comprehensive management information system, to provide information necessary to manage the CS scheme and evaluate its performance. | Identify and implement key performance indicators. |

Following the VFM review, new standard operating procedures were drafted and introduced by the Probation Service, with associated revisions of relevant policies, standard operating protocols and administrative procedures, and appropriate communication with relevant stakeholders, as well as updated staff training to support implementation. Community Service was 'rebranded' and relaunched, under the banner of a 'new model' of operation, aimed at being more efficient and effective, and implementing recommendations arising from the VFM Review. This 'rebranding' was communicated to the Judiciary, as well as to Service staff and partner organisations and other bodies. The new model included the introduction of same day assessment reports for courts, where appropriate and possible. This latter measure proved to be popular with many judges, with the annual number of same-day assessments for community service completed annually rising to several hundred[74] after the system was introduced in appropriate locations.[75]

## Strategic Review of Penal Policy

The Report of the Strategic Review of Penal Policy report published in 2014, acknowledged that following the enactment of the Community Service (Amendment) Act in 2011, encouraging the use of CSOs in cases where a custodial sentence of one year or less was being considered, as well as the launch of the more efficient 'new model' of community service, including the availability of same-day assessments, that '…there was an initial increase in the number of community service orders although the level of such orders is significantly less than in similar jurisdictions such as Scotland…'[76] That initial annual increase went from 1,413 community service orders made in 2008, to a high of 2,738 in 2011, then falling each year again to 1,938 in 2015. The annual number of CSOs made remained reasonably steady at around 2,000 for several years, before increasing again each year after 2016, up to 2019.[77]

The Strategic Review referenced community service as one of the 'advances in the area of non-custodial sanctions.'[78] The Review Report 'also considered the potential of community service to

---

74 See Probation Service Annual Reports for details.

75 Same-day Community Service Assessment Reports were to be made available in court locations where there is a probation officer present on 'court duty' at the court venue, where the officer has access (eg by phone) to their 'base' office, to check Probation Service and other records, where the presiding Judge requests such a report, all parties consent, and there is sufficient time to carry out the appropriate interview with the defendant, as well as any other enquiries on the day, and report back to the Judge within the same day/court sitting.

76 Department of Justice and Equality, *Strategic Review of Penal Policy: Final Report* (2014) 47.

77 The Probation Service Annual Report for 2019 records 2,791 CSOs made that year, the most recent full year for which statistics were available, at the time of writing.

78 Department of Justice and Equality (n 76) 21.

be more widely used as an alternative to prison' and whether 'a sanction imposing community service could not also require additional conditions, for instance, addiction treatment.'[79] In this context, the Review noted[80] that 'while not necessarily regarded as a sanction which focuses on rehabilitation, recidivism findings already demonstrate that community service is effective in reducing reoffending.'[81] The report of the Strategic Review included a proposal to support the introduction of so-called *integrated community service,* which would allow for the incorporation of more overtly rehabilitative elements into community service orders, where the supervising probation officer assessed that the individual's prospects of rehabilitation would be enhanced by encouraging such rehabilitative work through allowing 'credit' for this by way of a 'discounted' community service order.[82] It was established that up to a maximum of one third of an individual's CSO hours could be discounted in this way. This initiative had in fact been evolving at a practice level and after the strategic policy review, was progressed by the Probation Service in a more formalised way. Integrated Community Service was introduced by the Probation Service in practice, on a pilot basis, in 2016,[83] followed by commencement of the '...national roll out of the integrated model in late 2017.'[84]

## Community Service as Condition of Early Release from Prison

Community service work came to be used as part of temporary release of prisoners in certain instances following the Thornton

---

79 Department of Justice and Equality (n 76) 46-47.

80 The Strategic Review cites the Probation Service Recidivism Studies, 2007-2011 and 2008-2013, which provide relevant data — see Department of Justice and Equality (n 76) 47.

81 Recidivism studies carried out by the Central Statistics Office have shown that the annual population or group subject to Community Service annually have lower rates of reconviction than for those in other probation supervision cohorts, as well as when compared to those who served custodial sentences.

82 Department of Justice and Equality (n 76) 49.

83 Probation Service, *Annual Report 2016* (Probation Service 2017) 6, states that: 'Integrated Community Service allows for up to one third of Community Service hours to be used to facilitate a participant's attendance at programmes and support service, to address issues connected to his/her offending. For example, attendance at counselling, drug/alcohol treatment or educational / vocational programmes.'

84 Probation Service, *Annual Report 2017* (Probation Service 2018) 14. It is noteworthy that Guilfoyle (n 7) 202-203, has questioned the legality of the introduction of the Integrated CSO model.

Hall Review Report of 2011.[85] As documented by McNally and Brennan (2015), numbers in custody had been increasing during the first decade of the current century.[86] This precipitated the purchase of lands at Thornton Hall in North County Dublin, on which it was planned to build a large new prison, which would accommodate up to 2,200 prisoners and in turn ease pressure on bed-spaces across the prison estate. However, as pointed up by McNally and Brennan (2015), despite the rising prison population at the time, 'the serious economic downturn in 2008 in Ireland... and subsequent financial crisis...' forced a 'major restructuring of [Government] expenditure and changes in previously ambitious plans' – including those regarding the building of a so-called 'super-prison' in North County Dublin. As a result, in April 2011, the then Minister for Justice and Equality established a group to review the Thornton Hall proposal and specifically to consider how to address the issue of rising numbers in custody in other ways. The review group reported in July 2011, recommending *inter alia* the introduction of an 'incentivised scheme for earned temporary release coupled with a requirement to do community service under supervision.'[87] In October 2011, the probation and prison services commenced the new 'community return' programme in practice, initially as a pilot scheme.

'Community return'[88] was to be

> ...applicable to assessed prisoners who are serving sentences of between one and eight years' imprisonment. In a small number of instances persons serving sentences of longer than eight years were referred to the Community Return Programme, following a recommendation from the Interim Parole Board.[89]

---

85 Report of the Thornton Hall Project Review Group (Department of Justice and Equality 2011)

86 Gerry McNally and Andrew Brennan, 'Community Return: A Unique Opportunity' (2015) 12 Irish Probation Journal 141-159.

87 McNally and Brennan (n 86) 142. It should be noted however that there is no requirement for those released as part of the parole process in Ireland to undertake community service work as a condition of their parole.

88 The name of the initiative – *Community Return* – was suggested by one of the present authors (Geiran) during his time on the project planning group, as fulfilling a threefold message: indicating a person's *physical* return to the community; the paying back to the community by way of *reparative* return (by doing community service work); and reflecting the fact that a participant could be *returned* from the community, to prison, for non-compliance with the terms of their early release.

89 The Community Return programme was targeted at those serving prison sentences of between one and eight years. Those serving prison sentences of eight years or longer came within the remit of the Interim Parole Board (see

Those released on community return, following multi-agency assessment of suitability, were subject to a rigorous and reasonably strict work and supervision regime, being supervised in the community by probation officers, and their overall compliance overseen by an interagency (probation-prisons) team, co-located in probation service headquarters. As described by McNally and Brennan (2015):

> Participants in the Community Return Programme are required to complete three days' [community service] work each week. The working day is 9.30 am to 4.30 pm. Prisoners involved in the programme undertake the same type of work as people on court ordered community service. In many situations, the groups of offenders work side-by-side.

More recently, there have been expansions to the criteria for potential eligibility for the scheme. In particular, this has involved moving the point of earliest possible eligibility to half of one's remitted sentence, rather than half of the 'gross' sentence as initially designed.[90] The community return was subsequently evaluated, and the findings published in a joint Probation Service — Prison Service report, in 2014.[91] More information on community return and other early release programmes is provided in the separate conditional release chapter in this book.

The issues of participant compliance, as well as enforcement and dealing with non-compliance issues, are important considerations in the context of community service and community return, as much as with other community sanctions. The legal/procedural

---

separate chapter on Parole). Those serving prison sentences of less than one year are frequently released early anyway, and would be difficult to assess and manage in the structured way set out for Community Return. Given that those sentenced to short custodial sentences can present with significant personal and social challenges, and have statistically high rates of reoffending as a group, a scheme somewhat similar to Community Return– Community Support – was subsequently put in place for those serving prison terms of less than one year. More information on both Community Return and Community Support is included in the chapter on Conditional Release.

90 For example, given that there is a generally applicable remission of one quarter of any (determinate) prison sentence term, the change means that someone serving a four-year prison sentence would now be eligible to be considered for early release on Community Return once they have served one and a half years (ie the halfway point of their remitted sentence), as opposed to being eligible when they have completed two years (ie half of the 'gross' or unremitted length of the sentence).

91 Paul Donoghue, *Community Return: A Unique Opportunity: A descriptive evaluation of the first twenty-six months (2011-2013)* (Probation Service & Irish Prison Service 2014).

aspects and issues of managing compliance with a CSO have been described above. Such issues of compliance management, particularly where those on court-imposed CSOs are serving those orders alongside others released early from custodial sentences, under the Community Return programme, initially gave some cause for concern. Practitioners' concerns in this regard are heightened in the twofold context of wanting to treat both 'categories' of individuals with comparable procedural fairness, while acknowledging that the 'rules' of each scheme are different, allied to potential concerns that one group of offenders might have a demotivating effect on the other. This has not been proven to be the case, with both groups appearing to have a positive rather than negative effect on each other's levels of commitment, motivation and compliance. Simply from a legal-technical point of view, the person who is non-compliant with a court-ordered CSO must ultimately be returned to that *court* to be dealt with. The comparable action for the community return participant is much simpler: they can have their temporary release revoked much more easily and swiftly, and be returned to prison without recourse to court.

Guilfoyle has summarised 'the developments in the CSO since its introduction' as falling under two broad headings: 1. *Operational* and 2. *Legislative* changes.[92] Operational changes, implemented by the Probation Service in the main, followed findings and recommendations arising from research, the VFM report and the Review of Penal Policy, for example. Legislative changes aimed at increasing the use of CSOs by the courts, reducing committals to prison and substituting CSOs for fines. According to Guilfoyle,[93] neither of the legislative changes made (in 2011 and 2014) has changed the CSO itself, nor altered its core elements.

## Current Situation and Challenges

Guilfoyle suggested that: 'The international experience and the many variations of community service that now exist can create a degree of uncertainty and confusion when the Irish Community Service Order is discussed.' While McCarthy (2014) referenced a 'lack of reinforced clarity about its [CSO's] place in the rank of sentencing tariffs', giving rise to 'confusion about its optimal target population',[94] the Law Reform Commission suggests that the CSO is located between the *deferred sentence* (which is below

---

92 Guilfoyle (n 7) 197-201

93 Guilfoyle (n 7) 201.

94 McCarthy (n 59) 146-147.

the sentence of *immediate imprisonment*, the *part-suspended sentence* and the *fully suspended* [custodial] *sentence*) and the *fine* (with the conditional discharge and the dismissal coming in below these) in the 'hierarchy of criminal punishment.'[95] This is on the basis that 'the legislative provision and the judicial authorities expressly frame the suspended sentence as a non-immediate custodial sentence, whereas the CSO is expressed as an alternative to prison.'[96]

One of the key challenges and points of discussion in relation to community service in Ireland has been its use, as prescribed by the 1983 legislation, only in circumstances where it is employed as a direct alternative to a specified custodial sentence. Many commentators over the years since the 1983 legislation was enacted, including members of the judiciary, as well as the 1998 Expert Group on the Probation Service have reflected on this and voiced a view that community service should be possible to use as a standalone sanction in its own right.[97] This would avoid the need, statutorily required as things stand, that a judge theoretically imposed a specified custodial sentence in the first place, before substituting that with an alternative community service order. Such use of community service would mirror the comparable type of application in the UK for example.

Some members of the judiciary have expressed the view that community service could and should be used as a direct alternative to a formal and recorded sanction, in the context of a diversionary measure, at court stage. This would involve a defendant agreeing to undertake community service work at the stage where they were acknowledging their guilt but prior to the imposition of a formal sanction. Under this proposed approach, the offender would be given the opportunity to perform an appropriate amount of community service, after which the court might well decide to strike out the matter without penalty.[98] Such a diversionary type of approach is used in jurisdictions such as the Netherlands, where the Public Prosecution Service '…in the pre-trial stage… can settle of a case itself… in the form of (conditional) dismissal, a transaction or by way of a punishment order…' whereby: 'Many criminal cases are settled in this way out of court in the pre-trial stage, with a fine, a behavioural condition or community service.'[99] Community

---

[95] Law Reform Commission (n 39) 35-36.

[96] Law Reform Commission (n 39) 35.

[97] It is arguable that such a move would lead to further *net-widening*.

[98] Such an approach could be described as *reparative* – and potentially *restorative* – diversion. See separate chapter on Restorative Justice and Victims.

[99] Marco de Kok, Leo Tigges and Anton van Kalmthout, *Probation in Europe: The Netherlands* (Confederation of European Probation 2020) 22.

service is also used in a similar — alternative to prosecution — way as part of the 'checkpoint' diversionary programme in Durham in England. Checkpoint is described as

> a multi-agency pre-court diversion scheme used by Durham Constabulary for adult offenders who have committed ... "low-level crime"... It is a four-month programme... [and] takes the form of a contract which has several conditions... not to reoffend...a restorative justice element... and a community service condition...[100]

Opponents of such examples of the more widespread use of community service, for different purposes and at different points in the criminal justice process, would point to a perceived diluting of its value as a direct alternative to imprisonment, if community service where to be used in these other ways–either as a supervised community sanction in its own right, and particularly if used as a diversionary measure at the (pre)prosecution or pre-sentence stage. Such 'diluting' of the CSO as we know it to date in Ireland, is already under way, according to Guilfoyle, as a consequence of the implementation of the Fines (Payment and Recovery) Act 2014.[101]

As well as the studies described above[102] a number of doctoral theses have been undertaken in relation to community service in Ireland, including those by Riordan,[103] O'Hara[104] and Guilfoyle.[105] In addition, several significant related articles have been published, particularly in the Irish Probation Journal. Issues raised over the years since the introduction of the CSO in Ireland include those highlighted by Riordan from a judicial perspective, encompassing a reluctance by judges to strictly equate community service with a custodial sentence, as well as concerns regarding how well or otherwise CSOs may be monitored and enforced by the Probation

---

100 See UK Parliament – Hansard, Vol 802, 27 February 2020, available at: https://hansard.parliament.uk/lords/2020-02-27/debates/C4DA4DBD-0B73-408A-BD77-777242234D88/OffenderManagementCheckpointProgramme .

101 Guilfoyle (n 7) 200.

102 Including Walsh and Sexton (n 62) and Department of Justice, Equality and Law Reform (n 70).

103 David Riordan, *The role of the community service order and the suspended sentence in Ireland: a judicial perspective* (University College Cork, PhD Thesis 2009).

104 O'Hara, K. (2016) *Examining the comparative use, experience, and outcomes of community service orders as alternatives to short prison sentences in Ireland.* Thesis submitted in fulfilment of the requirements for the award of Doctor of Philosophy to Technological University Dublin, April 2016. doi:1021427/D7MG6W.

105 Eoin Guilfoyle, *An Examination of the Community Service Order in Ireland: Recommendations for Change* (University of Limerick, PhD Thesis 2018).

Service, in conjunction with criticism of the 'wide-ranging discretion unwittingly imported from [the] British legislation into the Irish Act [which] appears to undermine the purpose of the community service order as a penalty designed to act as an alternative to custody.'[106] The high degree of regulation of the (Irish) CSO, allied to 'the judiciary's aversion for the restrictive nature of the… [1983] Act', issues to which O'Hara and Rogan[107] had pointed, had also been alluded to previously by others.[108]

Some of the issues or 'dilemmas' raised by McCarthy include the sanction's 'more regulatory relationship between practitioners and … participants', its position 'as a sentencing measure with multiple variables' and 'multidimensional ambiguity,' 'a lack of reinforced clarity about its place in the rank of sentencing tariffs,' and concerns at community service's 'net-widening' properties, which in turn may be leading in some way to increased rather than reduced rates of imprisonment.[109] McCarthy concludes by commenting that 'consideration of the quality of the community service experience might yield greater benefits than a preoccupation with increased quantity.'[110]

## Discussion and Conclusions

Given what has gone before, it is difficult in the circumstances to 'square' some of the views and dilemmas described above with the view held by many, of community service as a sanction with a clear role and boundaries. Guilfoyle has pointed out that:

> It was clear that in Ireland the primary reason for introducing the CSO was to reduce the number of people sent to prison. To limit the potential for net-widening and increase the impact that the CSO would have on the expanding prison population, a requirement was added to the Irish legislation that allowed a CSO to be used only as an alternative to imprisonment and not as a sanction in its own right.

Geiran and Durnescu (2019)[111] have pointed out that:

---

106 Riordan (n 103) 146.
107 O'Hara and Rogan (n 72) 42.
108 Including Walsh and Sexton (n 62), Riordan (n 103), *supra*; Department of Justice, Equality and Law Reform (n 70).
109 McCarthy (n 59) 144-147.
110 McCarthy (n 59) 150.
111 Geiran and Durnescu (n 37) 54.

> Although the history of community service is one in which its value and credibility in the criminal justice system, and as part of what McCulloch (2010)[112] described as the often contentious matrix of community penalties, was often seen as its robust reparative nature, it has come to be valued over the years, in many jurisdictions, as a positively rehabilitative and reintegration sanction in its own right.

Community service is now a well-established supervised community sanction in Ireland, as much as in many other jurisdictions around the world. Its attractiveness as a sanction is undoubtedly linked to its perception as a practical demonstration of an offender making reparation for the harm they have caused through their offending back to the local community that has been impacted by the offending in the first place. Maruna and King have described this as — to a greater or lesser extent — 'symbolically transforming the probationer into a "giver rather than a consumer of help".'[113] In addition to being used as a direct, court-imposed sanction, community service work has also come to be used as part of certain early release programmes, in particular for prisoners on temporary release as part of the Community Return scheme. More recently, efforts have been made to substitute community service for those who default on fine payment.

Guilfoyle suggested that there is a need

> to provide clarity as to what exactly the CSO is in Ireland... in order to allow for the accurate assessment of the CSO's effectiveness and of its limitations and boundaries... and to provide a solid base for future discussions about the CSO and the potential role it can play in reducing the number of people sentenced to prison each year in Ireland.[114]

The use of community service in Ireland, in terms of the numbers of orders made by courts annually, has fluctuated from year to year at certain phases since its introduction as a community sanction four decades ago. Its value as a rehabilitative intervention for offenders has been increasingly acknowledged and demonstrated through the Central Statistics Office's recidivism studies. Debate in relation to whether community service should always, and only, be used

---

112 Trish McCulloch, 'Exploring community service, understanding compliance,' in Fergus McNeill, Peter Raynor and Chris Trotter (eds), *Offender Supervision: New directions in theory, research and practice* (Willan 2010) 384.

113 Shadd Maruna and Anna King, 'Selling the public on probation: Beyond the bib' (2008) 55(4) Probation Journal 337-351.

114 Guilfoyle (n 105) 190.

as a direct alternative to a named custodial sentence continues to surface from time to time. It seems though, that community service will continue to be a relatively popular sanction, notwithstanding the on-going debates about its purpose, its legal framework and other related issues.

CHAPTER SIX

# RESTORATIVE JUSTICE AND VICTIMS

## Introduction

As Geiran and Durnescu (2019) have pointed out:

> Traditionally, probation officers in many jurisdictions did not meet crime victims directly. Nevertheless, they might have been required or encouraged to take account of victims in a number of ways: through incorporating consideration of victim issues into their preparation of pre-sanction reports or considering victim awareness in offender programmes. At an organisational level, some information provision to victims of crime might have been the extent of direct contact with any victims, for many years.[1]

This is not to exclude the fact of course that many people who perpetrate crimes are also the victims of offending behaviour. There is not always, by any means, a neat dividing line between who might be described as 'offenders' and those identified as 'victims.' That said, in the context of a growing awareness of victim issues in criminal justice, '[w]hat has become known as 'restorative justice' has been growing in Probation and wider Criminal Justice practice in recent years.'[2] According to van Garsse (2016):

> The notion of restorative justice... found its way with remarkable ease through the UK and Western Europe to actually become a criminal policy approach that is well known everywhere and respected in circles both of the UN and the Council of Europe.[3]

Restorative Justice (RJ) in general describes a voluntary process characterised by the active participation of the victim(s), offenders

---

1 Vivian Geiran and Ioan Durnescu, *Implementing Community Sanctions and Measures: Guidelines* (Council of Europe 2019) 57.

2 ibid 58.

3 Leo van Garsse, 'Has Probation Any Impact in Terms of Reparation to Victims and Communities? Complicating a Simple Question,' in Fergus McNeill, Ioan Durnescu and René Butter (eds), *Probation: 12 Essential Questions* (Palgrave Macmillan 2016) 86.

and other stakeholders in the response to a crime. Whilst the benefits of RJ will be considered later in this chapter it suffices to say at this stage that research has indicated that it is a process that can help victims recover from the negative impact of crimes, reduce reoffending and save public resources and also benefit offenders by affording them an opportunity to be heard and to benefit from the re-integrative effects of this process. However before further analysing the development of RJ it is firstly necessary to consider in more detail what RJ is.

## Defining Restorative Justice?

Some commentators use the terms *restorative justice* and *restorative practice* interchangeably. Some of the differences between the two concepts have been discussed by Lauster[4] and Hunter[5] among others. For the present purposes, it is proposed to confine discussion to the (narrower) concept of *restorative justice,* while remaining conscious of the wider spectrum of associated applications in practice. Restorative justice is a concept which is centred on restoring the balance disturbed by crime and making good the harm caused to those concerned. In the Irish context it has generally been considered to require the perpetrator to face up to the harm that they have caused and to repair or make good the damage done, with the victim at the centre of the process.[6] The National Commission on Restorative Justice settled on defining RJ, in the Irish context, as:

> Restorative Justice is a victim-sensitive response to criminal offending, which through engagement with those affected by crime, aims to make amends for the harm that has been caused to victims and communities and which facilitates offender rehabilitation into society.[7]

The Council of Europe in their recommendation on restorative justice defined RJ as:

> … any process that enables those harmed by crime and those

4 Eileen Lauster and others, 'Practical Strategies for Coping with Child-to-Parent Violence: The Non Violent Resistance Programme in Practice' (2014) 11 Irish Probation Journal 208-221.

5 Christine Hunter, 'The Development of Restorative Practice with Adults Offenders in the Probation Board for Northern Ireland' (2015) 12 Irish Probation Journal 229-240.

6 National Commission on Restorative Justice, *Final Report* (2009) 29.

7 National Commission on Restorative Justice (n 7) 9.

> responsible for that crime, if they freely consent, to participate actively in the resolution of matters arising from that offence, through the help of a trained and impartial third party.[8]

The above definitions of RJ show, in their relative vagueness, that RJ is a concept that is not easily capable of being tied down. The fact that RJ is recognised as 'a global social movement with huge internal diversity'[9] amplifies the difficulty in placing it within the confines of a single definition. This difficulty, has given rise to the concern that as RJ has come to mean so many things to so many different people that there is a 'fear that it is beginning to cease to have any clear reference.'[10] Each of the definitions of RJ quoted above illustrate that RJ is a philosophy that includes a broad range of practices, which can differ in terms of when and how they are utilised however there are a number of fundamental tenets of RJ which include:

- The participation of those involved in and affected by an offence (the stakeholders – including the victim, the offender and the community);
- It is a victim-centred process;
- The participation of all parties, but especially that of the victim, is on a voluntary basis;
- The offender accepts responsibility and holds themselves accountable;
- There would be a facilitated encounter that implies a default face-to-face meeting of the victim and the offender;
- The aim of the process is addressing and repairing harm; and
- A focus on cultivating positive relationships.

RJ is also based on a number of key notions, one of which is that crime is to be viewed as a violation of the individual and a fracturing of social relations, rather than just as an offence against the State. Another is an acceptance that crime affects more than

---

8 Recommendation CM/Rec(2018)8 of the Committee of Ministers to member States concerning restorative justice in criminal matters (Adopted by the Committee of Ministers on 3 October 2018 at the 1326th meeting of the Ministers' Deputies) Rule 3

9 Gerry Johnstone and Daniel Van Ness, 'The Meaning of Restorative Justice' in Gerry Johnstone and Daniel Van Ness (eds), *Handbook of Restorative Justice* (Taylor and Francis 2013) 5.

10 Jennifer L Lanterman, 'Models versus Mechanisms: The Need to Crack The Black Box of Restorative Justice' (2020) 17(1) British J Community Justice 62, where this concept is explored further.

just the immediate victim, it also has an effect on the offender, the families of the victim and the offender, the local community and the State.[11] The above definitions of Restorative Justice provide clear evidence of a forward looking approach, offering the chance to translate a negative experience into a positive framework, which offers all parties the opportunity to become involved in establishing a basis from which to progress.[12] Utilising these key notions, RJ can be portrayed as a theory of criminal justice which focuses on crime as an act against another individual or the community, rather than against the State, in the first instance.

As RJ is such a wide, embracing notion it can best be initially considered as a philosophy, or a compass, guiding participants through a dialogue about wrongdoing rather than as a map, blueprint or particular programme.[13] With so many different definitions of RJ, it has frequently become the norm to discuss RJ by reference to what it is not, with a particular focus on contrasting RJ with the retributive focus of the traditional criminal justice system. In this regard RJ can take the form of alternative dispute resolution, involving the victim and the offender meeting and discussing the offence in a more informal setting than is available in a criminal court. The criminal courts in Ireland and the retributive justice system generally operated therein at the moment, is in stark contrast to that practiced using restorative justice principles. With the current traditional system, although court cases are conducted on behalf of the victim and the community, they can seem to many to operate mostly according to the requirements of the courts. The result is that many victims frequently feel distant and marginalised from 'their' process. There is often little sense of closure, forgiveness or encouragement for victims to get on with their lives by putting the damage caused by the crime behind them.[14] For offenders, the court process frequently does the opposite of what is intended in that it can also help distance them from their actions.

Although the spotlight is on the person in the dock, the offender– as well as the victim – frequently takes very little part in the

---

11 Acceptance of the basic facts of the case also has a protective effect – it affords an individual who denies a criminal accusation the due process of a trial and it also protects the victim from the re-victimisation of a suspected offender denying responsibility entirely during an RJ process. For further discussion see Ian Marder, 'Building restorative probation services', HM Inspectorate of Probation, Academic Insights 2020/04 (June 2020) 8.

12 Roger Graef, *Why Restorative Justice? Repairing the harm caused by Crime* (Calouste Gulbenkian Foundation 2001) 15.

13 Lanterman (n 10) 62 where this concept is explored further.

14 Graef (n 12) 13.

proceedings and generally watches passively as their lives are discussed by strangers in complex, legal language that they often do not understand. Frequently, if the offender pleads guilty, it is on legal advice that it will reduce the anticipated sentence rather than out of remorse and a desire to make good the harm they have done.[15] In contrast, RJ seeks to hold offenders accountable and reduce re-offending by relying on informal community involvement and varying forms of intervention and supervision.[16] It could be argued that the retributive, criminal court system allocates blame and punishment whilst the RJ system holds the perpetrator responsible and requires him or her to make things right. A key component of the application of restorative and community justice programmes is the aim of restoring victim dignity and to also facilitate offender reintegration. It could be stated that RJ is much more about responding to crime with a focus on addressing the causes of crime and the harm done by it than it is on punishment for the crime committed.

RJ frequently strives to achieve the aim of restoring victim dignity and facilitating offender reintegration through facilitated face-to-face meetings between victims, offenders and other relevant parties, such as members of their respective families. The bringing together of both parties lies at the core of RJ. This encounter enables victims to explain to their offenders the impact that the offence has had on them, while offenders are given the opportunity to acknowledge and to make right, in a practical way, the wrongs done to their victim or victims. The manner in which the offender and the victim are brought together is vital and such contact must take place on a voluntary basis and in a managed and safe setting.

At these meetings the victim is empowered to face the offender and highlight the hurt and injury the offender's behaviour has caused. The facilitated face-to-face meetings give victims the opportunity to get answers to questions that are of direct concern to them. It also gives them a chance to tell offenders of the effects and consequences of their actions. Aside from the possible physical

---

15 Nils Christie in referring to the fact that defendants generally have a lawyer to speak for them and consequently are required to say little or nothing for themselves and also that defending lawyers commonly regard it as their duty to attack the victim's credibility as a witness. If the offender is convicted his/or her lawyer generally denies or minimises the harm suffered by the victim so that the Court will impose a lighter sentence. Christie states, 'Conflicts belong to the people directly involved and should not be 'stolen' by professionals' in Nils Christie, 'Conflicts as property' (1977) 17(1) British J Criminol 1-15.

16 Kimberly de Beus and Nancy Rodriguez, 'Restorative Justice Practice: An examination of Program completion and recidivism' (2007) 35 Journal of Criminal Justice 337.

injury or financial loss attached to crime, psychological distress and increased suspicion can result in victims restricting their activities as a result, for example. In the retributive justice system where crime is defined as breaking the law or offending against the State, it is usual for the victim to have a limited role in the ensuing process, although it is acknowledged that the role of the victim and the respect and dignity afforded them in the criminal justice system has improved in recent times. Victims' views of the retributive justice system frequently record feelings of inadequate input, neglect and their role being reduced to that of a witness.[17]

In the RJ model the face-to-face meeting places the victim in a position to secure both explanations and assurances from the offender. The process may include an apology which many victims greatly value[18] or it may also allow the victim to receive some form of material and psychological reparation.[19] The use of RJ as a process has been shown to improve the experience of victims in the criminal justice system, particularly where fairness, respect and satisfaction levels are used as barometers of success.[20] It must however be recognised that RJ is not undertaken exclusively in the interests of the victim. It is concerned with providing constructive outcomes for the offenders, victims and the community. The victim's evidence has the added potential for creating an important impact in the RJ process, not least by the fact that an offender hearing directly from the victim how they have been affected by a crime is a more salutary experience for an offender than any second-hand account.

The offender also has a role to play and the RJ process gives the offender the chance to tell his or her side of the story. They may explain their actions and discuss how their own lives have been affected. A potentially greater impact however is the increased likelihood that the victim's involvement and contributions will impact upon the offender in a profound way. The offender, by proffering an apology and having it accepted, when that is appropriate, has the assurance that this offence can be placed in the past and that he or she can resume normal life in the community,

---

17 Sheena Norton, 'The Place of Victims in the Criminal Justice System' (2007) 4(1) Irish Probation Journal 63 where it is stated: 'Victims are often the forgotten parties in the criminal justice system, despite their involuntary and highly distressing involvement in the arena... however without the co-operation of the victim in reporting crime, furnishing evidence, identifying the offender and acting as a witness in court, most crime would remain unknown and unpunished.'

18 National Commission on Restorative Justice (n 6) 35.

19 Recent surveys have shown that before restorative justice mediation 25% of victims feared re-victimisation; after it only 10% did. See Graef (n 12) 30.

20 National Commission on Restorative Justice (n 6) 35.

thus mending fences. If the matter has reached the court stage when an RJ intervention is undertaken, the offender may frequently avoid a custodial sentence or other punitive sanctions, or at least have the RJ process taken into account in any consideration of sanction by the court.

The role of the community in the restorative justice process is also vital. The community in some situations may serve the role of victim representative and offender recipient, as well as being the collective connection between the two, and others who may have been impacted by the offence. Additionally, the community can have a positive influence on offenders such as to reduce stigmatisation, provide a sense of value, and create incentive for reform.[21] The community can play a significant role in that the community may have considerable power to influence the offender and help them to repair the harm which may have been caused. Unfortunately, the community can also hinder offender reintegration by labelling and ostracising offenders.[22] The goal of RJ is to restore a sense of community in the offender, the offender's family, the victim(s) and the community at large while at the same time holding the offender accountable for the offence.[23] RJ also facilitates the community in taking a particular problem-solving approach to offenders and offending, using a range of health and social service interventions, including mental health treatment, drug and alcohol treatment, job training etc with a view to minimising repeat offending. Greater community involvement, achieved through enhanced citizen involvement in the rehabilitation, sanctioning and surveillance of the offender, is likely to produce better outcomes than would be possible if the focus were solely on narrower approaches to offender supervision.

Research has reported participants of restorative justice as being extremely satisfied with the process and outcomes.[24] While RJ is

---

[21] David O'Mahony and Jonathan Doak, *Restorative Justice & Criminal Justice: International Developments in Theory & Practice* (National Commission on Restorative Justice 2009) 140, where it is stated that programmes that involved face to face contact between the offender and the victim were generally more successful in reducing offending, in many instances by 25%.

[22] de Beus and Rodriguez (n 16) 339.

[23] This sentiment is not a new one and is clearly reflected in the ancient African proverb (and subsequent title of a book by Hillary Rodham Clinton) 'It takes a village to raise a child'.

[24] de Beus and Rodriguez (n 16) 338. Analysis of thirty-five different studies has found significantly higher levels of satisfaction among victim and offender participants than other justice system alternatives. In addition the majority of victims participating in restorative justice conferences were willing to forgive offenders for their violation. Another school of thought however is that this

not appropriate in every case, the potential benefits for the victim, the offender and the community taking part in RJ have been evidenced. There is also a considerable dividend to the State as RJ programme costs are frequently less than those of other sanctions. The RJ process, when successful, may obviate the need for a costly trial and potentially the need to provide expensive prison capacity.[25] Benefits also arise from the potential for offenders concerned not to re-offend.[26] The benefit involves not only the saving in future criminal justice resources that might be needed to arrest, prosecute, defend, convict and imprison or otherwise sanction the offender, but also benefits from the absence of future injury and harm to victims and the community.

## The Stakeholders in Restorative Justice

There are four principal stakeholders in the RJ process.They are victims, offenders, communities and the State. The victims and offender are central to the process, which can often involve their families. Depending on the circumstances of a particular offence, and the restorative option being used, the local community may also play an important part. Additionally, where RJ is used in the criminal justice system itself, RJ can play a valuable role. Key features of each of the stakeholder participants are as follows:

*Victims* — RJ places the victim at the centre of the system, both in terms of process and outcome. Direct participation, preferably on a face-to-face basis, where victims are free to contribute on an entirely voluntary basis, is the goal of this process. On occasion surrogate victims are used (being a family member of the victim or someone who has previous victim experience of a similar type of offence). Research has found that victims who participate largely do so for altruistic reasons in the hope that their involvement will

process may not always be primarily in the interests of the victim but may be about reducing recidivism and promoting the reintegration of offenders into the community. This issue of 'secondary victimisation' is when the victims of crime experience further victimisation through their experience with agencies of the criminal justice system, which they may perceive as insensitive or even harmful.

25 The most recent (2019) figures available estimate the cost of keeping an offender in prison at €75,349 per annum (IPS Annual Report 2019, 12) whereas the cost of putting an offender through a RJ programme is estimated at €3,250 (National Commission on Restorative Justice (n 6) 90).

26 O'Mahony and Doak (n 21) 141, which states that in international studies of countries where the option of restorative justice rehabilitation programmes are available it was found that offenders who have received rehabilitative treatment have a recidivism rate of about 12% lower than offenders who do not receive such treatment programmes.

better assist offenders to understand the effects of their actions so that they might desist from further offending. Some victims decline to participate, perhaps due to a feeling that the matter has already been resolved; being too angry with the offender; not accepting the offender's remorse as being sincere or because they were afraid of the offender or their family/supporters.[27] Notwithstanding this, victims of crime who have met with the offenders are far more likely to be satisfied with the justice system and to be less fearful about re-victimisation. The high levels of satisfaction among participating victims appears to be irrespective of the seriousness of the offence or of cultural or geographic variations.[28] A sincere admission by an offender of responsibility and remorse has been shown to be important to a victim and such sincere admissions are much more likely to be given in a restorative setting than in court and are more likely to be regarded as sincere by the victim when given as part of a face-to-face encounter.[29] Furthermore, research has shown that participation in RJ reduces the incidence of subsequent emotional symptoms including PTSD associated with victimisation.[30]

***Offenders*** — For RJ to be effective, offenders must consent to participate and engage fully with the process. A key element of this is that offenders would admit their guilt and be open to understanding how their actions have affected the victim, their families and the community. Assuming responsibility and understanding the consequences of their actions are key in this regard. This needs to be followed through with a commitment to address the factors that led to their offending behaviour. In the process of RJ interventions that incorporate victim-offender dialogue, the offender will have the opportunity to take responsibility, to make amends, to seek the victim's forgiveness and to explain their side of the story.[31]

***Community Involvement*** — RJ projects have on occasion evolved from 'bottom-up' community initiatives where there was a communal sense that conventional criminal justice processes and institutions were failing to satisfactorily resolve local conflicts and address offending. Some of these schemes have developed independently of the criminal justice system and subsequently forged more formalised relationships with criminal justice agencies. Other projects have been established on a more formal basis, including on a statutory basis or in the role of a pilot scheme before

---

27 National Commission on Restorative Justice (n 6) 68.
28 ibid.
29 ibid 69.
30 Lanterman (n 10) 66.
31 National Commission on Restorative Justice (n 6) 69.

being placed on a formalised footing. The value of community involvement in RJ schemes is twofold — firstly by the community being close to the victim and offender they will be in a better position to support the victim and also will be in a better position to identify needs and support efforts to change behaviour on the part of the offender. Furthermore, the community by expressing disapproval of the offender's behaviour can encourage the offender to re-integrate into the community and to work to restore the trust and respect which was lost when the offence was committed.

***The State*** — The State has a key role in the RJ process and is often responsible, through its agencies for the functioning of the process. On a practical level, for the focus of the process to remain on the victim, it is often contended that the State's role should be limited to facilitating and resourcing community led programmes however the involvement of state agencies including the Probation Service and An Garda Síochána is vital for these programmes to operate efficiently. The State has a vested interest in ensuring RJ programmes are successful. It has the duty to ensure that justice is administered in the public interest and that appropriate human rights standards are maintained. In addition, it must ensure that victim's rights are appropriately vindicated. In addition the State benefits from the fact that RJ has been shown to be effective at reducing re-offending. Furthermore, RJ measures are amongst the less-expensive options open to the criminal justice system. Set against the cost of custodial sentences and even some sanctions involving supervision by probation officers, RJ may offer better value for money in appropriate cases.[32]

Despite the many positive facets of the RJ process, it must be acknowledged that this is an area in which further research is required. An example of an area which would benefit from further research is a study of who would be likely to benefit from RJ and for whom it would be counter-productive. Further research is also required into the causal mechanisms that may or may not produce positive outcomes.[33] It is now important to look at international developments in the area, particularly in terms of the relevant models of practice, international standards and the European criminal law context.

[32] National Commission on Restorative Justice (n 6) 96.
[33] Lanterman (n 10) 69.

## Restorative Justice — Models of Practice

The fact that there are multiple concepts of RJ has been explored earlier in this chapter, as has the situation that RJ is a theory and concept of practice as opposed to a clearly defined process. The fact that there is not a single method or set of methods in RJ but instead a diverse range of interventions and systems sharing some common characteristics has resulted in there being four main forms of RJ practice, with many other variants. The four most common forms of RJ include victim-offender conferences (VOC), restorative conferences (RC), reparation panels (RP) and circle processes.

VOCs employ a facilitator to bring together a victim and an offender to discuss the reason the offender committed the crime, the impact the crime has had on the victim, and, if possible, to agree to a resolution that addresses the victim's needs. These VOCs are also sometimes referred to as victim-offender mediation. These conferences normally involve a face-to-face meeting between the victim and the offender, after guilt has been admitted or settled. These meetings take place in a controlled environment, under the supervision of a trained mediator where the victim and the offender can talk to each other about what happened and devise a mutually agreed plan to repair the harm caused as a result of the crime. These conferences place the interests of the victim to the forefront and give the victim the opportunity to explain to the offender exactly how the offence has impacted their lives. It also provides the opportunity for the offender to provide an apology or some other type of reparation. On occasion, the victim may not wish to meet with the offender but still wants to engage with the process and in those circumstances the facilitator can engage in 'shuttle diplomacy' with the parties communicating through an intermediary.[34] The drawback of victim-offender mediation however is that it tends to not adequately engage the community in the process.

'Restorative conferences' (RCs) are similar to VOCs but they expand the group of participants to include victims' and offenders' supportive others, together with the aim to find their own solutions to conflicts. Part of the underlying rationale behind this process is that individuals, their families and associates often recognise their own needs and solutions better than professionals do. These conferences involve structured meetings of the offenders, victims

---

[34] See Recommendation CM/Rec(2018)8 (n 8). Rule 59 discusses RJ events which involve the application of RJ principles but which do not involve dialogue between the victim and the offender.

and their families and friends, in which they collectively deal with the consequences of the crime and decide how best to repair the harm caused. These conferences are different to the VOC process in that they involve more parties, the VOC process generally involves just the victim and the offender and a facilitator, whilst the RCs will frequently involve the victim, offender, members of their families/ close friends, community representatives and relevant community and State services. Also, unlike VOC, the RCs are outcome-focussed. This RC model is utilised in the Children Act 2001 which provides for the application of conferencing options by An Garda Síochána to deal with offenders and for cases referred by the Children Court for a family conference to the Probation Service.[35]

'Reparation panels' (RPs) generally comprise a small group of citizens and professionals who undertake face-to-face meetings with offenders. During these meetings panel members discuss with the offender the nature of the offence and its consequences. They develop a set of proposed actions which they consider with the offender and agreement is reached on the specific actions the offender will take within a given time to make reparation for the crime. Subsequently, the offender must document the progress that they have made in fulfilling the terms of the agreement. These panels are the form of RJ utilised in the 'community reparation panel', which originated in Nenagh, Tipperary and in the 'offender reparation panel', which originated in Tallaght, Dublin, both of which projects will be considered in greater detail later in this chapter.

The circle processes take two forms — peacekeeping/healing circles and sentencing circles. Peacekeeping circles are facilitated encounters that bring together victims, offenders and their family members, a judge, court personnel, police and community members to address victims' needs, whereas sentencing circles bring together victims, offenders, their families and traditional court actors to develop a sentencing plan that addresses the needs of victims, offenders and others who may have been harmed — directly or indirectly — by the crime.[36] There is an important distinction between healing and sentencing circles in practice. Healing circles 'seek to focus on the cause of the problem and address not only the harm caused but, wherever possible, the social and cultural basis as well.' Sentencing circles work in partnership with the criminal

---

35 See Chapter 9, on Children and Young People, for more on Children Act 2001 provision for family conferences.

36 For further discussion on this area see Lanterman (n 10) where each of these models is explored further.

justice system and use community direction 'as a basis for reaching consensus about the sentencing plans which are developed for responding to the problem at hand.'[37] Neither of the circles models of RJ are currently utilised in Ireland.

A common reference to RJ principles is frequently made in relation to the manner in which various police forces worldwide now issue police cautions and utilise RJ principles in this process. It must however be noted that the majority of these schemes do not typically involve direct victim participation, instead the police officer/facilitator conveys thoughts expressed by the victim to the offender or engages in a process whereby the purported thoughts and feelings of a victim are conveyed to the offender. Whilst these *cautions* frequently succeed in efficiently diverting offenders accused of less serious crimes from formal court processes and may have benefits in terms of reduced recidivism, the structure of these schemes render them less focussed on victims than other forms of RJ.[38] This chapter will now briefly consider international standards and European developments in the area before examining how RJ models of practice are utilised in Ireland, both in relation to young people and more generally in the criminal justice system.

## Restorative Justice — International Standards and European Developments

Appropriate units in both the United Nations (UN) and the Council of Europe have incorporated Restorative Justice principles and practices into their work programmes. At the level of international conflict, Art 33 of the UN Charter states that:

> The parties to any dispute, the continuance of which is likely to endanger the maintenance of international peace and security, shall, first of all, seek a solution by negotiation, enquiry, mediation, conciliation, arbitration, judicial settlement, resort to regional agencies or arrangements, or other peaceful means of their own choice.

At the interpersonal level, the UN has published a number of documents on the use of RJ in addressing such issues, specifically in the criminal justice field. A statement of basic principles on the

---

37 National Commission on Restorative Justice (n 6) 38-42 where each of these models is discussed in depth.

38 See Lanterman (n 10) 65.

use of RJ in criminal matters was published in 2002.[39] This document set out various definitions and principles, including that RJ should be available — on a voluntary participation basis — at every stage of the criminal justice process, and that practice guidelines should be available to practitioners. The UN subsequently published a handbook on RJ programmes in 2006, which offered:

> ...an overview of key considerations in the implementation of participatory responses to crime based on a restorative justice approach... prepared for the use of criminal justice officials, non-governmental organisations and community groups who are working together to improve current responses to crime and conflict in their community.[40]

A second, updated edition of the UN handbook was published in 2020.[41] This updated handbook similarly provides, in practice-friendly format, useful definitions, principles[42] and updates for practitioners in terms of what has proven to be effective in RJ practice, including covering provision of RJ interventions at different criminal justice process stages, types of processes and programmes, important components of successful programmes in terms of introduction and delivery, as well as appropriate RJ programme oversight, monitoring and evaluation.

The Council of Europe recognised the value of mediation and related approaches in criminal matters through its adoption of a Recommendation on mediation in criminal matters in 1999.[43] Two decades later, the Council of Europe issued Recommendation CM/Rec(2018)8 concerning RJ in criminal matters.[44] This Recommendation is not legally binding on member states of the Council of Europe but does provide for the recognised standards and good practices and principles in the area. The Recommendation sets out definitions and general operating principles for RJ. Rule 3 defines RJ and describes the process as one which enables those harmed by crime and those responsible for that crime, if they freely

---

39 United Nations (2002) Economic and Social Council resolution 2002/12 of 24 July 2002.

40 United Nations, *Handbook on Restorative Justice Programmes* (Criminal Justice Handbook Series) (2006).

41 United Nations, *Handbook on Restorative Justice Programmes* (Criminal Justice Handbook Series) (United Nations (UNODC)/Thailand Institute of Justice, 2nd Edn 2020).

42 ibid 17-20, Including summarising key UN and other international principles and standards documents.

43 Council of Europe, Recommendation No R (99) 19 concerning mediation in criminal matters (1999).

44 Recommendation CM/Rec (2018)8 of the Committee of Ministers (n 8).

consent, to participate actively in the resolution of matters arising from that offence, through the help of a trained and impartial third party. Rule 4 sets out the dialogue (direct or indirect) between the victim and offender and others. Rule 6 sets out the various stages of the criminal justice process at which referrals to RJ schemes can be made. The Recommendation sets out the forward looking nature of RJ, which response should be towards addressing and repairing the harm which crime causes to individuals, relationships and wider society (Rule 13). Furthermore, voluntariness, consensus, reparation and reintegration are acknowledged as key RJ principles (Rule 14). The principle of voluntariness is particularly emphasised, with it being stated that RJ should only take place if the parties freely consent, having been fully informed in advance about the nature of the process and its possible outcomes and implications (Rule 16). Furthermore, the process is confidential and any discussions in the RJ process may not be used subsequently, without participants' agreement (Rule 17) and that RJ should be a generally available service where the type, seriousness or geographical location of the offence should not, in themselves, and in the absence of other considerations preclude RJ being offered to victims and offenders (Rule 18). Additionally the Recommendation states that "the basic facts of the case should normally be acknowledged by the parties" (Rule 30).

Whilst the Recommendation envisages a much greater application of RJ principles and maps out processes for the implementation of such schemes it is clear that the fundamental tenets in this Recommendation substantially mirror the recommendations contained in the (Irish) National Commission on Restorative Justice in 2009 and the manner in which the RJ schemes in Ireland currently operate however it does present a roadmap for the wider and deeper implementation of RJ in the criminal justice system. There have been calls for the Irish criminal justice system to make RJ available 'by default' in both decision making and disposal of cases, rather than being the exception, while allowing for more traditional, including practitioner-led decision-making to be used where, for whatever reason, wider stakeholder participation in RJ is not possible.[45]

It is clear however that the wider application and availability of RJ will result in the Probation Service playing a crucial role. It will be necessary for the Probation Service to be in a position to ensure that their staff have the time and skills to facilitate RJ

---

[45] Ian Marder, 'Restorative Justice as the New Default in Irish Criminal Justice' (2019) 16 Irish Probation Journal 60-82.

according to best practice and make resources available for training, policy development, case supervision and other core features of an RJ service. Furthermore, where recommending cases for RJ intervention, it will be necessary for the Probation Service staff to be able to identify suitable cases, describe RJ accurately to prospective participants, and make reasonable, evidence-based judgements on the likely benefits and risks of proceeding with RJ in a given case.[46]

## Legislation in Ireland

There is relatively little by way of legislation regarding the role of the Probation Service in relation to victims of crime. The Criminal Justice Act 1993 does provide for the possibility of a sentencing court requesting a victim impact report to be provided by a probation officer, stating that:

> Section 5(1): In determining the sentence to be imposed on a person for an offence to which this section applies, a court shall take into account, and may, where necessary, receive evidence or submissions concerning, any effect (whether long-term or otherwise) of the offence on the person in respect of whom the offence was committed.[47]

This provision is used in some, although statistically few, cases each year. For example, there were 19 victim impact reports completed by probation officers in 2019, with 35 being completed in 2018 and 27 in 2017.[48]

The Criminal Justice (Victims of Crime) Act 2017, which gave effect to the EU Directive on Victims of Crime,[49] is the main piece of legislation setting out victims' rights in Ireland. As well as establishing victims' rights to information in relation to their case, particularly in the early stages of their contact with criminal justice agencies, the Act also outlines what an RJ process should look like, provides appropriate safeguards for participants and obliges

---

46 Marder (n 11) 7.

47 The Criminal Justice Act 1993, s 5(2) clarifies that the offences to which the provision is applicable are: sexual offences, violent offences and offences of attempting, conspiring, aiding or abetting, counselling, procuring or inciting the commission of such a sexual/violent offence.

48 Probation Service, *2019 Annual Report* (2020) 54.

49 Directive 2012/29/EU of the European Parliament and of the Council of 25 October 2012 establishing minimum standards on the rights, support and protection of victims of crime, and replacing Council Framework Decision 2001/220/JHA.

statutory agencies to inform victims about RJ, where available. In this regard, the Act defines a 'restorative justice scheme' as:

> ...any scheme administered for the time being under which, with the consent of each of them, a victim and an offender or alleged offender engage with each other to resolve, with the assistance of an impartial third party, matters arising from the offence or alleged offence.

The 2017 Act further stipulates that:

> Section 26(1) In respect of any offence or alleged offence, a body or other person shall administer a restorative justice scheme (in this section referred to as a 'scheme') only if the requirements of this section are complied with.
>
> (2) The offender or alleged offender shall –
> (a) acknowledge the basic facts of the offence committed or offence alleged to have been committed, as the case may be, against the victim, and
> (b) give his or her free consent to participating in the scheme.
>
> (3) The victim shall –
> (a) receive full and unbiased information about –
> (i) the scheme and the potential outcomes of participating in the scheme,
> (ii) the procedures for supervising and implementing any agreement that may be reached between the parties in the context of the scheme, and
> (iii) his or her right to withdraw at any time his or her consent to participating in the scheme,
> and
> (b) having received such information, give his or her free and informed consent to participating in the scheme.

Section 26 of the 2017 Act[50] further sets out key elements of the process to be followed in such RJ schemes, including in relation to informed consent, protecting the interests of victims and safeguarding them from secondary victimisation,[51] confidentiality, agreements reached between offenders (or alleged offenders)

50 The Criminal Justice (Victims of Crime) Act 2017, s 26, subsections 4, 5 and 6.

51 *Secondary victimisation* is defined in The Criminal Justice (Victims of Crime) Act 2017, s 2(1) as 'victimisation that occurs indirectly through the response of institutions and individuals to the victim.'

and victims and how these might be taken into account in court proceedings.

The 2017 Act, as amended, also places responsibilities on relevant agencies in relation to updating victims regarding the sentence management of those convicted of offences against the victim or victims in question. While there are not such specific provisions in the Act regarding the Probation Service management of sentences *per se*, clearly there are implications for probation and parole practice in the context of any Probation Service involvement in the management of custodial sentences – specifically having regard to post-custody supervision in the community, including parole. The Act also implies high levels of cooperation between the relevant justice agencies, in how they coordinate services, if the level of service to victims, envisaged by the Act, is to be realised.

## Development of Restorative Justice in Ireland

Restorative Justice was once common place in Ireland under the Brehon law system where the community had a direct say in the justice process and restitution by the offender was a common outcome of this system. Subsequent developments in Ireland paid little attention to this aspect of criminal justice until, as O'Donovan described it: 'Interest in restorative justice (RJ) began to "take off" in Ireland in the second half of the 1990s.'[52] Around then, An Garda Síochána, the Probation Service and several non-governmental organisations (NGOs), established RJ pilot projects (namely the Nenagh Community Reparation Programme and Restorative Justice Services [RJS] which developed a scheme initially in the Tallaght area of Dublin). These specific developments will be considered further later in this chapter. The successful operation of these projects was augmented by two further key developments in the area, namely the passage of the Children Act 2001, and the formation of a National Commission on Restorative Justice in 2007. An overview of the development of RJ in Ireland, North and South, is provided by O'Dwyer and Payne.[53]

The principles of the Children Act 2001, include that any child who accepts responsibility for his or her offending behaviour should be diverted from criminal proceedings, where appropriate and

---

52 David O'Donovan, 'The National Commission on Restorative Justice: A Review and Plan for Development' (2011) 8 Irish Probation Journal 165-184.

53 Kieran O'Dwyer and Brian Payne, 'Restorative justice' in Deirdre Healy and others (eds), *The Routledge Handbook of Irish Criminology* (Routledge 2016) 222-241.

also that due regard must be given to the interests of the victim. Additionally, RJ has become further embedded in the criminal justice system in Ireland with the passage of the Criminal Justice (Victims of Crime) Act 2017.[54] In 2018, a new Restorative Justice and Victim Services Unit (RJVSU) was established within the Probation Service. However, despite these developments, the provision of RJ in Ireland remains grossly underdeveloped, with most victims and offenders still not afforded the opportunity to participate.

## Victims, RJ and the Probation Service

The mission, values and the manner in which the Probation Service discharges its duties are key when considering its work in relation to victims and RJ in Ireland. The Service's Strategy Statement describes the organisation's mission as: 'To provide services to the courts and the wider criminal justice system through the delivery of effective community sanctions', while its vision is for: 'Safer and more inclusive communities where offending and its causes, are effectively addressed.'[55] As well as setting out the various ways the Probation Service works with offenders and others, promoting community safety, including 'providing professional, effective and evidence-based interventions', the Strategic Plan further describes the work of the Service as incorporating, *inter alia*: 'Addressing the harm caused from offending behaviours' and 'working with victims of crime through our Restorative Justice & Victims Unit.'[56] Under the accompanying Action Plan, the Probation Service commits to:

> 22. Develop a Probation Service Victim's Policy, reflecting the Service's commitment to being victim informed and integrate the victim perspective into the work of the Service.
>
> 23. In keeping with the Programme for Government commitment, review the implementation of Restorative Justice within the Service and take strengthening measures where possible.

The above vision and mission statement and the manner in which the Probation Service aims to deliver on them incorporates the idea of community building and indicates a belief in a clear link between the use of community sanctions, reduced recidivism and offender reintegration. It is also clear from the above that RJ is one

---

54 See more on the legislation below.
55 Probation Service, *Strategy Statement 2021-2023: Probation Works for Community Safety* (2021) 7.
56 ibid 6.

of the important ways in which the Probation Service can embed some of its the key values in practice, including by delivering on the key goal of 'promoting inclusion, through an organisational culture that recognises and supports diversity, integration and human rights…'.[57]

The role of the Probation Service in relation to victims is set out in s 10 of the Department of Justice Victims Charter.[58] This mainly covers the role of the Probation Service generally and what victims of crime can expect of the Service, information on probation interventions and contact details as well as other information relating to the RJ and Victims Services Unit of the Probation Service. Under the heading of work with offenders, the document includes the expectation that probation officers address victim empathy and related issues with offenders they are supervising, as well as taking victim issues into account in preparing pre-sanction assessments on offenders for courts.[59] In Ireland, as well as more widely, probation programmes that address general offending, as well as those addressing specific categories of offending — such as violent behaviour — routinely include victim awareness or victim empathy components as part of the programme.

The Probation Service response and approach to RJ specifically had evolved and developed somewhat organically from the 1990s onwards. That link to practice developments was supported through the Service's ongoing involvement with and development of expanded services in partnership with RJS and RJC (see below), development of other local RJ and RP initiatives that were supported where possible by probation officers, roll-out of the provisions of the Children Act, participation in the Commission on Restorative Justice and, increasingly in more recent years especially, an increased level of requests for RJ type inputs. In order to put more structure on RJ service delivery by probation officers, and to develop greater clarity, consistency and quality of service, the Probation Service published its Restorative Justice Strategy in 2013[60]

---

57 ibid 16.

58 Department of Justice, *Victims Charter* (2020) 60-64.

59 A small scale study, reported on by Andrea Bourke, 'Pre-Sanction Reports in Ireland: An Exploration of Quality and Effectiveness' (2013) 10 Irish Probation Journal 75-89, found overall good levels of compliance by probation officers with Probation Service standards for pre-sanction reports, but a relatively low level of compliance with Service standards regarding addressing victim issues in the reports reviewed. Further, more up-to-date research would be required to ascertain if this finding is still valid today. More detailed research might also shed light on why the standard might not be met — some of which are speculated upon in Bourke's paper.

60 Probation Service, *Restorative Justice Strategy – Repairing the Harm: A Victim*

and established a small, national Restorative Justice and Victims Services Unit (RJVSU) in 2018, based in its Dublin Headquarters Office.

The RJVSU produced, on behalf of the Probation Service, the following practice guide headings in relation to clarifying the established models of RJ practice, which the Service would seek to prioritise and make available across the country:[61]

> **Family/Restorative Conferences:** Structured and facilitated meeting of the offender, the victim, their family members and community and statutory representatives. Through discussion and collaboration, the conference aims to agree a plan to enable the offender to make amends for the harm caused. (Section 78 of Children Act 2001 makes provision for diversionary family conference).
>
> **Offender Reparation Panel:** Comprised of representatives from the community and state organisations who undertake face-to-face meetings with adult offenders at the request of the Court. The panel develops a set of proposed actions that seek to repair the harm caused to the victim and reflect the offender's willingness to make amends.
>
> **Victim Offender Mediation:** Victim-Offender Mediation (VOM) is a process that provides victims with the opportunity to meet their offender in a safe controlled setting with a mediator who facilitates a discussion between the parties to address/repair the harm done.
>
> **Bespoke Restorative Justice Intervention:** A tailored approach to restorative justice, constructed within the individual and social context of offending. Through the creative use of relevant community resources, the offender willingly participates in activities that highlight the impact of the harm caused and allows for either direct or indirect reparation to the victim and/or community. These activities could include, meeting with a victim advocacy service, a relevant charitable donation, a written reflective exercise.

On the question of when RJ interventions can be considered or take place in a probation work context, the briefing document states it

---

*Sensitive Response to Offending* (2013).

61 This is a summary from Probation Service, *Restorative Justice* (Internal Briefing Document 2019).

is available for consideration by a judge once guilt is established and prior to the imposition of sentence, including over:

i. a specific period of adjournment with a progress report back to the court,
ii. the period of statutory supervision,
iii. the course of a custodial sentence or as part of post release supervision.

Regarding the process of referral of a case to the Probation Service for RJ intervention, and what categories of case or types of offending are considered appropriate in principle, the Probation Service briefing clarifies these issues as follows:

> Process for referral:
>
> - A judge may request that an assessment for a restorative justice intervention be completed as part of a probation pre-sanction report and options will be addressed in the report.
> - Requests by the judge for participation in the offender reparation panel, where this model is available (Dublin Metropolitan area, Tipperary, Laois, Offaly), will be forwarded to the relevant project and the project will provide a report to the court on the outcome.
>
> Offences considered appropriate for pre/post sentence restorative justice:
>
> Restorative justice can be considered, as a sanction in itself or to complement other legislative sanctions; for any offence, with some caveats. The following conditions must be satisfied.
>
> (i) The offender must accept responsibility for the offence and be willing to participate in the process.
> (ii) Direct engagement by a victim, if willing to engage, must be based on voluntary and informed consent.
> (iii) It is a matter for the sentencing Judge to decide what weight, if any, to give to an offender's participation in a restorative justice process.

The briefing contains caveats in relation to the use of RJ interventions in cases involving sexual offending or domestic abuse or domestic violence. In cases of sexual violence, RJ should only be considered when a victim requests it or the court has been advised that the victim wishes to explore that option. In domestic abuse or violence cases, RJ is considered by the Probation Service to be generally inappropriate for RJ intervention, on the basis of the challenge for practitioners in detecting, assessing and managing issues of coercion and control, which at a minimum would be likely to mitigate against the need to uphold RJ principles of voluntary and safe engagement in the process.

While the Probation Service goal was to ensure the availability of all four models of RJ practice nationally — either through services provided directly by probation officers or by officers in conjunction with partner bodies[62] — it was accepted from the outset that it would not be possible — for various reasons — to achieve this level of coverage and availability across the country immediately. The briefing document set out the four models clearly, indicating an intention to make all four practice models widely available, as well as listing what services were available in each service region, while service capacity was built up nationally. The RJVSU has also worked in developing and ensuring good RJ practice standards and supporting staff locally to deliver the interventions listed. The Unit also acts as a single point of contact in relation to RJ and victims' issues with the Department of Justice, other governmental bodies and agencies, as well as with relevant NGOs, including those representing victims' or survivors' needs and interests. Lavin and Carroll (2014) published a case study of a probation-led RJ response to offending at local level. [63] The Probation Service and the Dublin-based organisation RJS have also produced a helpful and informative video showing a re-enactment of a community reparation panel in practice.[64]

Restorative Justice in Ireland can be considered in terms of both youth and adult offending and in this regard the RJ schemes currently operating in Ireland will now be examined in greater detail.

---

62 Marder (n 11) 6-7, has summarised the three models of probation-managed RJ provision as: (i) delivery where the probation agency is the national body responsible for RJ, (ii) where probation officers provide RJ interventions to clients of the service, and (iii) where RJ services are 'contracted out' to third party organisations, such as relevant NGOs. (ii) and (ii) above are the probation-manged models in Ireland.

63 Dermot Lavin and Claire Carroll, 'Restorative Justice in Practice: A Case Study' (2014) 11 Irish Probation Journal 245-253.

64 This Probation Service/RJS video is available at: https://www.youtube.com/watch?v=tpSlyNSibOU&t=1s . Other RJ resources are collected and available at the 'Restorative Justice: Strategies for Change' website: restorativejustice.ie.

## Restorative Justice for Youths in Ireland

Restorative justice is practiced in a number of ways in the Irish youth justice system. The main legislation covering children and the criminal justice system is the Children Act 2001. This Act focuses on diversion from the criminal justice system, rehabilitation and preventing criminal behaviour. The use of detention for a child is to be a last resort used only when all other alternatives have been explored and then deemed or held to be unsuitable. Despite the fact that the provisions of the 2001 Act facilitate the use of restorative justice, and include the principle that due regard must be given to the interests of victims, there is no explicit reference in the Act to restorative justice *per se*.[65]

Restorative justice in youth justice in Ireland encompasses the Garda Diversion Programme, restorative cautioning and conferencing and court referred Probation Service family conferences. Following the introduction of Part 4 of the Children Act 2001, the Juvenile Liaison Officer Scheme, which had been in place since 1963, was replaced by the Garda Youth Diversion Programme, to deal with children under the age of 18 who commit offences.[66] The purpose of the programme is to divert any child (a person under 18 years of age at the date of the offence) who takes responsibility for the offending behaviour from the traditional criminal justice system, by way of a caution.[67] It is also necessary that the child has not been cautioned previously or, if cautioned previously it would be deemed appropriate to administer a further caution. Consent is a vital component in these schemes and it is a prerequisite that the parents, guardians or persons acting in *loco parentis* agree to the terms of the caution. The 'garda juvenile liaison officer' (JLO) is trained in mediation and facilitation skills and will frequently arrange a restorative justice type meeting, which he or she will preside over, between the victim and the offender, at which the offender will be given the opportunity to take some action that will attempt in some way to right the wrong done by the commission of the offence.[68]

---

65 For more on the Children Act 2001 and its implications for Probation and Parole work, see Chapter 9 on Children and Young People.

66 The Children Act 2001, s 18 provides that any child who has committed criminal acts and accepts responsibility for the criminal behaviour will be considered for admission to the diversion programme, unless the interests of society would not be served by the diversion.

67 The caution may be either informal or formal and a formal caution will result in the child being placed under the supervision of a garda juvenile liaison officer (JLO) for a period of 12 months.

68 This action may take the form of an apology, compensation or a specific

The presence of the victim at a formal caution or family conference is provided for in the Children Act 2001[69] and it is here that the concept of restorative justice is introduced. Under the Garda Youth Diversion Programme, the cautioning allows for a discussion during which the juvenile may have to confront the effects of his or her behaviour and may be invited to apologise and make some form of reparation to the victim. If a child has been formally cautioned and is being supervised by a JLO a conference may also be convened.[70] The conference participants have a remit to examine a child's circumstances, reasons for offending and to discuss how the child might, with family support and community involvement be diverted from crime through the implementation of an action plan.[71] These conferences also have other restorative justice aims and goals.[72]

The court can also direct a Probation Service convened conference (see Chapter 9 in relation to Children and Young People for more on this). These conferences only take place where there are criminal charges pending against the child. It is again necessary for the defendant to admit to their offending behaviour and for the court to also consider it desirable for an action plan to be implemented in the case. This conference is organised by the Probation Service and generally involves the offender and members of his or her family, the victim and other participants.[73] If such a conference is unsuccessful, the criminal proceedings in court are re-activated.[74]

## Adult Restorative Schemes

The most widely-available restorative justice scheme for adult offenders in Ireland is the 'adult cautioning scheme' operated by An Garda Síochána. The parameters of the scheme are very similar to those which apply to the caution system operated by An

---

undertaking and the offender may agree a plan designed to help him or her avoid re-offending.

69 Children Act 2001, ss 26 and 29 respectively.

70 Children Act 2001, s 29

71 This conference may be convened only on the decision of the Director of the Garda National Juvenile Office and the conference facilitator must be a member of An Garda Síochána.

72 The purposes of these restorative conferences include:- establishing why the child became involved in the behaviour that gave rise to their admission to the programme; reviewing the child's behaviour since admission to the programme; mediating between the offender and the victim; and upholding the concerns of the victim and having due regard to the victim's interests.

73 These conferences are provided for in the Children Act 2001, s 78.

74 For further information, see Chapter 9 on Children and Young People, as well as the National Commission on Restorative Justice (n 6) 45.

Garda Síochána as part of the Garda Youth Diversion Programme. This scheme, which operates on a non-statutory basis, applies to adults against whom there is evidence of the commission of a criminal offence. The scheme adopts a diversionary approach, where prosecution of the offence is not considered necessary in the public interest.[75]

The other dedicated restorative justice programmes operating in the criminal justice system in Ireland, in relation to adults, are limited in number and geographical application. In the areas where these restorative justice schemes are in operation offenders may be referred to the relevant restorative justice programme by the local District Court.[76] However as these projects only operate in two locations, referrals of this type are generally limited to those specific geographical areas.[77] Funding for the two organisatuions (see below) comes through the Probation Service and their work is integrated into that of the Probation Service. When the District Court refers an offender to a restorative justice programme, a contract requiring the offender to address issues relating to the offending behaviour and to make reparation may be drawn up. The court finalises the case depending on how the contract has been honoured.

## Restorative Justice in the Community (RJC), Tipperary

RJC, originally designated the Nenagh Community Reparation Programme, started as a pilot RJ programme in June 1999. Offenders are generally referred to the project by the District Court, following establishment of their guilt. An essential part of this process is that the offender makes an informed decision to take part in the reparation programme. This initiative was modelled on

---

75 In considering whether or not to administer a caution a number of matters are considered by the Garda involved including the public interest and the views of the victim (although the consent/acquiescence of the victim are not necessary to enable such a sanction to be applied)

76 While it is true that restorative justice provision under the Garda Diversion Programme does not involve the judiciary, the other restorative justice applications in the criminal justice system do. Most RJ referrals originating from the courts come from the District Court. Nevertheless judges in other courts do refer cases for consideration of an RJ intervention from time to time.

77 The two restorative justice programmes currently operating in ireland are restorative justice in the community (RJC – previously designated the Nenagh Community Reparation Programme) and restorative justice services (RJS) which originated as a scheme in the Tallaght area and is now based in Dublin city centre and providing services in Dublin and surrounding counties. Both of these NGOs are funded by the Department of Justice, through the Probation Service.

a similar programme in Timaru, New Zealand[78] where offenders were provided with a means of making reparation to their victim or community.[79] This type of restorative justice system is traditionally perceived as having its roots among the indigenous people of Australia and New Zealand as these systems prevail to the present day. The clearest examples of success of the alternative, restorative approach to justice is still evidenced in the aboriginal communities in the State of Western Australia and also in the Maori communities of New Zealand where it is considered that the restorative justice processes and family-based problem solving skills are based on local culture, knowledge and experience.

The Nenagh Community Reparation Project was set up in an attempt to harness the moral resources and local knowledge of the community in identifying and prioritising the concerns surrounding problems of crime, disorder and crime prevention within the community. The project (now RJC) is a partnership of the community, An Garda Síochána, the Probation Service and other relevant stakeholders working together to address the underlying factors leading to problems caused by crime. By working together the aim is that the offender will be reformed and reintegrated back into the community in a spirit which seeks healing rather than retribution. This project does not regard itself as an alternative to the traditional justice system. Instead, it merely seeks to address some types of behaviour within the community rather than criminalise the offender at an early stage lest the offender be immersed in a cycle of re-offending. [80]

---

78 The establishment of the Nenagh initiative followed a visit to New Zealand by members of the Expert Group on the Probation Service (1997-1998), one of whom was Tipperary-based District judge Michael Reilly, who developed the Nenagh project with local community representatives and the support of An Garda Síochána and the Probation Service.

79 New Zealand introduced the restorative justice on a legislative basis with their ground-breaking Children and Young Persons' and Families Act 1989. They further enshrined the Restorative Justice Processes in legislation for adult offenders in The Sentencing Act of 2002, Parole Act 2002 and Victim Act 2002. These Acts lay down the principle that criminal proceedings should not occur if other methods of addressing the problem are available, measures that address offending behaviour should strengthen the family, sanctions should involve the least restrictive alternative and should take heed of the interests of crime victims.

80 The Nenagh Community Reparation Project carried out an extensive evaluation in 2004 which included feedback from key stakeholders outside of the project management which included the Judiciary, An Garda Síochána and solicitors. All of the feedback received was positive and it was illustrated that 84% of first time offenders who participated in the project had not re-offended. Nenagh Community Reparation Project, Evaluation 2004.

From its beginnings, the Nenagh Project has dealt in the main with matters involving:

- drug and alcohol abuse leading to violence and criminal damage
- assaults due to poor self-control or being under the influence of drugs or alcohol
- criminal damage arising from poor self-control or being under the influence of drugs or alcohol
- neighbourhood disputes (including fracas) leading to violence and assault charges

The programme process consists of three parts.

(a) The offender is asked to give an account of the offence, followed by a member of An Garda Síochána who will give the facts of the case as presented at Court.
(b) There follows a discussion with questions and possible ideas on how to resolve the matter, with particular emphasis on perceived behaviour issues such as poor self-control and/or addiction problems.
(c) The offender and possibly victim, participate in setting up a contract of reparation which must be doable and related to the offence. This contract requires the offender to address the issues which contributed to his/her offending behaviour and also make reparation to the community.

This contract is then presented to the Court by the Probation Officer and the case is adjourned to allow time for the conditions of the contract to be completed. The Court finally disposes of the case when the contract is satisfactorily completed.

## Restorative Justice Services (RJS), Dublin

Restorative Justice Services (RJS), Dublin, is the other main dedicated, operational restorative justice programme in this jurisdiction. It was established in 2000, is funded through the Probation Service and is managed by a partnership of stakeholders within the criminal justice system including the District Court, An Garda Síochána and the Probation Service, as well as victim support and community sector volunteers.

The RJS offers two separate restorative justice programmes, a victim offender mediation programme and also an offender reparation programme. With these two programmes all cases are court-referred at pre-sanction stage, at the discretion of the District Court judge and the court remains in charge of the process at all times. An Garda Síochána, The Probation Service, legal representatives and victim support groups may request the court to consider the appropriateness of reparation or mediation in a particular case.[81]

The victim offender mediation model is a significant part of the work of the RJS. It is victim focused and also seeks to make offenders more aware and understanding of the impact of their offending behaviour. The cases which this programme deals with include relatively serious offences in the areas of criminal damage, theft, assault and public order. The intended outcome is that the offender apologises, makes reparation and takes steps to help avoid future offending. This programme, like others in the RJ field, has had a practical difficulty in that the statistics clearly evidence an informed choice of many victims not to participate in these programmes.[82]

The Offender Reparation Programme has been in operation by the RJS since 2004. This programme concentrates on getting offenders to accept responsibility for their behaviour, to look at the effects on others and on the wider community, to address the consequences of their actions, to make positive changes to their lifestyles and to make reparation to the community. This programme focuses generally on public order offences and lower level assaults and criminal damage.[83]

Both of these programmes raise an important question — what types of crimes are appropriate to an RJ process? The debate about whether RJ should be confined to just behaviour which the law has elevated to a criminal offence or whether it should have a broader application is an ongoing one. Some RJ advocates have

---

[81] National Commission on Restorative Justice (n 6) 46.

[82] ibid 47 shows that of 51 referrals in the period 2004-2007, the completion rate was only 45%, largely as a result of the choice of victims not to engage in this process. This reflects an international trend and is comparatively a good participation rate. In the Thames Valley police-led restorative justice scheme, just 16% of victims participated. Of those that did not, 52% stated that they did not wish to do so, 30% wished to participate but were unable to do so and 15% say they were not invited to participate. A similar scheme operating in Northern Ireland found that victims only participated in 20% of cases. See O'Mahony and Doak (n 21) 113.

[83] National Commission on Restorative Justice (n 6) 47, which records that alcohol consumption was a notable factor in many cases and 85% of offenders undertook some form of alcohol awareness programme arising from the intervention. Over 95% of those referred to the Offender Reparation Programme were male.

argued that conflicts of all kinds should have RJ as a response to harms, including crimes, however such a position would go beyond the scope of this book, which is limited to harms which have been elevated to a level of a crime. This ongoing debate does however force consideration of the issue as to whether RJ is a viable alternative to the conventional criminal justice system or whether it should be viewed as a complementary set of practices or procedures that could exist alongside or, in some cases, within the criminal justice system.[84] A related debate is the one in relation to how serious the offences encompassed by RJ programmes should be. While most if not all Irish RJ programmes started out targeting 'lower level' offending, there has been a more recent trend towards including 'higher level' offences, including sexual and other violent offences, as potential matters for the inclusion of an RJ approach. Much of this latter movement has come about because of views and wishes expressed by survivors of violent and other serious crimes.

Having examined the operation of RJ in Ireland a number of questions remain — how do RJ schemes benefit the individual stakeholders; what types of crime are RJ processes most suitable for; and how can the needs of victims and offenders — as well as communities and wider society — be met through expanded use of RJ? Marder has considered how RJ might be used by agencies such as Probation and Parole[85] in working with various categories of offender, and indeed how RJ might usefully be made available as an option at every stage and across the full range of the Irish criminal justice system and concludes that:

> Restorative justice can represent a new direction for probation practice internationally. We know that almost everyone who commits an offence is also a victim at some point in their lives, and vice versa. Restorative justice gives us the language and the tools to overcome a zero-sum approach to meeting the needs of citizens engaged with the criminal justice process. Of course, barriers to change remain… Restorative justice represents a new philosophy of practice, requiring practitioners to step back 'from their traditional sovereign position as the owner of the conflict' (Clamp and Paterson, 2017).[86] Many will initially feel discomfort with engaging victims and devolving power to stakeholders. However, the research increasingly indicates

---

84 For further discussion on this area see Lanterman (n 10) where this issue is explored further.

85 Marder (n 11).

86 Kerry Clamp and Craig Paterson, *Restorative Policing: Concepts, Theory and Practice* (Routledge 2017) 168.

that the practical challenges are manageable, and the benefits for participants outweigh the risks.[87]

## Conclusion

Healy (2019) reviewed the literature on victims' interactions with the criminal justice system, specifically exploring the 'evidence on best practices that help to increase victim satisfaction, enhance victim wellbeing and encourage victims to participate in, or stay involved with, the criminal justice process,' and made recommendations in relation to various aspects and stages of the process, including a number that would impact on probation and parole practice.[88] Healy also 'highlighted many examples of practices globally' that achieve good outcomes and her recommendations revolve in the main around:

- Effective communication and information sharing.
- Coordinated, holistic and multi-disciplinary approaches.
- Supportive and victim-centred processes.
- Clearly defined victim participation mechanisms.
- Tailored approaches for victims with specialist needs and experiences.
- Equal access and enforcement of rights.

The extension of the provision of RJ across the stages of the criminal justice system offers opportunities to address the needs of victims, offenders and society. It does not represent anything like the panacea or 'silver bullet' that some would imply. Nevertheless, there is clearly a growing impetus to extend the availability of RJ in all applications of the term and across all phases of the criminal justice system, including probation and parole, and that can only be a good thing. In relation to the management of probation and parole themselves, it can no longer be assumed that RJ is an esoteric or hyper-specialised aspect of such work, an 'optional extra' in the probation officer's 'toolkit.' As Carr[89] emphasised, referencing the Council of Europe guidelines on training probation and prison staff:[90] the 'core components' of 'specialist training' for probation

---

87 Marder (n 11).

88 D Healy, *Exploring Victims' Interactions with the Criminal Justice System: A Literature Review*, (University College Dublin, October 2019).

89 Nicola Carr, *Recruitment, training and professional development of probation staff*, HM Inspectorate of Probation Academic Insights 2020/02 (HM Inspectorate of Inspection 2020) 8.

90 Council of Europe, *Guidelines Regarding Recruitment, Selection, Education, Training and Professional Development of Prison and Probation Staff* (CM 2019) 111.

officers 'should include mediation, restorative justice and work with victims.' A similar training need for other professionals operating in the area has also been identified.[91]

[91] Shane McCarthy, 'Perceptions of Restorative Justice in Ireland: The Challenges of the Way Forward' (2018) 8 Irish Probation Journal 187-201.

CHAPTER SEVEN

# PAROLE

## Introduction

All sentences of imprisonment imposed in Ireland include a possibility of early release. A key method of facilitating this is through the use of parole — an internationally recognised system which provides mechanisms for granting early or temporary release to prisoners before the formal expiry of their sentences. In Ireland, prior to the commencement of the Parole Act 2019 on 30 July 2021,[1] the granting of parole (or temporary release) was at the discretion of the Minister for Justice who was advised by the Interim Parole Board in relation to the administration of long-term and indeterminate prison sentences.[2] In certain categories of cases, the Interim Parole Board advised the Minister if, when, and under what conditions, a prisoner should be released from custody and granted 'parole'. The Parole Act 2019 changed the discretionary nature of this system of parole and replaced it with a statutory Parole Board. The enactment of the Parole Act 2019 has not resulted in the revocation of s 2 of the Criminal Justice (Temporary Release) Act 1960 and the existing temporary release system will remain in operation at least for non-Parole Board eligible prisoners. (The operation of this system of temporary release will be discussed later in this chapter.) However, it must be noted that even though the Parole Act has been commenced, the rules and procedures to inform how the parole system will operate have not yet been published, at the time of writing. This chapter will explore both the emergence and development of the concept of parole in Ireland and will examine the manner in which the Interim Parole Board discharged its functions and will also study, insofar as is currently possible, how the system will operate post the commencement of

---

1 SI No 405 of 2021 — Parole Act 2019 (Commencement) Order 2021 fixed 30 July 2021 as the date on which the Parole Board came into operation.

2 The eligibility criteria to be considered for parole are discussed later in this chapter. The Interim Parole Board reviewed the cases of prisoners sentenced to determinate sentences of eight years or more and also considered the cases of prisoners serving indeterminate (life) sentences. The Parole Act 2019 states that the eligibility of determinate sentenced prisoners to apply for parole will be prescribed by regulations enacted by the Minister for Justice following consultation with the Parole Board. As of the date of writing, the Parole Board will only review life sentenced prisoners, who have served twelve years of their sentence.

the Parole Act 2019. However, firstly, it is necessary to define parole and map its history and development.

## The Definition of Parole and its History in Ireland

The only definition of parole in Irish legislation is contained in the Parole Act 2019. In this Act, parole is defined as 'the release from prison pursuant to a parole order of a person serving a term of imprisonment prior to the expiry of that term'.[3] Internationally, 'parole' is typically taken to mean the procedure by which a prisoner is considered suitable for release and is released prior to the expiration of his or her sentence, to serve the balance of that sentence at large in society subject to some stated conditions, under supervision, and subject to return to prison if he or she fails to comply with the conditions governing his or her release.[4] This early conditional release of a prisoner can be difficult to justify in theoretical, philosophical or moral terms. This is especially so if a particular sentence is judicially chosen to give effect to a policy of 'just deserts,' deterrence or incapacitation, as it can be argued that such a sentence should, in principle, be served in its totality if its original purpose is not to be frustrated. With a 'just deserts' based system of sentencing, early release, especially where discretionary, can be seen as a process which upsets all of the fine-tuning of calculations of proportionality.[5] However, such early release can be most easily reconciled with a policy of rehabilitation,[6] with the parole system providing an opportunity to control and/or rehabilitate offenders on their release from prison.[7] Parole can also be seen as offering benefits to the community and public, by trading custodial time for the opportunity to either re-integrate the offender more successfully back into the community or to put conditions on the offender and allow the possibility of recall to prison for the purpose of public protection.[8]

The underlying principle of a penal system involving such discretionary early release arises from the belief that a prisoner's desire for self-improvement will increase significantly if their

3 The Parole Act 2019, s 2(1).

4 Canadian Committee on Corrections, *Report of the Canadian Committee on Corrections – Toward Unity: Criminal Justice and Corrections* (Queen's Printer 1969) 185.

5 Susan Easton and Christine Piper, *Sentencing and Punishment – The Quest for Justice* (2nd edn, Oxford University Press 2005) 147.

6 Thomas O'Malley, *Sentencing: Towards a Coherent System* (Thomson Round Hall 2011) 211.

7 Easton and Piper (n 5) 147.

8 ibid 147.

conduct directly affects their jail term, essentially placing the prisoner's fate into their own hands. Such a system allows prisoners to take charge of their own lives and to develop a sense of responsibility, as well as providing an incentive to serve their time productively, with a mind-set of moving forward.[9] A parole system gives prisoners hope, as well as an opportunity to change and encourages prisoners to adopt co-operative behaviour and to engage fully in the rehabilitative opportunities available to them. A parole system also has an essential role in the exercise of clemency and, in some cases, can also be utilised to deal with the futility of detaining certain prisoners beyond a point at which their continued custody serves no ostensible purpose.[10]

This chapter will examine rehabilitative effects of parole systems and study the overlap between parole and the work of the Probation Service. It is not proposed to examine the operation of remission in the Irish prison system in detail as this regime operates as the complete ending of a prisoner's sentence at a reduced point in time, with no attendant supervision or conditions. Remission provides, in theory, a structured system with criteria for prisoners to meet in order to encourage good behaviour, rehabilitation and self-improvement, with the ultimate benefit being the release of the prisoner. Remission does not apply to prisoners who are serving a life sentence, or those who are in prison as a debtor or as a result of contempt of court.[11] With remission, prisoners generally obtain a quarter off their whole sentence and whilst this reduction in their sentence is supposed to be dependent on good behaviour, it has become the practice that it is almost invariably granted. For all practicable purposes, standard remission is a right, which may be lost in whole or in part through bad behaviour while in prison rather than a privilege to be earned.[12] This right to remission appears to be a constitutionally protected right of the prisoner[13] with which the Minister for Justice is not in a position to interfere, except by means of 'a properly exercised discretion'.[14] Accordingly, remission in Ireland is granted without any particular consideration

---

9 See speech of Willie O'Dea TD, Minister of State at the Department of Justice, Equality and Law Reform, Dáil Éireann, Vol 557, 21 November 2002. Criminal Justice (Temporary Release of Prisoners) Bill 2001, Second Stage where the purpose of parole in Ireland is set out in such terms.

10 O'Malley (n 6) 212.

11 SI No 252 of 2007: Prison Rules 2007, Rule 59(3). See also Dermot TD, Minister of Justice, Equality and Law Reform, Dáil Debate – Written Answers, 18 November 2008.

12 O'Malley (n 6) 214.

13 *Ryan v Governor of Midlands Prison* [2014] IEHC 338, 340.

14 Raymond Byrne, Gerard Hogan and Paul McDermott, *Prisoners' Rights: A Study in Irish Prison Law* (Co-op Books 1981) 110.

of the extent to which the individual might pose a danger to the public upon release.

The Prison Rules 2007 incorporate a system for earning an enhanced remission and permits up to one-third remission for prisoners who have shown further good conduct by 'engagement in authorised structured activity' to such an extent as to satisfy the Minister that they are less likely to reoffend and will be better able to reintegrate into society.[15] However, there does not appear to be any administrative system in place at present to measure such engagement in authorised structured activity, as neither the Prison Rules themselves nor the primary legislation from which the rules are derived, offer any indication as to how the risk of reoffending is to be assessed for this purpose.[16]

Accordingly, the main distinctions between remission and temporary release or parole are that remission is granted, practically as of right, though one which can be forfeited in whole or in part through misbehaviour while in prison.[17] Temporary release/parole must be earned; it is a privilege within the gift of the Minister for Justice/the Parole Board that is, more or less by definition, granted at an earlier point in the sentence than remission. Unlike remission, the granting of temporary release or parole is subject to conditions, breach of which can lead to a recall to custody. As remission operates through the effluxion of time, as opposed to the considered process through which parole is granted, and as it is not applicable to prisoners serving life sentences, it is not proposed to study the rules applicable to remission, save and except where they interact with the parole process.

## The Legislation and Various types of Temporary Release

In examining how parole operates in Ireland, it is necessary to recognise that there are various types of temporary release granted to prisoners in the Irish prison system. The Criminal Justice Act 1960, s 2 gave the Minister for Justice power to make rules allowing for the temporary release of prisoners from all institutions,

---

15 SI No 252 of 2007: Prison Rules 2007, r 59(2).

16 Thomas O'Malley, 'The Ends of Sentence: Imprisonment and Early Release Decisions in Ireland.' Paper delivered at Fitzwilliam College, Cambridge, June 2008. The paper was later published in Nicola Padfield, Dirk Van Zyl Smit and Frieder Dünkel (eds), *Release from Prison. European Policy and Practice* (Willan Publishing 2010) 237-265.

17 ibid 24[illegible].

for whatever period he or she saw fit.[18] The Act permitted the granting of 'temporary release' rather than 'early release', and it was envisaged that the prisoner would be released for a defined period with the expectation that they would return to prison thereafter, unless granted a further extension. Such temporary leaves of absence were granted on compassionate grounds and were also advocated as a benefit for long-term prisoners to prepare them for release and possible employment.[19] The 1960 Act allowed wide discretion to the relevant Minister in deciding on criteria for granting temporary release, as well as to whom it may be granted, and in what circumstances. The Criminal Justice (Temporary Release of Prisoners) Act 2003 significantly updated the 1960 Act and stipulates the purposes for which temporary release may be granted. These purposes include assessing the prisoner's ability to be re-integrated into society,[20] preparing them for release on the expiry of their sentence,[21] to enable them to assist the Gardaí in investigating crime,[22] where there are circumstances where the release is warranted on health or humanitarian grounds,[23] where it is necessary, in the opinion of the Minister, to ensure good governance of the prison concerned[24] or to maintain good order in, and humane and just management of the prison concerned,[25] or where the Minister is of the opinion that the prisoner has been rehabilitated and is ready for reintegration into society.[26] It has been noted that, notwithstanding the enactment of this statute, essentially the system remains unaltered and the principal effect of the new statute was merely to render more explicit those factors and considerations which would probably have guided early release decisions in any case.[27]

The Criminal Justice (Temporary Release of Prisoners) Act 2003 not only sets out the purposes for which temporary release may be granted but also specifies the criteria and conditions to be utilised for the granting of temporary release. The Criminal Justice (Temporary Release of Prisoners) Act 2003, s 2(2) specifies what factors the

---

18 Mary Rogan, *Prison Policy in Ireland; Politics, penal-welfarism and political imprisonment* (Routledge 2011) 93.

19 Rogan (n 18) 93.

20 Criminal Justice (Temporary Release of Prisoners) Act 2003, s 2(1)(a)(i).

21 s 2(1)(a)(ii).

22 s 2(1) (a)(iii).

23 s 2(1) (b)(i)&(ii).

24 See O'Malley (n 16) 10, where he states that 'good governance of the prison concerned can safely be treated as an euphemism for relieving prison overcrowding.'

25 Criminal Justice (Temporary Release of Prisoners) Act 2003, s 2(1)(c)(i)&(ii).

26 Criminal Justice (Temporary Release of Prisoners) Act 2003, s 2(1)(d).

27 See O'Malley (n 16) 10.

Minister is required to take into account when reaching a decision on temporary release. These include the nature and gravity of the offence, the period of the sentence of imprisonment served by the person, the potential threat to the safety and security of members of the public (including the victim of the offence to which the sentence of imprisonment being served by the person relates) should the person be released from prison, prior convictions, the conduct of the person while in custody and any reports or recommendations made by the prison governor, An Garda Síochána or a probation officer (amongst others). Further matters which must be considered include the risk of the person committing an offence during any period of temporary release as well as the risk of the person failing to comply with any conditions attaching to his or her temporary release and the likelihood that any period of temporary release might accelerate the person's reintegration into society or improve his or her prospects of obtaining employment. (This list above is not exhaustive and reference must be made to the legislation for a full list of all of the considerations therein.)

Temporary release or parole, can be granted as a component part of the long term sentence management and release plan for a prisoner but it is more frequently granted for other purposes, such as for compassionate reasons. In addition, a further example of temporary release in operation is the 'Community Return' scheme, whereby prisoners serving sentences of over one year but fewer than eight years, may be deemed eligible to serve the balance of their sentence in the community, under strict supervision conditions.[28] Another example of temporary release in operation in the Irish prison system is the practice of releasing significant numbers of prisoners for the Christmas period.[29] Furthermore, the Irish Prison Service has stated that it is now policy to grant temporary release to the vast majority of prisoners at some point towards the end of their sentence, and only prisoners of a violent disposition or those serving sentences for particularly heinous crimes remain incarcerated until the last day.[30] This willingness and ability to grant temporary release, however, does not extend to every prisoner and these categories of prisoner who are not eligible for temporary release/parole will be discussed later in this chapter. It is important to note that whilst those serving determinate sentences will not be eligible for review by the Parole Board until certain regulations are made

---

[28] Mary Rogan, *Prison Law* (Bloomsbury 2014) 159. See also Chapter 5 on Community Service, for more.

[29] O'Malley (n 16) 246.

[30] Oireachtas Joint Committee on Justice, Defence and Equality, 2013 Report on Penal Reform. Appendix Five, 13 of the transcript of evidence of Kieran O'Dwyer, 1 February 2012.

by the Minister for Justice following consultation with the Parole Board, such prisoners remain eligible for temporary release at the discretion of the Minister for Justice. The eligibility criteria which operated for engaging with the Interim Parole Board, both in respect of life sentenced prisoners as well as in respect of prisoners serving determinate sentences, will now be examined as it can be envisaged that similar provisions in respect of determinate prisoners will be agreed in due course.

## Eligibility for Prisoners to be Considered by the Irish Interim Parole Board

A prisoner's eligibility to have his or her case considered by the Interim Parole Board was restricted in a number of regards. The principal limiting factor was that the Interim Parole Board only considered the cases of prisoners serving sentences of eight years or longer,[31] or if the prisoner was serving a series of shorter sentences consecutively which cumulatively totalled eight years, or longer. As referenced above, it is worth noting that the Parole Act 2019 states that the rules for eligibility for consideration for parole by the statutory Parole Board of determinate sentence prisoners are to be prescribed in legislation by the Minister for Justice after consultation with the Parole Board. The Act stipulates that this term cannot be less than eight years.[32] In relation to prisoners serving shorter sentences, the Minister for Justice frequently grants temporary release without any reference to the Parole Board, and the Minister for Justice will continue to have the power to grant temporary release to these prisoners and also to prisoners who have not engaged with the Parole Board if he/she deems the same to be appropriate. However, this chapter is only concerned with those who are considered for parole through the Parole Board process.

It must, however, be noted that the length of the sentence that the prisoner is serving is not the only eligibility criterion considered by the Parole Board. Certain prisoners who are convicted of offences and are subsequently deemed to be suffering from a mental illness necessitating their transfer to the Central Mental Hospital whilst serving their sentences are not eligible to have their cases reviewed by the Parole Board and are instead reviewed by the Mental Health (Criminal Law) Review Board.[33] In addition, prisoners serving

31 O'Malley (n 16) 246.

32 The Parole Act 2019, s 24(3)

33 Criminal Law (Insanity) Act 2006. It should however be noted that s 18 of this Act provides for the transfer of the prisoner back to the prison setting when they are no longer deemed to be in need of in-patient care. In such circumstances

sentences for a number of specified offences are also ineligible for parole.[34] In Ireland, those prisoners sentenced to a term of imprisonment for certain firearms offences[35] and for the possession of drugs under the Misuse of Drugs Act 1977, s 27(3A) and (3B), as amended by the Criminal Justice Act 1999, s 5 are not eligible to be granted temporary release. Other offenders who are generally ineligible for temporary release include those convicted of offences such as treason or attempted treason or murder or attempted murder to which the Criminal Justice Act 1990, s 3 applies (ie murder or attempted murder of a member of An Garda Síochána or the Irish Prison Service acting in the course of his or her duty); murder or attempted murder carried out in the course of furtherance of an offence under the Offences Against the State Act 1939, s 6 or in the course or furtherance of the activities of an unlawful organisation within the meaning of s 18 (other than paragraph (f) of that Act); murder or attempted murder, committed within the State for a political motive, of the head of a foreign state or of a member of the government or a diplomatic officer of a foreign State.[36] A person convicted of an aggravated murder as set out above must, in addition to being sentenced to life imprisonment, be ordered to serve at least 40 years in prison. An attempt at such a murder carries a mandatory minimum sentence of 20 years. Standard remission may be applied to the minimum term, which means, in effect, that a person convicted of aggravated murder can ordinarily expect to serve a prison sentence of at least 30 years. Special remission cannot be granted before the prisoner becomes eligible for standard remission. Temporary release may be granted but only for 'grave reasons of a humanitarian nature' and then only for such limited duration as is justified by those reasons.[37] However, it has been decided by the Courts that prisoners sentenced for offences under the Misuse of Drugs Act 1977, s 15A as amended, may apply for enhanced remission.[38] Notwithstanding that the ability to grant a parole order/ temporary release is currently prohibited in these cases, it appears that the Minister referred, on an exceptional basis, these cases to the Interim Parole Board where recommendations other than temporary release were considered.

---

the prisoner will once again become eligible to participate in the Parole Board process. For a full discussion of the law in this area see *M v The Parole Board and the Minister for Justice and Equality* [2020] IESC 24.

34 See Parole Board, *Annual Report 2002*, 6.

35 O'Malley (n 6) 219.

36 See Parole Board, *Annual Report 2002*, 6.

37 Criminal Justice Act 1990, s 5. For further discussion see O'Malley (n 16) 247.

38 *Hui v Governor of the Midlands Prison* (31 July 2013) High Court (per Hedigan J).

One practical consequence of this arrangement in so far as drug offences are concerned, is that such offenders now account for a significant proportion of the longer-term prison population.[39] There have been calls for a re-examination of the rules in relation to the statutory prohibition on the granting of temporary release to prisoners serving sentences for certain firearms and drug offences and it is a matter that the Minister for Justice has undertaken to review.[40] The Parole Act 2019, however, provides that the Board shall not make a parole order in respect of a parole applicant where the release of the parole applicant from prison is prohibited by or under any enactment, whether passed before or after the coming into operation of the Parole Act 2019.[41]

Minimum term sentences, such as those imposed under the Misuse of Drugs Act 1977, s 15A seem to ignore the fact that society is not damaged or threatened to exactly the same extent every time a given offence is committed, or that every offender who commits that offence will respond in the same way to the same penalty, or that the effect on public opinion in all cases will be the same. What is virtually certain is that legislatively imposed fixed term penalties for serious crimes should allow for the intervention of a Parole Board in the interests of clemency[42] as decisions affecting inmates should be tailored to them on a case-by-case basis, reflecting their individual progress towards rehabilitation.[43]

The total number of offenders participating in the parole process in Ireland varies from year to year, and in 2019 there were 350 cases at various stages of review by the Interim Parole Board.[44] As of 31 of December 2019, there were 3,950 prisoners in custody,[45] which indicates that the Interim Parole Board was engaged with approximately 8.9% of the prison population as of that date. On establishment, the statutory Parole Board had approximately 201 cases of prisoners serving life sentences who had served twelve years or more of their sentences and accordingly were eligible to have their cases reviewed,[46] representing approximately 8.9% of the prison population as of that date. Notwithstanding the fact that the

39 O'Malley (n 6) 219.

40 Penal Policy Review Group, *Strategic Review of Penal Policy: Final Report* (Department of Justice 2014) 86.

41 Parole Act 2019, s 27(3)(a).

42 Stanley A Cohen, 'An Introduction to the Theory, Justifications and Modern Manifestations of Criminal Punishment' (1981) 27(73) McGill L J 85.

43 Joel M Caplan, 'Protecting Parole Board Legitimacy in the Twenty-first Century: The Role of Victims' Rights and Influences' (2012) 7(1) Victims & Offenders 56.

44 Parole Board, *2019 Annual Report*, 8.

45 Irish Prison Service, *2019 Annual Report*, 2.

46 Parole Board, *2021 Annual Report*, 8.

Parole Board deals with a small portion of the prison population, it nevertheless carries out a vital role.[47]

## The Principal Functions of the Interim Parole Board and of the Statutory Parole Board

The Interim Parole Board's principal function was to advise the Minister for Justice on the administration of the sentences of persons whose cases were referred to the Board by the Minister and in those instances where temporary release is recommended, the conditions which should attach to any such release. It is important to remember that the Interim Parole Board's role was merely advisory and they did not issue any determinations. The Parole Act 2019 placed the Parole Board on a statutory basis, enabling it to issue determinations in the cases appearing before it.[48] The Interim Parole Board offered advice and guidance to the Minister for Justice on the conditions to attach to parole, enabling them to effectively frame the policies and practices relating to parole supervision. In addition, the Interim Parole Board also proffered advice about sentencing policies, new legislation and other matters. Many of these functions have been given a statutory basis in the Parole Act 2019 which provides that the Parole Board shall provide information to persons serving sentences of imprisonment, victims and members of the public in relation to its functions, assist the Minister in making and coordinating policy related to the release of persons from prison on parole and also undertake, commission and assist in research activities relating to the release of persons from prison on parole.[49] In addition, the Parole Board will, by the making of parole orders and by the conditions attached thereto, have a significant input into the manner in which parolees are supervised in the community. Furthermore, in considering and deciding on applications to revoke parole orders, the Parole Board will input into the ongoing behaviour of parolees in the community.[50]

Having studied the eligibility criteria for prisoner's cases to be reviewed by the Parole Board and the principal functions of the Parole Board, this chapter will now proceed to examine the process which was utilised by the Interim Parole Board prior to formulating its recommendations to the Minister for Justice.

---

47 For further discussion see John Costello, Chairman of the Parole Board, Submission to The Oireachtas Sub-Committee on Justice (2012) 2.

48 Parole Act 2019.

49 Parole Act 2019, s 9 (1)(a),(b) and (c).

50 Parole Act 2019, s 33

## The Parole Process in Ireland

The predecessor of the Interim Parole Board, the Sentence Review Group (SRG), operated from 1989 until the establishment of the Interim Parole Board in 2000. The SRG carried out a very similar role and function as the Interim Parole Board, also on a non-statutory, advisory basis and operated under remarkably similar processes and procedures as the Interim Parole Board. The Interim Parole Board operated from December 2000 to July 2021. The statutory Parole Board has yet to publish the rules and procedures which will be utilised under their process however it is envisaged that substantial elements of the process utilised by the Interim Parole Board will be retained. The process utilised by the Interim Parole Board had the stated intention of being open and inclusive. The process usually lasted approximately six months in duration and consisted of a seven stage process.

This seven stage process operated as follows:

**Stage 1:**

Referral — A prisoner did not apply for or submit an application for parole/temporary release. The Minister for Justice each year ascertained from the Irish Prison Service details of the prisoners who would become eligible for review by the Interim Parole Board in the following calendar year. The Interim Parole Board reviewed the cases of eligible prisoners sentenced to eight years imprisonment or more, including a life sentence, once the prisoner had served half their sentence or served eight years imprisonment, whichever event occurred sooner.[51] Prisoners who were serving a determinate sentence must have had at least twelve months of their sentence left to serve at the time of the commencement of the review process. The statutory Parole Board eligibility criteria have already been discussed in this chapter and it was noted that on commencement the Parole Board will initially only consider life sentenced prisoners for parole. The Parole Act 2019 provides that life sentenced prisoners will not be eligible to be granted parole until they have served twelve years of their sentence.[52] Under the statutory Parole Board system the process by which cases are referred to the Board is slightly different with an obligation on the Irish Prison Service to notify the Parole Board in writing at intervals of not more than one year of prisoners serving sentences of imprisonment who are

---

[51] O'Malley (n 16) 9.

[52] Parole Act 2019, s 24(1)(a).

eligible for parole or who will become eligible for parole within eighteen months following the notification.[53]

Under the Interim Parole Board system, the Minister could, if he or she so wished, refer a case to the Interim Parole Board for an early first review. It would appear that early consideration of a particular case is also possible under the Parole Act 2019 however the Parole Board would not be in a position to grant parole to any prisoner prior to the date on which the prisoner would be eligible to be granted parole under the Act.[54] In addition, it is worth re-iterating that the Minister had discretion whether to accept or reject any of the recommendations of the Interim Parole Board in any particular case, whereas now the decisions of the statutory Parole Board are determinative and no longer merely advisory.

**Stage 2:**

Invitation to Participate — The Secretariat of the Interim Parole Board wrote to each prisoner referred to the Board and invited the prisoner to participate in the review process, asking them to complete a form to indicate whether they wished to participate in this process or not. The Interim Parole Board only reviewed the cases of those who accepted this invitation. On occasion, prisoners decline to participate in the Interim Parole Board process however the vast majority of the refusals to participate in the parole process were from determinate sentenced prisoners[55] and accordingly the problem of prisoners declining to participate in the parole process is not one that the statutory Parole Board will be likely to experience to a significant degree. The Interim Parole Board, on being informed by the Irish Prison Service of a prisoner's eligibility to apply for parole, notified the prisoner in writing of the date on which they would become eligible to be considered for parole and notified the prisoner that they could make an application to be considered by the Board for parole. In the event that the prisoner applied to participate in the parole process, the Interim Parole Board proceeded to collate reports and other information to compile a review dossier.

**Stage 3:**

Assembling a Review Dossier — When a prisoner opted to participate in the review process with the Interim Parole Board, the Secretariat of the Interim Parole Board assembled a set of papers

---

53 Parole Act 2019, s 25(1)(a).
54 Parole Act 2019, s 26(4)
55 See Costello (n 47) 3.

(referred to as a Review Dossier), which included a number of reports from various agencies. Reports were sought from the Governor of the institution in which the prisoner was accommodated. These reports generally encompassed the behaviour of the prisoner in prison, how the prisoner occupied their time in prison (eg employment, education etc), engagement with services (such as Psychology/Probation/Addiction etc), the prisoner's disciplinary record and whether the prisoner had complied with the Minister for Justice's decision following the last Interim Parole Board review (if relevant).[56] A report was also furnished by the Prison Review Committee. These Prison Review Committees generally included prison management, probation officers, the chaplaincy service, the education service and representatives of the Irish Prison Service management. However, these committees did not have access to the full range of information available to the Interim Parole Board.[57] The Probation Service also provided a probation officer's report which generally incorporated a risk assessment as well as the probation officer's observations on the prisoner, what needed to be addressed to reduce risk of reoffending and assist the prisoner's reintegration in the community and information regarding work undertaken, ongoing or necessary in relation to rehabilitation and reintegration. It was noted that great importance was attached by the Interim Parole Board to these reports and the recommendations contained therein.[58] The Psychology Service also provided reports to the Interim Parole Board, where appropriate, setting out the progress of the prisoner in addressing their offending behaviour. These reports also frequently incorporated a risk assessment. It became the practice that the risk assessment would normally be prepared by whichever of the Probation Service or the Psychology Service was the lead agency at the time of the review, to avoid duplication, inconsistencies or contradictory risk assessments. Reports from a psychiatrist, in particular where the prisoner had been undergoing such treatment whilst serving his or her sentence, were also obtained when appropriate. In each and every case, a report was sought from An Garda Síochána, however these reports were often somewhat historical in nature as the information contained therein was generally informed solely by what the Gardaí knew of the crime and the perceived state of mind of the offender at the time of the commission of the offence.[59]

---

56 Parole Board, *2005 Annual Report* 6.

57 ibid 22, where it is stated that the Prison Review Committee does not have access to the medical/psychiatric reports, Psychology or Probation reports however each of these services is represented on the Prison Review Committee.

58 ibid 11.

59 Irish Prison Service, Examination of the Sentence Management of people serving Life Sentences (2017) 30.

A home circumstance report was also included, which dealt with the issue of where a prisoner to whom temporary release might be granted would be able to live. These reports were generally prepared by a probation officer and were generally incorporated into the report received from the Probation Service. The home circumstances report enabled the Board to assess the consequences of the offender returning to the environment from which they came and related issues.[60] The Review Dossier also contained any other material believed to be relevant, which on occasion included representations from the victim or the victim's family.

The dossier for the statutory Parole Board is expected to be similar to those utilised by the Interim Parole Board, with the Parole Board having the power to apply to the Courts Service for a transcript of a court hearing at which sentencing was considered,[61] as well as having the power to direct that a report be furnished by the Irish Prison Service, the governor of the appropriate institution where the prisoner is being detained, the Probation Service, An Garda Síochána, a psychologist, a psychiatrist or a medical practitioner.[62] When the Parole Board are utilising their discretion to direct the production of such a report there is an onus on them to specify in their directions the matters to be dealt with in that report.[63]

**Stage 4:**

Disclosure of Review Dossier — Once the reports (and any other material) were obtained by the Interim Parole Board, they were assembled into a Review Dossier and a copy was sent, under sealed cover, to the prisoner. Any person or organisation requested to provide a report was also informed that the report would be made available to the prisoner. The presumption in both Ireland and Northern Ireland is that all of the information contained in the dossiers received by the Parole Board/Parole Commissioners will also be provided to the prisoner.[64] There is, however, provision for the withholding of information or reports in very limited circumstances, such as in the interests of national security or on medical and/or psychiatric grounds. The Parole Act 2019 contains provisions for disclosure of the dossier to the prisoner 'other than

60 Parole Board, *2005 Annual Report*, 7.
61 Parole Act 2019, s 13(1)(h).
62 Parole Act 2019, s 13(2).
63 Parole Act 2019, s 13(3).
64 See Northern Ireland Parole Commissioners, *Parole Commissioners for Northern Ireland Handbook – A Guide for Parole Commissioners* (Undated) 25.

where the Board is of the opinion that exceptional circumstances exist that warrant such disclosures not being so given.[65]

In Ireland, on receipt of the dossier from the Interim Parole Board, all prisoners were then afforded an opportunity to submit written comments on the content of the Review Dossier. These submissions were frequently written on the prisoner's behalf by lawyers and, as well as commenting on the contents of the dossier, they also often provided any other information which the prisoner or their lawyer felt the Board should consider.[66] This other information, which often included testimonials, and all comments submitted by the prisoner were added to the dossier at this stage. The Parole Act 2019 also allows for written submissions by the parole applicant or their legal representative to the Parole Board.

**Stage 5:**

Interview — When the prisoner acknowledged receipt of the review dossier from the Interim Parole Board and submitted their written comments in respect of same, if necessary, arrangements were made for them to attend an interview with two members of the Interim Parole Board. It was always the practice of the Interim Parole Board for there to be an interview for a first review and the Interim Parole Board would then exercise its discretion as to whether or not to have an interview on the occasion of subsequent reviews. These interviews took place in the institution in which the prisoner was detained and the two members of the Interim Parole Board were accompanied by a member of the staff of the secretariat.[67] The process described in the Parole Act 2019 is similar and provides for the Parole Board to meet with a parole applicant for the purpose of interviewing them or receiving oral submissions from them or their legal representative.[68]

The Interim Parole Board did not allow legal representation at the interview and merely allowed a written submission from the prisoner's legal representative to the Board, as well as written representations from other relevant organisations and persons.[69] In addition to legal representation not being permitted before the Interim Parole Board, the courts held that a person appearing before the Interim Parole Board was not entitled to legal aid for

---

65 Parole Act 2019, s 14 (1)(b).
66 See Costello (n 47) 4.
67 Parole Board. 2004 Annual Report 4.
68 Parole Act 2019, s 13(1)(c).
69 The legality of this approach was upheld in the case of *Barry v Sentencing Review Group* [2001] 4 IR 167.

that purpose.[70] This situation changed utterly on the establishment of the Parole Board on a statutory basis. The Parole Act 2019 acknowledges that the availability of legal representation is a necessary element of ensuring that fair procedures are met before a statutory Parole Board. Legal representation before the Parole Board is permitted[71] and a legal aid scheme has been established to facilitate such representation.[72] The provision of legal representation reflects the jurisprudence of the European Court of Human Rights in instances where Parole Boards are determinative as opposed to merely advisory.[73] It is envisaged that the whole character of the procedure involved will be changed utterly by the introduction of legal representation in the process. However, offenders appearing before the Parole Board are frequently disadvantaged by their social background, by level of formal education, and occasionally by lack of fluency in the English language. Therefore, the case for all applicants to be legally represented appears unanswerable. Under the system utilised by the Interim Parole Board, prior to commencement of the interview, its structure and purpose was explained to the prisoner and the interview was then conducted in a relatively informal manner.[74] The Interim Parole Board members conducting the interview made efforts to use simple, plain language throughout to accommodate all literacy levels as well as various physical and mental health problems. Appropriate sensitivity to gender, ethnic, cultural and linguistic differences were maintained at all times, and, if necessary, an interpreter was provided to prisoners attending these interviews.[75]

The two Interim Parole Board members conducting the interview gave the prisoner an opportunity to make submissions in person to the Board, comment on the contents of the dossier and also to raise any queries or concerns they had in relation to the parole process. The prisoner was also afforded the opportunity to draw to the attention of the Interim Parole Board any positive features supporting their case for temporary release. The Interim Parole Board members then discussed the contents of the Review Dossier

---

70 *Grogan v Parole Board* [2008] IEHC 204.

71 Parole Act 2019, s 13 (1)(b).

72 Parole Act 2019, s 14 (1)(a).

73 See Černák v Slovakia (17 December 2013) ECtHR, no 36997/08 78 and also *Thynne v United Kingdom* (1991) 13 EHRR 666.

74 Parole Board, *2004 Annual Report*, 4.

75 See Parliamentary Question 394 on 9 July 2014, Clare Daly TD to Minister for Justice and Equality. This is an important consideration as there were 33 foreign nationals serving life sentences in the Irish prison system on 31 January 2017. Of these 33 foreign nationals, 25 were believed to not use English as their primary language. See Irish Prison Service (n 59) 7 and 40.

with the prisoner and sought any clarification or additional information required to deal appropriately with the prisoner's case.

The Interim Parole Board members conducting the interview ensured that all issues were fully explored in the interview with the purpose of the interview being to enable the two interviewers to report back to the Board on the prisoner before them and to consider what the Interim Parole Board's attitude to the prisoner should be.[76] To achieve this aim, the interview could be broken into four distinct segments, firstly, consideration and analysis of past behaviour, (as research has shown that what somebody has done in the past and how they went about doing it is an important predictor of what they might do in the future),[77] secondly, consideration of issues that might assist assessment of the individual's risk of causing harm in the future, thirdly, consideration of ongoing or necessary rehabilitative interventions and finally, a consideration with the prisoner of the likely recommendations that the interviewers would make to the Interim Parole Board.

In summary, the interview allowed additional facts or information about the case to be gathered, allowed verification of the accuracy of facts or information in the relevant file and afforded the prisoner the opportunity to provide their perspective. It also created an opportunity to evaluate the prisoner's release plan (if they had one) as well as providing a chance to encourage the prisoner to continue their positive activities and to motivate the prisoner to change behaviour or engage in risk reduction activities. The prisoner was also given an opportunity to raise relevant issues and ask questions relating to the parole process.

Following the interview, the secretariat prepared a written report on the interview and this report was furnished to the prisoner for their comments or to afford the prisoner the opportunity to provide any additional information. This interview report, together with any comments the prisoner made on the report and any further documentation the offender submitted, was added to the review dossier. It is worth noting that the Interim Parole Board, for second or subsequent reviews, did not always conduct an interview and, in appropriate cases, the Interim Parole Board monitored the prisoner's progress and considered their case further on the basis of reports from the various services with which they had been

---

[76] Gordon Holmes, 'Address to the Prison Law Seminar – The Parole Process' hosted by the Irish Penal Reform Trust, 26 March 2009.

[77] Christine Glenn, Christine and Elizabeth Rea, *Interviewing and Questioning Skills. Northern Ireland Parole Commissioner Training Manual* (2010) 4.

engaging. In these circumstances, the reports were disclosed to the prisoner in a new review dossier and the prisoner was allowed make written observations on the review dossier and also to submit any further documentation they wished to have included in the dossier when it was being considered subsequently.

The procedures envisaged under the Parole Act 2019 are similar to the procedures adopted by the Interim Parole Board save that the Parole Board will have the power to assign a legal representative to the parole applicant, unless the parole applicant themselves proposed to engage one.[78] An important additional step at this stage of the process introduced by the Parole Act 2019 is that the Parole Board will also have the power to meet with the relevant victim[79] for the purposes of receiving oral submissions from them or their legal representative.[80] The Parole Board also has the power to assign a legal representative to the relevant victim who proposes to make submissions to the Board, unless the relevant victim themselves propose to engage one.[81] The location of the interview with the parole applicant is described as 'in such place as the Board considers appropriate, including, where a person is detained in a prison, in that prison'.[82] The meeting between the Board and the relevant victim may be conducted 'in such place as the Board considers appropriate'.[83] It would appear inappropriate to meet the relevant victim within the prison where the parole applicant is detained and it would also appear inappropriate to meet the parole applicant outside the prison on account of security considerations. The Parole Act 2019 is silent as to whether the Parole Board members meeting the parole applicant and the relevant victim in the case should be the same two members of the Board and the publication of appropriate practices and procedures in this regard is currently awaited.

The Interim Parole Board members stated that they attached great value to the interview process. The fact that parole boards place such importance on the prisoner's performance at interview has been reported as a frustration for prison based professionals such as probation officers and psychologists, who have prepared detailed reports identifying a prisoner's risks, needs and strengths and have, perhaps, engaged in therapeutic interventions to reduce risks only for a Parole Board to make decisions that may be based more on the lay-person's intuition than on careful and considered professionals'

---

78 Parole Act 2019, s 13(1)(b).
79 'Relevant victim' is defined in the Parole Act 2019, s 2(1).
80 Parole Act 2019, s 13(1)(f).
81 Parole Act 2019, s 13(1)(b).
82 Parole Act 2019, s 13(7)(a).
83 Parole Act 2019, s 13(8)(a).

findings.[84] It would certainly be worrying if the gut reactions to a particular parole applicant by the non-expert interviewees received greater emphasis than the detailed reports from professionals who are trained in the assessment and management of risk and who ideally have had the benefit of working with the individual for a period of time so as to be well-placed to identify the positives and negatives about their progression within the prison system or indeed release.[85]

### Stage 6:

Board Meeting — The Interim Parole Board met monthly to review cases and to formulate recommendations to the Minister. Each Board Member was supplied, in advance of the meeting, with the full Review Dossier on each case for discussion. The Board discussed each case on an individual basis and when a matter came for consideration before them, the discussion was started by those Board Members who conducted the interview with the prisoner.[86] Both of these Board Members gave their opinions and outlined the impressions they formed of the prisoner.[87] An additional step with the statutory Parole Board is that it will also be necessary for the Parole Board members who interviewed the relevant victim to report back on this meeting.

The process at the Interim Parole Board was that in the course of discussing each case, the reports contained within the review dossier were discussed by the entire Board. The Interim Parole Board, following review of the dossier and discussion of an individual file, could decide to defer making a recommendation to seek further information; defer making a recommendation for other reasons (eg to await the outcome of an appeal or court review) or decide on a recommendation to the Minister. One extra step in the process post the commencement of the Parole Act 2019 is that there is a provision requiring the parole applicant to be given a copy of the draft decision of the Board in relation to their application for parole and to be enabled to make written submissions on the draft

---

84 Jane Mulcahy, 'The Parole Bill 2016: Courts, Quangos and the Risks of Conceptual Confusion', Submission to the Oireachtas Justice Committee (2017) 17.

85 ibid.

86 Diarmuid Griffin, *Killing Time: Life Imprisonment and Parole in Ireland* (Palgrave Macmillan 2018) 73 where members of the Interim Parole Board describe the impact of these oral presentations on the decision-making process.

87 Holmes (n 76).

prior to its finalisation.[88] The publication of procedures detailing how this will work in practice is currently awaited.[89]

In an international setting, however, research has concluded that a very high proportion of Parole Board's decisions can be predicted in advance on the basis of the information which is already recorded on the file, raising questions about the 'added value' which formal meetings of the Parole Board bring to the process except in formalising decisions.[90]

**Stage 7:**

Recommendations to the Minister/ Decision on Parole — On a practical level, the Interim Parole Board carried out its functions by making detailed recommendations (or in practice a detailed series of recommendations) to the Minister for Justice. The Interim Parole Board described the purpose of these recommendations as indicating steps the prisoner could take to improve their risk profile and accordingly increase their chances of early release.[91] The Interim Board appeared to consider its role to be primarily in managing the prison sentence and recommending temporary release when appropriate.[92] The Interim Parole Board made a variety of recommendations in the context of preparing a prisoner for release. These recommendations generally included suggestions in relation to therapy, education, work training, re-socialisation, transfer or temporary release. It was, however, noted that the parole process in Ireland was viewed as incremental whereby offenders took 'quite small steps' towards release at each review.[93]

The Interim Board's written recommendations were sent to the Minister who then considered the recommendations and arrived at a decision. The Minister had the discretion to accept the Board's recommendations; accept the Board's recommendations with conditions; accept part of the Board's recommendations or reject the Board's recommendations. Despite the fact that the Interim Parole Board's role was advisory only and the Minister was not obliged to accept any recommendation made by it, the statistics indicated that the Minister accepted the Interim Parole Board's recommendations in the vast majority of cases. Once the Minister

88 Parole Act 2019, s 14(1)(g).
89 Parole Act 2019, s 14(1), (2), and (3).
90 David Faulkner, *Crime, State and Citizen – A Field Full of Folk* (Waterside Press 2001) 198.
91 See Holmes (n 76) 2.
92 ibid.
93 Diarmuid Griffin, 'The Release and Recall of Life Sentence Prisoners: Policy, Practice and Politics' (2015) 53 Irish Jurist 25, 31.

decided to accept (in full or partially) or reject the Interim Parole Board's recommendation, the Minister's decision was subsequently conveyed to the prisoner, in writing.

The Parole Act 2019 has changed this procedure. The Parole Board now make the decisions on parole, deciding whether to grant or refuse a 'parole order'. The decision-making criteria applied by the Parole Board are discussed further below. The Parole Act 2019 contains provisions that all future refusals for parole by the Parole Board shall include reasons for the decision.[94]

In this regard it is worth noting that the Irish courts have recently established a series of principles in relation to the giving of reasons for decisions. These principles include that the essential rationale by which the decision was taken should be patent from the terms of the determination or be capable of being inferred from its terms and its context.[95] A failure to give reasons or to give the reasons in terms so vague or opaque that the underlying rationale cannot be properly or reasonably deduced will be criticised by the courts. Unless this is so, then the constitutional right of access to the courts to have a decision judicially reviewed could be rendered either pointless or so circumscribed as to be unacceptably ineffective.[96]

Having examined the manner in which the Interim Parole Board prepared for and conducted its interviews and board meetings, it is now necessary to look at what factors the Parole Board will take into account when making decisions on parole applications.

## Decision-Making Criteria Applied by the Parole Board

The Parole Act 2019 sets out in great detail the matters which should be considered by the statutory Parole Board in deciding whether a parole applicant should be released on parole. Before granting parole, the Board must be satisfied that the parole applicant would not, upon being released, present an undue risk to the safety and security of members of the public (including the relevant victim), and has been rehabilitated and would, upon being released, be capable of reintegrating into society, and that it is appropriate in all the circumstances that the parole applicant be released on parole.[97]

---

94 Parole Act 2019, s 30(1).

95 See *Meadows v Minister for Justice, Equality and Law Reform* [2010] IESC 3, 28 (Judgment of Murray CJ).

96 ibid.

97 Parole Act 2019, s 27(1).

The Parole Act 2019 further states that the statutory Parole Board, in deciding whether to make a parole order in respect of a parole applicant, shall have regard to a range of factors listed in the Parole Act. These factors include the nature and gravity of the offence to which the sentence of imprisonment being served by the parole applicant relates, the sentence of imprisonment concerned and any recommendation of the court that imposed that sentence in relation thereto, the period of the sentence of imprisonment served by the parole applicant, any offence of which the parole applicant was convicted other than the offence to which the sentence of imprisonment being served by him or her relates, the conduct of the parole applicant whilst serving the sentence or whilst previously on parole or temporary release, the risk of the parole applicant committing an offence while on parole, the risk of the parole applicant failing to comply with any conditions attaching to his or her release on parole, any treatment, education or training the parole applicant has undergone, or programmes he or she has participated in while serving the sentence of imprisonment, any report relating to the parole applicant prepared and furnished to the Board pursuant to a direction in that regard, any submissions made by the parole applicant or the victim in the course of their meetings with the Parole Board and the Parole Board can also have regard to any such other matter as the Board considers appropriate.

One matter which does not appear to have been addressed by the Parole Board in its current position, nor indeed in the Parole Act of 2019, but which is worthy of consideration is how the Parole Board deals with the possibility of a parole applicant having committed further crimes for which they were not convicted. The general position in sentencing is that a defendant is not to be sentenced for an offence unless it has been proved against them by admission or verdict.[98] It would be manifestly unfair if the Parole Board were to 'sentence' prisoners for offences for which they were not convicted by refusing them parole merely on the grounds that the Parole Board suspected the offender had committed further offences. It must be remembered that it is not the role of the Parole Board to determine the outcome of a criminal charge.[99] Nevertheless, evidence of other offending, whether resulting in convictions or not, can be considered as part of the global assessment of risk.[100] This issue is particularly relevant in the event of convictions only

---

98 *R v Kidd & Others* [1998] 1 WLR 604.

99 For discussion of this point in the context of England and Wales see *R (West) v Parole Board* [2003] 1 WLR 705.

100 *R (McGetrick) v Parole Board* [2012] 1 WLR 2488 and also [2013] 1 WLR 2064 (Court of Appeal).

being entered on sample charges or in circumstances where a *nolle prosequi* has been entered on some charges. In this regard, it is essential to re-iterate that it is not the function of the Parole Board to find a prisoner guilty or innocent of any offence — its function is to assess the risk that would be created if the prisoner is released on parole and, accordingly, it must take into account all information relevant to the offender.[101]

Whilst these considerations appear quite diverse, it has previously been considered that, both in Ireland and internationally, parole has been recognised as having a rehabilitative purpose.[102] The Parole Board, by holding forth the incentive of temporary release, attempts to get prisoners to engage in working towards their own rehabilitation.[103] The Interim Parole Board utilised this rehabilitative function in the past by stressing the importance that it attached in the parole decision-making process to offenders undertaking rehabilitative work and relevant programmes and courses to advance themselves whilst in prison. The Interim Parole Board also stated that any prisoner seeking release should have taken all the steps open to lead to his or her rehabilitation including completing anger management courses, substance abuse courses, sex offender courses or other such recommended courses.[104] It is worth noting, however, that in other jurisdictions, the effective 'precondition' of undertaking such treatment work has had the unanticipated result of demand for such treatment and courses greatly outstripping the ability of the prison and other services to supply such services, which has resulted in the continued confinement of prisoners who might otherwise be released.[105] It may be that the more judicious use of such treatment pre-conditions, particularly for low risk offenders, could relieve a significant portion of this problem.

Another factor which the Interim Parole Board stated that it utilised in the formulation of its recommendations to the Minister, and which is a matter which the Parole Board must have regard to under the Parole Act 2019, is a consideration of a prisoner's conduct whilst

---

101 See *Grogan v Parole Board* [2008] IEHC 204 where McMahon J states: 'The Parole Board is not there to determine the innocence or guilt of the applicant, much less to second guess the sentence imposed by the court. To attempt to do so would be to usurp the functions which reside elsewhere under our constitution.' For discussion of this point in the context of England and Wales see 'The Worboys Case'.

102 Tom Ellis and Peter Marshall, 'Does Parole Work? A Post-Release Comparison of Reconviction Rates for Paroled and Non-Paroled Prisoners' (2000) 33(3) Aust NZ J Criminol 301-302.

103 Costello (n 47).

104 Holmes (n 76) 15.

105 See Caplan (n 43) 57.

in custody. This consideration seems to assume that, if a prisoner offends, however rarely, in the supervised confines of a prison, then clearly, if released, they would pose a greater danger to the public.[106] It may be that too much importance is attached to this factor as research has shown that behaviour in prison is, at best, a very poor indicator of behaviour upon release as a person who reacts badly, for example, to prison discipline, is not necessarily violent or uncooperative in ordinary life.[107] By placing such emphasis on the conduct of prisoners, the fear has been expressed that parole is being used as a tool to make better prisoners rather than better residents of the community.[108] However, by encouraging more socially acceptable behaviours, prison management is not only developing more harmonious relations between inmates but, more importantly, they are also fostering pro-social modes of behaviour among prisoners that benefit society as a whole upon their release. The positive effects on prisoner behaviour through holding out the possibility of parole have long been acknowledged both internationally as well as in the Irish context.[109]

This relationship between disciplinary findings against a prisoner and adverse consideration in the parole process can give rise to a situation where there may be a disproportionate amplification of the consequences of the misconduct. Misgivings about the fairness of this amplification must, of course, be considered against the backdrop of the primary consideration of the Parole Board being the protection of the public. Nevertheless, the manner in which a disciplinary finding against a prisoner can impact on the consideration of that prisoner's application for parole becomes all the more concerning when considered in light of the prisoner's almost total lack of legal advice or legal representation in the conduct of the hearing of the disciplinary breach in the prison system.[110] It should, however, be noted that the European Court of Human Rights has held that a prisoner cannot be detained beyond the point where he or she would be entitled to release, even as a sanction for a prison disciplinary offence, if these 'extra days' have not been imposed by a court.[111] The most that a prisoner can be deprived of is remission. However, as remission is not applicable for prisoners serving life sentences, and life sentenced prisoners

---

106 Parole Board, *Annual Report* (2009) 4.

107 Nigel Walker, *Sentencing Theory, Law and Practice* (Butterworths 1985) 207.

108 Winthrop D Lane, 'A New Day Opens for Parole' (1933) 24(1) J Crim L & Criminology 92.

109 See Michael McDowell TD, Minister for Justice, Equality and Law Reform. Dáil Éireann, Written Answers – Prison Sentence Management, 9 October 2002.

110 Walker (n 107) 188.

111 *Campbell and Fell v United Kingdom* (1984) 7 EHRR 165.

do not have a date where they would be entitled to be released, this issue can be a very real problem.[112]

Furthermore, this approach of making conduct within the prison setting a major consideration in the parole decision-making process appears to ignore the fact that an offender who reacts badly to prison discipline is not necessarily violent or uncooperative in ordinary life and *vice versa*. It also ignores the fact that a 'good' prisoner may not, in fact, be in the best position to make the transition back to outside life.[113] Furthermore, international research has found that breaches of prison discipline do not necessarily predict recidivism, but may be indicative of future technical parole violations, such as a failure to keep parole appointments.[114] It appears that the Parole Act 2019 has adopted the position that conduct within the prison setting should be no more than one factor, of many, considered in the parole process. However, it is not clear what weight is to be applied to this factor in the decision-making process.

The parole system established by the Parole Act 2019 specifies decision-making criteria to be applied when considering applications for parole. These criteria look to both the past and the future and require consideration of the punitive and retributive aspects of the offence, including its seriousness, the length of sentence imposed and served by the prisoner up to the point of review. There is also a strong focus on the future behaviour of the offender, the likelihood of the offender reintegrating successfully into the community on release and the level of risk they present if release were to be granted.[115] A criticism of this approach is that, whilst the factors which should be considered when deciding to make a parole order are set out, there is no guidance as to whether any particular factors are to be treated as more important than others or whether other factors not listed above could be taken into account in the review process.[116] Regardless of the foregoing, however, the statutory parole system should introduce more transparency and accountability in the parole decision-making process than existed in the lifetime of the Interim Parole Board.

---

112 *Ezeh and Connors v United Kingdom* (2004) 39 EHRR 1.

113 Rob White and Santina Perrone, *Crime and Social Control* (OUP 2005) 257.

114 Ann Reade, 'Interviewing Prisoners for Parole Assessments', Training Material for the Parole Board (2013).

115 Griffin (n 93) 28.

116 See Costello (n 47) 9.

## The Supervisory Role in Relation to Parolees

The Irish Interim Parole Board did not have any role in the supervision of an offender once they were released on parole and this supervisory function was and is generally discharged by the Irish Probation Service.[117] The Irish Interim Parole Board did however on occasion express concern in relation to the in relation to the availability of services after release[118] and emphasised the need for the Probation Service to be adequately resourced in carrying out this aspect of its work.[119] The position in Ireland in which the Interim Parole Board had no role in the supervision of the parolee is in direct contrast with the situation in other jurisdictions where the contact between the parolee and the Board is maintained. The only mechanism the Irish Interim Parole Board had in relation to the control of parolees was in the setting, and possible reviewing of parole conditions. The statutory Parole Board will have an additional role in relation to the recalling of prisoners from parole however before examining that development this chapter will now examine the role and purpose of parole conditions in Ireland.

## Role and Purpose of Parole Conditions in Ireland

Programmes of temporary release, to be successful, must begin in prison itself with appropriate programmes of training, work experience and treatment, depending on individual needs. This is especially the case in relation to prisoners who have served lengthy prison sentences or who have been committed to prison for particularly serious offences. Public safety is enhanced by ensuring that, should these prisoners be granted temporary release that they have the life skills and competency to reintegrate into society and become law-abiding members of the community.[120] This situation perhaps best illustrates the basic paradox of prison: you cannot promote free will and expect released prisoners to act with self-control and foresight in the community by extinguishing free will in the prisons.[121] In this regard society must remember that the purpose of imprisonment is often stated to be rehabilitation — those who offend are placed in prison not in the spirit of revenge but in the fond hope that the experience will lead them to refrain from

---

117 Holmes (n 76) 4.

118 Parole Board, *Annual Report* (2002) 2.

119 John Costello, Chairman of The Parole Board, Evidence To The Oireachtas Sub-Committee on Justice, Defence and Equality (16 December 2015) 21-22.

120 Irish Prison Service (n 59) 3.

121 Gresham M Sykes, *The Society of Captives – A Study of a Maximum Security Prison* (Princeton University Press 2007) xxv.

criminal behaviour in the future.[122] The Interim Parole Board when advising the Minister for Justice on the sentence management of particular prisoners referred to them informed the Minister of the degree to which the offender had engaged with therapeutic and educational services whilst in prison. Such engagement will also be a consideration for the statutory Parole Board however, the benefits of engaging in these programmes is not just limited to the improved prospects of obtaining a parole order or being granted temporary release. Public safety is further enhanced when on the offender's release such persons are encouraged and assisted to settle back into the community and desist from further criminal activity.[123] The Parole Act 2019 gives the Parole Board, when considering an application for parole under the Act, the power to direct that a report in writing in respect of the relevant person be prepared and furnished to it by or on behalf of a number of specified persons/bodies including the Irish Prison Service.[124] The Parole Board also has the power to direct the Probation Service to prepare and furnish such reports.[125] The power to direct the preparation of such reports is critical in ensuring that prisoners are making positive use of their time spent in prison.[126] Sentence management is a critical component for the successful reintegration of the prisoner[127] and research conducted on the Irish prison system has concluded that 'a well-functioning sentence planning and sentence management process is the glue that holds together any rehabilitative oriented correctional process'.[128] When directing the preparation of these reports the statutory Parole Board may specify that the reports should address the conduct of the offender[129] and the risk or likelihood that the offender would reoffend or present an undue risk to the safety and security of the public if released.[130] In addition, such reports can be directed to address the extent to which the person has been rehabilitated and would, if released on parole, be capable of reintegrating into society.[131] It is anticipated that such reports would be persuasive as to the granting of a parole order to the prisoner or not. Key to the granting of a parole order

---

[122] ibid xxxi.
[123] O'Malley (n 6) 223.
[124] Parole Act 2019, s 13(2)(a).
[125] Parole Act 2019, s 13(2)(c).
[126] Irish Prison Service (n 59) 4.
[127] Irish Penal Reform Trust, Progress in the Penal System – A framework for penal reform (2017) 81.
[128] Frank Porporino, 'A Review of the Psychology Service within the Irish Prison Service'. *New Connections: Embedding Psychology Services and Practice in the Irish Prison Service* (T3 Associates Inc 2015).
[129] Parole Act 2019, s 13(3)(b).
[130] Parole Act 2019, s 13(3)(c).
[131] Parole Act 2019, s 13(3)(c)(ii).

is the consideration of risk of committing further criminal offences, failing to comply with conditions attaching to the parole order or presenting an undue risk to the safety and security of members of the public (including the relevant victim).[132] It is accordingly vital that prisoners are in a position to show that they have been properly prepared for eventual release and given whatever help or incentives they need to refrain from crime once they are at liberty.[133] This assistance, from the Probation Service and other prison based therapeutic services, focuses on the prisoner's offence focussed needs, as identified by the application of risk assessment processes and matches the offender's needs to therapeutic interventions to aid rehabilitation. Today, there are targeted treatment programmes in operation and research has demonstrated that many drug and alcohol, sex offending and violence treatment programmes are effective. The parole process and/or the prospect of obtaining temporary release or a parole order provides an incentive for offenders to participate in such programmes in the knowledge that their failure to do so will reduce their chances of parole or temporary release significantly.

The role and purpose of conditions attaching to a grant of temporary release or a parole order in Ireland are generally achieved through a combination of general and specific conditions. In recommending the imposition of conditions attached to such releases the Parole Board are engaging in short-term risk management and also trying to effect long-term behavioural reform. Currently, all prisoners obtaining temporary release are required to keep the peace, be of good behaviour and sober habits and comply with any additional conditions which may be set.[134] The Parole Act 2019 sets out a non-exhaustive list of conditions which include that the parolee submit to supervision by the Probation Service, that the person resides or remains in a particular district or place in the State, refrains from attending at such premises or other place as the order may specify and refrains from having any contact with such person or persons as the order may specify.[135] These suggested conditions however, do not impinge on the powers of the statutory Parole Board to set any conditions they feel appropriate having regard to the circumstances of the case.[136] Such an approach can be criticised as being vague

[132] Parole Act 2019, s 13(3)(c).
[133] Thomas O'Malley, *Sentencing Law and Practice* (Thomson Round Hall 2006) 41.
[134] See Prisoners (Temporary Release) Rules 2004: SI No 680/2004. See also Speech of Noel Teacy TD, Minister of State at the Department of Justice, Seanad Debates Volume 128 – 16 May 1991, Prison Services.
[135] Parole Act 2019, s 28(4).
[136] Parole Act 2019, s 28(1)(d)(i).

and allowing for too much discretion by the authorities.[137] By recommending conditions, the Irish Parole Board is attempting to ensure that offenders are provided with supervision and support levels proportionate to their level of perceived risk and the likelihood of reoffending. However, it is clear these conditions may waver between help and regulation with control orientated conditions perhaps taking precedence.[138] Prior to the enactment of the Parole Act 2019 the Irish courts confirmed the Minister for Justice's entitlement to attach conditions to the granting of temporary release, subject to such conditions not being capricious, arbitrary or unjust.[139] The Minister's powers in this regard were specifically considered in the case of *Breathnach v Minister for Justice, Equality and Law Reform*[140] where the applicant was granted temporary release on condition that he remained handcuffed during his release. The applicant challenged the right of the Minister for Justice to impose such a condition however the court rejected this challenge and concluded that the setting of conditions was at the Minister's discretion 'subject to any conditions which he wishes to impose',[141] and it was not necessary for the Minister to give reasons for the imposition of conditions attaching to the grant of a period of temporary release. It remains to be seen whether the statutory Parole Board will have so wide a discretion in the imposition of conditions when it is operating in a determinative capacity as opposed to merely advising the Minister for Justice in the exercise of a discretionary power and it appears that the conditions attached to such parole orders must be necessary and proportionate for the purposes of ensuring public safety and/or prevention of crime.[142] Additionally, it should be noted that if refusing an application for parole the Parole Board is required to include reasons for the decision and similarly, if the Parole Board varies a condition attaching to a parole order such a decision must be in writing and include reasons for the decision.[143] Accordingly, it appears that

---

137 Diarmuid Griffin and Ian O'Donnell, 'The Life Sentence and Parole' (2012) 52 Brit J Criminol 611–629.

138 Keith Jobson, 'Fair Procedure in Parole' (1972) 22(4) Univ Toronto L J 267-303, 282.

139 See judgment of Murray CJ in *Lynch & Whelan v Minister of Justice* [2010] IESC 34; [2012] 1 IR 1, where he quotes from Fennelly J in *Dowling v Minister for Justice Equality and Law Reform* [2003] 2 IR 535.

140 [2004] 3 IR 336.

141 ibid, 343 per Ó Caoimh J.

142 James Mehigan, 'Parole Reform and the ECHR', Address to IPRT Prison Law Seminar (22 October 2012) 10, where *R (Craven) v Secretary of State for the Home Department and the Parole Board* [2001] EWHC 850 (Admin) is discussed.

143 Parole Act 2019, s 31(3).

fair procedures could also dictate that reasons are required for the attachment of onerous conditions to a parole order.[144]

A key purpose of parole conditions, in addition to long-term behavioural change, is that of on-going risk management. It must be remembered that risk of serious harm is a dynamic concept and it is vital that it is kept under regular review. The conditions attached to the granting of parole enables the risk assessment process to be ongoing throughout the period of temporary release and allows the supervising personnel (the Probation Service) to respond quickly to deteriorating behaviour and hence escalating risk. Factors which are highly relevant in this regard include whether the offender is already failing to comply with the conditions attached to their parole order and also whether the circumstances in which the offender has committed harmful acts in the past are now reappearing. As previously stated, life sentence prisoners are released on temporary release and for the rest of their natural lives they are liable to recall to prison to serve the balance of their sentence in prison[145] without necessarily committing any further offence, but simply on the grounds that their behaviour has given cause for concern. In Ireland, to date, it has been the practice of the Interim Parole Board to take cognisance of the facts which gave rise to a revocation of temporary release regardless of whether such facts disclosed a criminal offence or not; on occasion they have based their refusal of a further grant of parole on the existence of 'suspicious circumstances'.[146] The Parole Act 2019 states that a parole order can be revoked if the parolee 'poses an undue risk to the safety and security of the public' and if such a risk justifies the revocation of the parole order.[147] This assessment and management of the risk of harm is an area where tensions between the rights of the offender and risks to the community are often present. The right of a person to privacy and to a fresh start after a custodial sentence are balanced against the rights of the wider public to be protected from harmful offenders. In this regard a parole order must be considered a 'conditional release' as opposed to 'early release'. The general principle appears to be that public and victim protection outweighs the offender's rights and this is justified on

---

144 Parole Act 2019, s 30(1)(c).

145 See National Probation Service – West Midlands. Handbook on 'The Life Sentence', 13 which states that 5% of people serving life sentences in the United Kingdom are recalled licencees.

146 Gordon Holmes, 'The Parole System in Ireland – an Overview' a speech given at the Judicial Studies Institute, Annual Supreme Court and High Court Conference (19 June 2009). See also Wheatley Balme and others, *Observations on the Treatment of Convicts in Ireland* (Simkin Marshall & Co 1862) xiii.

147 Parole Act 2019, s 33(1)(a)(i).

the basis of 'risk of harm'.[148] International research has clearly shown that a managed parole programme after release, subject to imminent recall to prison for default, is three to four times more effective in preventing reoffending when compared with releasing the offender at the end of their sentence without parole conditions and supervision.[149]

When Parole Boards attach conditions to parole orders they are attached with the dual aim of fostering short-term risk management and also long-term behavioural reform.[150] To the extent that conditions attached to the granting of a parole order create a 'roadmap' for future actions by the offender the placing of conditions upon offenders is one of the most fundamental things that releasing authorities do.[151] The earliest uses of 'parole', in the original French context of *parole d'honneur* was utilised with prisoners of war and it had merely one condition — do not take arms up against us again — however in the current use of the term parole it appears the criminal justice system has become preoccupied with the idea of meeting many objectives and curing many ills by attaching ever increasing numbers of conditions

---

148 See Hazel Kemshall, Bernadette Wilkinson and Gill Mackenzie, *Risk of Harm Guidance and Training Resources* Version 4.36 (De Montfort Univ 2011). See also *R (Brooke) v Parole Board* [2008] EWCA Civ 29, where the English courts stated: 'Judging whether it is necessary for the protection of the public that a prisoner be confined is often no easy matter. The test is not black and white. It does not require that a prisoner be detained until the board is satisfied that these is *no* risk that he will reoffend. What is necessary for the protection of the public is that the risk of reoffending is at a level that does not outweigh the hardship of keeping a prisoner detained after he has served the term commensurate with his fault. Deciding whether this is the case is the board's judicial function.' See also *R v Parole Board ex parte Watson* [1996] 1 WLR 906, 916-917 where the English courts stated: 'In exercising this practical judgement {whether or not to grant release] the board is bound to approach its task under the two sections in the same way, balancing the hardship and injustice of continuing to imprison a man who is unlikely to cause serious harm to the public against the need to protect the public against a man who is not unlikely to cause such injury. In other than a clear case this is bound to be a difficult and very anxious judgment. *But in the final balance the board is bound to give preponderant weight to the need to protect innocent members of the public against any significant risk of serious injury.*' (emphasis added).

149 Agnieszka Martynowicz and Martin Quigley, 'It's like stepping on a landmine...' Reintegration of Prisoners in Ireland (Irish Penal Reform Trust 2010) 12.

150 Mario Paparozzi and Roger Guy, 'The Giant That Never Woke: Parole Authorities as the Lynchpin to Evidence-Based Practices and Prisoner Re-entry' (2009) 25(4) J Contemporary Crim Justice 405.

151 R Stroker, 'Imposing Conditions Driven by Evidence Based Practices', Paper delivered at Association of Paroling Authorities International Annual Conference, Providence, Rhode Island (21 May 2013) 3.

to the granting of parole.[152] It appears that there are standard conditions imposed with all grants of parole and the number of these standard conditions varies by jurisdiction. The Parole Act 2019 empowers the Parole Board to specify conditions, where it considers it appropriate, to which all parolees, or a specified class of parolees, shall be subject.[153] These conditions are in addition to the requirement that the person does not commit an offence while on parole.[154]

Internationally, in addition to these standard conditions frequently there are special conditions which are additionally imposed in particular cases creating extra requirements or prohibitions for the offender.[155] It is envisaged that the situation in Ireland will reflect this international norm and the Parole Act 2019 provides for the attachment of conditions to the parole order 'as may be specified… having regard to the circumstances of the case.'[156] In many jurisdictions it appears that over time the standard conditions have expanded and it seems that an attitude of it being better to add to general conditions rather than to take some away has developed giving rise to the question — is it *necessary* to have all of these standard conditions in *every* case?[157] Research has shown that the sheer weight of numerous conditions makes it more difficult for the average parolee to succeed and may encourage the parolee to believe that they cannot meet all of the requirements.[158] The benefits in imposing only conditions directly relevant to an individual's case as opposed to imposing standard conditions on everybody is that such conditions appropriately proportion punishment to offence severity and by only imposing relevant 'special' conditions monitoring is much more focussed on these risk factors rather than the offender's general behaviour.[159] In England there is established jurisprudence that any conditions imposed cannot be overly broad in their restrictions of a person's movement or activity and a 'blunderbuss' approach restricting all sorts of behaviour is not permitted.[160] Such a 'blunderbuss' approach would appear to ignore the principle set out in the European Prison Rules that

---

152 Stroker (n 151) 28.
153 Parole Act 2019, s 14(1)(i).
154 Parole Act 2019, s 28(1)(d)(iii).
155 Stroker (n 151) 25.
156 Parole Act 2019, s 28(1)(d)(i).
157 Stroker (n 151) 37.
158 Stroker (n 151) 40.
159 Joan Petersilia and Susan Turner, 'Intensive Probation and Parole (1993) 17 Crime and Justice 323.
160 *R v Boness and Babbington and Others* [2005] TLR 1, as discussed in Mary Rogan, 'The Innocence Rights of Sentenced Offenders' (2011) 55 Irish Journal of Legal Studies 64.

'restrictions placed on a person's liberty should be the minimum necessary and proportionate to the legitimate objective for which they are imposed'.[161]

## Problems with Parole Conditions

An overarching consideration when a Parole Board is setting conditions is the nature of the offences committed by the offender, as well as the individual characteristics and needs of the particular offender. In this regard it must be noted that the Irish prison population is not only characterised by disproportionately representing a relatively limited range of socio-economically disadvantaged areas, but also by having a disproportionate prevalence of mental illness, addiction issues and similar markers of disadvantage.[162] In considering parole conditions, it must be remembered that the individuals to whom they will apply may face challenges in relation to critical life skills and may possess antisocial values and attitudes. Furthermore, they frequently display a lack of history of success with jobs, education and relationships and may have difficulty following rules. Parolees may have been ill prepared for regular employment before being incarcerated and the prison experience in many cases will further damage their likelihood of obtaining employment.[163] The traits which make employment difficult to obtain for many parolees are often combined with housing and other immediate re-entry problems as well as drink and drug dependence issues.[164] As well as discrimination, if an average offender has such numerous problems and needs it is likely that such issues have evolved over many years. It is also likely that only some of these issues may be related to criminal behaviour and accordingly it is worth considering how many of these substantial issues one person can work on at the same time? Examples of inappropriate condition setting include overloading the offender with multiple conditions that are each difficult to achieve and in some cases may be completely irrelevant to the offence for which the offender was committed.[165] It must be recognised that if a Parole Board expects a parolee to get a job, or go to school, or to

[161] The European Prison Rules 2006, No 3. This rule applies to persons deprived of their liberty but the principle applied is the same.

[162] Oireachtas Joint Committee on Justice, Defence and Equality (n 29) at Appendix Five, 8, in the transcript of Liam Herrick's evidence of 23 November 2011. See also Inspector of Prisons, Healthcare in Irish Prisons – Report by Judge Michael Reilly, Inspector of Prisons (2016) 13.

[163] John K Irwin, *The Warehouse Prison – Disposal of the New Dangerous Class* (Roxbury Publishing Co 2005) 198.

[164] Stroker (n 151) 27.

[165] ibid 14.

participate in a treatment programme, some time has to be spent doing that. In addition to the things that a Parole Board might expect, the parolee may have to be a parent, care-giver, or perform some other important duties.[166] It must be considered that by attaching numerous parole conditions even more opportunities for the offender to fail whilst under supervision are created. Simply put, the more numerous and the more demanding the parole conditions are, the more likely the parolee will be found to breach the conditions.[167] Accordingly, if the Parole Board is not conscious of the need and value of each condition attached to a prisoner's release the conditions may be a recipe for failure as opposed to a roadmap for success.[168]

Research has shown that in order to encourage a person to work towards a goal that person must believe that the goal is both achievable and appropriate. In this regard it is worth considering that short-term goals may be the best way to help a person move forward towards larger goals.[169] This gives rise to the consideration as to the manner in which the Irish Interim Parole Board traditionally recommended conditions to attach to parole with the entirety of the conditions being decided on a long term basis with no further alterations being possible without the offender being deemed in breach of his conditions, being recalled and new conditions being set after a possibly lengthy remand in prison. The Parole Act 2019 creates the possibility of a different means of deciding these conditions. The Parole Act 2019 provides that the Board may at any time, of its own motion or on application of a specified person (including the Probation Service), vary a condition attaching to a parole order, whether by the alteration, addition or revocation of a condition.[170] This provision provides the opportunity for the Parole Board to consider short-term goals, with appropriate conditions drafted, and the Parole Board setting review dates to subsequently modify these conditions as appropriate.[171]

The relevance of the conditions being imposed on a parolee must also be considered.[172] International research has shown that where

---

166 ibid 35.

167 Ioan Durnescu, 'Experiencing Supervision; From 'Sparing the First Offenders' to 'Punishment in the Community' and Repairing the Harm Done' In Fergus McNeill, Ioan Durnescu and René Butter (eds), *Probation: 12 Essential Questions* (Palgrave Macmillan 2016) 210.

168 Stroker (n 151) 12.

169 ibid 54.

170 Parole Act 2019, s 31(1)(a).

171 Stroker (n 151) 62.

172 ibid 60.

onerous parole conditions are imposed and supervised many offenders chose not to participate in such programmes and instead opt to remain in prison.[173] It seems reasonable that when offenders return to their communities they expect, to a large extent, to return to something akin to their old lives. However intensive probation supervision can transform those old lives radically and the necessity for intense supervision is a matter which the Parole Board is also required to consider.[174]

There is however a balancing act between the exercise of control over the offender on temporary release or parole and fostering the rehabilitation of the offender when drafting these conditions. When designing the conditions to attach to a grant of parole or conditional release it appears that particular emphasis is placed on protective factors which are likely to reduce the risk of reoffending, including family and relationship supports in the community.[175] Notwithstanding the fact that some conditions are drafted as therapeutic aids in the treatment of underlying causes of criminal behaviour, such as conditions in relation to intoxicants,[176] it must nevertheless be understood that the purpose of some other conditions appears to be control focused and consist of *ad hoc* surveillance measures. The use of parole conditions as surveillance and control measures will now be briefly examined.

## The Use of Parole Conditions as Surveillance and Control Measures

As previously noted, parole conditions are frequently utilised as risk management tools and act as control and *ad hoc* surveillance measures. Examples of parole conditions being utilised as control and surveillance measures include conditions requiring reporting to the police, or requiring permission before leaving an area, changing jobs or address.[177] It is worth noting that, in addition, recent developments in electronic tracking devices allow such devices to incorporate not only the tracking of the location of the offender wearing the device but also the drug and alcohol consumption

---

173 Joan Petersilia, 'When Probation Becomes More Dreaded Than Prison' (1990 54 *Federal Probation* 23. See also Petersilia and Turner (n 159) 324.

174 Petersilia and Turner (n 159) 324.

175 Arthur Taft, 'Parole: Principles and Practice of a Prison Release Procedure' (NYU PhD thesis PhD Thesis 1941) 89.

176 Jobson (n 138) 281.

177 ibid 281. See also Koichi Hamai and others, *Probation Round the World – A Comparative Study* (Routledge 1995) 41.

of the offender.[178] The non-statutory Irish Interim Parole Board appeared to approve of the use of such electronic tagging when they stated, in 2009, that electronic tagging could become a consideration for the Board in drafting parole conditions.[179] In this regard the Interim Parole Board further stated that they had no doubt that if a prisoner voluntarily agreed to such tagging it would be easier for them to recommend parole. However, 'implications' would be drawn from a prisoner's refusal to agree to be released subject to being tagged.[180] This issue of electronic tagging is dealt with in greater detail elsewhere in this book (Chapter 10).

In addition to the use of electronic devices as surveillance methods as *ad hoc* parole conditions, other jurisdictions have placed even more onerous conditions on parolees which are aimed at reducing the risk of reoffending behaviour.[181] Examples of such onerous conditions include a prohibition in some jurisdictions on the ownership of computers or of offenders using the internet without permission of their parole officer.[182] It has been noted that the more onerous conditions attached to the granting of parole are frequently matched to the offence profile of the parolee.[183] The Parole Act 2019 envisages conditions being attached based on the offence profile of the applicant and it is stated that the conditions in the parole order will be both applicable to the person to whom the order relates and/or the class of persons to which he or she belongs.[184] This new function of parole appears to have its roots in the media fuelled demand and perceived public need for the community to be protected from criminals which has influenced, if not largely dictated, the shape of recent parole development and the conditions now attached to parole.[185]

Internationally, parole supervision is generally entrusted to probation officers and this is also the position in Ireland. It has however been commented that internationally the probation officer's objectives have appeared to become more identified with societal needs to control, punish, change, and manage offenders

---

178 See George Drake, 'Emerging Technologies for Community Corrections', Paper delivered at Association of Paroling Authorities International Annual Conference, Providence, Rhode Island (21 May 2013).

179 See Parole Board, Annual Report (2009) 6. See also Hamai (n 177) 41.

180 See Parole Board, Annual Report (2009) 6.

181 See Frank Abagnale, *The Art of the Steal* ( Broadway Books 2001) 154 -155.

182 Drake (n 178).

183 John Watt, 'Parole in Ireland – The Way Forward; Experiences from Other Jurisdictions', Paper delivered at Parole Conference, Dublin (25 October 2013).

184 Parole Act 2019, s 28(1)(d)(ii).

185 See Vivian Geiran, 'Defining What We Do: The Meaning of 'Supervision' in Probation' (2011) 8 Irish Probation Journal 19.

who have begun to be seen in the new narrative as risk entities.[186] To the extent that custodial sentences are partially commuted, the general public are demanding continued assurance of protection via the mandatory supervision and surveillance of released prisoners until the expiration of their sentences.[187] As a consequence, the supervision of parolees which advocates of the rehabilitative theory of parole would largely justify as aid and assistance for the resettlement of offenders, has instead come to be seen by many as a simple transfer of control from prison into the community ('custody without bars').[188] In other jurisdictions it has been argued by researchers that parole is now largely being perceived as a cost effective way of imposing long term management on the dangerous.[189] This evolution in the purpose of the parole supervisor from being purely to support the resettlement of an offender to one where the role of the parole supervisor is viewed predominantly as a means of controlling prison populations creates a risk that the supervisory aid and assistance element that the parole supervisor should be providing is at risk of being forgotten or downplayed.[190] The perception that the role of the probation officer has changed is not limited to academics and elements of the general public — research in England and Wales has shown dramatic changes in offender's views of their probation officers with 78% of offenders regarding surveillance as opposed to rehabilitation as the primary purpose of probation.[191]

English researchers have stated that the growing involvement of probation in the political web of punishment is manifested in a much greater preoccupation with risk and harm, public protection, punishing and controlling offenders via tougher and demanding community sentences, and stricter enforcement arrangements.[192] It has been stated in the Irish context that an apparent manifestation of a similar change in approach was the change in nomenclature from the 'Probation and Welfare Service' to the 'Probation Service',[193]

---

[186] ibid.

[187] Keith A Bottomley, 'Parole in Transition: A Comparative Study of Origins, Developments and Prospects for the 1990s' (1990) 12 Crime and Justice 366.

[188] Standing Senate Committee on Legal and Constitutional Affairs, Parole in Canada (Information Canada 1974) 4.

[189] Malcom Feeley and Jonathan Simon, 'The New Penology' in John Muncie, Eugene McLaughlin and Mary Langan (eds), *Criminological Perspectives: A Reader* (Sage Publications 1996) 369.

[190] O'Malley (n 6) 229. See also Anne Worrall, *Punishment in the Community: The Future of Criminal Justice.* (Longman 1997) 64.

[191] Durnescu (n 167) 200.

[192] Philip Whitehead, *Exploring Modern Probation – Social Theory and Organisational Complexity* (The Policy Press 2010) 87.

[193] See Criminal Justice (Community Service)(Amendment) Act 2011, s 13 which

with the withdrawal of emphasis on the welfare function coinciding with increased responsibility for post-release supervision orders and risk assessments.[194] The evolving of the 'Probation and Welfare Service' to the 'Probation Service' has resulted in the services provided to people on probation changing significantly in the last ten years.[195] It has been argued in respect of the similar changes in England and Wales that the shift in the role discharged by the Probation Service in that jurisdiction has left the criminal justice system unbalanced, with too much emphasis on punishment and a void where there should be an agency dedicated to values of befriending and assisting.[196] It has been further stated in respect of the Probation Service in England and Wales that by focussing on risk assessment tools, which are stated to be 'easy' to complete, there is a de-skilling of staff and a loss of people skills.[197] These people skills — such as building relationships, engaging with individuals and probation officers exercising autonomy and discretion when formulating judgements and making decisions about people — have been replaced with a new rationality orientated towards the efficient containment and control of risky populations.[198] This goal of the efficient containment and control of these parolees has led to a concentration on 'measurable indicators of performance', which often tends to remove or substantially curtail the exercise of discretion by individual parole officers and has been shown to make revocation of parole for a technical violation more likely than heretofore.[199]

The use of parole supervision to reduce opportunities to commit crime has reached its zenith in the United States where the concept has been heavily applied in the introduction of intensive supervision programmes (ISPs), a system which employs random

states that: 'officers of the Minister assigned to perform functions in the part of the Department of State for which the Minister is responsible commonly known as the Probation and Welfare Service before the coming into operation of this section shall, on and after that date, be known as the Probation Service and, references in any enactment to the Probation and Welfare Service of that Department of State shall be construed accordingly.'

194 Martynowicz and Quigley (n 149) 36.

195 Anthony Cotter and Carmel Halton, 'Reforming, Reframing or Renaming Irish Probation Practice in the 21st Century', in Alastair Christie and others (eds), *Social Work in Ireland: Challenges and Continuities* (Palgrave Publishing 2015).

196 Whitehead (n 192) 154. See also Gwen Robinson, 'Late-Modern Rehabilitation: The Evolution of a Penal Strategy' (2008) 10(4) Punishment and Society 436 where the replacement of the title 'Probation Officer' with the term 'Offender Manager' is noted.

197 Philip Whitehead, *Modernising Probation and Criminal Justice – Getting the Measure of Cultural Change*. (Shaw & Sons 2007) 88.

198 Whitehead (n 192) 87.

199 Feeley and Simon (n 189) 370.

officer visits, frequent mandatory check-ins and tight curfews to limit parolees' opportunities to break the law.[200] Empirical data seems to validate these intensive supervision programmes, particularly where surveillance and control techniques are combined with rehabilitative services such as drug treatment and support groups.[201] Such an approach, with the emphasis on surveillance of the offender as opposed to assisting the offender's rehabilitation into the community, abandons the view that parole is to act as a normalising influence on the offender to counteract the negative effects of the institutional experience.[202] While on paper 'intense supervision will restrict free time and help foster a structured environment', in practice 'reintegration rarely flourishes in this type of environment' since it promotes 'the continuation of institutionalisation'.[203] The use of such intensive supervision programmes appears to be based on the premise that there is no such thing as an ex-offender, but instead only offenders who have been caught before, will strike again, and accordingly must be kept under constant surveillance.[204] Accordingly, and partially to maintain confidence in the criminal justice system, supervision in the community is considered to be a vital safeguard in the parole system, for after all what is the purpose of attaching conditions to the granting of parole if compliance with those conditions is not subsequently monitored?

## Measuring the Success of Parole Supervision

Research undertaken in America has shown that prisoners who are discharged from prison with no supervision and with no parole conditions are half as likely to be returned to prison as those released on parole with conditions attached. It is clear that increased monitoring provides opportunities for breaches of parole conditions to be discovered and frequent drug testing alone is likely to generate high rates of technical violations.[205] Similarly, the difficulties in complying with onerous parole conditions, including supervision conditions, can in itself create difficulties and make

[200] See Jordan Baker and others, 'A Solution to Prison Overcrowding and Recidivism: Global Positioning System Location of Parolees and Probationers' (Univ Maryland PhD Thesis 2002).

[201] ibid 21.

[202] Public Safety Canada (Archived Content), *History of Conditional Release* (1987) 10.

[203] Dirk Van Zyl Smit and Alessandro Corda 'American Exceptionalism in Parole Release and Supervision' in Kevin R Reitz (ed), *American Exceptionalism in Crime and Punishment* (OUP 2018) 23.

[204] David Garland, *The Culture of Control* (OUP 2001) 142.

[205] Irwin (n 163) 182.

reintegration more difficult for the released prisoner.[206] The total effect of many separate parole conditions may be to create another layer of challenge to what is an already daunting situation for the parolee.[207] The chaotic lives that some former prisoners lead may make breaches of some parole conditions, with such breaches often resulting in minor criminal convictions, particularly likely. In light of this, it is also likely that yet further costly and ineffective short sentences will be imposed on these parolees arising from these minor criminal convictions and attendant breach of their parole conditions.[208] It appears that the interpretation of recidivism rates has changed utterly. High rates of parolees being returned to prison once indicated programme failure, however now it is offered as evidence of efficiency of parole as a control apparatus and the effectiveness of the parole supervision.[209]

Approximately half of those released on parole in America fail to complete their parole successfully and of those parolees returned to prison one third were returned for committing a new crime whilst two thirds of these were returned for violating the conditions of their parole.[210] The number of revocations of parole is increasing and the rate of failure of offenders on parole has given rise to the situation where revocations are now the fastest growing category of prison admissions in America.[211] Approximately half of all the prisoners in American prisons are persons who are imprisoned as a result of violating either the conditions attached to their probation or to their parole,[212] with approximately 40% of those admitted to prison as a consequence of parole violation being incarcerated for violations of the technical conditions of their release.[213] Some research has shown the presence of a historical trend in which the percentage of offenders returned for violation of parole has steadily increased.[214] It is interesting to note that this is not an entirely new phenomenon. Of the offenders who were released under Crofton's system, between 1856 and 1861, who had their parole revoked 36% had their parole revoked because they led 'irregular lives' or had a technical breach of the conditions

---

206 Christine Scott-Hayward, 'The Failure of Parole; Rethinking the Role of the State in Re-entry' (2011) 41(2) New Mexico L Rev 422.
207 ibid 422.
208 Rogan (n 160) 64.
209 Feeley and Simon (n 189) 369.
210 Stroker (n 151) 16.
211 ibid 17.
212 ibid 18.
213 See Matthews, Roger and Young, Jock, Ed. *The New Politics of Crime and Punishment* (Willan Publishing 2003) at 228. See also Elliott Currie, *Crime and Punishment in America* (Metropolitan Books, Henry Holt & Co 1998) 173.
214 Irwin (n 163) 190.

attaching to their licence as opposed to having committed a fresh crime.[215] The current situation, in America, is that in excess of half of new prison admissions result from revocation of community supervision and not from conviction for a new crime.[216] A possible explanation of the increase in revocations for technical breaches of parole as opposed to recidivist actions is a change in management style. It has been noted that courts and other social agencies have been seen to decouple performance evaluation from external social objectives, such as a reduction in crime, and have instead moved to systems which tend to measure their own outputs as indicators of performance. This change in management style has led to a new emphasis on value for money, performance indicators and evaluation of outcomes. Furthermore, probation officers being required to adhere to these management principles will enjoy less discretion than previously.[217] It has been argued that this focus on the quantifiable has led probation officers to neglect some of their less well-defined functions and emphasise the measurable over the holistic, emphasising outputs over outcomes.[218] Similarly, there has been a move away from rehabilitation and treatment to a language of probability and risk and a move away from ideals and values associated with people, towards managerial, technocratic and bureaucratic procedures.[219] These statistics suggest that, in the American context at least, rather than serving as an alternative to imprisonment, community supervision is often no more than continued incarceration in a different setting.[220]

The statistics relating to parole revocation in the United States are all the more startling when it is considered that of the half of individuals who 'succeed' in completing parole many have had violations of conditions and compliance issues at some time during their parole period. In a significant number of instances, breaches are deemed too minor to warrant imprisonment or revocation;[221] so

215 See Wheatley Balme and Others (n 146) 108 in this regard. See also Elizabeth Eileen Dooley, 'Sir Walter Crofton and the Irish or Intermediate System of Prison Discipline' in Ian O'Donnell and Finbarr McAuley (eds), *Criminal Justice History, Themes and Controversies from pre-Independence Ireland* (Four Courts Press 2003) 205.

216 Cecelia Klingele, 'Rethinking the Use of Community Supervision' (2013) 103 J Crim Law & Criminology 1020.

217 Durnescu (n 167) 203.

218 Shane Kilcommins and others, *Crime, Punishment and the Search for Order in Ireland* (Institute of Public Administration 2004) 32.

219 Whitehead (n 197) 46.

220 Klingele (n 216) 1020.

221 Ernest W Burgess, 'Is Prediction Feasible in Social Work – An Inquiry Based upon a Sociological Study of Parole Records' (1928) 7(4) Social Force 536 which details research indicating that even in the 1920s as many parole agreements

accordingly, very few offenders are in complete compliance with all of the conditions of their parole all of the time.[222]

The starkness of the figures indicating failure to complete parole successfully in America are not replicated in Canada where for day parole the success rate was 89.1% with a revocation for breach of condition in 9.3% of cases and a revocation for a non-violent offence in 1.5% and for violent offending in 0.1% of cases. The figures in respect of full parole in Canada indicate a success rate on parole of 76.6%, with revocation for breach of conditions in 17.3% of cases, revocation for committing a non-violent offence in 5.3% of the cases and for committing a violent offence in 0.8% of cases.[223]

It has been shown internationally that there is an onus on paroling authorities to develop strategies to identify offenders who are at a high risk of revocation of parole and ensure these offenders have the appropriate level of support in problem solving techniques to increase their chances of successfully completing parole.[224] Having examined the manner in which the success of the process of supervision is examined it is now necessary to study the systems dealing with breaches of parole conditions and the possible subsequent recall of parolees in Ireland.

## Breaches of Parole Conditions and Recall

The conditions of parole/temporary release, violation of which would provide the basis of parole termination, were historically fault orientated as opposed to treatment orientated. However, in many jurisdictions the revocation clauses now include provisions for revocation if arrest is necessary or desirable not only for a breach of parole but also for the rehabilitation of the offender or the protection of society.[225] Under the Parole Act 2019 the grounds for recall are both fault based, (that the parolee has breached a condition attaching to the parole order)[226] or are treatment based (that the parolee poses an undue risk to the safety and security of

---

were violated on minor and technical grounds as were violated on major grounds.

[222] Stroker (n 151) 34.

[223] Renee Collette, 'Protecting the Community Through the Structured Reintegration of Offenders', Unpublished speech delivered at the 2011 Association of Paroling Authorities International Annual Conference 31.

[224] Renee Collette, 'Few notes for the workshops at the 2006 Annual Conference of the International Corrections & Prisons Association (ICPA) in Vancouver, British Colombia, Canada', unpublished (obtained directly from author).

[225] See Jobson (n 138) 273.

[226] Parole Act 2019, s 33(1)(a)(ii).

the public).[227] The Parole Board additionally have wide powers to vary a condition attaching to a parole order, whether by the alteration, addition or revocation of a condition, subject to such decisions being reasoned and in writing.[228]

The restrictions under which a parolee lives include that the person does not commit an offence while on parole.[229] Additional conditions typically oblige the person to also refrain from certain behaviour not in itself criminal, as well as requiring of him certain behaviour not required, by law at least, from his unconvicted neighbours. An example of this would include abstinence from alcohol.[230] In some jurisdictions, other than Ireland, it has unfortunately been noted that parole conditions are frequently so vague that technical violations are inevitable.[231] It is worth noting however that the Irish courts have stated, in the context of bail, that if a court order potentially results in the loss of liberty the order should be carefully prepared, with any ambiguity being read in favour of the bailee.[232] There is no reason to believe that this principle would not be equally applicable in the context of parole conditions. It should be noted that breaches of the conditions of parole render the parolee liable to be returned to prison and if the breach involves the commission of an act which is an offence in itself, the prisoner may also be sentenced in respect of same. The Parole Act 2019 specifies that a parole order must be in writing and must specify the conditions attached to the conditional release.[233] Having reviewed the role and purpose of conditions attached to a conditional release it is now worth considering how breaches of parole conditions can result in recall from parole and the process by which such an outcome is reached.

## Breaches of Parole Conditions and Recall in Ireland

Similarly to the international position described above, breaches of temporary release conditions in Ireland can result in a recall to the custodial setting. Prior to the enactment of the Parole Act 2019 the Irish Minister for Justice stated that prisoners who had been released to serve their sentences in the community, did so under

---

227 Parole Act 2019, s 33(1)(a)(i).
228 Parole Act 2019, s 31.
229 Parole Act 2019, s 28(1)(d)(iii).
230 Stephen White, 'Alexander Maconochie and the Development of Parole' (1976) 61(1) J Crim Law & Criminology 74.
231 Jobson (n 138) 299.
232 *J O'G v Governor of Cork Prison* [2007] 2 IR 204.
233 Parole Act 2019, s 28(1)(d)(iii).

conditions, and stressed that a breach of any of these conditions would lead to an automatic ending of the temporary release and a consequential return to custody without the necessity of any court proceedings.[234]

In relation to those granted a parole order the situation post the enactment of the Parole Act 2019 is somewhat similar save that the parolee will have the opportunity to present their case at a recall hearing. This process will be described subsequently in this chapter however it is nonetheless vital that a prisoner would not only understand their obligations whilst on either temporary release or parole but also that any release conditions would be realistic and capable of being fulfilled, having regard to the circumstances and characteristics of the person being released.[235] In Ireland, on being granted parole or temporary release the prisoner signs a form acknowledging that they are aware of the terms and conditions of the release, that the terms and conditions have been explained to them and that they are aware of when the period of release expires.[236] Under the Parole Act 2019 recall from parole is made on foot of an application to revoke a parole order. This application can be initiated by the Parole Board at any time, of its own motion or on application by the Probation Service, the Irish Prison Service, the Commissioner of An Garda Síochána, the Minister for Justice or such other person as the Board considers appropriate.[237] In other jurisdictions there are temporal safeguards such as mandating that a revocation hearing by the Parole Board would be held within a specified period of time however there are no such safeguarding time limits within the Irish system save that the matter should be considered by the Board 'as soon as practicable.'[238] The Board, in considering whether to revoke a parole order, shall have regard to such matters as it considers appropriate, including the circumstances giving rise to the consideration of the revocation, any reports requested/furnished, details of any meeting with or representations from the parolee and any representations or submissions from the victim.[239] If the Parole Board is not satisfied that the parolee poses an undue risk to the safety and security of the public, or has breached a condition attaching to the parole order and the revocation of the order is not justified by the gravity of the

[234] See Dáil Debates Vol 528, 12 December 2000 – Written Answer of John O'Donoghue TD, Minister for Justice, Equality and Law Reform to Paul Connaughtan TD.
[235] O'Malley, Thomas (n 133) 296.
[236] Schedule to the Prisoners (Temporary Release) Rules 1960 (SI No 167 of 1960).
[237] Parole Act 2019, s 33(2).
[238] Parole Act 2019, s 36(2). See also Jobson (n 138) 294.
[239] Parole Act 2019, s 33(3).

risk or breach of the condition, as the case may be then the Parole Board may decide to vary some of the conditions attached to the parole order, if appropriate.[240] This related issue of 'risk' is dealt with elsewhere in this book (Chapter 3).

If a parolee has their parole order revoked, to a large extent these prisoners are ineligible for further periods of temporary release until their case has been reconsidered by the Parole Board. The Board, when making the order to revoke parole will include reasons for the decision in their order as well as the time and date at which the revocation shall take effect, and the place to which, the person is to return to prison, and a date, not later than two years after the date of the making of the decision, on which the person shall become eligible again for parole.[241] This further consideration of the case by the Parole Board will necessitate the preparation of further up to date reports and a new hearing.[242]

Research was quoted earlier in this chapter which indicated that approximately half of offenders released on parole in America fail to complete their parole successfully and of those parolees returned to prison one third were returned for committing a new crime whilst two thirds of these offenders were returned for violating the conditions attached to their probation/parole.[243] The disparity in the figures in this regard between the American system and the Canadian system were noted. It should be further noted that the American situation also significantly contrasts with the European norm, where research has shown that approximately 6.3% of committals to prison are as a result of the suspension, revocation or annulment of conditional release.[244] The system relating to the recall of parolees outlined in the Parole Act 2019 has not yet become operational however the rates of recall of parolees from temporary release in Ireland per the system previously operated by the Interim Parole Board were relatively low. In Ireland, of the 18 life sentence prisoners recalled from parole during the period 2001 to 2016, six (33 per cent) were recalled having been charged with a new offence (one theft offence, one burglary offence, one firearm offence, one arson offence and two drug offences).[245] It is unclear whether these

---

[240] Parole Act 2019, s 33(4).

[241] Parole Act 2019, s 33.

[242] John Olden, Report of Mr John Olden on the Management of the Sentences of Thomas Murray, Life Sentenced Prisoner, 2 April 2001. See also Michael McDowell TD, Minister for Justice, Equality and Law Reform, Dáil Éireann, Written Answers – Prison Sentence Management, 9 October 2002.

[243] Stroker (n 151) 16.

[244] Van Zyl Smit and Corda (n 203) 2.

[245] See Griffin (n 86) 93.

charges were pursued to conviction or whether they were simply treated as a breach of conditions following an inquiry by the prison governor. The remaining recalled parolees were recalled for failing to be of sober habits or breach of an 'other' condition.[246] These statistics, together with the official statistic that only one offender reoffended in the first six years of operation of the Interim Parole Board may possibly be misleading as on occasion when offending behaviour is brought to the attention of the gardaí they may not always charge the parolee with the appropriate offence, for example such as being drunk and disorderly or theft, but instead revoke their temporary release.[247] It is however important to note that whilst the recalls of prisoners analysed herein is for the period 2001 to 2016 the recalls may relate to prisoners released prior to the establishment of the Interim Parole Board in 2001 and may not accordingly be an accurate indicator of the success or failure of the decision-making of the Interim Parole Board. By way of contrast, in England and Wales in 2012 an additional charge for an offence was the reason for the recall of life sentence prisoners in 25 per cent of cases.[248]

It is unclear whether the remarkably low rate of reoffending in Ireland by offenders released on parole is because of the threat of recall or due to some more positive feature of supervision.[249] Regardless of the reason for such a low rate of reoffending, it should be noted that this figure compares very favourably to the statistics for the general prison population in Ireland which shows a much higher overall recidivism rate for offenders after three years.[250] However, the rate of recalling prisoners released on parole in Ireland may be higher than the official statistics would suggest with the discrepancy being explained by the fact that some prisoners have their parole cancelled by merely not being given further temporary release, as opposed to being recalled from temporary release.[251] The system established under the Parole Act 2019 should bring greater transparency to this situation in relation to prisoners granted parole orders at least.

---

246 Griffin (n 93) 34.

247 ibid.

248 ibid.

249 Walker (n 107) 206.

250 Probation Service, Recidivism Study 2008-2013 (Probation Service Research Report 4, 2013) 6, which states that the figure for the 2008-2013 cohort was 41%. The CSO updated this figure for the 2009 cohort on 14 December 2015 which declared a recidivism rate of 47.5%. See Central Statistics Office. www.cso.ie/en/releasesandpublications/er/prir/prisonerrecidivism2009cohort/. 6 July 2018.

251 See Seán Aylward, 'Observations on Olden Report by Director General of the Irish Prisons Service', July 2001, reproduced in John Olden, Report of Mr John Olden on the Management of the Sentences of Thomas Murray, Life Sentenced Prisoner, 2 April 2001.

Whilst the Parole Act 2019 provides certainty to prisoners granted a parole order prisoners who are not eligible for consideration by the Parole Board may continue to be granted temporary release by the Minister for Justice under the Criminal Justice Act 1960, s 2. In circumstances where it is necessary to revoke the temporary release status of a prisoner granted temporary release (as opposed to not granting further periods of temporary release) the legal basis for such a recall is the Criminal Justice Act 1960, s 6(1) which sets out that a person on temporary release is regarded as being unlawfully at large if the period for which they were granted temporary release has expired or if a condition to which their release was made subject was broken. A member of the Garda Síochána may arrest without warrant a person whom they suspect to be unlawfully at large[252] and the fact that the consequences for non-compliance with the parole conditions are so draconian emphasises the need to ensure that appropriate temporary release conditions are set.[253] In the event that it is required to consider recalling these offenders from temporary release it is necessary to consider what process is required pursuant to the Criminal Justice Act 1960, s 6(1) in this regard.

If circumstances arise in which it is necessary to consider revoking temporary release in Ireland both the High Court and the Supreme Court have held that fair procedures are required in respect of any such revocation.[254] This position results from the fact that a person who has been granted temporary release is entitled to their freedom unless the period of their release has expired or a condition of which their release was subject to has been broken.[255] Having regard to the effect on the prisoner of the revocation of their temporary release a hearing into an allegation that they were in breach of the terms of a condition attaching to their temporary release is required. This is also the situation in other countries[256] and has given rise to the distinction of there being no entitlement to due process being created when applying for temporary release whereas there is a right to due process in circumstances where temporary release is being revoked.

---

252 Criminal Justice Act 1960, s 6(3).

253 Stroker (n 151) 5.

254 *State (Murphy) v Kielt* [1984] IR 458, sub nom *State (Murphy) v Governor of St Patrick's Institution* [1982] ILRM 475 (HC) and [1985] ILRM 141 (SC).

255 Cathal O'Braonáin, 'Stone Walls do not a prison make' (2007) 101(5) GLSI 40 where the circumstances of *State (Murphy) v Governor of St. Patrick's Institution* are discussed.

256 Dirk Van Zyl Smit and Alessandro Corda (n 203) 9, where it is noted that the American Supreme Court has ruled that parolees have only limited rights to due process when being considered for parole but have extensive due process rights in the event of revocation of parole in their jurisdiction.

There is a crucial difference between release on temporary release and revocation of temporary release, the distinction is between being deprived of a liberty which one has, as in temporary release, and being denied a conditional liberty which one desires.[257] Similarly to other countries,[258] these temporary release revocation hearings are not required to be anything in the nature of a judicial determination and an informal procedure is all that is required. However, such a procedure should ensure that any evidence against the prisoner is presented to them and that they be given sufficient time to prepare and present their defence.[259]

In Ireland, prisoners who have been granted temporary release and in whose cases it is proposed to revoke their temporary release are only afforded the benefit of the hearing of their case before the Prison Governor. In this informal hearing the pertinent finding to be made by the Prison Governor is whether a condition of the temporary release has been breached, and if so, the temporary release is revoked.[260] In deciding to revoke temporary release it is not necessary that the conduct which is being utilised to justify the recall has resulted in successful criminal proceedings[261] nor that the nature of the conduct alleged be of a criminal nature in itself.[262] In cases of recall where the focus may be on behaviour that is deemed to be a pattern of conduct posing considerable risk to the community but which may not in itself be either a criminal offence or a breach of specific temporary release conditions, then a full temporary release revocation hearing is desirable in terms of promoting both transparency and accountability. Frequently in such circumstances the person who has obtained temporary release may be relatively poorly educated, without adequate resources and in need of legal representation if they are to have any real influence on the discretionary decision affecting their future liberty.[263] Internationally, it has been argued that the issue to be

257 Paul A McDermott, *Prison Law* (Round Hall 2000) 418, where the judgment of Burger J in *Greenholtz v Inmates of the Nebraska Penal and Correctional Complex* (1979) 442 US 1, 9 is quoted.

258 Thomas G Blomberg and Karol Lucken, *American Penology – A History of Control* (Aldine Transaction 2010) 158, where the position in America is noted as there being very significant safeguards for the offender whose parole status is being revoked however these due process standards do not reach the level afforded at a full criminal trial.

259 McDermott (n 257) 410 – 414.

260 Griffin (n 93).

261 See also Taft (n 175) 17.

262 See Jon van Dyke, 'Parole Revocation Hearings in California: The Right to Counsel' (1971) 59 (1215) *California L Rev* 1215-1217 which discusses the case of *In Re Tucker* 5 Cal 3d 171, 486 P2d 657, 95 Cal Rptr 761 (1971).

263 See Jobson (n 138). See also MacBride, Sean, *Crime and Punishment* (Ward River Press, 1982) at 40

decided at revocation of temporary release hearings should not be whether there has been a breach of the conditions attached to the temporary release but whether the breach of conditions has been so significant as to constitute a serious threat to the community or not. In such hearings it has been stated that in identifying what evidence is relevant, in correcting errors and in identifying mitigating factors, the opportunity of a hearing with the assistance of a lawyer would be of major assistance to the offender who had been granted temporary release.[264]

This mechanism of revocation of temporary release is replete with numerous problems, including uncertainty over the standard of proof to be applied. To overcome these problems the Department of Justice introduced a system of merely not granting further periods of temporary release as opposed to revoking a grant of temporary release. This system incorporated a policy of granting very short periods of (reviewable) temporary release rather than one extended period of release. The Department of Justice then set themselves the regular task of deciding whether to grant the parolee a fresh period of temporary release as opposed to deciding whether an extended period of temporary release should be revoked. In the normal course of events, in the event of a failure to renew a period of temporary release the parolee has no real chance to refute the charges against them or to present evidence of mitigating circumstances, has no right to counsel, nor a right of confrontation and cross-examination or the right to an independent, impartial adjudication of the facts.

The constitutionality of this practice was upheld in the case of *Ryan v Governor of Limerick Prison*[265] however it was held in the subsequent case of *Sherlock v Governor of Mountjoy*[266] that if an applicant was granted the renewal of their temporary release on a sufficient number of occasions they may well develop a legitimate expectation to get a further renewal of their temporary release. In the event that they do not do so then they are entitled to be furnished with the reasons for the failure to renew the temporary release and to answer any allegations so put.[267] This system operates in practice by the Probation Service, where applicable, providing a report to the Prison Service reporting on reintegration, resettlement and risk management issues arising or the breach of any conditions

---

[264] Jobson (n 138) 299-300.
[265] [1988] IR 198.
[266] [1991] 1 IR 451.
[267] McDermott (n 257) 415-416.

of release.[268] In practice, a life sentence prisoner on 'reviewable temporary release' was unlikely to be recalled or refused additional periods of temporary release unless there was a breach of the conditions attached to a previous temporary release.[269] However the Irish Prison Service have stressed, following advice from the Attorney General, that life sentenced prisoners must remain amenable to supervision and recall by the Minister for Justice during the currency of their temporary release.[270]

The issues of fair procedure identified above have been largely dealt with in the manner in which recall hearings will be held for the holders of parole orders however the issues remain in respect of prisoners who have been released on temporary release. An example of the operation of this system is the Community Return Scheme where a failure to adequately engage in the scheme will lead to the Temporary Release not being renewed. This procedure has the attraction that it does not involve any hearing or enquiry to which the rules of constitutional justice would apply, whereas the revocation of an existing temporary release does.[271] It is worth comparing the situation faced by these released prisoners with the analogous situation of proceedings to terminate probation, which proceedings are conducted in a judicial manner complete with a fair hearing, right to representation and the right to introduce evidence and to conduct cross-examination of witnesses before the court. There is a recognition, in this instance, that where an action is being taken which could affect the individual's rights and liberty, it is imperative that such actions are in accordance with the rules of fundamental fairness and natural justice. The similarities between the prisoner on temporary release and probationer are that both are at liberty in the community under supervision, subject to certain conditions and it is difficult to adduce a persuasive reason for granting a hearing and due process in one case and not in the other.[272] The procedural safeguards introduced in the Parole Act 2019 for those prisoners granted a parole order affords this cohort of prisoners some certainty however issues of procedural fairness can still arise for those released on temporary release.

## Conclusion

Having considered a definition of parole, this chapter mapped

---

[268] Griffin (n 86) 32.
[269] ibid.
[270] Irish Prison Service (n 59) 13.
[271] McDermott (n 257) 413.
[272] Jobson (n 138) 296. See also the US case of *Morrissey v Brewer* (1972) S Ct 2593.

the development of parole and proceeded to differentiate parole from remission and other forms of early release from custodial sentences in the Irish criminal justice system. This chapter examined the various types of temporary release granted in Ireland and considered the eligibility criteria for being considered for parole both in the previous non-statutory system operated by the Interim Parole Board and also pursuant to the Parole Act 2019. The principal functions of the Irish Parole Board were examined and an in-depth examination of the processes utilised by both the Irish Parole Board and the Interim Parole Board were considered. In addition, this chapter then studied the decision-making criteria previously utilised by the Interim Parole Board and the Minister for Justice and further considered the statutory criteria contained in the Parole Act 2019.

As this book is focussed on the role of probation and parole in the Irish criminal justice system this chapter examined the reintegration of prisoners into the community in Ireland and the supervisory role and function discharged by probation officers in relation to parolees and those on temporary release. In this regard the purpose of release conditions in so far as it affects the cohort of prisoners who have been granted temporary release or a parole order following review by the Parole Board was studied. This examination of parole conditions in Ireland included studying the types of conditions which can be set by the Parole Board. Various problems which can arise from the imposition of parole conditions were considered, including the use of these conditions for purposes other than the aiding and assisting of the parolee and instead as a surveillance and control tool. The manner in which 'success' on parole is measured was considered and the chapter proceeded to examine breaches of parole conditions and the attendant recall of parolees and persons on temporary/conditional release and the processes utilised therein. Whilst there was a focus in this chapter on what happens when breaches of conditions attached to a parole order occur many of the issues raised in this regard are also relevant to the breach of probation orders and other supervisory functions which the Probation Service discharges.

An examination of the nature of the supervisory role discharged by the Probation Service in relation to parole orders and temporary release as disclosed in this chapter clearly set out the conditional nature of parole. In the next chapter, other forms of post-release supervision will be examined and placed within the criminal justice system.

CHAPTER 8

# OTHER TYPES OF CONDITIONAL RELEASE AND POST-RELEASE SUPERVISION

## Introduction

It has been suggested that supervision of offenders on probation and parole, and other forms of post-release supervision of offenders, may only be effective in reducing further offending while the person is actually on supervision and the sanction of recall to either the criminal courts or prison is possible.[1] In relation to those who receive custodial sentences for their offending, international studies have shown that there is a significantly lower reconviction rate for offenders released on parole, for example, compared to those who have not been paroled.[2] In this regard, it must be remembered that the mandatory life sentence for murder[3] ensures that those who obtain temporary release from such a sentence are subject to the possibility of being recalled to prison for any breach of conditions pertaining to their release and are subject to supervision by a probation officer for the rest of their lives.[4] If the parolee or person on some other form of supervised conditional release is serving a sentence of imprisonment for a determinate term only, the possibility of recall to prison has effect until the sentence of imprisonment expires.[5]

Similarly, the threat of recall to the criminal courts on foot of a breach of a probation order is limited to the duration of the order.

---

1 Tom Ellis and Peter Marshall, 'Does Parole Work? A Post-Release Comparison of Reconviction Rates for Paroled and Non-Paroled Prisoners' (2000) 33(3) Aust NZ J Criminol 309.

2 Ellis and Marshall (n 1) 310 and 311.

3 Criminal Justice Act 1990, s 2.

4 See Parole Board, Annual Report (2016) 43. See also *Lynch and Whelan v Minister for Justice* [2012] 1 IR 1 where Murray CJ stated: 'It is a sentence which subsists for the entire life of the person convicted of murder. That person may, by virtue of the discretionary power vested in the executive be temporarily released under the provisions of the relevant legislation on humanitarian or other grounds but he or she always remains liable to imprisonment on foot of the life sentence should the period of temporary release be terminated for good and sufficient reason.'

5 Parole Act 2019, s 28(3)(i).

The actual practice of supervision of life-sentenced offenders who are serving their sentences under licence in the community is undertaken by the Probation Service in accordance with a protocol agreed between the Probation Service, the Irish Prison Service and An Garda Síochána. The Probation Service also supervises other offenders in the community who have been released on parole/conditional release/temporary release. In addition, the Service supervises those who have been convicted and receive a post-release supervision order, which is different in a number of ways to the various types of conditional release from a custodial sentence. Chapter 7 considered in detail the history, development, law and practice regarding the specific conditional release programme that is parole. The present chapter will discuss other types of early/conditional release that incorporate probation supervision, as well as post-release supervision under the Sex Offenders Act 2001. The specific provisions for supervision of children and young people following a period of time in custody, under the provisions of the Children Act 2001, are addressed separately in Chapter 9 on Children and Young People.

## Categories of Early and Conditional Release and Post-Release Supervision

For many years, the Criminal Justice Act 1960 (as amended) provided the only legislative basis for early release from a custodial sentence — *temporary release* — which could be used for a variety of reasons including specifically for resocialisation, rehabilitation and reintegration in the community of the person in custody. The Criminal Justice Act 1960, and specifically its provisions for the granting of temporary release, are addressed in more detail, specifically with regard to how the provision is used in relation to parole decisions, in Chapter 7, on Parole. A key aspect of temporary release, whether supervised by the Probation Service or not, is that the process of deciding on and managing such release, including the issue of recall where that may arise, is ultimately a matter for the Executive — the Minister, Department of Justice or the Irish Prison Service, subject to the rules requiring fair procedure as outlined in Chapter 7. The recall of prisoners released on foot of a parole order is a matter for the Parole Board, using the recall procedures described in Chapter 7.

Temporary Release may be granted for any period of time with or without supervision conditions attached. Additional conditions to the 'standard' ones may also be imposed, in both cases involving supervision and those without supervision. The present publication is only concerned with conditional release that incorporates supervision by a probation officer as one of its conditions of being granted. Over time, the provisions of the 1960 (temporary release) legislation proved themselves quite flexible and adaptable to a range of new schemes and programmes. Temporary telease came in turn, to be further adapted as the legislative basis for the community return (see more on this in Chapter 5, on Community Service) and community support programmes, as well as the Joint Agency Response to Crime (JARC) initiative (see Chapter 11) and electronic monitoring as a condition of early release from prison in certain cases (see Chapter 10 on Electronic Monitoring). All of these latter programmes have been founded on and facilitated, either fully or in part, by the 1960 temporary release legislation. The issue of early or conditional release of those under eighteen years of age is covered in Chapter 9 on Children and Young People.

## Other Forms of Court-Ordered Post-Release Supervision

While the post-release supervision described in the two immediately preceding paragraphs all involve an executive decision to release someone who still has part of their prison sentence to serve, before they have reached their remission date, there are two other types of post-release supervision, which have very different legislative bases and other key differences in their imposition as well as in relation to issues of breach and recall. These are the post-release supervision order under the Sex Offenders Act 2001 and the part-suspended sentence supervision order under the Criminal Justice Act 2006. The former of these is *additional* to a custodial sentence, while the latter involves the *suspension* of a portion of the custodial sentence itself, on certain conditions.

## Post-Release Supervision Orders Under the Sex Offenders Act 2001

Probation Service supervision of sex offenders in the community, following their release from prison at the expiry of their custodial sentence, is covered by the seven sections of part 5 of the Sex Offenders Act 2001. Specifically, the Sex Offenders Act 2001, s 28 mandates that a sentencing court in specific cases *must* consider imposing a post-release supervision order, as set out in the following section of the Act:

> 28. – (1) In determining the sentence to be imposed on a sex

offender in respect of the sexual offence concerned, the court shall consider whether to impose a sentence involving post-release supervision.

(2) In considering that matter, the court shall have regard to –

(a) the need for a period, after the offender has been released into the community, during which his or her conduct is supervised by a responsible person,

(b) the need to protect the public from serious harm from the offender,

(c) the need to prevent the commission by the offender of further sexual offences, and

(d) the need to rehabilitate the offender.

(3) For the purposes of this section, the court may, if it thinks necessary to do so, receive evidence or submissions from any person concerned.

The early-identified implications of the Sex Offender Act 2001 for the work of the Probation Service, specifically in relation to the management of those persons convicted of sexual offences, were outlined and discussed by Cotter *et al*,[6] who highlighted the emphasis of such legal provisions on maximising offender rehabilitation and reintegration, as well as their goal of '... enhancing public safety by protecting the community and reducing victimisation.'[7]

Section 29 of the 2001 Act sets out the powers of a court in imposing a post-release supervision order and the 'terms and conditions' of such orders. A post-release supervision order, while it must be imposed at the time of sentencing, is effectively a separate component of the sentence (to the custodial element), and qualitatively different to a part-suspended supervision order (see below). The duration and conditions of such a post-release supervision order are left, under the terms of the 2001 Act, to the discretion of the sentencing judge. Nevertheless, the post-release supervision period shall be for the purposes identified in s 28(2) of the Act (see above), and be 'for a specified term', during which 'the offender shall be under the supervision of a probation and welfare officer and requiring the offender to comply with such conditions

---

6 Anthony Cotter, Úna Doyle and Paul Linnane, 'Sex Offenders Act 2001: Implications for the Probation and Welfare Service, Policy and Practice' (2005) 2(1) Irish Probation Journal 78-83.

7 Cotter, Doyle and Linnane (n 6) 78.

as are specified in the sentence for securing that supervision.' [8] In addition, 'the aggregate of the sentence of imprisonment... and the supervision period shall not exceed the duration of the maximum term of imprisonment that may be imposed in respect of the sexual offence concerned'[9] and 'the term of the sentence of imprisonment... shall not be less than the term the court would have imposed if it had considered the matter apart from the provisions of this Part.'[10] So, the post-release supervision is to be additional to — rather than replacing — the punitive / custodial element of the sentence, or any part thereof.

As mentioned above, s 29 of Act allows considerable discretion to the sentencing judge regarding the duration and conditions attaching to any post-release supervision order. Section 30 meanwhile outlines additional provisions that may be included in a sentence involving post-release supervision, as follows:

> 30.–(1) In addition to the conditions referred to in *section 29 (1) (b)*, a sentence involving post-release supervision may include such conditions as the court considers appropriate for the purposes of *paragraphs (a)* to *(d)* of *section 28 (2)* and having regard to the needs of the sex offender.
>
> (2) Without prejudice to the generality of *subsection (1)*, there may be included in a sentence involving post-release supervision –
>
> (a) a condition prohibiting the sex offender from doing such one or more things as the court considers necessary for the purpose of protecting the public from serious harm from the offender, and
>
> (b) a condition requiring the sex offender to receive psychological counselling or other appropriate treatment provided by the probation and welfare service or any other body which it appears to the court, having regard to any submissions made to it on behalf

8 Sex Offenders Act 2001, s 29.

9 Sex Offenders Act 2001, s 29(2). Where a post-release supervision order is imposed, the aggregate of the custodial sentence imposed, combined with the period of post-release supervision, cannot exceed the duration of the maximum term of imprisonment provided in law for the sexual offence in question. Some sexual offences such as rape, carry a potential maximum sentence of life imprisonment. Because of this, the period of post-release supervision in matters involving conviction for rape for example, can be for anything up to a maximum of a lifetime.

10 Sex Offenders Act 2001, s 29(3).

of the probation and welfare service, is an appropriate body to provide such counselling or treatment.

(3) A condition referred to in *subsection (1)* or *(2)* shall have effect during the whole or a specified part of the supervision period as the court considers appropriate and specifies in the sentence concerned.

There have been a number of issues with imposing and implementing conditions of post-release supervision, for example where conditions imposed have been unclear or even open-ended. These have implications for breach and recall procedures, which will be considered further below.

## Part-Suspended Sentences, With Supervision

The Criminal Justice Act 2006 (as amended) provides a statutory basis for courts to suspend — either fully or in part — custodial sentences, at the time of sentence being imposed, as follows:

> 99.–(1) Where a person is sentenced to a term of imprisonment (other than a mandatory term of imprisonment) by a court in respect of an offence, that court may make an order suspending the execution of the sentence, in whole or in part, subject to the person entering into a recognisance to comply with the conditions of, or imposed in relation to, the order.
>
> (2) It shall be a condition of an order under subsection (1) that the person in respect of whom the order is made keep the peace and be of good behaviour during –
>
> (a) the period of suspension of the sentence concerned, or
>
> (b) in the case of an order that suspends the sentence in part only, the period of imprisonment and the period of suspension of the sentence concerned,
>
> and that condition shall be specified in the order concerned.

Subsequent subsections of s 99 outline how supervision and other conditions of fully or part-suspended sentences are to be imposed and managed:

> (3) The court may, when making an order under *subsection (1)*, impose such conditions in relation to the order as the court considers –

(a) appropriate having regard to the nature of the offence, and
(b) will reduce the likelihood of the person in respect of whom the order is made committing any other offence,
and any condition imposed in accordance with this subsection shall be specified in that order.

(4) In addition to any condition imposed under *subsection (3)*, the court may, when making an order under *subsection (1)* consisting of the suspension in part of a sentence of imprisonment or upon application under *subsection (6)*, impose any one or more of the following conditions in relation to that order or the order referred to in the said *subsection (6)*, as the case may be:

(a) that the person co-operate with the probation and welfare service to the extent specified by the court for the purpose of his or her rehabilitation and the protection of the public;
(b) that the person undergo such–
  (i) treatment for drug, alcohol or other substance addiction,
  (ii) course of education, training or therapy,
  (iii) psychological counselling or other treatment,
  as may be approved by the court;
(c) that the person be subject to the supervision of the probation and welfare service.

(5) A condition (other than a condition imposed, upon an application under *subsection (6)*, after the making of the order concerned) imposed under *subsection (4)* shall be specified in the order concerned.

(6) A probation and welfare officer may, at any time before the expiration of a sentence of a court to which an order under *subsection (1)* consisting of the suspension of a sentence in part applies, apply to the court for the imposition of any of the conditions referred to in *subsection (4)* in relation to the order.

Courts can and do impose fully-suspended custodial sentences with conditions of supervision by a probation officer. The Law Reform Commission has suggested[11] that in terms of severity, the partly and fully-suspended custodial sentences respectively fall just below a sentence to immediate imprisonment in the hierarchy

[11] Law Reform Commission, *Report: Suspended Sentences*, (LRC 123) (Law Reform Commission 2020) pp 34-36.

of criminal sanctions. From a practice — and practical — point of view, the fully suspended sentence with supervision is generally treated by the Probation Service as similar in nature to a probation order under the Probation of Offenders Act 1907, although the two are legally quite different. That is, someone on a fully-suspended custodial sentence with probation supervision will experience that probation supervision and any associated interventions in a similar way to someone on a probation order *per se*.

The provisions of the 2006 Act, particularly in relation to part-suspended custodial sentences with supervision conditions attached, are applicable to sex offenders, as to those convicted of other categories of offence. As a result, it is not unusual for someone convicted of a scheduled sexual offence, to have a custodial sentence, partly-suspended on certain conditions, combined with a post-release supervision order under the Sex Offenders Act 2001, s 28. The manner in which supervision conditions attaching to part-suspended sentences, as well as to post-release supervision orders, are set out and how they may be subsequently managed by the Probation Service and others, has caused some challenges in implementation, from time to time, for various reasons. These have included for example supervision conditions that are not sufficiently clear, defined and specific, or where there is an ambiguity or open-endedness in the timeframes involved. Over time, probation officers have worked towards focusing on proposing specific, realistic and enforceable supervisions to courts, by way of inclusion as proposals in pre-sanction assessment reports prepared for court by probation officers. These issues can be further complicated in cases where both a part-suspended sentence and a post-release supervision order are applied. It is also worth noting that some of the original provisions of the 2006 Act, s 99 including for example subss 9 and 10, in relation to what should happen to persons who are subsequently convicted of an offence during the time an earlier custodial sentence is suspended, have been ruled unconstitutional.[12]

## Reintegration of Prisoners into the Community in Ireland

The managed release of prisoners with special programmes enabling them to make the transition from life in prison to a law-

[12] The 2006 Criminal Justice Act, s 99 (9) and (10) were declared unconstitutional by *Moore v DPP* [2016] IEHC 244. The Criminal Justice (Suspended Sentences of Imprisonment) Act 2017 (4/2017) was enacted as a consequence.

abiding life in the community is vital. This position is reflected in the European Prison Rules.[13] The European Prison Rules further state that this form of managed release is particularly necessary in the case of prisoners with longer sentences and in these instances steps should be taken to ensure a gradual return to life in free society.[14] An example of such a system operating in an international context is the Canadian system of 'day parole' which is a programme designed to introduce inmates to the outside world prior to them being able to apply for full parole. This programme allows inmates move into a community housing setting, to attend educational, vocational and treatment programmes, with the prisoners having to return to the prison at a set time.[15] Studies of these programmes have shown them to be successful with 85% of the inmates who successfully completed day parole proceeding to fulfil the full parole obligations without any intervention from the criminal justice system.[16] Such research clearly indicates that getting prepared for release is essential if parole, early release or non-parole release is to be achieved with the most positive outcomes however research conducted some years ago on some uses of the Irish system of temporary release has shown that proper preparation for release has in the past often been absent completely or stymied due to early release decisions for some prisoners being expedited to relieve pressure on prison spaces.[17] It must however be noted that similar systems to the Canadian 'day parole' model are successfully operated in Ireland by the PACE[18] organisation, with the support of the Probation Service.[19]

An examination of the role of PACE and others serves as a useful reminder that the assistance provided to offenders is not just based within the prison and aiding released offenders has a long history in Ireland. During the 1960s, probation officers were supervising individuals after release from prison however, it does not appear that this supervision was conditional. Instead, the probation officers

---

13 European Prison Rules 2006, r 107.1.

14 ibid, r 107.2.

15 Public Safety Canada, History of Conditional Release (Archived Content 1987) 16.

16 Rob White and Santina Perrone, *Crime and Social Control* (OUP 2005) 255.

17 This was frequently referred to as the 'revolving door' approach to prison committals and release management. For example, see Agnieszka Martynowicz and Martin Quigley, 'It's like stepping on a landmine...' Reintegration of Prisoners in Ireland (Irish Penal Reform Trust 2010) 37.

18 Prisoners Aid through Community Effort (PACE).

19 See PACE, Annual Report (2016). PACE Organisation http://www.paceorganisation.ie/wp-content/uploads/2017/06/PACE-Annual-Report.pdf. 18 March 2019 for further information in relation to the services provided by PACE.

who were part of what was then known as the Welfare Service worked with community organisations to provide services for people leaving prison; what are now more widely known as re-entry services.[20] These supports seem to have been provided in an attempt to 'befriend and assist', however, from the same period, forms of conditional post-custody supervision also began to appear. The first modern form of temporary release was established by the Criminal Justice Act of 1960 and refined in 2003 by the Criminal Justice (Temporary Release of Prisoners) Act. The manner in which the Probation Service assists the reintegration (often gradual) of prisoners into the community and supervises their compliance with any release conditions imposed will now be considered in greater detail.

## Supporting Prisoner Reintegration

The operation of gradual release programmes in the Irish criminal justice system acknowledges the fact that leaving prison is one of the most vulnerable periods for prisoners and lack of supports upon release can result in reoffending behaviour.[21] The Irish Interim Parole Board stated that the gradual reintegration of a prisoner back into the community is the best way of enabling a life sentenced prisoner, or someone serving a relatively long custodial sentence, to re-settle successfully into society.[22] Such a gradual release process has been noted in other jurisdictions to provide re-assurance to the paroling authorities in testing the robustness of the risk assessment in a calibrated, gradual manner.[23] The release process is critical to reducing the risk of recidivism and reoffending rates. It has been noted that in the past there frequently was a failure to properly plan for such early release, resulting on occasion in prisoners being given very short notice of their release, with many released at times when accessing support was particularly difficult such as on Friday evenings or on Saturdays.[24] Short notice of release can undermine the preparatory work being done with a prisoner prior to release and ignores the need for the granting of temporary release to be timed to coincide with the completion of education

20 Gerry McNally, 'Probation in Ireland: A Brief History of the Early Years' (2007) 4(1) Irish Probation Journal 21.

21 Irish Penal Reform Trust, *Progress in the Penal System – A framework for penal reform* (2017) 81.

22 Parole Board, Annual Report (2017) 4.

23 *R (on the Application of DSD and NBV & Ors) v The Parole Board of England and Wales & Others and John Radford (formerly known as John Worboys)* [2018] EWHC 694 (Admin) (commonly known as 'The Worboys Case')

24 Martynowicz and Quigley (n 17) 38.

and other vocational or training programmes.[25] It may also result in vital support needed in the first few days post-release not being provided at all.[26]

Similarly, the failure to provide adequate support to these prisoners is most acutely felt in relation to provision of accommodation by local authorities and provision of medical treatment, including addiction and mental health treatment for example, upon release.[27] Similarly, lack of fixed release dates also appears to have prevented a number of prisoners from registering on housing lists and makes it difficult for community-based service providers to offer appropriate support.[28] Likewise, vulnerable persons who may have addressed offending behaviour while in prison, for instance underlying addiction problems, may be cut off or distanced from these supports on release (unless subject to post-release supervision) and would therefore be more likely to return to problematic lifestyles on release.[29]

An unplanned approach towards the granting of temporary release does not appear to balance the interests of the community, the victim and the offender and ignores the fact that if the state has seen fit to remove a person from society by placing them in prison, it equally has an obligation and interest in aiding their reintegration into society.[30] Above all, a system of unprepared and unassisted release of prisoners into the community is inconsistent with the principles of rehabilitation and reintegration which are central principles of probation and parole.[31] It should however be noted that the failure to properly prepare prisoners for temporary release was more a feature of the temporary release system in the past and particularly in relation to prisoners primarily from categories of relatively less serious offending, serving shorter sentences and who did not appear before the Interim Parole Board and who do not appear before the Parole Board[32] as opposed to prisoners who had participated in the parole process. Furthermore, in relation to paroled life-sentenced prisoners it should be noted that these parolees remain under the supervision of the Probation Service for

---

25 Public Safety Canada (n 15) 8.

26 Martynowicz and Quigley (n 17) 38.

27 ibid 3.

28 ibid 44.

29 Penal Policy Review Group, *Strategic Review of Penal Policy: Final Report* (Department of Justice 2014) 80.

30 White and Perrone (n 16) 256.

31 Penal Policy Review Group (n 29) 80.

32 Thomas O'Malley, *Sentencing: Towards a Coherent System* (Thomson Round Hall 2011) 218.

the rest of their lives and accordingly may find longer term access to such supports.

It should further be noted in relation to prisoners who are released without the benefit of support from the Probation Service that the Irish Prison Service have appeared to address many of the problems arising in respect of the release process in their relatively newly introduced Integrated Sentence Management system.[33] Nowadays, it is the goal of the Irish Prison Service, the Probation Service and partner organisations that as far as possible all releases from custody should be planned and allow for maximum take-up of appropriate services by the person being released. As a result, the current Integrated Sentence Management ensures that all persons committed to prison are assessed at or as soon after committal as possible and an appropriate sentence plan put in place, which includes targets for preparation for release. Releases from prison, early or otherwise, generally now take place on a planned and coordinated basis, so that for example releases on Fridays or at weekends are avoided and connections are made with appropriate community based services by or on behalf of the prisoner. Even with those serving short sentences (under twelve months), the community support scheme is available for this group across the prison estate and means that at a minimum those who need it are connected with support staff from partner organisations, who develop initial contact with the prisoner in custody and provide mentoring and practical support in the community after release. This is particularly important because those serving shorter sentences have been found through research — in Ireland and internationally — to have some of the highest reconviction rates after release, compared to those who have served longer sentences.[34]

Research in America has shown that prior to release most prisoners have made up their minds to live a non-criminal lifestyle. However difficulties they encounter on release, including in relation to obtaining employment and accommodation, regularly derail them from these good intentions.[35] Frequently the stigma of imprisonment seriously prejudices future prospects for legitimate advancement, thereby undermining the potentially positive influences towards a

---

[33] For further in relation to the operation of this system see Irish Prisons Service. 'Integrated Sentence Management'. https://www.irishprisons.ie/prisoner-services/integrated-sentence-management/

[34] See, for example, relevant research carried out in Ireland and reports published by the Central Statistics Office.

[35] John K Irwin, *The Warehouse Prison – Disposal of the New Dangerous Class* (Roxbury Publishing Co 2005) 172.

more law-abiding lifestyle.[36] Research in California disclosed that whilst there was a very low rate of unemployment in the general society, over 70% of their parolees remained unemployed.[37] Such difficulties in obtaining employment can result in offenders who may have been optimistic in prison about finding a job becoming disillusioned when faced with the harsh realities of high-unemployment and perhaps finding the 'leisure of freedom' only slightly less boring than the 'leisure of incarceration'.[38]

## The Importance of Employment

International research has shown that the single main factor which appears to reduce reoffending appears to be having a job to go to on release.[39] The maintenance of schemes to assist prisoners to obtain employment on their release from prison is very important as research has shown that those released from prison frequently have very poor access to jobs and employers overwhelmingly prefer job applicants with 'clean' records over those with criminal convictions, even in the best case scenario in which the former prisoners are well presented, well-spoken, educated and possessing a decent work history.[40] Released prisoners may also not be perceived to be 'jobs ready', which has created a need for systems of 'supported employment'.[41] These schemes of supported employment provide prisoners with the necessary skills and confidence to secure and keep employment and act as a stepping stone to mainstream work.[42]

## The Time Immediately After Release

The first few days after release can be extremely stressful however these first few days post-release are considered some of the most crucial in terms of successful reintegration into the community. Whilst the Probation Service frequently assists prisoners to manage their release into the community the prisoners' statutory rights are limited to the governor of the prison in which they were

---

36 Paul O'Mahony, *Criminal Chaos – Seven Crises in Irish Criminal Justice* (Round Hall Sweet & Maxwell 1996) 107.

37 Irwin (n 35) 178.

38 Nigel Walker, *Sentencing Theory, Law and Practice* ( Butterworths 1985) 215.

39 Roger Matthews and Jock Young (eds), *The New Politics of Crime and Punishment* (Willan Publishing 2003) 229.

40 Gresham M Sykes, *The Society of Captives – A Study of a Maximum Security Prison* (Princeton University Press 2007) xxii. See also Joan Petersilia, *When Prisoners Come Home* (OUP 2003) 116.

41 The National Economic and Social Forum, *Re-integration of Prisoners: Forum Report No 22* (Government Publications Sales Office 2002) 90.

42 ibid.

detained being obliged to ensure the 'prisoner has sufficient means for travelling to their destination within the State, has adequate clothing and sufficient means of subsistence'.[43] In practice the prisoner needs much more to successfully manage the transition from life in prison to life in the community.[44] This is all the more so in situations involving the release of life sentenced prisoners and the European Prison Rules 2006, specifically acknowledge that 'in the cases of prisoners serving long sentences in particular, steps are required to ensure a gradual return to life in free society'.[45] The European Prison Rules 2006, further 'require prison authorities to work closely with services and agencies that supervise and assist released prisoners to enable all sentenced prisoners to re-establish themselves in the community, in particular with regard to family life and employment'.[46]

In Ireland the importance of assisting prisoners to obtain employment on their release from prison has long been recognised. In Ireland there is a long history of utilising temporary release to permit prisoners to participate in work outside the prison, with this work playing an important role in preparing prisoners for their eventual release and reintegration.[47] Additionally, temporary release is provided to prisoners to enable them to attend workshops and training courses outside of the prison they are detained in.[48] Frequently, the purpose of a programme of such short-term release is to reduce the effects of institutionalisation, help familiarisation with the outside world and for the prisoner to meet with family and relatives.[49]

## Development of the Training Unit at Mountjoy Prison

The issue of assisting prisoners to be in a position to obtain employment on their release is one that has been frequently addressed by the Department of Justice and as early as 1962 an inter-departmental committee was established which recommended consideration of the use of temporary release for attendance at vocational courses and apprenticeships as well as the expansion of the prison industries to include a 'training unit' to ensure

---

43 Prison Rules 2007, Rule 61 as quoted by Oireachtas Joint Committee on Justice, Defence and Equality, Report on Penal Reform (2013) 17.

44 Oireachtas Joint Committee on Justice, Defence and Equality (n 43). Appendix 5.12.

45 European Prison Rules 2006, r 107.2.

46 ibid, r 107.4.

47 Prison Act 2007, s 39(1).

48 The National Economic and Social Forum (n 41) 85.

49 ibid 84.

the skills that could be learned by prisoners whilst incarcerated would be relevant to them in their efforts to obtain employment on release.[50] The development of the Training Unit was ahead of its time and pre-empted the European Prison Rules which state that '[p]rison authorities shall strive to provide sufficient work of a useful nature',[51] 'the work provided shall be such as will maintain or increase a prisoners' ability to earn a living after release'[52] and 'vocational training shall be provided for prisoners able to benefit from it'.[53]

The training unit project was further extended in 1965 by then Minister for Justice, Brian Lenihan, when he implemented a plan of his predecessor, Charles Haughey and established an 'after-care committee' at Mountjoy Prison which was composed of a number of business men and was designed to assist prisoners to obtain employment and accommodation on discharge from prison. Whilst this committee was originally lauded for its efforts in finding work for prisoners on their release, it became inactive in 1967 after holding eleven meetings and finding work for six prisoners, and was never re-established.[54] In 1998 the CONNECT project, which was designed to increase the employability of prisoners on release was given funding in a national development plan however despite this project being reported to be extraordinarily successful[55] its funding was subsequently cut and the project was discontinued.[56]

Attempts to assist in the re-settlement of released prisoners are still continuing. The Irish Association for Social Inclusion Opportunities (IASIO)[57] currently operates two services in the Irish prison system in this regard. The first service, 'the gate service', is a vocational resettlement service which explores what the person wants and is able to do, the barriers to this and organises 'placements', or incremental steps towards achieving that end. This assistance provided to released prisoners to obtain employment is all the more vital as research conducted in Ireland has found

---

50 Mary Rogan, *Prison Policy in Ireland: Politics, Penal-Welfarism and Political Imprisonment* (Routledge 2011) 101 -104.

51 European Prison Rules 2006, r 26.2.

52 ibid, r 26.3.

53 ibid, r 26.2.

54 Rogan (n 50) 111-112.

55 See Nuala Haughey, 'Extraordinary crime reduction reported to have resulted from prison project', The Irish Times (6 July 2001) where it is reported that the recidivism rate of offenders completing this project was 5% as opposed to an average recidivism rate of 70% amongst the general prison population.

56 Rogan (n 50) 201.

57 Previously known as the 'Irish Association for the Social Integration of Offenders'.

that unemployed ex-prisoners are twice as likely to reoffend as those in full or even part time employment.[58] The second project operated by IASIO in the Irish prison system is designed to assist the reintegration of the offender and this project, 'the resettlement service', is a primary needs resettlement service that develops with the person a realistic plan that includes the housing, welfare and social aspects of a stable return to their original community or a new one.[59] The resettlement service is all the more vital because, as noted previously, homelessness and the provision of suitable accommodation is one of the most frequent difficulties facing prisoners and the service providers supporting them on release.[60] The role discharged by the resettlement service mirrors the onus in the European Rules to 'ensure that on release … prisoners are assisted in finding suitable accommodation and work'.[61]

A prominent social commentator has stressed the importance of prisoners obtaining both employment and other assistance on release from prison as a means of reducing recidivism and in this regard quoted the ancient Nigerian proverb 'if your neighbour is hungry, your chickens aren't safe' to emphasise his point.[62] The Irish research which concluded that unemployed ex-prisoners are twice as likely to reoffend as those in full or even part time employment replicates long standing trends in other jurisdictions.[63] The importance of parolees having employment was also emphasised in Ireland where for many years the practice was that parole was only granted to enable an offender to take up employment.[64]

Additionally, in terms of education, research has shown that those former prisoners who attend vocational educational programmes on their release from prison are substantially less likely to return to prison than similarly situated offenders who did not participate in such educational programmes.[65] Furthermore, research data also

---

58 Martynowicz and Quigley (n 17) 18.

59 See Irish Prison Service, Examination of the Sentence Management of People Serving Life Sentences (2017) 26.

60 See John Costello, Chairman of the Parole Board, Submission to The Oireachtas Sub-Committee on Justice (2012) 9 where a 2010 report by the Irish Penal Reform Trust is quoted. See also Irish Penal Reform Trust (n 21) 81.

61 European Prison Rules 2006, r 33.7.

62 See Peter McVerry, Speech at the launch of Combat Poverty's 20th Anniversary Photo Exhibition (29 May 2007).

63 Arthur Taft, Parole: Principles and Practice of a Prison Release Procedure (NYU PhD Thesis 1941) 86.

64 Seán MacBride, *Crime and Punishment* (Ward River Press 1982) 40.

65 Oireachtas Joint Committee on Justice, Defence and Equality, Report on Penal Reform (n 43) 20, Appendix 5.8 of the transcript of evidence of Ian O'Donnell (24 October 2012). See also R Stroker, 'Imposing Conditions Driven by Evidence

indicates that offenders who had known substance abuse needs and received treatment returned to prison at a much lower rate during the first year after release than those who did not receive treatment.[66] This assistance through the first period after release is all the more vital when one considers that research shows that most offenders who fail parole do so within the first six months following release.[67]

## Other Obstacles to Prisoner Reintegration

It must however be noted that the difficulties outlined above such as obtaining employment and accommodation are not the only obstacles faced by those on release. Releases and attempts at reintegration can often be difficult, for a variety of reasons. Some of those newly released may find it difficult to live independently and in a prosocial way, including meeting the conditions of early release and avoiding old behaviours and unhelpful situations and relationships. They may have become accustomed to being told exactly what to do and how to do it in prison, and having to make decisions again can be challenging. They may have unrealistic expectations of their supervising probation officers and others and be disappointed when their expectations are not met.[68] Some may not form trusting relationships with those who supervise them, with research finding that most parolees, for example, resent supervision but prefer it to remaining in prison. This lack of a trusting relationship between the parolee and their supervisor is most noticeably present in cases where the parolee has been recalled to prison.[69]

Research has however shown that parolees serving a life sentence generally liked their probation officers and where mutual trust existed were prepared to confide, at least in a limited way, in these officers.[70] As previously stated, in the event that a person serving a life sentence be returned to the community on reviewable

Based Practices', delivered at Association of Paroling Authorities International Annual Conference, Providence, Rhode Island (21 May 2013) 71.

66 Stroker (n 65) 72.

67 ibid 69.

68 Ian Crow, *The Treatment and Rehabilitation of Offenders* (Sage Publications 2001).

69 Ioan Durnescu, 'Experiencing Supervision; From 'Sparing the First Offenders' to 'Punishment in the Community' and Repairing the Harm Done' in Fergus McNeill, Ioan Durnescu and René Butter (eds), *Probation; 12 Essential Questions* (Palgrave Macmillan 2016) 203.

70 Anthony E Bottoms and Roy Light (eds), *Problems of Long-Term Imprisonment* (Cambridge Studies in Criminology 1987). See also White and Perrone (n 16) 255.

temporary release or following the granting of a parole order, they will be supervised by the Probation Service for the remainder of their life. Supervision of persons serving life sentences differs from other types of supervision because of the nature of the offence, the indeterminate term of supervision and the high degree of sensitivity and responsibility involved. This supervision is usually characterised by high levels of compliance on the part of the person serving the life sentence with close supervision sustained over many years.[71] In other cases, as is to be expected, the intensity of the supervision necessary in any given case will depend on the personal circumstances and characteristics of the particular offender,[72] as well as other factors such as their assessed level of risk of reoffending or of causing further harm. The fostering of this relationship between the supervisee and their supervisor is important as research has shown that where the probation officer is perceived as a helpful figure, the more positive post-release outcomes are reported.[73]

It is important to note however that supervision by the Probation Service means more than mere surveillance and instead requires the supervising Probation Officer to assist the person with the difficult business of returning to and reintegrating in the community.[74] The process of reintegration for returning offenders whose prospects may be quite limited, while the challenges they face are significant – often made more difficult by long separations from families and communities – is often inevitably difficult and hazardous.[75] Several studies have shown the vital importance and the positive and therapeutic benefits of the relationship between released prisoners and probation staff, particularly in the case of prisoners who have served long terms of custody and who may have few remaining positive ties in the community as a result.[76]

Research has further shown that the first few weeks of freedom are the most stressful for ex-prisoners and if they return to family life both they and their families must re-adjust to each other.[77] This situation has been described by a former prisoner as meaning that:

---

71 Irish Prison Service (n 59) 4.
72 O'Malley (n 32) 230.
73 Durnescu (n 69) 209.
74 Jane Mulcahy, 'The Parole Bill; Courts, Quangos and the Risks of Conceptual Confusion', submission to the Oireachtas Justice Committee (2017) 14.
75 See Susan Herman and Cressida Wasserman, 'A Role for Victims in Offender Re-entry' (2001) 47(3) Crime & Delinquency 428.
76 O'Malley (n 32) 223.
77 See Walker (n 38) 215.

For many people, leaving prison is often the point where the formal judicial punishment ends and the real suffering begins.[78]

## Accommodation

It is clear that the difficulties people released from prison experience in obtaining employment and accommodation are merely two of a myriad of barriers they may encounter in their attempts to successfully transition from custody back to life in the community. It should however be noted that the need to secure accommodation is particularly vital. Research has shown that managing the release process is critical to reducing the risk of recidivism and reoffending rates[79] and releasing a person from prison who has no accommodation or, at best, inadequate temporary accommodation serves neither a rehabilitative purpose nor supports reintegration.

It is unquestionable that prisoners released back into homelessness or unsuitable accommodation are generally more likely to reoffend.[80] Furthermore, homelessness impedes a person from maintaining contact with community supervision or treatment programmes, where applicable.[81] In some instances, the difficulty in securing accommodation may not be as severe for those released after serving a short sentence because it is not long since they left their homes and it may have been possible to maintain relationships with their families who may have continued to occupy the home but for many long-term prisoners this often presents a significant problem.[82] This problem is magnified in the cases of those who have been sent to prison for certain specific types of offences. One particular category of prisoner for whom securing accommodation on release is particularly problematic is that of sex offenders considering they will rarely be able to go back to their family homes or even the communities where they lived prior to conviction.[83] Additionally, and particularly in high-profile cases, placements may be perceived as threatening to the local community, as press and media occasionally disclose the details of

---

78 The National Economic and Social Forum (n 41) 83.

79 See Irish Penal Reform Trust (n 21) 81.

80 Oireachtas Joint Committee on Justice, Defence and Equality (n 43) Appendix 5.4, in the transcript of Lisa Cuthbert's evidence (23 November 2011).

81 Penal Policy Review Group (n 29) 77.

82 Oireachtas Joint Committee on Justice, Defence and Equality (n 42) Appendix 5.25 where the evidence of Judge Michael O'Reilly (1 February 2012) is reproduced.

83 Martynowicz and Quigley (n 17) 6.

the location.[84] It can accordingly be seen that a carefully managed reintegration programme is necessary to aid the transition from prison to the community.

## Conclusion

This chapter clearly set out the legal basis for, the processes and benefits of various types of conditional release and post-release supervision. It examined the effectiveness of this system in reducing further offending while the offender is on supervision and the sanction of recall to either the criminal courts or prison is possible.[85] The international position in this regard was also studied and it was shown that there is a significantly lower reconviction rate for offenders released on supervision compared to those who have not been supervised after release.[86] The chapter also examined various categories of early and conditional release as well as studying the area of the post-release supervision of those convicted under the Sex Offenders Act and the post-release supervision of those with partly suspended sentences who are subject to supervision. The chapter also focused on the reintegration of released prisoners into the community, including an examination of the manner in which post-release supervision can aid prisoner reintegration. In this regard the importance of employment and the crucial period just after release were studied. Other obstacles to prisoner reintegration were also studied and the manner in which various initiatives, including the establishment of the training unit, to aid reintegration was examined. A particular focus was placed on the difficulties in released prisoners obtaining accommodation, and steps taken to aid and support them in this regard were considered. In examining all of these issues this chapter mapped the myriad roles that a probation officer must discharge in the successful re-integration of a conditionally-released person into society.

84 ibid. See also *Murray v Newsgroup Newspapers Ltd & Ors* [2010] IEHC 248.
85 ibid 309.
86 ibid 310 and 311.

CHAPTER 9

# CHILDREN AND YOUNG PEOPLE

## Introduction

As Seymour[1] has pointed out:

> Involvement in anti-social and offending activity for the majority of children is adolescent-limited behaviour that most cease to engage in as they make the transition into adulthood (Barry, 2006;[2] Rutherford, 1992[3]). In the interim period, the challenge for any progressive youth justice system is to balance its response, by holding children accountable for their actions without being overly punitive or stigmatising them in a way that reinforces a criminal identity.

This chapter will deal with children and young people as a specific category of service user in the probation and parole context. The concept and practice of parole *per se* does not really apply to those under eighteen years of age in Ireland. The Parole Act 2019 *is* applicable to those who received a custodial sentence as a child and who are subsequently transferred, on becoming an adult in the course of that sentence, to an adult prison to complete the remainder of the sentence. In relation to such cases, please refer to Chapter 7 on Parole for more information regarding the parole process. While always a key group for attention in probation practice throughout its century-plus history, probate practice with children and young people, and its underlying legislative foundation, changed significantly following the passing of the Children Act 2001.

## Definitions and Terminology

The issue of definitions, terminology and language generally is often fraught when discussing crime, offending and those who perpetrate or may be at the receiving-end of such anti-social or

1 Mairéad Seymour, 'The Youth Justice System,' in Claire Hamilton, *Irish Social Work and Social Care Law* (Gill Education 2011) 165.

2 Monica Barry, *Youth Offending in Transition: The Search for Social Recognition* (Routledge 2006).

3 Andrew Rutherford, *Growing Out of Crime: The New Era* (Waterside Press 1992).

aggressive behaviours. This challenge of language is particularly present, if not indeed heightened, in the context of considering children and young people. As will be described below, there are challenges in arriving at mutually acceptable definitions of what constitutes a 'child,' a 'juvenile,' a 'young person' or a 'young adult,' particularly in the context of international comparisons. International standards instruments, specifically those of the United Nations and the Council of Europe, tend to have to adopt definitions that accommodate international differences among their member states, while also seeking to establish appropriate, and also workable, standards of practice, based on the broader framework of internationally accepted values and principles, human rights and the rule of law.

There is also a further problem with applying labelling terms — like *offender* — to people generally, and especially so with children. Through the rest of this chapter, the authors have used terminology that reflects the reality of what is written in legislation, or in international standards documents for example, while where possible in the text, what the authors believe may be more appropriate language and terminology, is used. Readers are encouraged however to bear in mind the wider issues involved and not necessarily accept what is written here, or elsewhere, uncritically. This may not be completely satisfactory, nor to all readers' satisfaction, but it is in recognition of the complexity of the challenges involved, while also seeking to acknowledge the individual human and other rights of those involved. The challenging issue of terminology and language used in probation and parole is also addressed in other parts of this book.

So, while the terminology used to describe and refer to people who have been identified as having committed criminal offences, and specifically those who are being or have been dealt with by the organs of the criminal justice system is fraught in the best of circumstances, the comparable challenges are heightened even more when we describe or refer to children and young people who have been found to have committed criminal acts. In probation work, particularly in Ireland, such individuals are generally referred to as *children* or *young people*, with anything they may have done added afterwards, if needs be, in their descriptor: eg *child found guilty of a homicide*, or *young person in detention* and so on. In this regard, children are accorded their overarching status *as* a child, rather than having the additionally negatively impactful nomenclature of offender for example, become their defining characteristic.

## International Standards — United Nations Convention on the Rights of the Child (UNCRC)

Policy and practice in relation to children and young people who commit criminal offences is underpinned by a strong framework of international standards. A comprehensive overview of international standards in this area of law and practice, which focuses *inter alia* on the development and implementation of a rights-compliant youth justice strategy, is provided in Forde.[4] In relation to any organ of the state dealing with children, the United Nations Convention on the Rights of the Child is a hugely significant international instrument, to which Ireland 'signed up' in 1992. The UNCRC defines a child as a person under the age of eighteen years of age, and enumerates 41 articles, which it has been suggested, can be grouped under the following themes:

1. *Survival rights:* include the child's right to life and the needs that are most basic to existence, such as nutrition, shelter, an adequate living standard, and access to adequate medical services.
2. *Development rights:* include the right to education, play, leisure, cultural activities, access to information, and freedom of thought, conscience and religion.
3. *Protection rights:* ensure children are safeguarded against all forms of abuse, neglect and exploitation, including special care for refugee children; safeguards for children in the criminal justice system; protection for children in employment; protection and rehabilitation for children who have suffered exploitation or abuse of any kind.
4. *Participation rights:* encompass children's freedom to express opinions, to have a say in matters affecting their own lives, to join associations and to assemble peacefully. As their capacities develop, children should have increasing opportunity to participate in the activities of society, in preparation for adulthood.[5]

The Children's Rights Alliance go on to point out that:

> The UN Convention includes four articles that are given special emphasis. These are also known as 'general principles.'

---

4 Louise Forde, *The International Standards Relating to Youth Justice: An Overview* (Department of Justice and University College Cork 2020).

5 Children's Rights Alliance webpage: *The United Nations Convention on the Rights of the Child,* accessible at: https://childrensrights.ie/childrens-rights-ireland/un-convention-rights-child, accessed on 26 June 2021.

These rights are the bedrock for securing the additional rights in the UN Convention:

- that all the rights guaranteed by the UNCRC must be available to all children without discrimination of any kind (Art 2);
- that the best interests of the child must be a primary consideration in all actions concerning children (Art 3);
- that every child has the right to life, survival and development (Article 6); and
- that the child's view must be considered and taken into account in all matters affecting him or her (Art 12).

Similarly, a range of EU and Council of Europe legal instruments and standard-setting texts promote and protect children's rights. These include the European Convention on Human Rights, which upholds the rights of all, including children.[6] All of the Council of Europe's provisions in relation to children reflect and support the UNCRC provisions.

## United Nations Standards

There are a number of international standards applicable to criminal justice system responses, and specifically probation work interventions and parole, in relation to children. The main relevant foundational United Nation Standards in this area are known collectively as 'The Beijing Rules.'[7] Two other United Nations instruments in relation to children and young people, and the criminal justice system the so-called 'Riyadh Guidelines'[8] and the 'Havana Rules'[9] — followed the Beijing Rules. The present section will focus on the Beijing Rules, as they deal in detail with how

[6] The European Convention on Human Rights is available on the Council of Europe website, at: https://www.echr.coe.int/Documents/Convention_ENG.pdf–accessed on 26 June 2021.

[7] United Nations, Standard Minimum Rules for the Administration of Juvenile Justice (The Beijing Rules), Adopted by General Assembly resolution 40/33 of 29 November 1985.

[8] United Nations, Guidelines for the Prevention of Juvenile Delinquency (The Riyadh Guidelines), Adopted and proclaimed by General Assembly resolution 45/112 of 14 December 1990. This instrument discusses measures that should be taken to prevent offending by juveniles, that is — in the main, social, educational and other policies and programmes that should be provided to children in general, to reduce their risk of subsequently getting caught up in the criminal justice system.

[9] United Nations, Rules for the Protection of Juveniles Deprived of their Liberty, Adopted by General Assembly resolution 45/113 of 14 December 1990. These

children and young people should be treated within the criminal justice system, including when subject to supervised community sanctions. The Beijing Rules, in common with other international instruments dealing with the welfare of children, emphasise the broader well-being, developmental issues and rights of children and their families, as well as social justice and wider social policy. The authors of the Beijing Rules were clearly conscious of national differences in defining a child, with the age at which one moves from childhood to adulthood varying from some countries to others. As a result, the document avoids setting any generalised age limits, but rather uses the (broader) terminology of a 'juvenile' and referring to systems of 'juvenile justice'. In this respect, a juvenile is defined as follows:[10]

> A juvenile offender is a child or young person who is alleged to have committed or who has been found to have committed an offence.[11]

They also set out the scope of the provisions of the Rules as applying to any '...child or young person who, under the respective legal systems, may be dealt with for an offence in a manner that is different from an adult.'[12]

The general principles of the UN's Beijing Rules incorporate the goal of furthering the wellbeing of the young person and their family, in the context of a:

> ...comprehensive social policy in general and aim at promoting juvenile welfare to the greatest extent, which will minimize the necessity of intervention by the juvenile justice system, and in turn, will reduce the harm that may be caused by any intervention. Such care measures for the young, before the onset of delinquency, are basic policy requisites designed to obviate the need for the application of the Rules. [13]

The same document further points to:

> ...the important role that a constructive social policy for juveniles will play, inter alia, in the prevention of juvenile

---

rules deal with how juveniles are to be treated in police custody, pre-trial detention and custodial sentences.

10 United Nations (n 7) Scope of the Rules and definitions used, 2.2 (c), p.2.

11 ibid at 2.2(b): 'An offence is any behaviour (act or omission) that is punishable by law under the respective legal system.'

12 ibid, Scope of the Rules and definitions used, 2.2 (a), 2.

13 ibid, General Principles, Commentary.

> crime and delinquency… [with] juvenile justice as an integral part of social justice for juveniles… [allied to] the necessity of constantly improving juvenile justice, without falling behind the development of progressive social policy for juveniles in general and bearing in mind the need for consistent improvement of staff services.

The Beijing Rules set out the aims of juvenile justice as follows:

> 5.1 The juvenile justice system shall emphasise the well-being of the juvenile and shall ensure that any reaction to juvenile offenders shall always be in proportion to the circumstances of both the offenders and the offence.[14]

As well as defining their scope and terminology, including emphasising the need for national systems of juvenile justice *per se*, advice on setting national age limits for criminal responsibility, and urging the application of their provisions to young adults where possible, the Beijing Rules include overarching standards regarding:

- The scope of discretion in proceedings involving children and young people,
- The rights of juveniles (including presumption of innocence, and the rights to be informed of charges, to remain silent, to have counsel and the presence of a parent or guardian, to confront and cross-examine and to appeal, at all stages), and
- Protection of privacy.

The Beijing Rules also address matters in relation to investigation and prosecution of offences, including contacts with young people, through arrest, court proceedings, diversion,[15] specialisation within police services, detention pending trial,[16] adjudication and disposition by competent authority,[17] legal counsel, parents and guardians, guiding principles in adjudication and disposition,[18]

---

14 United Nations (n 7), r 5.

15 To be used (r 11.1) '…wherever appropriate, to dealing with juvenile offenders without resorting to formal trial by the competent authority…'

16 To be used (r 13.1) '…only as a measure of last resort and for the shortest possible period of time.'

17 In Ireland, this is the appropriate court – '…according to the principles of a fair and just trial' (r 14.1).

18 These principles include: proportionality, limits to restrictions on personal liberty, deprivation of liberty as a last resort, the well-being of the young person to be a guiding factor, no capital or corporal punishment, and courts to have the authority to discontinue proceedings at any point.

least possible use of institutionalisation,[19] avoidance of delay,[20] record-keeping,[21] professionalism and training of staff,[22] effective oversight and implementation of decisions and measures,[23] as well as separate sections on institutional treatment[24] and on research, planning, policy formulation and evaluation.[25] The provisions in the Beijing Rules regarding custodial detention of juveniles were subsequently updated in the UN's 'Havana Rules.'[26] In the context of the present publication, the Beijing Rules list a number of possible 'disposition measures' which include: care, guidance and supervision orders; probation; community service orders; financial penalties, compensation and restitution; intermediate treatment and other treatment orders; orders to participate in group counselling and similar activities; orders concerning foster care, living communities or other educational settings; or other relevant orders – while 'no juvenile shall be removed from parental supervision, whether partly or entirely, unless the circumstances of his or her case make this necessary.'[27]

Commenting that: 'Social inquiry reports (social reports or pre-sentence reports) are an indispensable aid in most legal proceedings involving juveniles', the UN Rules state that:

> 16.1 In all cases except those involving minor offences, before the competent authority renders a final disposition prior to sentencing, the background and circumstances in which the juvenile is living or the conditions under which the offence has been committed shall be properly investigated so as to facilitate judicious adjudication of the case by the competent authority.[28]

The importance and value of such social inquiry or pre-sanction reports to the courts and sentencing and other decisions, prepared by probation officers, is repeated in other standards and specifically in the relevant Irish legislation, as will be discussed below.

---

19 United Nations (n 7), r 19: 'Institutionalisation' in this context refers to confinement in residential/custodial institutions that involves a loss of liberty for the individual confined.
20 United Nations (n 7), r 20.
21 ibid, r 21.
22 ibid, r 22.
23 ibid, r 23.
24 ibid Part five, rr 26-29.
25 ibid Part six, r 30.
26 United Nations (n 9).
27 United Nations (n 7), r 18.2.
28 United Nations (n 7), r 16.

## Council of Europe Standards

The main Council of Europe (CoE) standards document specifically dealing with children and young people who have been accused or convicted of criminal offences dates from 2008,[29] although there are also important references to these categories of persons in the 2010 European Probation Rules[30] and the 2017 European Rules on Community Sanctions and Measures.[31] The CoE's 2008 standards in relation to juveniles address the management of juveniles and young adults both in the community and in detention. The sections dealing with community based sanctions and measures do, in contrast to the UN's Beijing Rules, provide some more specific definitions regarding to whom they refer, defining 'juvenile offender' as '...any person below the age of 18 who is alleged to have or who has committed an offence...' and a 'young adult offender' as '...any person between the ages of 18 and 21 who is alleged to have or who has committed an offence and who is subject to these rules because he/she falls under the provisions of Rule 17...'[32] These Rules also set out a number of important overarching principles, which apply to all settings in relation to sanctions and measures following offending behaviour, specifically including:

1. Treatment with respect for human rights.
2. Implementation of sanctions affecting juveniles to be in accordance with law.
3. Sanctions must be imposed by a court, determinate in nature and duration,[33] imposed for the minimum necessary period and, if imposed by another authority, must be subject to prompt judicial review.
4. 'The minimum age for the imposition of sanctions or measures... shall not be too low and shall be determined by law.'

---

[29] Council of Europe, Recommendation CM / Rec (2008) 11 of the Committee of Ministers to member States on the European Rules for juvenile offenders subject to sanctions and measures.

[30] Council of Europe, Recommendation CM / Rec (2010) 1 of the Committee of Ministers to member States on the Council of Europe Probation Rules.

[31] Council of Europe, Recommendation CM / Rec (2017) 3 of the Committee of Ministers to member States on the European Rules on Community Sanctions and Measures.

[32] Council of Europe (n 29) Rule 17 states that: 'Young adult offenders may, where appropriate, be regarded as juveniles and dealt with accordingly.'

[33] The life sentence, which can be imposed for example for murder convictions on children in Ireland, would appear to be at odds with this Council of Europe provision. Nevertheless, the Irish court practice of reviewing long sentences — including life sentences — imposed on children (see below) would appear to mitigate this. The debate around this issue, however, is beyond the scope of the present publication.

5. Imposition and implementation of sanctions and measures must be based on the best interests of the young person, as well as proportionate and taking account of the individual young person's circumstances (principle of 'individualisation').
6. Relevant authorities should have adequate discretion without resulting in inequality of treatment.
7. Juveniles should not be humiliated or degraded by sanctions imposed.
8. Sanctions and measures should not be unduly afflictive, nor risk causing physical or mental harm.
9. They should be implemented without undue delay and only for the specified length of time (principle of 'minimum intervention').
10. Deprivation of liberty (especially pre-trial detention) to be a last resort and only used for the shortest period possible.
11. Principle of non-discrimination – on any grounds – in relation to sanctions and measures.
12. Mediation and restorative justice to be encouraged at all stages.
13. Juveniles should be encouraged to participate effectively in all proceedings affecting them and have the same level of rights as adults in similar circumstances.
14. Relevant systems should take due account of the rights and responsibilities of parents and guardians, as well as other family members and the wider community, where appropriate and involve them in proceedings, sanctions and measures, except where that would not be in the best interests of the young person.
15. A multi-agency and multi-disciplinary approach, integrated with other relevant social systems, should be adopted (principles of 'community involvement' and 'continuous care').
16. The juvenile's right to privacy to be respected at all stages.
17. Young adults, in the criminal justice system, may be regarded and treated as juveniles, where appropriate.
18. Recruitment, training and working conditions of relevant staff must facilitate appropriate standards of care and service delivery.
19. Sufficient staffing and related resources must be provided, to ensure meaningful and effective interventions are provided. Conversely, lack of resources cannot justify human rights infringements.

The Council of Europe defines community sanctions or measures[34]– insofar as they are applied to juveniles, as:

> ...any sanction or measure other than a detention measure which maintains juveniles in the community and involves some restriction of their liberty through the imposition of conditions and/or obligations, and which is implemented by bodies designated by law for that purpose. The term designates any sanction imposed by a judicial or administrative authority and any measure taken before or instead of a decision on a sanction, as well as ways of enforcing a sentence of imprisonment outside a prison establishment.[35]

The relevant part of the Council of Europe Rules dealing with community sanctions and measures clusters detailed rules around the three headings of (1) the Legal Framework, (2) Conditions of Implementation and (3) Consequences of Non-compliance, summarised as follows:

*Legal Framework:*[36]

- A wide range of community sanctions and measure should be provided, taking different stages of juveniles' development into account.
- Priority to be given to sanctions and measures that are educational and restorative.
- National law shall specify the characteristics of community sanctions and measures, including: definitions and mode of application; associated conditions and obligations; clarity regarding cases that require the young person's consent before imposition of a sanction or measure; duties and responsibilities of authorities that impose, modify or implement sanctions and measures; grounds for modification of sanctions and measures; scrutiny procedures in relation to implementation authorities; the requirement that national law shall clarify the obligations on competent authorities to explain sanctions and measures to young people and their parents or guardians, to maximise cooperation with young people and their parents or guardians, as well as the rights of

---

34 Council of Europe (n 29) 21.4.

35 It should be noted that in Ireland a child cannot be committed to a prison. Custodial sanctions or measures in relation to children are provided through the children detention school structure only.

36 Council of Europe (n 29) rr 23-25.

and restrictions on parents and guardians regarding the imposition of sanctions and measures.

- Imposition and revocation of community sanctions and measures shall only be taken by judicial authorities or other authorities as laid down by law, and shall be subject to the possibility of judicial review.
- Provision should be made in law for the possible reduction of duration or of obligations of a sanction or measure, in the event of progress made by the young person.
- Other legal rights, such as in relation to education, training, physical/mental health, care, safety or social security should not be adversely affected.
- Any consent required of young people or their parents/guardians must be informed and explicit.
- Failure to comply with a community sanction or measure should not automatically constitute an offence and should not lead automatically to deprivation of liberty but preferably to modified or new community sanctions or measures.

*Conditions of Implementation:*[37]

- Community sanctions and measures should be implemented in a meaningful way, contributing to young people's educational and social skills development.
- Young people should be encouraged to discuss matters affecting them with relevant authorities.[38]
- Implementation should respect young people's existing constructive social and family relations.
- Young people should be informed, in appropriate language, regarding their rights and responsibilities.
- They should be entitled to make oral or written representations prior to any formal decisions being made affecting them.
- Individual case records should be established and maintained up to date. These records — should only contain relevant information; should as far as possible and reasonable be made accessible to the young person, their parents or guardians, who should in turn have a right to contest their contents; should only be disclosed — on as limited a basis as necessary — to those with a legal

---

37 Council of Europe (n 29) rr 31-45.

38 This principle is frequently referred to as ensuring that 'the voice of the child' is listened to and heard.

right to receive them; and should be destroyed or kept in archives with access to these appropriately restricted and regulated.

- Only relevant information regarding young people shall be shared with third-party organisations (eg those providing education, training or other assistance).
- Community service work placements for young people shall be in accordance with national health and safety regulations and the young people must be insured or indemnified against accident, injury or public liability.
- Costs of implementation of community sanctions and measures shall not be borne by young people or their families.
- Implementation shall be based on individualised assessments and evidence-informed intervention methods that adopt a range of approaches.
- Restrictions of liberty shall be proportionate and only used to the extent necessary for proper implementation.
- Staff involved must receive clear instruction regarding implementation and where possible a continuous and long-term relationship between the staff and young person should be facilitated.
- Attention should be given to appropriate interventions for linguistic or ethnic minorities and for young people who are foreign nationals.
- Where available, provision to transfer or expel young people who are foreign nationals should ensure that appropriate liaison is established with competent agencies in the other jurisdiction.
- Young people should be encouraged as far as possible to make reparation for their offending behaviour, within the scope of the relevant community sanctions or measures.

*Consequences of Non-compliance:*[39]

- Young people, their parents or guardians should be informed of the rules, conditions and obligations, as well as the potential consequences of non-compliance with community sanctions or measures.
- Procedures for dealing with non-compliance shall be clearly defined.
- Minor transgressions should be noted but not necessarily

[39] Council of Europe (n 29) rr 46-48.

reported to the deciding authority,[40] but rather dealt with on a discretionary basis.

- Significant non-compliance should be reported promptly in writing to the deciding authority, detailing how and in what circumstances the non-compliance occurred, as well as the personal situation of the young person, with the deciding authority only making a ruling after a thorough examination of the facts.
- Young people, as well as their parents/guardians where appropriate, should have an opportunity to examine evidence presented in relation to non-compliance and to present their own observations.
- Where revocation or modification of a community sanction is being considered, due account should be taken of the extent to which the young person has already fulfilled the requirements of the original sanction or measure and where a sanction or measure is to be revoked or modified there should be an option available for judicial review.

## The Council of Europe Rules in Relation to Detention of Children

The sections of the CoE Rules dealing with detention[41] are collectively quite expansive and comprehensive, covering issues such as those under the following headings:

- *Overall approach:* (including) principles, possibility of early release, provision of meaningful activities, continuity of care, physical and mental integrity and well-being, and specific needs of those detained.
- *Institutional structure:* range of facilities, conditions with least restrictive controls as necessary, 'normalisation,'[42] desirability of small institutions and appropriate locations.
- *Placement:* type of care, individualised approaches,

---

[40] In the context of Ireland, the *deciding authority* is generally the sentencing court.

[41] Council of Europe (n 29) Part III- Deprivation of liberty: rs 49.1 to 107.2, as well as F. Special Part, dealing with matters in relation to juveniles in police custody, pre-trial detention and other forms of deprivation of liberty prior to sentencing; as well as sections (F.3) dealing with detention in welfare institutions, and in mental health institutions (Section F.3).

[42] Although the term *normalisation* itself is not used here, that is —in the way it has come to be in relation to adult custodial facilities — r 53.3 provides that: 'Life in an institution shall approximate as closely as possible the positive aspects of life in the community.'

family accessibility, least restrictive level of security, mental health issues, consultation with young people and their families, specific facilities for young people (not with adults), assessment systems, age-related issues, educational and other needs.

- *Admission:* legal and security issues, information gathering and sharing, induction process, medical examination and facilities, psychological, educational and social assessments, development of individual plans for education, training and other programmes.
- *Accommodation:* Conditions to respect human dignity and privacy, health and hygiene issues, individual bedrooms as far as possible, effective yet unobtrusive supervision by staff and effective alarm systems for protection of individuals.
- *Hygiene:* proper maintenance and cleaning, ready access to sanitary (including bathing/showering) facilities, cleanliness and tidiness of bedrooms.
- *Clothing and bedding:* those detained allowed to wear their own clothing where possible, provision of appropriate clothing as required, provision of separate, appropriate and clean bed and bedding.
- *Nutrition:* nutritious diet appropriate to age and health etc, regular meals and self-catering where possible.
- *Health:* international standards on medical care to be applied, comparability of services to those in the wider community, particular hazards to be addressed, preventive care and health education provision, regarding medical interventions and medications, particular client needs, coordinated multi-disciplinary care.
- *Regime activities:* all interventions to be designed to promote juveniles' development and their participation and to meet individual needs, consistent with proven professional standards and best practice, variety of activities should be provided—aimed at education, personal and social development, vocational training, rehabilitation and preparation for release (with a range of examples provided in the text). Also, schooling, training and treatment interventions to be given priority over work, juveniles should attend local schools where possible, and where schooling is provided within the institution, it should be provided by external bodies. There should be appropriate links with external educational, training and accreditation bodies,

individualised learning plans, regularly updated, with social and physical exercise activities and out of bedroom time maximised. Meaningful activities to be provided at weekends and holiday periods. Work opportunities to be provided, which is both stimulating, of educational value, and rewarded.

- *Contact with the outside world:* communications by letter or other form, with families and friends to be facilitated, as well as visits, which should encourage development and maintenance of family relations and aimed at social reintegration.
- *Freedom of thought, conscience and religion:* must be respected, with detainees' rights to practise their religion and follow their beliefs, without any compulsions on these issues.
- *Good order:* including a wide range of rules on the safe and secure environment, protecting vulnerable juveniles and preventing victimisation, dynamic approaches to safety and security, as well as sections on searching detainees, use of force, physical restraint and weapons, separation of juveniles for security and safety reasons, discipline and punishment, and transfer between institutions.
- *Preparation for release:* measures to be in place for preparation for and transition back to life in the community, including by specialised forms of interventions in individualised planning and gradual return by the individual to the community, provision of help with family and other relations, accommodation, education, training and employment, social and health-care and monetary assistance, post-release, including in post-release supervision and assistance.
- *Foreign nationals:* to be treated in the same way as others, to be facilitated in extended visits where appropriate, to be allowed contact with embassy and consular representatives, and to be helped with reintegration in their own countries, if returning there.
- *Ethnic and linguistic minorities:* whereby special arrangements should be made to meet the needs of juveniles in question, including that they be facilitated to continue cultural practices, and that interpreters, appropriate written materials and language courses be provided as far as possible.
- *Juveniles with disabilities:* should be accommodated in ordinary facilities, that are adapted as appropriate.

> Where their needs cannot be met in this way, they should be facilitated in specialised institutions.

This latter section of the relevant Council of Europe Rules also provide for consultation with individual detainees and their families or caregivers, insofar as possible, in relation to the broad range of issues impacting on their detention. Nevertheless, for the purpose of the present chapter, the primary focus will remain on the application of community sanctions and measures with juveniles and young adults.

## Relevant Policy in Ireland

The Irish Youth Justice Service was established in December 2005, originally as an office of the Department of Justice, Equality and Law Reform, on foot of a recommendation of the Working Group on Youth Justice, which identified a need for a lead or coordinating agency to oversee and coordinate the implementation of the changes arising from the Children Act 2001.[43] The governance and structure of the Irish Youth Justice system, and specifically the Irish Youth Justice Service (IYJS) has been summarised by Seymour as follows:

> The aim of the Irish Youth Justice Service is to provide a co-ordinated approach to the delivery of youth justice in Ireland. Included in its remit are: responsibility for the development of youth justice policy; the development and implementation of a national youth justice strategy with links to other child-related strategies; responsibility for the detention of offending children under 18 years of age; implementation of the provisions of the Children Act 2001 relating to community sanctions, restorative justice, conferencing and diversion projects; and the co-ordination of service delivery at both national and local level.[44]

The first National Youth Justice Strategy was published in 2008, and the establishment of the Department of Children and Youth Affairs (DCYA) followed in June 2011. As described by Seymour, the role of the DCYA was '…to lead the development of harmonised policy and quality integrated service delivery for children and young people across a range of sectors, including health, education, youth

---

43 Department of Justice, Equality and Law Reform, *Report on the Youth Justice Review* (2006).

44 Seymour (n 1) 168.

justice, sport, arts and culture.'[45] While the IYJS transferred from the Department of Justice to the DCYA, it subsequently transitioned back to the Department of Justice. The Department of Justice had retained responsibility for all aspects of crime policy and detection, criminal proceedings, diversion and community sanctions — as well as the work of An Garda Síochána and the Probation Service, throughout. Following the 2020 general election and the subsequent reorganisation of some Government departments, the IYJS transferred back to the Department of Justice, with a new Department of Children, Equality, Disability, Integration and Youth also being established.

A new Youth Justice Strategy, covering the years 2021-2027, was launched by the Department of Justice in April 2021.[46] The strategy document was accompanied by the publication of three 'companion' research documents: on young people at risk,[47] an overview of international standards on youth justice[48] and a review of the previous (2014-2018) youth justice action plan.[49] The Youth Justice Strategy builds on the previous strategic plans and sets out, among other goals, to:

- Provide a developmental framework to address key ongoing challenges, as well as new and emerging issues in the youth justice area;
- Preventing offending from occurring and diverting children and young adults who commit a crime away from further offending and involvement with the criminal justice system;
- Provide for enhanced criminal justice processes, detention and post-detention measures to provide consistent support to encourage desistance from crime and promote positive personal development for young offenders. [50]

Actions in the strategy, related to probation work, include:

---

45 ibid.

46 Department of Justice, *Youth Justice Strategy 2021-2027* (2021)

47 Department of Justice, *Young People at Risk: YPAR Case Study* (2020).

48 Forde (n 4).

49 Ursula Kilkelly and Louise Forde, *Looking Back at Tackling Youth Crime: Youth Justice Action Plan 2014-2018: A Review of Progress Achieved and Lessons Learned* (2019).

50 According to the statement by the Department of Justice, on 15 April 2021, available at: http://www.justice.ie/en/JELR/Pages/PR21000079. Accessed on 29 June 2021.

- Specific training for and deployment of suitably qualified probation officers, in conjunction with training of other relevant professionals;
- Establishment of clear interagency procedures to ensure that all relevant children and young people are fully and appropriately dealt with, including through the provision of community sanctions, restorative justice and the use of coordinated case management approaches;
- Identification of and support at an early stage for those children and young people at risk of becoming serious offenders, including through the development of community projects under the auspices of the Probation Service;
- Cooperation by the Probation Service and partner community-based organisations in the development of the Garda Youth Diversion Projects and alignment of the development of Probation and Garda projects, to maximise learning and effective use of resources;
- Probation Service contribution to interagency case management processes, and risk and need assessments, to help children in detention and in relation to release and post-release, incorporating community sanctions, post-release supervision and support, continuum of interagency supports, as well as family engagement;
- Provision of enhanced and effective services for 18 to 24 year-olds on release from prison;
- Probation cooperation in the Bail Supervision Scheme;[51]
- Provision of appropriate information to assist young persons throughout the court process;
- Prioritisation of the management and processing of cases involving children and young people as far as possible;
- Maximising opportunities to support children and young people through supervision and interventions in the community; and
- Ensuring that a comprehensive range of sentencing options for the court are available, including restorative and personal development approaches, extending

[51] Although previously envisaged by some commentators (eg Sinead Freeman, 'The Experience of Young People Remanded in Custody: A Case for Bail Support and Supervision Schemes' (2008) 5 Irish Probation Journal 91-102) as a measure that might be managed by the Probation Service, the Bail Supervision Scheme as implemented from 2016, has been managed by an NGO – EXTERN (see: https://www.extern.org/bail-supervision-scheme-ireland and Catherine Naughton, Sean Redmond, and Barry Coonan, *Evaluation of the Bail Supervision Scheme for Children (Pilot Scheme)* (Department of Children and Youth Affairs, and the University of Limerick 2019).

the Bail Supervision Scheme, and developing other sentencing options, including in the context of any revision to the Children Act.

As well as participation by the Probation Service in the planned strategic and policy governance and oversight structures, other actions arising, such as cooperation with relevant agencies in Northern Ireland, would involve Probation Service input. The strategy also envisages the development of a revised Children Act, which would incorporate changes that would specifically impact on the work of the Probation Service, or at least be likely to do so.[52] These would include:

- widening and improving the provision of family conferences convened by probation officers,[53]
- faster processing of cases before a Children Court, including earlier Probation Service involvement;
- effectively consolidating or 'streamlining' the range of community sanctions, supervised by the Probation Service, available under the Act;[54]
- considering provision of a right to post-release (from a sentence of detention) aftercare support; and
- provisions for suspended sentences (particularly if this involved Probation supervision as a condition of the suspension).

## Practice Developments

Probation practice with children and young people has been influenced by wider evolution of research and evidence-based practice in relation to children and young people in the fields of social work, psychology and education for example. Similarly, approaches to work with children and young people in the criminal justice system have been influenced in major part by the growing body of research and other evidence regarding 'what works' in probation and parole work generally. In that context, since the earliest origins and foundations of probation and parole practice

52 Department of Justice (n 46).

53 See more on Family Conferences below.

54 This refers to ss 115, 118, 124-126, 129, 131, 133 and 137 of the Act and would seem to imply making provision for a 'generic' supervised community sanction, within which any required conditions as might for example be recommended in a probation officer's pre-sanction report to court, could be included. To a large extent, this proposed change would seem to reflect the reality of current practice in terms of how Children Courts actually frame such orders.

and organisation in Europe and North America, over a century ago, there has been a recognition that younger people who commit criminal offences should be treated in ways that differ to some extent from the treatment of adults in similar situations. This is on the basis of taking account in practice of the unique stage of development of the child or young person and the implications of this from a therapeutic as well as legal perspective. This has led to the introduction and implementation of more nuanced or targeted approaches with the younger group of service users, even though the overall approach to and organisation of such work, including the goals of work with younger people is otherwise the same as with all probation clients, that is the aim of reducing reoffending, offender reintegration and making good the harm done by offending.

## The Law in Ireland — The Probation of Offenders Act 1907

Chapter 4 — Probation work — deals in detail with the legislation underpinning probation work generally in Ireland, with the Probation of Offenders Act 1907 as the statutory foundation of such work. Before moving on to discuss the specific legislative provisions in relation to children who offend, contained in the Children Act 2001, it is important to point out that the foundational 1907 Act comprehended the fact that probation as a system would include, and indeed be aimed at, children and young people. Indeed, age is listed as one of the factors that is recognised as being taken into account in a court's decision to consider that it might be '... expedient to release the offender on probation...'.[55] The 1907 Act went on, in the section dealing with the appointment of probation officers, to specify that:

> There shall be appointed, where circumstances permit, special probation officers, to be called children's probation officers, who shall, in the absence of any reason to the contrary, be named in a probation order made in the case of an offender under the age of sixteen. [56]

The general provisions of the Probation of Offenders Act 1907 applied to adults and children alike.[57] While the legislative basis for probation practice with adults remains the 1907 Act, the specific

---

[55] Probation of Offenders Act 1907, s 1(1) and s1(2).

[56] Probation of Offenders Act 1907, s 3(2).

[57] For more on the implications and practice of the Probation of Offenders Act 1907, see Chapter 4.

legislative provisions in relation to probation and other community sanctions and measures, as applied in cases involving children, has been modernised and updated through the Children Act 2001.

## The Law — The Children Act 2001

Those who framed the Probation of Offenders Act 1907 envisaged, as described above, its application to children and young people, as well as to adults, and sought to make a number of specific provisions for the former. Following almost a hundred years without significant change, the legislation regarding how children are to be treated by the justice system was overhauled and updated at the start of the current century. The Children Act 2001 is a comprehensive piece of primary legislation, governing the full spectrum of responses to those persons under eighteen years of age, who come into conflict with the law. The 2001 Act was not commenced in full for several years.[58] Nevertheless, the passing of this statute signalled a sea-change in the responses to offending by young people in Ireland.

A decade and a half after the passage of the Children Act 2001, a significant change was also made in the Irish Constitution, Bunreacht na hÉireann, in relation to the constitutional position of children. Originally according similar rights to children as to other citizens, the Irish Constitution was amended in 2015 to provide specific rights for children, including through the addition of Article 42A of the Constitution, to the effect that:

> The State recognises and affirms the natural and imprescriptible rights of all children and shall, as far as is practicable, by its laws protect and vindicate those rights.[59]

The Children Act 2001 is an extensive piece of legislation, comprising 271 sections, divided into thirteen parts. The present chapter will confine itself to highlighting and discussing briefly only those elements of the legislation that most impact on the workings of probation and parole.

---

[58] The Children Act 2001 is available in full on the Oireachtas website at: http://www.irishstatutebook.ie/eli/2001/act/24/enacted/en/html .

[59] The 31st Amendment to the Constitution. The relevant referendum was held on 10 November 2012, with the implementing legislation giving effect to the change in the Constitution being signed into law on 28 April 2015 (following a legal challenge to the Amendment that was heard in the High Court and the Supreme Court).

The Children Act gives legislative effect to the principle that custody must only be used as a sanction of last resort in cases involving children who have offended, stating explicitly that:

> s 96 – (1) Any court when dealing with children charged with offences shall have regard to –
>
> (a) the principle that children have rights and freedom before the law equal to those enjoyed by adults and, in particular, a right to be heard and to participate in any proceedings of the court that affect them, and …

in the context of protecting a child's rights and access to education, training, employment, relationships with parents and family members, as well as facilitating as far as possible that families resolve their own issues and challenges, that:

> (d) …any penalty imposed on a child for an offence should cause as little interference as possible with the child's legitimate activities and pursuits, should take the form most likely to maintain and promote the development of the child and take the least restrictive form that is appropriate in the circumstances; in particular, a period of detention should be imposed only as measure of last resort.

In addition:

> s 143 – (1) The court shall not make an order imposing a period of detention on a child unless it is satisfied that detention is the only suitable way of dealing with the child and… that a place in a child detention school is available for him or her.
>
> (2) Where an order is made under *subsection (1)*, the court making the order shall give its reasons for doing so in open court.

The Act deals, *inter alia*, with pre-court child welfare, treatment of children in police custody, diversion from prosecution, the Children Court and its powers and proceedings, through community sanctions supervised by the Probation Service and on to children's detention, as well as more general themes such as the age of criminal responsibility, child protection and various other miscellaneous provisions. The present chapter will highlight some of the key features of the Children Act 2001, specifically those impacting on probation and parole work and managed by Probation Service personnel. It will concern itself in the main with Part 9 of the Act, which is headed *Powers of Courts in Relation to Child Offenders*, and includes significant sections[60] on *Proceedings in Court*,[61] *Probation Officer's Reports*,[62] as well as in relation to *Community Sanctions*.[63] Where appropriate, the chapter will refer to other provisions of the Children Act that are relevant to probation officer duties and the role of the Probation Service.

## The Age of Criminal Responsibility

Children are deemed to be different to adults, specifically in the sense of legal responsibilities for example. In addition, there are general assumptions that children under a certain age are incapable, because of their age and developmental stage in their life, of meeting the criteria of legal responsibility and of being held completely responsible for their actions. In that sense, legal systems tend to have a 'cut-off' age, below which one is not considered to be legally responsible for their actions. This is known as the age of criminal responsibility. The Children Act 2001 raised the age of criminal responsibility in Ireland from seven to twelve.[64] This measure was brought into effect in 2006, but with an amending legislative clause that while the general age of criminal responsibility would be twelve, someone aged ten or eleven could also be charged with murder, manslaughter, rape or aggravated sexual assault.[65] The 2006 legislation also removed the previous provision that children up to the age of fourteen enjoyed a rebuttable presumption that they were incapable of committing a crime.[66] Thus, there are now three categories of children who offend:

1. Children under the age of ten, who are considered completely legally incapable of committing a criminal offence;
2. Children who are not less than ten years but under twelve, who are fully legally capable of committing murder, manslaughter, rape or aggravated sexual assault (but not other crimes); and
3. Children aged twelve years and under eighteen years, who are fully legally capable of committing any crime.

---

60 ss 99 to 107.

61 Part 8 – *Proceedings in Court* – includes sections on the provision of family conferences convened by probation officers.

62 ss 99 to 107.

63 ss 115 to 141.

64 Children Act 2001, s 52.

65 Criminal Justice Act 2006, s 129.

66 Known in law as the principle of *doli incapax*, that is, incapable of forming the intent to commit a crime.

The Youth Justice Strategy 2021-2027 highlights a number of the Children Act 2001 provisions to be considered for amendment. These include the provisions in relation to the age of criminal responsibility.[67] Referencing the fact that a child aged 10 to 11 could be charged with homicide and serious sexual assault, the Strategy states that: 'This provision has never been used' and that:

> The Act also provides that a child aged 12 to 13 can be charged with a crime, but only with the express consent of the Director of Public Prosecutions, and unfortunately this provision has had to be used, including for some of the most heinous crimes. However, for most crime and most purposes the effective age of criminal responsibility in Ireland is 14.

The strategy concludes that while the Children Act 2001 provisions in relation to the age of criminal responsibility will be kept under review, 'Ireland's rights-based and child-centred youth justice system ensures that children are prosecuted only as a last resort.'[68]

## The Role and Duties of Probation Officers under the Children Act 2001

Section 259 sets out succinctly the duties of probation officers, including – as summarised by McDermott and Robinson — imposing '…a statutory duty on probation officers to maintain a working relationship with any child placed under their supervision',[69] as follows:

> s 259. – While a child remains under the supervision of a probation and welfare officer pursuant to this Act, whether in accordance with an order of a court or otherwise, the officer shall, subject to the directions of the court, where appropriate, and in addition to the terms of and any conditions attaching to any particular placement –
>
> (a) visit, assist, advise and befriend the child, and where feasible, the child's parents or guardian or other adult in whose residence the child may be residing,
>
> (b) see that the child observes the terms and any conditions attaching to the supervision, and

---

[67] Department of Justice (n 46) 33. See more on the Youth Justice Strategy earlier in this chapter.

[68] Department of Justice (n 46), 33.

[69] PA McDermott and T Robinson, *Children Act 2001* (Thomson Round Hall 2003), 226-227.

(c) when necessary and appropriate, endeavour to find the child suitable employment and accommodation.

These duties are quite close, in spirit and even wording, to the duties of probation officers as set out in the original Probation of Offenders Act 1907.[70] Nevertheless, there are three small, but potentially quite significant differences between the two pieces of legislation, although this is to be expected, at least in part, because while the 1907 Act was to govern probation practice with both adults and children, the 2001 Act specifically deals with children. These key differences are:

1. The 2001 reference to visiting the child – places an emphasis on the probation officer having more of a focus on meeting the child where they live, rather than only meeting them in probation offices or other similar facilities away from the child's home;
2. Dropping the provision – included in the 1907 Act – of the duty to 'report to the court as to his [sic] behaviour' – this would appear to reflect the change in approach to providing 'update' reports to courts once a probation supervision order was made;[71] and
3. The inclusion of the reference in the 2001 Act to finding accommodation (with finding employment) for the child. This would seem to reflect the enduring value identified with probation officers providing practical assistance to their clients, as well as recognising the fact of the challenges of homelessness for many of those on probation supervision.

Other than these aspects, the duties as expressed in 2001 are virtually identical to those enumerated in 1907. Both the duties of the probation officer, as well as the approach to probation practice, expressed in the Children Act 2001, are very close to the ideals and practice of probation as envisaged over a century ago. Modern probation practice with children and young people is defined by many probation officers as incorporating a *reach not breach*[72]

---

70 Probation of Offenders Act 1907, s 4.

71 This practice — whereby probation officers periodically reported back to sentencing courts regarding probationers' progress or otherwise, was not unusual up to the 1980s, before it was discontinued on the basis of its inappropriateness — legally and otherwise.

72 A reluctance among probation officers working with children to be overly prescriptive or strict in dealing with non-compliance; using discretion and being more flexible in understanding and adapting to a child's needs, rather than rushing to return matters to court pre-emptively or rigidly.

approach to professional intervention with service users, one that incorporates treating children always as children first, 'going the extra mile' in terms of maintaining the professional relationship, adopting the guiding principle of *one good adult*,[73] and never giving up on the child or young person, no matter what; all the while holding this approach within the traditional balance of care and control.[74]

## Family Conferences Convened by Probation Officers

The Children Act has sometimes been described, by practitioners and others, as a piece of legislation with a 'restorative' focus, and yet the term 'restorative' is not specifically used anywhere throughout its text.[75] One of the reasons that the 2001 Act has attracted the description of being 'restorative' is probably down to its provisions for a number of different, but similar, types of family conference. These conferences are aimed at involving significant people in the child's life, with a view to identifying relevant issues and harnessing the collective positive energy that may be available to assist the child and their family and others to move forward in a positive way. The Children Act provides for three types of family conference: (1) those convened by the child protection and welfare services,[76] (2) those run by An Garda Síochána[77] and (3) those run by the Probation Service.[78] It is the latter category of family conference that is of concern to the present chapter.

Section 78 of the Children Act 2001 provides for the introduction of an innovative practice — the *family conference*, convened and managed by the Probation Service — as follows:

> s 78. – (1) Where, in any proceedings in which a child is charged with an offence –
>
> (a) the child accepts responsibility for his or her criminal

[73] The concept of 'one good adult' is based on the premise that the positive impact of having even one dependable and committed adult in their life (at a time when there may not otherwise be such a figure present) can have a significantly positive impact on a child in trouble.

[74] See Chapter 4 on Probation Work for more on this.

[75] See Chapter 6 on Restorative Justice and Victims for more on the relevant aspects in relation to probation and parole, including the involvement of victims and others more widely in restorative interventions.

[76] *Family Welfare Conferences* — covered by Part 2, ss 7 to 15. These were to be convened by health boards at the time of the passing of the Act. The health board child protection and welfare duties have since passed to Tusla.

[77] In Part 4 — *Diversion Programme* — ss 29 to 43; Holding of conference in respect of a child.

[78] In Part 8 — *Proceedings in Court* — ss 78 to 94.

behaviour, having had a reasonable opportunity to consult with his or her parents or guardian and obtained any legal advice sought by or on behalf of him or her,

(b) it appears to the Court that it is desirable that an action plan for the child should be formulated at a family conference, and

(c) the child and the child's parents or guardian, or members of the child's family or relatives of the child who in the opinion of the Court could make a positive contribution at a family conference, agree to attend such a conference and to participate in its proceedings,

the Court may direct the probation and welfare service to arrange for the convening of a family conference in respect of the child and adjourn the proceedings until the conference has been held.

Legal proceedings against the child in the Children's Court are effectively 'paused' while the family conference is given an opportunity to find a way of dealing with matters productively and potentially without proceeding to a traditional criminal court conclusion. Section 79 goes on to stipulate that the family conference shall be convened, by a designated probation and welfare officer, '...not later than 28 days after the date of the direction of the Court.' Section 80 provides that:

> 80. – (1) A family conference shall endeavour to formulate an action plan for the child in respect of whom it has been convened.

In terms of the practicalities of these family conferences, convened and managed by probation officers, the Act stipulates that a family conference '...may regulate its procedure in such manner as it sees fit', that the convening probation officer should '...ensure, as far as is practicable, that any information and advice required by the conference to carry out its functions are made available to it,'[79] as well as that the Probation Service must ensure that the necessary 'administrative services' be made available '...to enable a family conference to discharge its functions.'[80] The Children Act, in establishing that a family conference should '...endeavour

---

[79] s 86 (1).
[80] s 87.

to formulate an action plan...'[81] references[82] an earlier section of the Act[83] dealing with the other – Garda Síochána Diversion Programme – conferences, in clarifying what might be included in an action plan arising from a family conference.

Those present at the conference (and specifically the child and their parent/s or guardian/s) are required to formulate an *action plan,*[84] which should as far as possible, be unanimously agreed by those at the conference, and may include provision for any one or more of the following undertakings by the child:

a) an oral or written apology to the victim,
b) financial or other reparation,
c) participation in some appropriate sporting or recreational activity,
d) attendance at school or work,
e) participation in a training or educational programme,
f) being at home at specified times,
g) staying away from a specific place or person,

As well as anyone involved –

h) 'taking initiatives within the child's family and community that might help to prevent the commission by the child of further offences, and
i) any other matter that in the opinion of those present at the conference would be in the child's best interests or would make the child more aware of the consequences of his or her criminal behaviour.'[85]

Following the conference, an action plan agreed by those present at the conference[86] should be written up by the convening probation officer '...in language that can be understood by the child,'[87] who should also sign the action plan, as should the probation officer and by one other person present.[88] The relevant probation officer must then either:

a) submit the action plan to the court,

---

81 s 80(1).
82 s 80(2).
83 s 39(1) to (3).
84 s 80 and s 39(1) to (3).
85 Children Act 2001, s 39(3).
86 s 39(2).
87 s 39(4).
88 s 39(5).

b) inform the court that the conference did not reach agreement,
c) apply for an extension of time, or
d) inform the court that the conference has not been held and that there is little likelihood of it being held. [89]

Where an action plan is submitted to court, the court may approve or amend it, and order that the child comply and be supervised by the probation officer accordingly.[90] The court will also set a date, no more than six months later, to review compliance with the plan.[91] At that review, the Act sets out that the court '…may, if it is satisfied that the child has complied with the plan, dismiss the charge against the child on its merits.'[92]

Where the probation officer reports that an action plan has not been agreed, but the court believes that one is appropriate and might succeed, it may put one in place and order that the child comply with it and be supervised by the probation officer. Alternatively, in such instances, the court may 'resume the proceedings in respect of the offence with which the child is charged.'[93] Similarly, where a probation officer seeks more time or reports to the court that it seems unlikely that a conference will be held successfully, the court may either (a) grant an extension of time to convene a conference or (b) resume court proceedings.[94]

In terms of managing compliance with a family conference action plan, the Children Act provides[95] that:

> 83 – Where the Court has ordered a child to comply with an action plan and, on application by the probation and welfare officer who convened the relevant family conference, it appears to the Court that the child has, without reasonable cause, failed to comply with the terms of the plan, the Court may resume the proceedings in respect of the offence with which the child is charged.

In terms of good practice, such a conferencing approach should represent a unique and positive opportunity to engage with both the child in question and their family, as well as their victim or

---

89 s 81.
90 s 82(1).
91 s 82(4).
92 s 84.
93 s 82(2).
94 s 82(3).
95 s 83.

victims, and any significant others where appropriate, in addressing relevant issues in a strengths-based and restorative practice way.

McNulty[96] outlined the evolution and practice of probation-convened family conferences, including its threefold focus on: '... diversion of children and young people from the court, convictions and custody... the role and responsibility of parents and the interests of victims.'[97] The same author described the development of the measure in terms of planning and practice in the Probation Service, from the initial establishment in 2003 of a cross-grade group to develop thinking on youth justice approaches to be used by probation officers, in the context of the Children Act 2001, as well as describing how conferences themselves were prepared, convened, facilitated and managed. Nevertheless, and despite the Probation Service investing significantly in preparing for the implementation of this intervention, including through extensive planning and training a significant cohort of the agency's staff, this provision has been used in relatively small numbers of cases, since the legal provision was commenced. For example, in 2019, there were only seven such conferences completed following a court's request, with 22 having been held in 2018 and 23 in 2017.[98]

## Probation Officers' Assessment Reports for Court

At a very basic level, and leaving aside for a moment the specific rationale and requirements of the Children Act 2001, Pitts suggests that one reason a Judge might ask for a pre-sanction report is to establish the extent to which the young person may be held responsible for their actions"[99] and cites Matza whose view:

> suggests that this task is problematic in practice because young offenders seldom, if ever, resemble either the free legal subject so dear to the hearts of lawyers, or the determined social object beloved of cognitive behavioural psychologists... young offenders are neither wholly free nor wholly determined [and] [m]ost youth crime is, in reality, an ill-conceived shambles.[100]

---

[96] Brian McNulty, 'The Introduction of Family Conferencing to the Probation and Welfare Service' (2005) 2(1) Irish Probation Journal 42-51.

[97] ibid 43.

[98] Probation Service, Annual Report 2019 (2020) 54.

[99] John Pitts, *Working with Young Offenders,* in Jo Campling (series ed), *Practical Social Work* series (2nd edn, Macmillan/British Association of Social Workers 1999) 72.

[100] David Matza, *Delinquency and Drift* (Wiley 1964).

That said, as well as reports that probation officers provide to the Children Court on foot of any family conference they may have convened, the Children Act also makes specific provision for probation assessment reports on children before the Court, as follows:

> 99 – …where a court is satisfied of the guilt of a child, it –
> (a) may in any case, and
> (b) shall, where it is of opinion that the appropriate decision would be to impose a community sanction, detention (whether or not deferred under section 144) or detention and supervision,
>
> Adjourn the proceedings, remand the child and request a probation and welfare officer to prepare a report in writing (a "probation officer's report") which –
> (i) would assist the court in determining a suitable community sanction (if any) or another way of dealing with the child, and
> (ii) would contain information on such matters as may be prescribed, including any information specifically requested by the court.

Section 99 also deals with matters regarding the circumstances in which a probation officer might be asked to address issues in relation to any parental contribution to the child's offending behaviour;[101] as well as to victim impact reports;[102] situations where a court would be justified in *not* requesting a probation officer's report;[103] and the court's authority to summon witnesses in relation to any assessment reports presented to it. The Act also provides for the possibility of a court making a parental supervision order, to be supervised by a probation officer, for up to six months, and as part of which a range of supervision conditions such as participation by the parent/s on an appropriate training course or alcohol or drug treatment programme, in any case in which a child has been found guilty of an offence and the court '…is satisfied that a wilful failure of the child's parents to take care of or control the child contributed to the child's behaviour.'[104] It is not clear whether any such parental

---

101 s 99(2).

102 s 99(3).

103 s 99(4): where the penalty for the offence in question is fixed by law, or where there was a probation officer's report prepared on the child not more than 2 years previously and where the child's attitude and circumstances were similar on the previous occasion to what they are now; and where the previous report is available to the court.

104 s 111.

supervision orders have ever been made under Section 111 of the Children Act

Regarding the preparation and construction of pre-sanction reports prepared by a probation officer on behalf of the Children Court, or any other court dealing with criminal matters alleged to have been committed by a child, Quigley has described the process as follows:

> Pre-sentence reports are constructed in a narrative format based on interviews with the offender and, where appropriate, other relevant persons. The report informs the court on the personal and social history of the young person, their family, accommodation circumstances, education and/or training. It provides information and assessment relating to the current offence and any offending history. It assesses the young person's attitude to the offending behaviour and, where applicable, to the victim, and the level of risk of reoffending in the future. Based on this information, the report will propose a programme for the management of the young person in the community.[105]

Quigley concludes the analysis of her research findings by asserting that:

> ...the process of pre-sanction report preparation in the Children Courts has undergone substantial formalisation since its origins as a practice of special pleading to the Court [in early twentieth-century probation practice]... The streamlined approach, particularly evident over the past five to eight years, which has incorporated risk-oriented approaches, illustrates a changing field in pre-sentence report preparation... The changes, at practice level... are best understood as a gradual change in how the individual is assessed rather than a sudden discernible ideological shift. Many of the changes discussed operate in parallel with practices more aligned with traditional approaches that incorporate treatment ideals, utilise professional judgement and operate an informal approach to information gathering and communication... [T]he pre-sentence report preparation process in the Irish youth justice system, while adopting elements of the risk approach, may be described as a dual welfare/risk model. It would appear that YPP [Young Persons Probation] officers are achieving a

105 Etain Quigley, 'Pre-Sentence Reports in the Irish Youth Justice System: A Risk to Risk-Oriented Practice?' (2014) 11 Irish Probation Journal 63-86.

balance between risk-oriented approaches on one hand and fulfilling the broader needs of young offenders on the other.

The probation officer's report is recognised as a vital component in Children Court proceedings. This is reflected from a legal standpoint in the clarity of the legislation in question, including the fact that a court must request such an assessment report when considering a supervised community sanction, a custodial sentence, or a combination of the two. A pre-sanction assessment report is also generally considered (see also Chapter 4 on Probation Work) an essential pre-requisite to a period of probation or parole supervision to be undertaken by a probation officer with any individual. This is considered to be even more important where such a case involves a child or young person. In addition, while not *required* to do so by law, it has been the policy of the Probation Service for some time that a probation officer should be in attendance for all sittings of the Children Court, hearing criminal business, unless there are extraordinary reasons why this is not possible in relation to a particular court sitting.[106] This approach has been adopted because of the status of children and their potential vulnerability and the view that on the spot advice or access to relevant services should be facilitated by the probation officer's attendance at Children Court.

## Community Sanctions Supervised by the Probation Service

The Children Act 2001 makes provision for the imposition of penalties as follows:

> s 98 – Where a court is satisfied of the guilt of a child charged with an offence it may, without prejudice to its general powers and in accordance with this Part, reprimand the child or deal with the case by making one or more than one of the following orders:
>
> a) a conditional discharge order,
> b) an order that the child pay a fine or costs,
> c) an order that the parent or guardian be bound over,
> d) a compensation order,
> e) a parental supervision order,

[106] This is especially important where for example probation officers' pre-sanction reports are to be presented in Children Court. The probation officer attending and presenting such reports in court may not — for various reasons — be the author of the report in question. Nevertheless, the officer in court should be in a position to clarify any issues arising in relation to the assessment report and to make any follow-up enquiries or inputs as appropriate on the day.

f) an order that the parent or guardian pay compensation,
g) an order imposing a community sanction,
h) an order (the making of which may be deferred pursuant to section 144) that the child be detained in a children detention school or children detention centre, including an order under s 155 (1),[107]
i) a detention and supervision order.

The present chapter is predominantly concerned with those provisions of the Children Act 2001 that lead to a child being subject to probation intervention and supervision. In the context of the above list of potential penalties available under the Act, these are mainly those referred to as *community sanctions* at s 98(g) above. That said, there are potential supervisory responsibilities arising out of parental supervision orders (s 98(e)) and specifically in detention and supervision orders (s.98(i)) above. The range of community sanctions supervised by the Probation Service, provided for in the Children Act 2001 are listed in s 115, which describes a community sanction, being those sanctions '...which may be made by a court on being satisfied that a child is guilty of an offence' as follows:

a) A *community service order,*[108] '...in the case of a child of 16 or 17 years of age...';
b) A *day centre order,*[109] prescribing attendance at a day centre, run by or on behalf of the Probation Service, for up to 90 days, '...targeted at children who have moderate to high risk scores on the risk of re-offending scale and where other sanctions have been unsuccessful', [110] and at which centres they can participate in appropriate activities that are '...likely to be beneficial and supportive of the child's development;'
c) A *probation order* under the Probation of Offenders Act 1907, s 2;
d) A *probation (training or activities) order*, that is, an order 'that a child shall undertake and complete a programme of training or specified activities...' as recommended

[107] The Children Act 2001, s 155 deals with punishment of children, by sentences to detention, of certain indictable offences.

[108] Imposed under the provisions of the Criminal Justice (Community Service) Act 1983.

[109] For more, see ss 118-123 of the Children Act 2001, as well as PA McDermott and T Robinson (2003), *supra* n 69, pp 127-133.

[110] Seymour (n 1) 179.

as being productive for the child and their future good behaviour, by a probation officer, to the court;[111]

e) A *probation (intensive supervision) order*, comprising a probation order with additional requirements, including intensive supervision by the probation officer, residence at a specified location and participation at assigned education, training or treatment programmes for up to a maximum of 180 days;[112]

f) *A probation (residential supervision)* order, which can be for up to one year is one that requires '...that a child shall reside in a [designated] hostel residence[113]...;'

g) A *suitable person (care and supervision) order*, whereby 'a court may by order assign a child to the care of a person, including a relative of the child concerned (a 'suitable person')...;'[114]

h) A *mentor (family support) order*,[115] through which 'a court may... assign a child to a person... including a relative of the child concerned (a 'mentor'), to help, advise and support the child and the child's family in its efforts to prevent the child from committing further offences and to monitor the child's behaviour generally;'

i) A *restriction on movement order*, '...provides for the imposition of a restriction on movement order (or what is popularly known as a curfew). Typically, a child who has been engaged in criminal activity and perhaps substance abuse will be restricted to leaving his or her residence

---

111 Children Act 2001, s 124.

112 As prescribed in Children Act 2001, s 125(6)(c), where the period of intensive supervision is to exceed 90 days, it must be reviewed by the court after 60 days operation.

113 According to Children Act 2001, s 126(4)-(6) such hostel residences may be provided by the Probation Service or other provider and either way must be certified as suitable by the head of the Probation Service.

114 This provision, under the Children Act 2001, s 129, '...can only be made where the parents or guardian... consent in writing "and "...effectively substitutes a suitable person into the place of the parents or guardian' according to PA McDermott and T Robinson (2003), *supra* n 69, p 139. Such an order can be for up to two years. While it is in operation, the child must also be under the supervision of a probation officer.

115 Children Act 2001, s 131: must be made with the consent of the child and their parents or guardian, for up to two years and during which the child must remain under the supervision of a probation officer. In practice, and as described by Seymour (n 1) 179, 'Mentoring for children under the supervision of the Probation Service is facilitated by the Le Chéile Mentoring Project... Trained volunteers from the community are matched with children and the role of the mentor is to act as a positive role model to the child and to complement the work of the probation officer in reducing reoffending... Mentoring is also available as part of a standard probation order.'

during the daytime and will be prohibited from going out at night';[116] and

j) A *dual order*, whereby 'a supervision order or a day centre order can be combined with a restriction on movement order where the former orders would not be sufficient on their own to reduce the likelihood of the child committing further offences.'[117]

The Act explains that an order under *d, e,* and *f* above[118] '...shall for all purposes be a probation order, with the addition of [additional] requirements.' Section 116 of the Act details the manner and context in which a community sanction is to be imposed by a court, where the court considers that a community sanction is appropriate. These include:

- consideration of the probation officer's report,
- hearing the evidence of anyone whose attendance has been requested,
- giving the child's parent, guardian or relative an opportunity to give evidence,
- explaining to the child, in open court and in clear language, the meaning of the order and its 'terms and conditions.'

Section 116(3) also addresses the issue of what should happen in any case where a child does not express their willingness to comply with a community sanction and any conditions attached, the court may deal with the matter in any other way open to it. Section 116(4) addresses the issue of where a child fails to comply with a community sanction or where the sanction is revoked, stating that the court must not impose a custodial sanction as the alternative, unless that is the only suitable way to deal with the matter.

As described by McDermott and Robinson (2003), s 117:

> sets out a non-exhaustive list of the conditions which may be incorporated in a community sanction. The list is a broad one and the conditions may relate to any matters that the court considers appropriate in relation to the child.

The list of specific conditions that may be attached to a community sanction includes those relating to: attendance at school,

[116] PA McDermott and T Robinson (2003), *supra* n 69, p 142.
[117] PA McDermott and T Robinson (2003), *supra* n 69, p 145.
[118] Children Act 2001, s 124(2), s 125(2) and s 126(2).

employment, reducing risk of reoffending, place of residence, counselling or medical treatment, association with peers or others, attendance at specified premises, consumption of intoxicating substances, and any other matters the court may deem relevant or appropriate. Every community sanction (except community service orders and unless it has otherwise terminated) expires '…6 months after the child in respect of whom the order was made attains the age of 18 years.'[119] Where a child is found guilty of a new offence, while still on a community sanction, '…the court can impose a new sanction either in place of or in addition to the existing one.'[120]

## Probation Services Provided to those Sentenced to Detention and After Release

The Children Act 2001 makes extensive provision for and regulation of sentences involving detention of the child. Probation officers provide services, including assessment, interventions to help reduce risk of reoffending and facilitating reintegration into the community, to those detained in the Oberstown Children Detention Campus in Dublin. Under s 144, a court may — for any reason, but particularly if there is no suitable detention place available — defer the making of a detention order, during which time the court must adjourn the hearing and place the child under the supervision of a probation officer, who must then prepare a report for the court at the resumed hearing, at which point the sentence to detention can be activated, reduced or suspended. In addition:

> s 151 – (1) Where a court is satisfied that detention is the only suitable way of dealing with a child who is between 16 and 18 years of age, it may, instead of making a children detention order, make a detention and supervision order.
>
> (2) A detention and supervision order shall provide for detention in a children detention centre followed by supervision in the community.

Half of a detention and supervision order must be spent in detention and the other half under supervision in the community, with the latter supervision being provided by a probation officer. Simply put: 'This hybrid order provides for the first part of the time of the order to be spent in detention and the second half of

[119] Children Act 2001, s 138.

[120] PA McDermott and T Robinson (2003), *supra* n 69, p 145, regarding Children Act 2001, s 139.

the order to be spent in the community under supervision.'[121] It is also worthy of note that suspended and part-suspended sentences are otherwise not now legally applicable to children, although sentence can be deferred.

Two other forms of post-release supervision of children by the Probation Service are deserving of mention:

> (1) *'placing out' a child, under supervision in the community*[122] — whereby the Director of a children detention school may, following consultation with the Director of the Probation Service, and continuity of appropriate education and training being available, and any other conditions – such as regarding residency — being put in place, a child may be released early, under probation supervision; and
>
> (2) *voluntary aftercare* — '...allows a child, on release from a children detention school, to opt for supervision by a probation and welfare officer, if the Director [of the school] in consultation with the principal [probation] officer, considers that this would help the child reintegrate into society and resist committing further offences.'[123]

## Extreme Offending by Children and Young People

Thankfully, criminal cases involving very extreme offending by children – including crimes such as rape and homicide — are relatively rare. When they do occur, they tend to attract considerable attention from the news media and from the wider public. Although such extreme cases can be viewed as very much some of the negative features of modern times, they have been known through many decades, if not centuries.[124] There has been a small number of such homicide cases in particular, in Ireland in modern times. When such matters come before the courts, they call for particular responses, in terms of the court processes, sentencing and case management and supervision.

The Children Act 2001 is silent on the issue of children who commit

---

[121] PA McDermott and T Robinson (2003), *supra* n 69, pp 152-153.

[122] Children Act 2001, s 207.

[123] PA McDermott and T Robinson (2003), *supra* n 69, pp 192-193.

[124] One example, from a previous century is the killing by Robert Coombes (then aged 13 years) of his mother Emily Coombes in London, England, as described by Kate Summerscale, *The Wicked Boy: An infamous Murder in Victorian London* (Bloomsbury 2016).

very serious crimes, and specifically in the case of homicides. As discussed above, the general age of criminal responsibility in Ireland is now twelve years, while ten years is the age of criminal responsibility in relation to certain offences, including rape and homicide. Irish legislation deems that a conviction for the crime of murder carries a mandatory life imprisonment. The Children Act 2001 did not address how such a sentence should be applied to children. Nevertheless, the courts have developed their own responses in practice, in such cases.[125] The absence of relevant specific provision in the Children Act would appear to mean that when a child is convicted of murder, the court may impose a sentence of detention up to and including a life sentence. According to Gray, in such cases involving the sentencing of children: 'The practice of imposing a sentence, with an inbuilt review mechanism became fashionable among sentencing judges.'[126]

Regarding extreme offending by children — of whatever age — a number of recent cases in Ireland demonstrate particular aspects of the approach taken by Irish courts in some such cases. One of the most publicised and commented-on cases of recent times was that involving the killing of 14-year-old schoolgirl Ana Kriegel, following which two young[127] boys were sentenced at the Central Criminal Court; 'Boy A' to life in custody[128] with a review scheduled after twelve years, and 'Boy B' to 15 years, with a review to take place after 8 years. In an earlier case, White J, in the Central Criminal Court, sentenced a boy to life imprisonment for the murder of another boy, with a review after ten years – in 2014, after which the perpetrator was released in 2016, under the supervision of the Probation Service.

The practice of sentencing courts reviewing custodial sentences after a portion of the sentence has been served, once quite common,[129] was subsequently found by the Supreme Court to be unconstitutional as such reviews infringed the separation of powers doctrine and specifically the Executive powers of commutation of sentences.[130] These "Butler Order Reviews", however survive in the

---

125 See, for example, *State (O) v O'Brien* [1973] IR 50, discussed in Thomas O'Malley, *Sentencing Law and Practice* (Round Hall 2016).

126 Darren Gray, Sentencing & Children (2020) post on O'Sullivan Kenny LLP website, at: https://www.osullivankenny.ie/post/sentencing-children , accessed on 26 June 2020.

127 They were 13 years of age at the time of the offences.

128 'Boy A' was convicted of murder and aggravated sexual assault, 'Boy B' was convicted of murder.

129 Known as 'Butler Orders' after the practice was introduced in 1969 by Butler J in the case of *State (Woods) v Attorney General* [1969] IR 385.

130 *People (DPP) v Finn* [2001] 2 IR 25. For a discussion of this case, see O'Malley, T.

consideration of prisoners serving sentences following conviction of possession of drugs for supply under s 15A of the Misuse of Drugs Act 1977. In these cases, where the Minister for Justice is statutorily prohibited from granting temporary release, the court may, when imposing sentence, enquire if the offender was addicted to one or more controlled drug at the time of committing the offence. If the Court is satisfied that the offender was so addicted at the time of the offence and that such addiction was a significant factor in the commission of the particular crime, the Court may list the sentence for review after the expiry of one half of the custodial term imposed. When reviewing a sentence in accordance with this provision, the Court may suspend the balance of the sentence on such conditions as it thinks fit and may have regard to any factors they think appropriate. In limiting the opportunity to apply for review to cases involving addiction it is clear that the purpose of this evaluation is rehabilitative in nature. Another instance in which the sentencing courts review their own decisions after the offender has served part of their sentence is in cases of young persons convicted of murder, who have received a mandatory life sentence. The sentencing practice by judges in cases involving murders perpetrated by children, incorporating custodial sentences with inbuilt reviews, would appear to follow the spirit and intent of the Children Act 2001 but particularly in the absence of specific statutory provision, may be open to potential challenge from a constitutional point of view.

Despite the earlier Supreme Court finding that such reviews in general are unconstitutional, the courts have continued to use them in cases involving children. Indeed, the Court of Criminal Appeal upheld such a sentence in *DPP v DG*.[131] A person receiving a custodial sentence while still a child, and which will involve their remaining in custody after they become an adult, will serve the first part of that sentence in Oberstown Children Detention Campus until they pass 18 years of age, at which stage they will transfer to an adult prison. After this, and unless a sentence review has been ordered by the sentencing court, as described above, the person's subsequent release will become a matter for the Minister for Justice, or for the Parole Board in life sentence cases.[132]

---

'The Ends of Sentence: Imprisonment and Early Release Decisions in Ireland,' paper delivered at Fitzwilliam College, Cambridge, June 2008, later published in Nicola Padfield, Dirk Van Zyl Smit and Frieder Dünkel (eds), *Release from Prison: European Policy and Practice* (Willan Publishing 2010) 237-265.

131 *DPP v DG* (2005) Court of Criminal Appeal 198/04, 27 May 2005 (Murray CJ, O'Sullivan J and O'Leary J.

132 One of the most high-profile cases in the United Kingdom involving children convicted of murder was that of two 10-year-old boys, Robert Thompson and

## Desistance from Offending and the Age-Crime Curve

It has long been recognised that the majority of identified crimes are committed by persons in their teens and early to mid-twenties, with most of those maturing out of offending behaviour as they grow older, mature and develop a stronger stake in society. As Healy summarised:

> Longitudinal studies reveal that criminal activity tends to peak in adolescence and then tapers off in young adulthood. This phenomenon, known as the 'age-crime curve,' shows that by the age of 28, most offenders have ceased to be involved in crime. [133]

The concept and reality of the age-crime curve '...is one of the few criminological constants, which has been found in very similar shapes in different countries for a hundred years or more.'[134] The age-crime curve and its connection with desistance from crime are considered in more detail in Chapter 4 on Probation Work. The concept and reality of the age-crime curve are pointed to here because of the obvious implications for how any youth justice system responds to offending by children and young people in the first instance.

## Delineating Childhood and Adulthood

It is widely accepted in probation practice, as well as in social work and psychology for example, that one does not reach full human developmental maturity and become a fully functioning adult when one reaches one's eighteenth birthday, or — as is often said to illustrate this point – just at the point 'when you blow out the candles on your eighteenth birthday cake.'[135] Psychological and wider human development is now understood to continue for some

---

Jon Venables, both convicted for killing two-year-old James Bulger. Originally sentenced to detention 'at Her Majesty's pleasure' with a recommendation that they serve at least eight years, the Lord Chief Justice increased this to 10 years, with the Home Secretary subsequently increasing it again to at least 15 years – a decision later criticised by the European Court of Human Rights.

133 Deirdre Healy, *The Dynamics of Desistance: Critical pathways through change* (Willan 2010) 4.

134 Joanna Shapland and Anthony Bottoms, 'Desistance from crime and implications for offender rehabilitation,' in Alison Liebling, Shadd Marunavand Lesley McAra (eds), *The Oxford Handbook of Criminology* (6th edn, OUP 2017) 745-746.

135 Paraphrasing Dame Anne Owers, in the foreword to *Transition to Adulthood: Pathways from Crime: Ten steps to a more effective approach for young adults in the criminal justice process* (T2A Alliance/Barrow Cadbury Trust 2012) 2.

years after one turns eighteen, at least up to the early twenties, if not further. Nevertheless, for our purposes, eighteen years of age is when a person achieves legal maturity and all the accompanying responsibilities that go with it. However, acknowledging the above observations in relation to human development and maturation issues, the Probation Service has, for some years, adopted an approach of dealing as far as possible with service users who are over eighteen but under twenty-one with the same practice approaches taken with those under eighteen. In this respect, and to the extent that it is applied, Irish Probation practice accords with the provisions of the Council of Europe's Rules regarding juvenile offenders, which state that:

> [Rule 17] Young adult offenders may, where appropriate, be regarded as juveniles and dealt with accordingly.[136]

This is in a context where the same European Rules state the following definitions:

- [Rule 21.1] 'juvenile offender' means any person below the age of 18 who is alleged to have or has committed an offence… [and]
- [Rule 21.2] 'young adult offender' means any person between the ages of 18 and 21 who is alleged to have or has committed an offence and who is subject to these rules because he/she falls under the provisions of Rule 17…

Nevertheless, for reasons associated with overall resource limitations and the goal of maximising organisational efficiency, as well as the need to prioritise resources primarily on the basis of assessed risk of reoffending, the Irish Probation Service's enhanced approach to work with 18 to 21-year-olds tends to be confined to:

1. Those who are referred to the Service when they were still under eighteen, and who continue under probation supervision for a period of time after their eighteenth birthday, and
2. Those who are referred to the Service when they are between the ages of eighteen and twenty-one but who were previously service users while children.

The above provisions are principles rather than hard and fast rules and are subject to the exigencies of the Probation Service. The Irish

---

136 Council of Europe (n 30) rr 17, 21.1 and 21.2.

Penal Reform Trust published a report (IPRT, 2015) detailing the case for a bespoke or tailored approach to young adults (18-24) right across the criminal justice system, which advocated inter alia for a separate Justice strategy for 18 to 24-year-olds. [137] The General Scheme of the Community Sanctions Bill 2014 singles out the unique position of 18 to 21-year-olds to the extent that the Bill envisages that one of the situations in which a sentencing court would be required to requisition a probation officer's pre-sanction assessment report would include where the court is considering:

> (s. 2 [b]) imposing a sentence of imprisonment, and the person concerned –
> (i) is aged at least 18 years of age but under the age of 21 years, and
> (ii) has not previously been sentenced to a term of imprisonment of 12 months or more.

It should be noted that such strategies for and approaches to young adults, and particularly where they result in young adults being treated similarly to children, are not without their own unique challenges. For example, there would be an understandable reluctance among those managing penal sanctions (in the community or in custodial settings) to mix service users who are under 18 with those over 18. In that respect, some commentators might lament to some extent the policy and legal changes that have effectively removed the conceptual category of *juvenile* (16 to 21-year-olds) from the criminal justice system, even though there were very good reasons for doing so. A full discussion of these and related issues is beyond the scope of the present publication. Suffice to say that those managing and delivering relevant services can struggle to delineate services for those defined as children by law, while seeking to recognise and respond to developmental and other issues faced by those in their late teens and early twenties, in the context of managing community-based and other sanctions.

## Young People's Offending — Individual Responsibility and the Community Dimension

From time to time, in Ireland as elsewhere, there have emerged widespread concerns in relation to spates of very public or publicised offending. This can occur in any number of contexts, sometimes linked to specific individual serious crimes and at other

[137] Irish Penal Reform Trust, *Turnaround Youth: Young Adults (18-24) in the Criminal Justice System – The case for a distinct approach* (IPRT 2015).

times triggered by protracted periods of public or visible offending, perhaps in one identifiable town, neighbourhood or geographical area, and frequently attributed to 'out of control' or 'lawless' young people. One such report — on *Urban Crime and Disorder* — in one particular area of Dublin in 1992, was established to address the issue of persistent 'Dublin Juvenile Vandalism' in that area.[138] A number of research projects[139] and Lord Mayor's commissions and reports — such as Dublin City Council[140] — have focused on similar issues in their respective areas. More recently, studies by Nolan[141] and Geiran[142] were commissioned by Dublin City Council and the Department of Justice respectively, to provide analyses and recommendations in respect of two identified geographical areas, not exclusively confined to youth offending but incorporating significant concerns regarding the involvement of young people in serious, drug-related crime.

In reality, such concerns and the response to them have not only emerged in recent times, although that can appear to be the case. By way of illustrating this fact, over forty years ago, Rottman[143] quoted a report from almost six decades earlier (1925) by the General Prisons Board, in relation to crime in Ireland, which stated that:

> We have, within the last few years, to deal with an entirely new class of criminal, composed of half-educated youths who would appear to have escaped early from parental control. They have grown up in lawless habits, and the streets and the cinema have been the main sources of their moral education. Full of new and unsatisfied desires, these youths have been dazzled by sensational reports in newspapers of large sums of money obtained by organised robbery… Formerly a series of convictions for minor offences preceded offences of a grave

---

138 Interdepartmental Group, *Urban Crime and Disorder: Report of the Interdepartmental Group* (1992) 13.

139 For example, see Niamh Hourigan, 'Juvenile Justice, Crime and Early Intervention: Key Challenges from the Limerick Context' (2012) 9 Irish Probation Journal 64-74.

140 Dublin City Council, Lord Mayor's Commission on Anti-Social Behaviour (2012).

141 Jack Nolan, *Darndale: A Long View of an Enduring Challenge, A Socio-Economic & Community Plan* (Dublin City Council 2020).

142 Vivian Geiran, *Drogheda: Creating a Bridge to a Better Future (Community Safety and Wellbeing: Report of a Scoping Review for the Department of Justice)* (Department of Justice 2021).

143 DB Rottman, *Crime in the Republic of Ireland: Statistical Trends and Their Interpretation (ESRI Paper No 102)* (Economic and Social Research Institute 1980) 141.

> nature. Now the first offender starts with the more serious form of crime (quoted in Molony,[144] 1925-26, 183).

The overarching point here is that while acute concerns regarding offending by young people emerge from time to time, they are not new in historical terms. The acknowledgement of these concerns however serves to point up the fact that criminal behaviour by young people is about more than simply what Pitts has described as:

> the tedious rhetoric of 'individual responsibility' [that] belies a stark reality in which growing numbers of young people are being driven to desperate, often self-destructive, lengths in order to salvage a livelihood and a plausible identity from an increasingly barren social and economic environment.[145]

While Pitts acknowledges that 'the proclivities of individuals play a significant role in the problem of crime, it is also clear that crime is not reducible to the inability of some parents to instil a capacity for self-control in their children.'[146] In this context, he emphasises a need to include 'local analysis… and the participation of residents in the local and regional economies' in localised strategies aimed at crime prevention.[147] Such wider considerations — including peer group and local community dimensions, as well as extended kinship connections — need to be taken into account and addressed in dealing with offending by young people. One benefit of the various localised analyses and responses to youth offending that have been carried out from time to time has been repeated efforts to improve interagency cooperation at local and national levels. Similarly, one very practical and useful example of how such issues in relation to offending by young people as part of criminal networks themselves, can be and continue to be addressed is reflected in the cutting-edge Irish research and practice initiatives arising out of the Greentown project[148] (and related research and practice initiatives).[149] This research and the implications for practice have been incorporated into the Youth Justice Strategy, and the actions — by various

---

144 Thomas Molony, 'The Probation of Offenders' (1925-26) XV (Cont) Journal of the Statistical and Social Inquiry Society of Ireland 181-196.

145 Pitts (n 99) 33-34.

146 Pitts (n 99) 116.

147 ibid 33.

148 Sean Redmond, *Lifting the Lid on Greentown: Why we should be concerned about the influence criminal networks have on children's offending behaviour in Ireland* (Department of Children and Youth Affairs/University of Limerick 2016).

149 See also: Sean Redmond (2015) 'The Greentown Crime Network: Introducing its Cast of Principal Actors' (2015) 12 Irish Probation Journal 205-228.

relevant agencies concerned with child offending, protection and welfare — arising from that.[150]

## Probation Service — Organisational Responses and Other Operational Approaches

In broad terms, the generic work of probation officers aimed at achieving organisational goals and specifically interventions focused on reducing reoffending by service users, whether they are legally children or adults, is as set out in the other relevant chapters, particularly in Chapter 4 on Probation Work. While the Probation of Offenders Act 1907 had envisaged the designation of certain probation officers as 'children's probation officers,' the practice over many decades since then was that probation officers working in the courts and the community tended to carry generic caseloads, comprising adults and children under supervision. In some areas of the country, particularly the larger urban centres, it also was not unusual for individual probation officers on generic community teams to supervise most or all of the children on probation in that area. This made sense for example because of the fact that such probation officers developed strong links with relevant services in the area, including schools and training centres, educational welfare and psychology, child protection and welfare services, child and adolescent mental health professionals and so on. In addition, clearly those probation officers working over those years in custodial institutions catering for children, specialised in that area of work for the duration of their assignments there.

Following the introduction of the Children Act 2001, however, a decision was made to establish a specialised operational division — Young Persons Probation (YPP) — within the Probation Service. In the years immediately after the introduction of the Children Act, YPP comprised five specialised teams, with two teams based in Dublin, and one each in Cork, Limerick and Waterford. Following a comprehensive review of Probation Service operations in 2006, YPP was further strengthened, with an increase in the number of its teams and personnel assigned, and its designation as a national 'region' within the Probation Service, headed up by an Assistant Director.[151] Under this structure, all YPP probation officers were assigned to YPP teams, operating within and managed by the overarching YPP management structure, with the relevant Assistant

---

150 Department of Justice (n 142).

151 Probation Service, *An 'As Is' Audit of Probation Operations in Ireland, July – October 2006* (Probation Service 2007).

Director reporting in turn to the Probation Service's Director of Operations. This structure facilitated the development of Service practice in this area, a clearer 'mapping' of YPP with other bodies such as An Garda Síochána and the Irish Youth Justice Service, as well as a more focused engagement with the courts and relevant partner agencies and organisations. It also created a clearly identifiable line of sight and responsibility for probation practice with children, within the Probation Service. In addition, certain community-based organisations funded through the Probation Service were identified as specific YPP resources and managed and developed accordingly.

In 2009, there were 1,098 court referrals for probation officer assessment reports of all kinds on children, with 844 orders for supervision of children, and 32 referrals for (probation-run) family conferences under the Children Act.[152] A decade later, in 2019 by contrast, the courts made 651 referrals for assessment of children to the Probation Service, with 581 supervision orders of all types being made, and seven referrals for family conferences. In terms of the annual sum-total of a collection of specific 'pieces of work' requested of the Probation Service by the Children Courts, the above represents a drop of 37 percent in such referrals. This fall-off in numbers of referrals of children to the Probation Service over the decade in question may be for a number of reasons. These may be related to changes in crime statistics and reporting, increased diversion of young people from prosecution and the courts system, and even a decline in the number of young people in the general population. There may also be issues in relation to the ways the youth justice system operated in the relatively immediate aftermath of the operationalisation of the Children Act, as well as potentially any number of other reasons. The economic recession of a decade or so ago, the consequent reduction in available public service resources, as well as any number of other factors, may also have had an impact on numbers of referrals of children for supervised community sanctions.

Particularly since the establishment of YPP, the Probation Service has recognised, through a number of internal workload agreement frameworks agreed between Service management and staff representatives of the relevant trade union, that the standard caseload of a YPP probation officer has generally been set at somewhere around 50% to 60% of the comparable caseload of adults under probation supervision by an individual probation officer. This has been done to reflect the needs and rights of children

---

152 Probation Service, *Annual Report 2009* (2010) 28.

and young people, their potential vulnerability and lifecycle stage, as well as where they may be on the 'age-crime curve,' and their consequent prioritisation within the overall Probation Service caseload, so as to divert them from the criminal justice system, and particularly from harsher sanctions and all that might imply, as early as possible

## Probation Practice with Children and Young People

'The founding principles, operational functioning and impact of the institutions which have evolved across the four nations in the United Kingdom to deal with children and young people who come into conflict with the law,' as well as the shifting paradigms and 'patterns of control which have emerged' there, have been discussed by McAra (2017),[153] who also sets out a matrix of the various paradigms in youth justice in the United Kingdom, and their implications.[154] Those paradigms and patterns are of interest in the context of the present publication, given our shared history and legal system with our nearest neighbouring jurisdictions. In Ireland, a comprehensive exploration of the history and paradigms employed at various times in relation to youth justice in this country has been carried out by Sargent (2010[155] and 2014[156]) as well as by Convery and Seymour.[157]

In many respects, the approach to probation and parole practice with individual children and young people is structured in similar ways to the principles and frameworks described in other relevant chapters, and particularly in Chapter 4 on Probation Work. Internationally, the trend in probation and parole policy and practice has been to adopt specialised structures, methods and approaches to assessment, interventions and programmes and indeed all aspects of probation and parole work with children and young people. A number of different interventions and programmes have been trialled or prioritised in probation work with children and young people. Such approaches would tend to be provided in the context of the prevailing paradigms (or the

---

153 Lesley McAra, 'Youth Justice,' in Alison Liebling, Shadd Maruna and Lesley McAra (eds), *The Oxford Handbook of Criminology* (6th edn OUP 2017) 938-966.

154 ibid 942.

155 Paul Sargent, *A History of Youth Justice in Ireland: Opening up the Space of Government* (PhD Thesis, Trinity College, The University of Dublin 2010).

156 Paul Sargent, *Wild Arabs and Savages: A history of juvenile justice in Ireland* (Manchester University Press 2014).

157 Una Convery and Mairéad Seymour, 'Children, crime and justice,' in Deirdre Healy and others (eds), *The Routledge Handbook of Irish Criminology* (Routledge 2016) 2423-260.

mixture of paradigms and 'treatment' goals arising) in youth justice. While a range of different approaches and interventions have been tried, some of those that have been favoured more recently include educational approaches,[158] intensive supervision,[159] family work,[160] restorative practice,[161] as well as the application of Core Correctional Practices[162] with juveniles,[163] among others and in addition to the 'standard' menu of probation interventions and approaches as described elsewhere in this chapter as well as in Chapter 4. A number of recent commentators (eg Brierley[164] and Fullerton[165]) have re-emphasised the absolute importance of the worker-child professional relationship in probation and youth justice work with young people, as well as the need for workers to be trauma-aware in their work with all probationers, but with young people in particular.

According to the Irish Probation Service's website:

> The Probation Service knows that working with young people who offend is different to working with adults who offend. As a result, we have developed a division of trained staff – Young Persons Probation (YPP) to work with children and teenagers between the ages of 12 and 18 who come before the Courts or who are in the Children Detention Schools/Centre. Young people make up a good proportion of new referrals to our services and we support and work with a range of

---

158 Geoff Hayward, Martin Stephenson and Maggie Blyth, 'Exploring effective educational interventions for young people who offend,' in Ros Burnett and Colin Roberts (eds), *What Works in Probation and Youth Justice: Developing evidence-based practice* (Willan 2004) 88-108.

159 Robin Moore, 'Intensive supervision and surveillance programmes for young offenders: the evidence so far,' in Ros Burnett and Colin Roberts (eds), *What Works in Probation and Youth Justice: Developing evidence-based practice* (Willan 2004) 159-179.

160 Chris Trotter, *Collaborative Family Work in Youth Justice,* HM Inspectorate of Probation, Academic Insights 2021/02 HM Inspectorate of Probation 2021).

161 Ian Marder, *Building Restorative Probation Services,* Academic Insights 2020/04 (HM Inspectorate of Probation 2020).

162 See more about Core Correctional Practices (CCPs) in Chapter 4.

163 Pamela Ugwudike and Gemma Morgan, 'Evidence-based skills in Welsh youth justice settings,' in Pamela Ugwudike, Peter Raynor and Jill Annison (eds), *Evidence-Based Skills in Criminal Justice: International research on supporting rehabilitation and desistance* (Policy Press 2018) 291-316.

164 Andrew Brierley, *Connecting with Young People in Trouble* (Waterside Press 2021).

165 Deirdre Fullerton, John Bamber and Sean Redmond, *Developing effective relationships between youth justice workers and young people: a synthesis of the evidence,* REPPP Review (University of Limerick 2021).

> programmes to help young people at a critical time in their lives.[166]

The Probation Service also identified four specific community-based organisations dealing with young persons on probation supervision that have been co-funded by the Irish Government and the European Social Fund (ESF) as part of the ESF Programme for Employability, Inclusion and Learning, 2014-2020. The organisations are Le Chéile, which is a nationwide mentoring service, Céim ar Chéim and Southill projects based in Limerick City and Dóchas don Óige based in Galway. These and other partner organisations collaborate with YPP officers in the various aspects of their role as summarised below, particularly in relation to assisting young persons to achieve long-term desistance from offending.

Seymour summarises the various elements of the particular role of YPP probation officers as follows:

> Social workers employed by the Probation Service as Young Persons Probation (YPP) officers have direct input into all aspects of children's progression through the youth justice system. Their role ranges from court liaison work, through to: convening family conferences; assessing children's suitability for community-based sanctions; managing children's cases while they are under supervision in the community; addressing the factors related to offending behaviour; providing support to children's families; and working to provide for the needs of offending children in conjunction with statutory, community and voluntary organisations.[167]

Probation practice approaches adopted with children and young people have emphasised interagency cooperation at all levels[168] and included family-focused interventions such as the Strengthening Families Programme,[169] and child and parent mentoring, among others. Since 2017, a number of young people aged 16 to 21-years of age, identified as persistent and prolific offenders have been included in pilot programmes in Dublin and Cork initially aimed at

---

166 Probation Service webpage on Young Persons Probation (YPP): http://www.probation.ie/EN/PB/WebPages/WP16000038 accessed on 5 July 2021.

167 Seymour (n 1) 164.

168 For example: Catherine McGowan, 'The Ballymun Network for Assisting Children and Young People' (2009) 6 Irish Probation Journal 124-134.

169 For more information on the Strengthening Families Programme, see: http://sfpcouncilireland.ie/strengthening-families/. See also Mary McGagh, Emma Gunn and Rachel Lillis, 'Strengthening Families Programme: An Interagency Approach to Working with Families' (2009) 6 Irish Probation Journal 113-123.

managing and addressing problematic behaviour and helping the young people involved to move away from crime. This programme is known as Y-JARC, or Youth-Joint Agency Response to Crime.[170] These and other similar initiatives and programmes reflect the specialised approach to providing services to children and young people who have offended.

## Conclusion

This chapter has described key elements of the law and practice in relation to probation and parole services for children and young people who have committed criminal offences. Such practice with children and young people is founded in large part on the progressive and modern statutory provisions of the Children Act 2001, which in turn builds on the provisions of earlier legislative provisions such as the Probation of Offenders Act 1907 and the Criminal Justice (Community Service) Act 1983. At the time of writing, the Children Act 2001 is undergoing review by the Department of Justice, with a number of potential areas for change flagged in the current youth justice strategy.[171] It remains to be seen what legislative changes may follow from that review process, as well as their implications for future practice in this area. What seems certain is that work to reduce children's and young people's risk of and actual involvement in offending will continue to be a high priority for government, government departments, their agencies and other relevant organisations.

Clearly, a number of children and young people do come before the courts, charged with having offended, sometimes seriously and/or persistently. Because our modern youth justice system has a range of options that serve to divert children from the formal, court process where possible, it is generally only those for whom there is deemed to be no other option, who end up in court. Even then, every effort should be – and is – made to use diversion options at that stage, for example through the availability of measures such as family conferencing and the use of detention options as a last resort. Thankfully, as Pitts[172] has pointed out:

> Most children and young people grow out of crime…If we

---

[170] Y-JARC is a multi-agency case management process, with similarities to the Integrated Offender Management initiatives in the United Kingdom and elsewhere. For more, see–http://www.justice.ie/en/JELR/Pages/Joint_Agency_Response_to_Crime .

[171] Department of Justice (n 46) 33-36.

[172] Pitts (n 99) 97.

> can hang on, and encourage others to hang on as well, we can often see a child or young person through their offending and out the other side (Rutherford, 1986[173])... Our responses to young offenders must reflect the reality of growth and change.

This reality is as applicable at the court stage and with those children and young people who experience probation supervision as it must with those who are managed at other points along the criminal justice process.

[173] Andrew Rutherford, *Growing Out of Crime* (Penguin 1986).

CHAPTER 10

# ELECTRONIC MONITORING[1]

## Introduction

Electronic Monitoring (EM) of offenders, as well as of accused persons in some situations, has been in use in a range of jurisdictions, including those of our nearest neighbours (United Kingdom), for some years. Nevertheless, Ireland had not moved to introduce EM technology as an offender management tool in practice up to 2004, when Michael McDowell TD, then Minister for Justice, announced in a speech to the annual conference of the (Irish) Prison Officers Association (POA) that he intended to introduce 'electronic tagging of criminals… as an alternative to custodial sentences, to free up prison places.'[2] The Minister also cited the perceived value of EM, that he favoured the greater use of non-custodial measures, including EM, particularly for first time offenders and relatively minor offending. Legislation to introduce EM was, in fact, enacted two years later, and EM has subsequently been used in Ireland for over a decade and a half. Nevertheless, the approach to its usage in offender management has been cautious, its introduction has been slow, and its usage in practice has been quite limited. This chapter will outline the relevant legislation on EM and consider the use of the measure in Ireland, in practice, having first provided a short description of the historical development of EM internationally.

## The History and Development of EM Internationally: Its Growth and Uses

Electronic monitoring of offenders can evoke visions of criminal justice *utopia* or *dystopia*, depending on one's point of view. From its original conception, EM has sought to offer — at the utopian end of the conceptual spectrum — a relatively cheap and efficient means for monitoring or restricting the location and movements of persons accused or convicted of crimes. For those who view

1 An earlier version of this chapter appeared as an article ('Electronic Monitoring in Ireland: Disruptive Innovation, Affordance, or a Technology in Search of a Rationale?'(2021) 18 Irish Probation Journal 49-72.

2 Conor Lally, 'Electronic tags on prisoners proposed', *The Irish Times*, 7 May 2004, available at: https://www.irishtimes.com/news/electronic-tags-on-criminals-proposed-1.1139386 (accessed 7 November 2021).

EM from a more dystopian perspective, it appears to epitomise the 'coercive connectivity'[3] or 'ambulant or mobile punishment'[4] of the modern day, technology-facilitated *panopticon*.[5]

As summarised by Nellis, 'EM was an American invention', where '…the notion that the locations of convicted criminals could and should be pinpointed and/or tracked had been imagined by science fiction writers and futurologists' going back to the 1950s and '60s, before becoming '…an experimental, notionally rehabilitative, technology in the hands of behavioural psychologists Ralph and Robert Schwitzgebel (later Gable) at Harvard University in the 1960s.'[6] Lilly and Nellis have traced the origins of EM to the work of the Schwitzgebels, as well as others, who developed the technology to make EM possible in practice.[7] Nevertheless, '…none of the technologies were adopted by criminal justice agencies, or subject to further research and development, nor did they find commercial sponsors… There was no governmental or professional attempt to revive interest in the work of the Schwitzgebels…' until '…EM as we came to know it arrived almost surreptitiously' through its unilateral introduction by Albuquerque (New Mexico, USA) Judge Jack Love.[8] Judge Love had become interested in the concept of EM as a potential way of facilitating early release from custody, since 1977 and particularly following a penitentiary riot in 1980.

3 Mike Nellis, 'Electronically monitored offenders as "coercive connectivity": Commerce and penality in surveillance capitalism,' in Tom Daems and Tom Vander Beken (eds), *Privatizing Punishment in Europe?* (Routledge 2018) 124-142.

4 Fergus McNeill, *Pervasive Punishment: Making Sense of Mass Supervision* (Emerald Publishing 2019) 5, citing Christine Morganstern, '"Der Resozialisierungsgrundsatz" — Social reintegration as the dominant narrative for community punishment in Germany,' in Gwen Robinson and Fergus McNeill (eds), *Community Punishment: European Perspectives* (Routledge 2016) 72-94.

5 According to Richard J Butler, *Building the Irish Courthouse and Prison: A political history, 1750-1850,* (Cork University Press 2020) 167-168, '…Jeremy Bentham invented "the panopticon", an architectural device that brought together the concept of complete moral control of prisoners with its author's widely publicised utilitarian theories… It was somewhat similar to Blackburn's radial plan [for the construction of 18th and 19th century prisons] but with the crucial difference that all the cells opened facing the inspection tower, allowing the gaoler to see not only the common yards but also – and critically – the entire interior of every cell.'

6 Mike Nellis, 'The Electronic Monitoring of Offenders in the European Penal Imaginary,' in Eoin Carroll and Kevin Warner (eds), *Re-imagining Imprisonment in Europe: Effects, Failures and the Future* (The Liffey Press 2014) 220-221.

7 Robert Lilly and Mike Nellis, 'The limits of techno-utopianism: electronic monitoring in the United States of America,' in Mike Nellis, Kristel Beyens and Dan Kaminski (eds), *Electronically Monitored Punishment: International and Critical Perspectives* (Routledge 2013) 21-43.

8 ibid 24.

Judge Love succeeded in introducing EM as a way of monitoring a 'home detention' condition of probation supervision, before he was eventually stopped from doing so by his judicial superiors. Despite this, other US states and commercial organisations developed and introduced the technology over the following years, which also then '…spread steadily from the US to Canada, Australia, England and Wales, Sweden and the Netherlands.'[9] Britain was the first European jurisdiction to introduce EM. That introduction was not instigated in the first instance by 'the conventional channels of penal innovation' but rather by the efforts of 'Sunday Times journalist and prison visitor Tom Stacey' on the basis of his view '…that most alternatives to prison were inadequate', which in turn prompted the Home Office to follow up Stacey's idea, visit American programmes '…and then "constructed" EM as the logical extension of tracking and curfews.'[10] According to Mair, '[t]he first use in England and Wales of electronic monitoring as a tool in the criminal justice process took place during 1989-90 in the course of a six-month trial of electronic monitoring as a condition of bail.'[11] Since then, EM has been developed and implemented in all the UK's jurisdictions, as well as those in various European countries and elsewhere.[12]

EM programmes can utilise '…a range of distinct-but-related surveillance technologies', as well as different supporting infrastructures or contexts of implementation. In terms of the technology, these fall broadly under the following headings, as summarised by Nellis (2016):

- *Radio frequency* (RF) systems: '…the original and still most widespread… which require a signalling device (colloquially, a "tag") to be fitted to the ankle or wrist…' of a person '…and for them to remain in close proximity to a transceiver in their home, which relays data about their presence or absence to a monitoring centre, either by a landline or, increasingly, the cellular telephone system.'[13]

---

9 Mike Nellis (n 6) 223.

10 Mike Nellis, 'Electronic monitoring and the community supervision of offenders,' in Anthony Bottoms, Sue Rex and Gwen Robinson (eds), *Alternatives to Prison: options for an insecure society* (Willan 2004) 228.

11 George Mair, 'Technology and the future of community penalties,' in Anthony Bottoms, Loraine Gelsthorpe and Sue Rex (eds), *Community Penalties* (Willan 2001).

12 For example, see Lilly and Nellis (n 7).

13 Mike Nellis, 'Electronic Monitoring and Probation Practice,' in Fergus McNeill, Ioan Durnescu, and Renee Butter (eds), *Probation: 12 Essential Questions* (Palgrave-Macmillan 2016) 217-243.

- *Voice verification* systems: '...use the uniqueness of a person's voice to identify them during a phone call, by matching it with a biometric voiceprint already stored, at the point of sentence, in the monitoring centre's computer, and tallying this with the location from which the phone call is made.'[14]
- *Global positioning systems* (GPS): 'The preferred, and increasingly popular, means of tracking an offender's movements relies on geo-location satellites... The precision and accuracy of satellite tracking systems, which require ankle-worn devices that both pick up GPS signals and transmit location data to monitoring centres, is invariably augmented by – and could not operate efficiently without – cellular telephone systems, and can be supported by night-time curfew requirements which require the defendant/offender to go home and charge the battery.'[15]

In addition,

- *Remote alcohol monitoring*, which allows consumption of alcohol to be monitored and measured remotely, through breath or sweat analysis via the anklet or other device in the subject's home for example, has also been trialled or used in a number of jurisdictions.[16]

EM can also be used in a number of different ways or contexts. According to Beyens and Roosen, there are basically two different models of EM: [1] '...the models where EM is part of an integrated sentence and where EM is applied in combination with other supervisory conditions that are followed up by probation officers, and' [2] 'those where EM is a standalone measure.'[17] Interestingly, in some jurisdictions, EM is used in prison, for example as a means of tracking the whereabout of inmates in open or semi-open facilities.

The early history and development of EM of offenders, in the comparative international context, has been documented in Nellis (2013[a])[18] for example. In the introduction to that publication, the

---

14 ibid 219.
15 ibid 219.
16 ibid 218.
17 K Beyens and M Roosen , 'Electronic monitoring and rehabilitation,' in P Ugwudike, H Graham, F McNeill, P Raynor, F Taxman, and C Trotter, *The Routledge Companion to Rehabilitative Work in Criminal Justice*, (Routledge 2020) , p 895.
18 M Nellis, K Beyens and D Kaminski (eds) (2013[a]) (n 7).

authors summarised that, at that time, EM had been introduced as a penal measure in over thirty countries since the 1980s, "having originated in the United States."[19] While many studies of EM have focused on its use in individual, specific jurisdictions, more recently, some researchers have focused on comparative studies of a number of jurisdictions and their use of EM. For example, Graham and McIvor,[20] Hucklesby and others,[21] Beyens[22] and Hucklesby and others[23] have authored international comparative studies on the uses of EM in different jurisdictions, primarily in Europe.

In what was described by Nellis and others as 'a very generic definition.' Nellis and Rossell proposed that: 'EM technology must be understood as nothing more or less than a form of remote surveillant control, a means of flexibly regulating the spatial and temporal schedules of an offender's life.'[24] Nellis, in his Handbook for the Council of Europe, defines the purpose of EM as follows:

> Electronic monitoring technologies enable judicial and executive authorities to restrict, regulate and enforce a suspect or offender's spatial and temporal activity (their locations, movements and schedules) at a distance, often in 'real time', potentially in a very finely calibrated way, for periods of variable duration.[25]

Crucial, in terms of understanding EM as a concept and practice, is the assertion by Nellis and others that:

> EM Is not one single thing, technologically speaking. Different

---

19 M Nellis, K Beyens and D Kaminski. (2013[b]) 'Introduction: making sense of electronic monitoring,' contained in M Nellis, K Beyens and D Kaminski (eds) (2013[a]), (n 7).

20 Hannah Graham and Gill McIvor, *Scottish and International Review of the Uses of Electronic Monitoring* (Scottish Centre for Crime & Justice Research (SCCJR) Report No 8 2015).

21 Anthea Hucklesby and others, 'Creativity and effectiveness in the use of electronic monitoring: A case study of five jurisdictions' (2016) 27(2) Journal of Offender Monitoring 31-47.

22 Kristel Beyens, 'Electronic monitoring and supervision: A comparative perspective' (2017) 9(1) European Journal of Probation 3-10.

23 Anthea Hucklesby, Kristel Beyens and Miranda Boone, 'Comparing electronic monitoring regimes: Length, breadth, depth and weight equals tightness' (2020) *Punishment & Society* 1-19.

24 Mike Nellis and NT Rossell, *Electronic Monitoring and Probation: Offender rehabilitation and the reduction of prison populations* (Report on 7th European Electronic Monitoring Conference, 5-7 May 2011, Évora, Portugal).

25 Mike Nellis, *Standards and Ethics in Electronic Monitoring: handbook for professionals responsible for the establishment and the use of Electronic Monitoring* (Council of Europe 2015).

> types of technologies are being used and innovation continues. The first and still most dominant type uses radio frequency (RF) to ensure an offender – fitted with a signalling device on his ankle (or more rarely wrist) – remains within proximity of a transceiver in his home, which relays his presence (or absence) via landline or mobile phone technology to a monitoring centre which may be hundreds of miles away. By such means, and with a number of anti-tamper mechanisms built into the device, curfews or house arrest can be affected.[26]

For a succinct, and simultaneously all-encompassing, definition of EM, one might consider Simon's, which suggests that EM is '...designed to enforce spatialized exclusion on those deemed low enough risk to be out in public either on a pre-trial release, or as part of a sentence of parole following imprisonment, or on probation as an alternative to imprisonment.'[27] Nellis summarises that 'Electronic Monitoring (EM) is the use of remote surveillance technologies to pinpoint the locations and/or movements of offenders and/or defendants'; and that EM '...was first used in Europe a quarter of a century ago, and has become an established — although by no means ubiquitous or dominant — feature of the continent's collective "penal imaginary".'[28]

According to Hucklesby and Holdsworth:

> England and Wales was the first European jurisdiction to deploy electronic monitoring (EM) technology in 1989 and its use has since grown both in terms of numbers and modalities. England and Wales remains one of the largest and most enthusiastic users of EM in the world. At the time of writing, EM is used mostly to enforce curfew requirements and is deployed as a condition of bail, a requirement of community and suspended sentence orders and as a form of early release under the Home Detention Curfew scheme.[29]

Some years ago, and in a context where EM had already been in use in a range of European jurisdictions for twenty years or more, Nellis and others suggested that: '[t]here is as yet no settled view as to EM's nature or significance, its constructive potential or its

---

26 Nellis *et al* (2013[b]), (n 19), p 5.

27 Jonathan Simon, 'Punishment and the Political Technologies of the Body,' in Jonathan Simon and Richard Sparks (eds), *The Sage Handbook of Punishment and Society* (Sage 2013) 80.

28 Nellis. (n 6) (2014) p 217.

29 Anthea Hucklesby and Ella Holdsworth, *Electronic Monitoring in England and Wales*, (Centre for Criminal Justice Studies, University of Leeds 2016) 3.

dangers.'[30] Since then, EM has remained and indeed grown, in terms of usage, as an instrument of offender monitoring, management and rehabilitation.

Before moving to summarise the legislative situation in Ireland, it is worth mentioning the international standards on EM, as enunciated by the Council of Europe (CoE) Standards. The introduction of Council of Europe standards on EM,[31] were finalised in 2014 and have been further elaborated on by Nellis.[32] The development of those European standards was instigated by the Confederation of European Probation (CEP)[33] and developed in the context of the growth in the widespread use of EM in Europe; and according to Nellis (2016), 'undoubtedly influenced EM's development for the better in Europe,' as well as setting out a '...human rights framework for implementing EM.'[34]

## The Law on Electronic Monitoring in Ireland

There have been three pieces of enacted legislation enabling EM to be introduced in Ireland. In addition, at the time of writing, there is another Bill before the Houses of the Oireachtas, and which would provide for extended use of EM in this country. These four pieces of legislation are:

1. The Criminal Justice Act 2006; and
2. The Criminal Justice Act 2007;
   as well as
3. The Criminal Justice Act 2017; and
4. The Sex Offenders (Amendment) Bill 2018 and the Sex Offenders (Amendment) Bill 2021.

The first piece of legislation that provided for EM in Ireland, and under which EM has actually been introduced, was the Criminal Justice Act 2006. This was a significant addition to statute law. Among its various provisions, the Act specifically provides

30 Nellis and Rossell, (2013) (n 24) pp 14-16.

31 Council of Europe, Recommendation CM/Rec (2014) 4 of the Committee of Ministers to member States on electronic monitoring, adopted by the Committee of Ministers on 19 February 2014 (Council of Europe).

32 Mike Nellis, *Standards and Ethics in Electronic Monitoring: Handbook for professionals responsible for the establishment and the use of Electronic Monitoring* (Council of Europe 2015).

33 As pointed out by Mike Nellis (2016) (n 13) p 217, the CEP has convened a series of European conferences on EM, since 1998; for more information on these: https://www.cep-probation.org/knowledgebases/electronic-monitoring/.

34 Mike Nellis (2016) (n 13) pp 217-218.

a clear legislative basis for fully or part-suspended custodial sentences, with or without probation supervision — as well as the first provision in law for electronically monitored restriction on movement orders — focused on offender rehabilitation.[35] As its explanatory memorandum explained, the Act, particularly Part 10:

> ...provides for changes in sentencing arrangements by increasing and clarifying the options available to the courts so that they will be better able to respond to the circumstances of the offender and in cooperation with other agencies, such as the Probation & Welfare Service, they will enhance the prospects for the rehabilitation of offenders.[36]

The 2006 Act provides for two types of EM in Ireland:

(1) EM as an alternative to imprisonment in certain cases, and
(2) as a condition of early release from a custodial sentence.

Sections 101-105 of this Act provide for electronic monitoring of *restriction of movement* orders, imposed by a Court as an alternative (community based) sanction to imprisonment for specifically scheduled offences, including certain public order offences,[37] and a number of summary offences under the Non-Fatal Offences against the Person Act 1997.[38] Provision for such orders was envisaged in cases involving conviction of a person aged eighteen years or more, for a scheduled offence, with the offender's consent,[39] and the consent of other adult/s living with them,[40] and where the court was considering a custodial sentence of at least three months.

While offenders subject to EM would be required to wear a 'tag' for the duration of the court ordered community sanction, up to six months in duration,[41] they could not be required to remain in one place (eg in a home detention curfew context) for more than twelve hours in any one day.[42] The legislation also provided that

---

35 Up to then, suspended sentences, while used relatively frequently by the courts in Ireland, were imposed on a common law basis, rather than being statutorily underpinned.

36 Criminal Justice Act 2006; Explanatory Memorandum 23 (http://www.irishstatutebook.ie/eli/2006/act/26/enacted/en/pdf ).

37 Using threatening, abusive or insulting behaviour in a public place, failure to comply with the directions of a police officer, trespass, affray, and to assault or obstruct a peace officer.

38 Including assault, assault causing harm, coercion or harassment.

39 s 101(11).

40 s 101(9).

41 s 101(3).

42 s 101(2).

a sentencing court should not make a restriction on movement order, with EM, unless it is satisfied that the offender is a 'suitable person' and 'for that purpose… [the court] may request a probation and welfare officer to prepare a report in writing in relation to the offender', and 'shall make a provision making an authorised person responsible for monitoring the offender's compliance with it.'[43] The Act defined an 'authorised person' as '...a person who is appointed in writing by the Minister, or a person who is one of a class of persons which is prescribed, to be an authorised person…'[44] This would appear to allow for a Probation Officer, or such other person or 'class of person' — presumably potentially including a person employed by a commercial company or other organisation providing EM services, if so designated by the Minister — to supervise restriction on movement orders, or aspects of such orders. As well as providing for 'curfew' type restrictions on movement, as described above, the 2006 Act also provided that a restriction on movement order might be one that required '…the offender *not* [emphasis added] to be in such place or places, or such class or classes of places, at such time or during such periods, as may be specified.'[45] Orders with such conditions included are sometimes referred to colloquially as 'exclusion orders.'

In addition to the provisions regarding court ordered use of EM as part of a community sanction, the Criminal Justice Act 2006, ss 108 to 112 updated the Criminal Justice Act 1960, which provides the legislative basis for temporary release of prisoners, to include the potential inclusion of EM as a condition of temporary release from prison. It has been these sections of the 2006 Act that have been used to implement EM, where it has in fact been used, in Ireland. It is perhaps at least questionable as to whether such specific legislative provision for inclusion of EM as a condition of temporary release from prison was strictly necessary, given that the Minister already had, under the relevant 1960 legislation[46] introducing temporary release,[47] considerable discretion regarding specific conditions that might be applied to an order for temporary release.[48] It is also noteworthy, that while the 2006 legislation provided for the inclusion of EM as a specific condition of a temporary release

---

43 s 102(a).

44 s 98.

45 s 101(2)(b).

46 As amended, specifically by the Criminal Justice (Temporary Release of Prisoners) Act 2003, available at: http://www.irishstatutebook.ie/eli/2003/act/34/enacted/en/print.html .

47 See Chapters on Parole and Other Post-Release Supervision.

48 See, for example, *Breathnach v Minister for Justice and Law Reform* [2004]3 IR 336 at 343.

order, such usage of the measure did not extend in practice to the work of the (non-statutory) Interim Parole Board.[49] While the Interim Parole Board, as an advisory rather than decision making body, did not have any explicit power in this regard, that did not stop them considering the potential use of EM as part of parole. For example, in 2010 the then Chairman of the Parole Board stated that electronic tagging could become a consideration for the Board. The Board Chairman further stated that they had no doubt that if a prisoner voluntarily agreed to such tagging, it would be easier for the Board to recommend parole, however, 'if prisoners do not wish to be tagged implications can be drawn from this.'[50] Nevertheless, despite such consideration of the applicability or otherwise of EM as a condition of parole, the Interim Parole Board did not in fact use such provision in practice, in terms of the recommendations it made for the early release of prisoners within its ambit.

## Electronic Monitoring and Bail

Subsequent to the Criminal Justice Act 2006, the Criminal Justice Act 2007, ss 11-13 amended the Bail Act 1997, to enable a court considering the granting of bail in serious offence cases, to order EM as a bail condition. The Bail Act 1997 had given effect to the sixteenth amendment to the Irish Constitution, providing that a court can refuse bail to a suspect where it fears that the suspect would commit further offending while otherwise at liberty. The 2007 Act, which also provided for various aspects of how EM should be applied and managed in such cases, had not been commenced when, three years later, Charity[51] raised concerns, suggesting that 'the presumption of innocence has been consistently compromised since the introduction of the Bail Act of 1997', and pointed to issues arising from the use of EM in similar circumstances in Britain, concluding that it was '...certainly evident that the legislature has envisaged a move towards electronic monitoring... and (citing Grolimund and Durac[52]) that it appeared '...that the increasing concern of the Oireachtas in reforming the bail system, "is crime control and not the preservation of liberty".' Charity further pondered: 'It remains to be seen when the legislation dealing with

---

[49] See Chapter 7 in relation to Parole.

[50] Parole Board, 2009 Annual Report (2010) 6.

[51] JD Charity, 'Electronic Tagging of Applicants for Bail' (2020) 15(5) The Bar Review (Journal of the Bar of Ireland).

[52] Marc Thompson Grolimund and Leonard Durac, 'Counting the Cost: Stiffer Irish Bail Laws and the Sacrificing of the Principle of Liberty', (2009) 19(2) 51-55 ICLJ 55.

electronic monitoring [in bail cases] will be commenced and how it will be enforced.'

Five years later, that legislation had not been commenced when, on 23 July 2015, Enda Kenny TD, the Taoiseach, and Frances Fitzgerald TD, the Minister for Justice and Equality, announced a further new Bail Bill, publishing its General Scheme. The accompanying press release explained, *inter alia*, that the new legislation would update and extend the legislative basis for the electronic monitoring of persons on bail, with An Taoiseach commenting that as well as being '…the first comprehensive review of Bail law since 1997', the Bill '…demonstrates this Government's ongoing commitment to crack down on crime.'[53] The Bail (Amendment) Bill, when passed, would limit the power of the Courts to order EM, to those cases where the prosecution requests it as a condition of the bail. This would represent a significant change to the legislation on granting bail.

This appears to have been a relatively non-controversial proposal, from both a parliamentary and public opinion point of view. That is not to say that some concerns were not voiced in the policy discussions on the use of EM as part of the system of measures to enforce bail conditions, especially as an alternative to remand in custody. For example, the Irish Penal Reform Trust[54] published their submission on the General Scheme of the Bail Bill.[55] This submission included comment on the specific provisions for EM in the Bill, referencing both the European Convention on Human Rights, and decisions of the European Court of Human Rights, as well as the Council of Europe (2014) Recommendation on EM, for precedents and standards in relation to how this issue should be approached and managed.

Citing the Council of Europe's 2014 standards document[56] as '…the first guidance on this [EM] internationally,' the IPRT highlighted a number of the Council of Europe standards as being important to consider in the Irish context.[57] These include: the

53 Press release and related notes available at: http://www.justice.ie/en/JELR/Pages/PR15000430 .

54 IPRT describe (IPRT website homepage: http://www.iprt.ie accessed on 28 April 2017) their organisation as: a '…non-governmental organisation campaigning for rights in the penal system and the progressive reform of the Irish penal system.'

55 Irish Penal Reform Trust, *IPRT Preliminary Submission on General Scheme of the Bail Bill* (August 2015).

56 Council of Europe (2014) (n 25) 25.

57 IPRT (2015), (n 55) p 8.

need for judicial decision making in imposing or revoking EM, the dangers of 'net-widening',[58] proportionality of implementation of EM, potential impact of EM on families and others, the personal circumstances and quality of life of those subject to EM, potential negative impacts of EM, taking time spent on EM into account in subsequent sentencing decisions, and the use of personal and other data gathered in the course and framework of EM. The IPRT submission on the Bail Bill concluded by suggesting that, up to the time of their submission, '...none of these safeguarding factors appear to have been considered in the current General Scheme.'[59] The IPRT document recommended that: 'any proposed scheme for pre-trial electronic tagging be reviewed for compliance with Council of Europe Recommendation CM/Rec (2014) 4 before being introduced into legislation.'[60]

Subsequently, the Department of Justice and Equality strategic plan,[61] as well as the Programme for Government,[62] both published in 2016, included a commitment to introduce electronic tagging for those on bail, where requested by gardaí, with a view towards reducing the risk of reoffending, and that this legislation would be fast-tracked. What became the Criminal Justice Act 2017 was enacted on 28 June 2017. Its purpose, according to a statement by the Department of Justice and Equality,[63] was to strengthen the law on bail, including as its main provisions:

- In refusing bail, a court may take into account persistent serious offending and the likely future risk posed by the accused,
- Strengthening police powers in dealing with bail,
- Courts may hear victim's views regarding possible interference with them by the accused,
- Courts to give reasons for refusing bail, and
- Including electronic monitoring among the range of bail conditions that might be imposed by a court granting bail.

---

58 The IPRT (2015) (n 55) p 8, defines 'Widening the net' as referring to '...the practice by which instead of electronic monitoring being a genuine alternative to pre-trial detention it instead becomes a widely imposed condition of bail.'

59 IPRT (2015) (n 55) p 8.

60 IPRT (2015) (n 55) p 8.

61 Department of Justice and Equality, *A safe, fair and inclusive Ireland: Strategy Statement 2016-2019*, (2016) 29.

62 Government of Ireland, *A Programme for a Partnership Government* (2016) 100-102.

63 Statement on the Department's website, at: http://www.justice.ie/en/JELR/Pages/Criminal_Justice_Act_2017. Accessed on 7 November 2021.

A key element of this legislative provision was that EM could only be included by a court, as a condition of bail, on the application of the prosecution. In December the same year, Jim O'Callaghan TD introduced his Bail (Amendment) Bill 2017, as a private member's bill. The proposed legislation sought to amend the existing bail laws to enable a court to refuse bail if it considered it 'necessary to prevent the commission of a serious offence by that person.' Burglary-related offending was specifically targeted in the Bill, which would also require a court, in admitting someone to bail in such circumstances (ie of a prior history of such offending) to have 'an electronic monitoring device attached to his or her person, either continuously or for such periods as may be specified.' The Bail Bill was referred to the Joint Committee on Justice and Equality for scrutiny and was the subject of a discussion in Committee session on 5 December 2018, which included a number of academics and advocacy and interest groups in the Committee's discussions.[64] In one particularly interesting contribution to the discussion, Dr Mary Rogan, Associate Professor at Trinity College Dublin, suggested that:

> The most important question is what will it [electronic monitoring] be for… An important question, which has not been answered in Ireland, is what the purpose of electronic monitoring is. Is it to reduce pre-trial detention rates or is it something else?

While concerns about serious reoffending by accused persons on bail have been raised from time to time, other concerns have also been raised by others, including the then Justice Minister,[65] in relation to the proposals in the 2017 Bail Bill. Such concerns centred on what the then Minister expressed as government concerns about the constitutionality of Deputy O'Callaghan's Bill, its potential for contravention of 'ECHR[66] case law', the potentially negative impact its enactment, given its perceived 'technical flaws', and that such legislation might also breach the Council of Europe Guidelines on the use of electronic monitoring. The Justice Minister, in reply to a Dáil question on 5 March 2019, stated that: 'Extensive preparations are underway to ensure these provisions [for EM of certain persons on bail] can be implemented and more importantly, to ensure they

64 Joint Committee on Justice and Equality debate (5 Dec 2018) available at: https://www.oireachtas.ie/en/debates/debate/joint_committee_on_justice_and_equality/2018-12-05/5/. Accessed 7 Nov 2021.

65 The Minister's statement of 27 June 2018 is at: http://www.justice.ie/en/JELR/Pages/SP18000214 . Accessed 7 Nov 2021.

66 European Convention on Human Rights.

can be effective.'[67] The private member's Bail Bill did not progress beyond Second Stage in the Dáil and lapsed with the dissolution of the Oireachtas on 14 January 2020. The legislative provision for EM as a condition of bail has not been commenced up to the time of writing.

## Electronic Monitoring and Sex Offenders

In 2009, the Department of Justice and Equality published a discussion document on the management of sex offenders.[68] In considering a range of issues on this theme, the discussion document identified EM as one option, and reviewed how it might be used, in different ways. The discussion document records that EM '... has not yet been implemented in this jurisdiction...' and expressed the view that EM '...does not provide a supervisory regime as such but provides a tool that may support a particular regime.'[69] In addition to describing different types of EM and highlighting cost, technical and other challenges with its implementation, as well as cases of serious further offending by a number of offenders on EM in Britain, as well as the planned introduction of EM in Northern Ireland, the document identified EM (particularly GPS)[70] as being potentially valuable for use with otherwise uncooperative sex offenders. The document's author/s suggested that EM could already be imposed on a sex offender, under existing legislation as a condition of post-release supervision: either as part of a post-release supervision order under the Sex Offenders Act 2001; or as a specific condition of a part-suspended sentence supervision order under the Criminal Justice Act 2006, s 99. EM has not been used in Ireland, in either of these ways, to date.

Since the 2009 paper was published, the potential use of EM as part of the supervision of sex offenders in the community, has been debated on a number of occasions in the Oireachtas. For example, in a parliamentary debate on the Criminal Law (Sexual Offences) Bill 2015, on 3 November 2016, David Stanton TD, Minister of State at the Department of Justice and Equality, responding to questions regarding a perceived need '...to enhance the monitoring of sex offenders following release from prison', said that the government proposed that:

---

67 Dáil Question on 5 March, available at: https://www.oireachtas.ie/en/debates/question/2019-03-05/234/. Accessed 7 Nov 2021.

68 Department of Justice and Equality, The Management of Sex Offenders: A Discussion Document (2009).

69 ibid 34-36.

70 Global Positioning System.

> 'Provisions are to be brought forward in a sex offenders (amendment) Bill which will significantly strengthen such monitoring. These will include electronic monitoring of certain sex offenders on release…'[71]

In November 2018 the Oireachtas Joint Committee on Justice and Equality held hearings with a number of bodies, including the Probation Service, the Police Service of Northern Ireland, the Rape Crisis Network Ireland, and an academic expert, in the context of pre-legislative scrutiny of the General Scheme of the Sex Offenders (Amendment) Bill 2018, which was '…intended to update the Sex Offender Act 2001 in light of a 2010 Review into the Management of Sex Offenders'[72] and included provision for the court-ordered EM of convicted sex offenders, as a condition of post-release supervision orders in certain cases. The Committee's report, published in early 2019,[73] found support for the efficacy of EM as part of a comprehensive plan for prisoner resettlement, cautioned against 'seeing EM as a "silver bullet" for preventing reoffending', concluding that: 'Submissions received… suggest that evidence as to the effectiveness of electronic monitoring generally is mixed,'[74] and recommended that:

- … Given the financial investment required, the Department [of Justice & Equality] may wish to assess, in light of international evidence, how successful the proposed measures are likely to be in achieving their policy aim (ie reducing reoffending),
- That a provision [requiring the consent of persons habitually resident with an offender] be added to the General Scheme, in light of Council of Europe guidance… and evidence to the effect that electronic monitoring can have significant effects on the family of a sex offender or on others living in the same property, and that
- Electronic monitoring should also be available for monitoring compliance with conditions imposed for a part-suspended sentence under the Criminal Justice Act 2006, s 99.[75]

---

71 Dáil Éireann Debate, Vol 927 No 2 – available at: https://www.oireachtas.ie/en/debates/debate/dail/2016-11-03/6/ — accessed on 12 December 2020.

72 Joint Committee on Justice and Equality, Report on pre-legislative scrutiny of the General Scheme of the Sex Offender (Amendment) Bill 2018 (2019) 14.

73 ibid 47.

74 ibid 51.

75 As well as part of a Post-Release Supervision Order under the terms of the Sex Offenders Act 2001.

This legislation lapsed with the dissolution of the Oireachtas in January 2020. Nevertheless, the legislative proposals for electronic monitoring of sex offenders in certain instances post-release, were reintroduced with the publication and presentation to the Oireachtas (on 12 November 2021) of the Sex Offenders (Amendment) Bill 2021. The Bill, among a range of new developments, includes (s 15) provision in certain circumstances for electronic monitoring of sex offenders on Sex Offender Orders, where the person in question is over 18 years of age, for up to six months at a time. These proposed legislative provisions would mean someone subject to such an order could be required to remain *in* or *away from* specified locations or places for the duration of the order.

## Evolution of Electronic Monitoring Practice in Ireland

While legislative provision for the use of EM to monitor the movements of offenders has been in place since 2006, it was some four years later before it was used in practice. The legal provisions for the use of EM, as part of a supervised community sanction such as probation supervision, have not yet been commenced or utilised in Ireland. On the other hand, the provisions of the 2006 Act allowing for the use of electronic monitoring as a restriction on movement order, as one of the conditions of early release from a custodial sentence ('temporary release,' as provided for under the Criminal Justice Act 1960, as amended), for up to six months after release, have come to be used.[76]

This initially came about as a short, time-limited pilot, from August to December 2010. The pilot programme was initiated at the behest of Dermot Ahern TD, then Minister for Justice and Law Reform,[77] and was overseen by a multi-agency Project Board that included representatives of the Prison Service, Probation Service, An Garda Síochána and the Department of Justice. The pilot itself had its origins in an earlier multi-agency working group that considered the potential application of EM: at the court/bail stage, for early release from prison and for sex offenders, post-release. The initial proposal from that earlier working group was that the first application of EM in Ireland should target early release from prison and that it be piloted for up to 300 participants on that basis.

[76] ss 108-110.

[77] Demct Ahern TD had also made the relevant Ministerial Order commencing the relevant provisions of the 2006 Act, for 'a restriction of movement condition applying to the granting of temporary release' (see: the following Minister, Alan Shatter TD's contribution to Dáil Éireann Debate Vol 754, No 3, 70 on 7 February 2011).

That initial proposal was scaled back to the much smaller number who took part in the actual pilot itself. This was on the basis that identifying the higher number originally envisaged might present difficulty, including potentially raising the risk level of those released, and/or potentially not really adding value to those who might have been given early release anyway.

The short 2010 EM pilot included thirty-one prisoners, with a maximum of eighteen being on early release, with EM, at any one time, mainly subject to home detention curfews.[78] This was undertaken on the legislative basis of the Criminal Justice Act 2006 provision for EM. In practical terms, EM in such cases was used as a specific condition of temporary release, itself granted under the terms of the Criminal Justice Act 1960, as amended.[79] The pilot was reviewed by the project oversight group, and deemed a success with reference to all indicators, particularly the management and behaviour of participants and the efficacy of the technology itself. The evaluation concluded that EM delivered some (albeit small-scale) value to the management of offenders, post-release in Ireland, and could usefully offer such added value in certain cases. The pilot evaluation report recommended a further, two-year trial of EM, for a limited number of prisoners on Temporary Release, including (as appropriate) those in hospitals or nursing homes,[80] as well as those for whom — on a case-by-case basis — EM might be assessed as offering added value in terms of public protection and/or compliance with the terms of their temporary release. The report also recommended that the number on EM at any one time be 'capped,' to a suggested daily maximum of 30-40 prisoners.

Alan Shatter TD, then Minister for Justice and Equality, in a reply to a Dáil[81] question in February 2012,[82] referred to the establishment of the 2010 pilot programme and stated that the issue of expanding the implementation of EM would be considered by 'a group to carry out an all-encompassing strategic review of penal policy', that: 'We are not looking at it [EM] in isolation,' that: 'The Probation Service engages with a considerable number of prisoners before

---

[78] The pilot used GPS technology to monitor compliance with (mostly) home detention curfew, and exclusion zone compliance (in some cases).

[79] For the background to the introduction of 'temporary release' as a measure, see Mary Rogan, *Prison Policy in Ireland: Politics, penal welfarism and political imprisonment* (Routledge 2011) 92-94.

[80] Who might otherwise require expensive — and probably otherwise unnecessary, from a public protection viewpoint — round-the-clock escorts by prison officers.

[81] Irish equivalent of a Parliamentary Question.

[82] Dáil Éireann Debate Vol 754, No 3, 70, available at: https://www.oireachtas.ie/en/debates/debate/dail/2012-02-07/9/. Accessed 24 September 2019.

they are released' and while he expected EM 'might have a role in the future... no final decision has been made as to whether we will proceed further with tagging in 2012 or 2013 or whether priority will be given to other forms of intervention.'[83] Although the Department of Justice and Equality's 2014 strategic review report was not completed and published until two years later, a media report in April 2012 stated that the Irish Prison Service had 'put forward a tender notice on the e-tenders website, searching for a company who can provide such a service through satellite tracking.'[84] The same media outlet reported in August 2013 that there were 'currently just two people who have been electronically tagged in Ireland', after '[e]lectronic tagging began in Ireland in March' that year and that '[t]he Irish Prison Service signed a two-year contract with Chubb Ireland on 15 February', this 'following a long consultation period.'[85]

The Irish Prison Service subsequently decided to implement EM on an expanded but still limited basis, and in early 2014 issued an EU request for tenders, with a contract for the provision of up to fifty 'tags' at any one time being awarded in May 2014. The new contract saw some new features incorporated, including the use of GPS and GSM, as well as RF[86] technology, using one-piece, waterproof units. The service-level agreement incorporated monitoring 24:7, with 'real time' update reports provided daily. Tags are fitted by the contracted service provider within forty-eight hours of being requested. Up to the end of September 2016, sixty-two prisoners on temporary release had EM as one of the release conditions. Twenty-three of these had been 'tagged' while attending hospital outside the prison, thirty-one had been on home detention curfew and eight had been released early on the 'community return' or 'community support'[87] programmes.

---

83 ibid.

84 Sinead O'Carroll, 'Electronic monitoring of prisoners to be introduced,' thejournal.ie (13 April 2013) at: https://www.thejournal.ie/electronic-monitoring-of-prisoners-to-be-introduced-416415-Apr2012/ . Accessed 7 Nov 2021.

85 Christine Bohan, 'Here's how many people are electronically tagged in Ireland,' thejournal.ie (24 August 2013) at: https://www.thejournal.ie/electronic-tagging-numbers-ireland-1050470-Aug2013/ . Accessed on 7 Nov 2021.

86 Global Positioning System, Global System for Mobile communication, and Radio Frequency technology.

87 *Community Support* is structured early release for prisoners serving prison sentences of up to twelve-months. Whereas post-release supervision under the Community Return scheme is provided by the Probation Service, it is usually community and voluntary sector organisations, funded and contracted jointly by the Probation and Prison Services, that provide resettlement assistance and mentoring etc under the Community Support programme. See Chapter 8 for more on this.

In a reply to a Dáil question on 29 March 2018, Charles Flanagan TD, then Minister for Justice and Equality, confirmed that the Prison Service's EM contract, which had commenced in 2014, was 'used to monitor prisoners who have been granted Temporary Release including for the purpose of the Community Return/Community Support scheme' as well as being used 'to monitor some hospital in-patients who have been granted Temporary Release from prison.'[88] The Minister further confirmed that: 'During 2017, there were 59 prisoners electronically monitored while on Temporary Release', with the total cost in 2017 being €166,117. 'Electronic tagging devices were deployed 4,616 times, involving 59 prisoners at an average cost of €36 per deployment', according to the Minister. In one follow-up media comment to the Minister's parliamentary statement, it was pointed out that: 'Laws to allow electronic tagging as a bail condition have yet to be fully implemented. Last year, it emerged that 13% of all crimes were committed by people who were out on bail.'[89]

The organisational policy on the current use of EM in Ireland is contained in an Irish Prison Service (2017) document.[90] This policy document outlines the qualifying criteria and procedures for implementation of:

- A clear, consistent and best practice approach to the selection and management of prisoners who may be suitable for EM,
- Circumstances whereby EM is considered, and
- Restrictions that may be imposed.

The document lists those prisoners coming within the scope of the EM scheme, as including: hospital inpatients, prolific offenders, prisoners who, due to the nature of their offence and history of offending, may require additional controls to ensure that they obey the conditions of their temporary release. It also provides clarity on a range of related matters including the aim, purpose and scope of the scheme, procedures for implementation, as well as including a copy of the relevant consent form and a 'user guide.'

---

88 Dáil Éireann Debate, 29 March 2018, Questions 207, 208, 209) at: https://www.oireachtas.ie/en/debates/question/2018-03-29/208/. Accessed on 28 March 2020.

89 Garreth MacNamee, 'Electronically tagging 59 prisoners last year cost the State €116,000 [*sic*],' thejournal.ie (4 April 2018) at: https://www.thejournal.ie/electronic-tags-3938140-Apr2018/. Accessed 7 November 2021.

90 Irish Prison Service, *Electronic Monitoring: Policy Document* (2017) 1. (Available at: https://www.irishprisons.ie/wp-content/uploads/documents_pdf/Irish-Prison-Service-Electronic-Monitoring-Policy.pdf).

## Recent Policy and Political Consideration of EM in Ireland

From before Michael McDowell TD's 2004 statement of intent to introduce EM in Ireland,[91] as well as since then, EM has remained consistently on the political agenda, as a part of a standard 'be tough on crime' toolkit of measures in response to offending. It is also likely that other policy positions and directions have served to lend support to at least part of the attractiveness of EM summarised by Nellis as a 'cool brand', 'self-evidently modern' and part of the ' … global ubiquity of computer-mediated action-at-a-distance, real-time communication, digital transparency and connectedness…'[92]

Recent and current penal policy is encompassed in the findings of the comprehensive review of all aspects of penal policy, established in 2012, with its deliberations and report completed two years later, published by the Department of Justice and Equality and accepted by government.[93] As part of its programme of discussions and consultations, the Review group considered the issue of EM. While noting that EM was already being used on a small scale, in the context of early release from prison, the group was of the view that EM's potential applicability was limited, and concluded that it did '...not propose to recommend extending resources relating to electronic monitoring (EM) to non-custodial sanctions beyond that proposed to be introduced in relation to sex offenders.'[94]

To an extent, it seems plausible that the official view and approach to EM in Ireland has been that encapsulated in a senior Justice official's presentation to the Oireachtas Joint Committee on Justice, Defence and Equality discussions on penal reform, in 2013.[95] The Committee in its deliberations had taken a broad range of submissions. EM was referenced in the Committee's discussions, including a contribution by a senior Departmental official to the effect that: 'Although we have tested electronic monitoring we have not used it as we are not sure it is viable', adding that: 'International evidence suggests that it can be expensive and does not necessarily enhance rehabilitation. While it provides some insurance to the public, it does not necessarily prevent people from

91 Conor Lally (2004) (n 2).

92 Mike Nellis, 'Electronic Monitoring and Penal Reform: Constructive Resistance in the Age of "Coercive Connectedness"' (2016) 14(1) British Journal of Community Justice 113-132.

93 Department of Justice and Equality, *Strategic Review of Penal Policy: Final Report* (2014).

94 ibid 50-51.

95 Joint Committee on Justice, Defence and Equality, *2013 Report on Penal Reform* (31/JDAE/009).

committing offences.'[96] The resulting report incorporated wide-ranging recommendations including: reduced prison numbers, commutation of custodial sentences of less than six months, increased standard remission of sentence, one single piece of legislation to provide for early release and measures to address prison conditions including overcrowding.[97] In the context of such limited exchanges on EM, the Committee's final recommendations did not refer explicitly to EM, either way.

A subsequent Joint Committee on Justice and Equality report on penal reform and sentencing again reflecting wide-ranging discussions and a variety of contributions, made equally wide-ranging recommendations, once again without referencing EM in either its discussions or recommendations.[98] The following year, it was reported by at least one media outlet that '[a] tender issued by the Irish Prison Service shows that €680,000' had been 'set aside for the tagging and monitoring of prisoners who are on temporary release', with the plan being for potentially 'up to 50 prisoners [being] tagged at any one time.'[99] This can be compared with the average costs of keeping someone in prison in Ireland — in 2019, for example, this was €75,349 per bed-cell space *per annum*.[100]

There has been relatively little academic analysis or research to date that has directly addressed consideration of EM in Ireland. One academic analysis was carried out by Moss, who concluded that in the context of '...the ongoing use but unclear purpose of EM' as well as '...the exceptionalism of the Irish criminal justice model', both '...EM purpose, performance and probation oversight...' have been '...overlooked in research in Ireland.'[101] A small number of studies have considered EM in the Irish context, as part of exploring what works in offender management and what might be transferable in practice to Ireland. Seymour carried out a review of the use and effectiveness of community sentencing as an alternative to imprisonment in Ireland.[102] As part of this review, Seymour considered EM and concluded, under a grouping of suggested 'Less

---

96 ibid.

97 Joint Committee on Justice, Defence and Equality (n 103) 9.

98 Joint Committee on Justice and Equality, *2018 Report on Penal Reform and Sentencing* (32/JAE/19).

99 Seán McCárthaigh, '€680k to be spent on the electronic tagging of prisoners,' Irish Examiner (22 April 2019) at: https://www.irishexaminer.com/breakingnews/ireland/680k-to-be-spent-on-the-electronic-tagging-of-prisoners-919178.html . Accessed 7 Nov 2021.

100 See Irish Prison Service, *2019 Annual Report*, 10.

101 Brian Moss, 'Electronic monitoring and monitoring probation: The case of Ireland,' (2018) 10(2) 120-135 *European Journal of Probation* 131.

102 Mairead Seymour, *Alternatives to Custody* (Report for Business in the

Successful Approaches,' that '…despite being more expensive than other sentencing alternatives, there is extremely limited data to suggest that punitive measures including electronic monitoring is effective in reducing recidivism…'.[103] Seymour went on to express concern at the planned inclusion of EM in the provisions of the then-proposed Criminal Justice Bill 2004.[104] In a Department of Justice sponsored literature review and report, O'Donnell considered what approaches and interventions to reduce reoffending have been demonstrated through research findings to be either effective, or ineffective, or to have shown some promise.[105] EM was included in the latter category, with O'Donnell citing Hucklesby's conclusion that: 'For at least some offenders, curfew orders have the capacity to facilitate desistance during the time the curfew order is active'[106] and in support of O'Donnell's finding that EM '…may offer limited benefits to offenders who are inclined towards desistance and need support to break criminal habits.'[107]

On 5 March 2019, Justice Minister Charlie Flanagan TD stated in the Oireachtas that, in the context of 'extensive preparations' to implement EM:

> My Department is chairing a Working Group on Electronic Monitoring which includes the Irish Prison Service, the Probation Service, the Courts Service, An Garda Síochána and the Director of Public Prosecutions (DPP). The Working Group submitted a report to my Department's Management Board and those recommendations were considered. Following on from this, my Department has been engaging with the Office of Government Procurement (OGP) to try and identify a suitable expert to advise the Department on Electronic Monitoring pre-market consultations. Discussions between the Department and the OGP in this regard remain ongoing.[108]

To date, any such 'extensive preparations' already carried out have so far not resulted in further implementation of EM in Ireland. On 17 December 2021, a newspaper article reported that the Irish

---

Community Ireland [BITC] and the Irish Penal Reform Trust [IPRT], supported by the Cyril Forbes Fund at the Community Foundation for Ireland 2006).

103 ibid 23.

104 ibid 26.

105 Ian O' Donnell, *An Evidence Review of Recidivism and Policy Responses* (Department of Justice and Equality 2020)

106 Anthea Hucklesby, (2008) 'Vehicles of Desistance? The Impact of Electronically Monitored Curfew Orders,' (2008) 8(1) 51-71 Criminology & Crim Justice 67.

107 O' Donnell (n 105) 73-74.

108 Dáil Éireann Debate, Tuesday, 5 March 2019, Question 234, available at: https://www.oireachtas.ie/en/debates/question/2019-03-05/234/

Prison Service had '...abandoned the use of electronic tagging for offenders 12 years after it was first introduced, citing concerns about value for money'.[109]

## Conclusion

According to Nellis, 'EM has often been glibly described as 'science fiction come true,' but 'not always in a good way.'[110] Of all the penal sanctions and measures available anywhere, EM, whether used for surveillance, monitoring, management or rehabilitation and reintegration of offenders, or some combination of these potential goals, tends to evoke unrealistic expectations in commentators, including politicians, the media and the wider public, on the one hand. Some stakeholders, on the other hand, tend to raise concerns about its potential intrusiveness, risks of net-widening, unreasonably expanding usage, ineffective implementation, and commercial contractual difficulties, among such issues. Nellis and others have suggested that:

> It is not difficult to conjure a dystopian vision out of EM. Both house arrest and the tracking and tracing of one's every move by the state have long been potent totalitarian tropes, and although the precise contours of the world that Orwell (1949)[111] envisaged in Nineteen Eighty-Four never materialized, there have been many subsequent iterations of the view that in Weber's 'iron cage' lie all our futures.[112]

According to Laurie and Maglione, EM has emerged, in reality, '...as a multi-layered policy instrument geared toward governing segments of populations, according to specific political logics.'[113] That said, there is ample evidence in the international research of EM's potential to make a positive contribution to the effective management of offenders and assisting their desistance from crime. This is particularly the case where EM is used selectively and applied as part of a wider range of community sanctions and measures, whose goals and methods are clearly focused and supported and where EM is used in such ways as to support other aspects of offender supervision.

---

[109] Conor Gallagher, *Irish Times*.

[110] Mike Nellis (2014) (n 6) p 224.

[111] George Orwell, *Nineteen Eighty-Four: A Novel* (Secker & Warburg 1949).

[112] M Nellis, K Beyens and D Kaminski (2013[b]) (n 19) p 14.

[113] Emma Laurie and Giuseppe Maglione, 'The Electronic Monitoring of Offenders in Context: From Policy to Political Logics' (31 Oct 2019) Critical Criminology (published online). Retrieved at: https://link.springer.com/article/10.1007/s10612-019-09471-7 .

While EM may well have become an established part of the collective penal imaginary in Europe, including to some extent in Ireland, an imagery reinforced through usage of the technology in practice in many jurisdictions, its use in Ireland has been a slow and relatively recent development, now ceased. That is despite the fact that EM has been a recurring feature of Irish political and penal policy debate and media attention for over twenty years. The use of EM as a means of monitoring and restricting the movement of offenders, or those awaiting trial for criminal offences, has been considered at different times in Ireland over the past quarter of a century. It has been provided for in legislation for over ten years. Nevertheless, while EM was used on a small scale for around ten years, as a condition of early release, its proposed wider use in Ireland, particularly as (a) an alternative to remand in custody (pre-trial detention) and as a condition of bail, and (b) as part of post-release for sex offenders has yet to progress through or beyond the legislative process. It remains to be seen whether there will be any appetite to revive the early release, let alone the community sanction EM option, while the bail and sex offender supervision options appear set to remain on the political, media and public agenda for the foreseeable future.

It is difficult not to acknowledge that EM can add value to the supervisory and surveillance aspects of offender management in certain cases. Beyens and Roosen '...conclude that EM is not rehabilitative in itself but is able to facilitate other rehabilitative measures.'[114] Fitzalan Howard, in the context of exploring the lived experience of EM, similarly concludes that 'EM seems to have clear, rehabilitative potential', as well as a '...potential to promote compliance and to contribute to rehabilitation and desistance.'[115] It is also clear however, from experience in other jurisdictions, that EM in and of itself, will not prevent offending, and should not be seen as a panacea. Nevertheless, like other technological advances, EM as an aid to the management of penal sanctions and measures, wherever it has been introduced, in Ireland as well as elsewhere, is here to stay. The legislative foundations already in place, as well as those planned, and its practical applications to date, will likely ensure that this platform for EM as an adjunct to more 'traditional' forms of offender supervision, will form the basis for further consideration in this field.

---

114 K Beyens and M Roosen (2020) (n 17) p 898.

115 Flora Fitzalan Howard, 'The Experience of Electronic Monitoring and the Implications for Effective Use' (2020) 59(1) 17-43 Howard J Crime & Justice 32-34.

CHAPTER 11

# SOME OTHER ISSUES AND CHALLENGES IN PROBATION AND PAROLE

## Introduction

The whole area of policy and practice in probation and parole work is complex and many issues and areas of practice as well as legislation and policy etc, intertwine and overlap with each other. The foregoing chapters have attempted to deal with key aspects of probation and parole practice, as they have evolved and developed in Ireland and reflecting international trends and influences. There are a number of issues that impact probation and parole, some of which are not necessarily the policy nor statutory responsibility of the probation and parole authorities. Some indeed do not fall within the formal remit of any part of the justice system. At the same time, these issues must be considered and incorporated in the context of developing and delivering the most appropriate and effective response to those who have offended. Most, if not all, of the issues addressed in this chapter could be the subject of separate books in their own right. Indeed, many of the issues considered in the following sections have been dealt with in dedicated publications of their own. The various subjects highlighted and discussed summarily in this chapter, while identifying and exploring in minimal detail a number of key issues impacting on probation and parole work, do not comprise an exhaustive list of such themes. Similarly, while the critical issues are addressed in brief here, *all* relevant aspects of the issues below cannot be covered exhaustively, nor is the list of relevant subject headings in itself exhaustive.

## Emerging Trends in Crime and Offending

There can be certain widely-held perceptions regarding the categories and 'types' of offender with whom probation and parole services traditionally have dealt or with whom such organisations should appropriately deal and be most effective. These perceptions or 'world views' have varied at different points in time. They can also differ from one jurisdiction and culture to another. In the context of Ireland for example, at times such categories of groups widely considered appropriate for engagement by the Probation Service have included young people and those presenting with substance misuse issues. The focus for probation and parole services has also traditionally been seen to be those who have committed 'traditional' types of crime, such as stealing, minor assaults, drug or alcohol-related offending and so on. Much more recently, other less 'traditional' forms of offending facilitated by technology and modern means of communication, have become more prevalent and have led to increases in so-called 'white-collar offending' and 'cybercrime,' as well as to consideration of the most appropriate ways of responding to such crimes and those who commit them. Other and newer 'constructions' or designations of specific types of activity as unique crimes in themselves, have emerged from a range of wider socioeconomic and even political issues. These include various types of organised crime and so-called 'white-collar crime,' 'cybercrime,' production and sale of child abuse images, human trafficking and modern slavery, and various manifestations of violent extremism, among others.

## The Wider Social Context and Social Policy Issues

Similarly, it has become increasingly recognised and acknowledged that the criminal justice system cannot, on its own, address offending and victimisation, much less the issue of fostering social justice, without the cooperation and real 'buy-in' of the other agencies of the state and wider civil society.[1] In that context, it is increasingly recognised that, as a society, we cannot just police ourselves into a safer society. Issues of socio-economic and other forms of poverty and deprivation, including access to employment and accommodation, as well as access to social, health and mental health services are a common challenge in this respect. Unless these issues are adequately addressed for example, the criminal justice response to those who commit certain offences will not in itself overcome the negative outcomes of such deprivation and exclusion down the line. In addition, aspects of the criminal justice system can themselves be 'criminogenic.'[2] For example, there is a clear and lasting negative impact of criminal records on real reintegration of those who have offended in the past.[3] Similarly, spending time in

---

1 For example, see: Penal Policy Review Group, *Strategic Review of Penal Policy: Final Report* (Department of Justice 2014), and Cecilia Klingele, *The Role of Human Service Providers During Community Supervision* (National Institute of Justice 2021)

2 Criminalising or crime-causing.

3 In 2020, the Department of Justice initiated a review of the Criminal Justice (Spent Convictions and Certain Disclosures) Act 2016.

prison can have a brutalising effect on the individual, as well as their family and community, in addition to the negative impact of such experience of custody on their subsequent reintegration efforts.[4]

## Multi-disciplinary Work and Interagency Cooperation

While individual practitioners in various criminal justice agencies and services have always had to communicate with each other (for example, probation officer to police officer or prison officer) as well as with colleagues in other agencies (eg education and training, drug treatment, accommodation providers and so on) the need for maximising interagency and multi-disciplinary cooperation in offender assessment and management has come increasingly to the fore internationally in more recent years, including in Ireland.[5] This cooperation has been especially evident and practised in relation to certain issues and specific categories of offender or of offending. Examples of the former include children and young people, and of the latter – sexual offending, domestic abuse and violence,[6] and other groups of individuals with histories of serious and/or prolific offending.

Canton and Dominey, who also highlight the dangers and weaknesses in single-agency approaches to risk assessment and management state for example, citing Rumgay:

> Inter-agency work involves sharing information, collaborative risk assessment and management and the rational deployment of skills and resources to reduce risk. Agencies with their different responsibilities, authority, knowledge, skills and resources should achieve much more in a coordinated endeavour than when working separately.[7]

---

4 Fiona Donson and Aisling Parkes, 'Weighing in the balance; Reflections on the sentencing process from a children's rights perspective.' *Probation Journal* 63 (3) (2016): 331-346.

5 For example, see Paul Senior, 'Integrated Offender Management: Pooling Resources and Expertise and Creating Effective Working Partnerships' (2014) 11 Irish Probation Journal 7-28.

6 See David Morran, 'Programme Integrity or Programme Integration: The need for a co-ordinated approach to work with domestic violence offenders' (2005) 2 Irish Probation Journal 57-67; John Devaney, Anne Lazenbatt and Maurice Mahon, 'The Role of Theory in Promoting Social Work Values and Its Potential Effect on Outcomes in Work with Domestically Violent Men' (2009) 6 Irish Probation Journal 151-170; and John Devaney and Stephanie Holt, 'Understanding domestic abuse and sexual violence: prevalence, policy and practice,' in Deirdre Healy and others (eds), *The Routledge Handbook of Irish Criminology* (Routledge 2016) 70-88.

7 Judith Rumgay, 'Partnerships in probation' in Loraine Gelsthorpe and Rod

At a strategic level, interagency cooperation in offender management in Ireland is evidenced in the four-way[8] strategic plan, published by the Department of Justice in 2019.[9] Specific interagency initiatives have also focused on particular groups, including young people.[10] Issues in the assessment and management of those who have committed sexual offences, as discussed by Cotter,[11] have given rise to the development and pooling of dedicated inter-agency resources, resulting in the establishment of the Sex Offenders Risk Assessment and Management (SORAM) structure, as described by Wilson.[12] Another important inter-agency initiative has been the Joint Agency Response to Crime (JARC), initially aimed at prolific adult offenders involved mostly in burglary offences, which started in a number of locations in 2015. Following an evaluation of its success in the initial three areas, the JARC programme was extended for adults in a number of additional areas, and for young people in two new locations. [13]

## Substance Use and Misuse

Substance use and misuse issues are central to much offending and to probation and parole work in general. The Misuse of Drugs Acts 1977 and 1984, as amended, as well as the National Drugs and Alcohol Strategy form the legislative and policy foundations for work in this respect. The prevalence of alcohol and substance misuse amongst the adult population on probation supervision is a subject that has been researched by the Irish Probation Service

---

Morgan (eds), *Handbook of Probation* (Willan 2007) cited in Rob Canton and Jane Dominey, *Probation*, (2nd edn, Routledge 2018) 171.

8 Signed off by the Department of Justice, Probation Service, An Garda Síochána and the Irish Prison Service.

9 Department of Justice, *Action Plan for the Joint Management of Offenders, 2019-2021: Enhancing Community Safety Through Collaborative Management of Priority Offenders* (Department of Justice 2019) available at: http://www.justice.ie/en/JELR/action-plan-for-the-joint-management-of-offenders.pdf/Files/action-plan-for-the-joint-management-of-offenders.pdf .

10 For example, see: Mary McGagh, Emma Gunn and Rachel Lillis, 'Strengthening Families Programme: An Inter-Agency Approach to Working with Families' (2009) 6 Irish Probation Journal 113-123; Catherine McGowan, 'The Ballymun Network for Assisting Children and Young People: A Local Model for Inter-agency Working' (2009) 6 Irish Probation Journal 124-134.

11 Anthony Cotter, Úna Doyle and Paul Linnane, 'Sex Offenders Act 2001: Implications for the Probation and Welfare Service, Policy and Practice' (2005) 2(1) Irish Probation Journal 78-83.

12 Mark Wilson, John McCann and Robert Templeton, 'SORAM: Towards a Multi-agency Model of Sex Offender Risk Assessment and Management' (2013) 10 Irish Probation Journal 177-192.

13 Department of Justice, *Critical review of initial evaluations on the three J-ARC pilot projects* (Department of Justice 2018).

at different times. Probation Service research reported in 2012 disclosed that 89% of those adults on probation supervision had misused drugs or alcohol either 'currently' (at the time of the survey) or in the 'past'. Of the 89% of those who misused either alcohol/drugs, 27% misused drugs only, 20% misused alcohol only and 42% misused both drugs and alcohol.[14] This research further disclosed that both male and female adult offenders exhibited similar drug and alcohol misuse levels.

This study identified a considerable link between drug misuse and the current index offence committed. Based on the probation officers' professional judgment, for 74% of drug-misusing offenders on supervision misuse was linked to their current offending. Additionally, 71% of alcohol-misusing offenders had their misuse linked to the current offence committed. Drug-misuse linked to the offence is more pronounced in the younger age categories in this survey. Each of the age categories 18-24, 25-34 and 35-44 have in excess of a 70% link to offending while the 45-54 and 55-64 age groups have a 50% or less link to offending. The research also disclosed differences between the offence categories of offenders based on whether their offences were related to the problematic use of drugs or alcohol. The majority of drug-related offences were either for drug offences (31.8%) or acquisitive crimes such as Theft (32.8%). The majority of alcohol-related offences were crimes against the person and public order offences at almost 40%.

More recent (2021) research in relation to the same issues analysed the response of 81% of probation officers, providing data on 3,096 persons nationally. [15] The research found that 81% of the sample (comprised of both adult and young persons on supervision) were reported to have misused alcohol and/or drugs, with 50% having misused both drugs and alcohol. The study found that 14% had misused alcohol only and 17% drugs only, while 19% of those under probation supervision had either no history of substance abuse (10%) or any such history was unknown (9%). The highest level of substance misuse was recorded among those in the 25 to 34-age bracket. In other significant findings, for 53% of service users, there was a reported direct link between alcohol abuse and the relevant offence, while the comparable figure was a 48% direct link between drug misuse and the relevant offending.[16] The author

[14] Probation Service, *Drug And Alcohol Misuse Among Adult Offenders On Probation Supervision In Ireland* (Research Report May 2012).

[15] Louise Rooney, 'Substance Misuse and Supervision: An Examination of Drug and Alcohol Misuse Among Probation Service Clients' (2021) 18(1) Irish Probation Journal 153.

[16] Louise Rooney, 'Informing & Supporting Change: Drug and Alcohol Misuse

of this research report made a number of key recommendations regarding the Probation Service's approach to substance misuse issues. These include the need for 'structured and coordinated engagement' between the health and justice sectors; increased and focused training for probation officers; 'gender-informed research, policy and practice'; 'Cultural Awareness and Sensitivity Training... [for] all Probation Service staff'; and increased access for service users to appropriate programmes and interventions.[17]

In the context of parole, it is vital that parolees are properly prepared for eventual release and given whatever help or incentives they need to refrain from crime once they are at liberty.[18] This assistance, from the Probation Service and other prison based therapeutic services, focuses on the prisoner's offence focussed needs, which may include substance misuse issues, as identified by the application of risk assessment tools and matches the offender's needs to therapeutic interventions to aid rehabilitation. Today, there are targeted treatment programmes in operation in prisons and research has demonstrated that many such treatment programmes are effective. Parole assessments (as in the case of probation) provide an incentive for offenders to participate in such programmes in the knowledge that their failure to do so will considerably reduce their chances of being granted parole.[19] It is worth noting that, in addition, recent developments in electronic tracking devices allow such devices to incorporate not only the tracking of the location of the offender wearing the device but also the drug and alcohol consumption of the offender.[20] Such technology has not, to date, been used with those on probation or parole in Ireland.

## Accommodation Issues and Homelessness

Homelessness amongst individuals in the criminal justice system has a number of direct implications at all stages for the system, from the first point of contact with the police, to arrest, prosecution

---

among People on Probation Supervision in Ireland', (Probation Service Research Report 8, July 2021).

17 ibid.

18 Thomas O'Malley, *Sentencing Law and Practice* (Thomson Round Hall 2006) 41.

19 The Honourable Justice JW Gendall, 'International Perspectives on Parole: Transition from Defence to Prosecution Counsel to Judge to Parole Board Chair and Handling Public Criticism' delivered at Association of Paroling Authorities International Annual Conference, Providence, Rhode Island (21 May 2013) 3.

20 See George Drake, 'Emerging Technologies for Community Corrections' delivered at Association of Paroling Authorities International Annual Conference (21 May 2013).

and charge, through court-ordered community-based sanctions, imprisonment and on to release from prison. Indeed, it is well documented that homeless individuals tend to be overrepresented in the prison population, as well as among those under probation supervision. According to Carlen (1983) this occurs for two main reasons, firstly, homeless individuals have a higher reconviction rate than domiciled offenders and secondly their housing status may be instrumental in the court's decision to remand them in custody and sentence them to imprisonment.[21]

In considering the relationship between crime and homelessness a key question relates to whether homelessness leads to offending or *vice versa*. The multiplicity and complexity of risk factors relating to crime and homelessness highlights the importance of not adopting one causation model. The most accurate assumption to be made is that crime potentially is both a cause and an effect of homelessness. Whether homelessness precedes crime or occurs as a result of offending behaviour, a significant body of emerging literature suggests that accommodation difficulties are related to a higher risk of re-offending.

By discussing the link between homelessness and its impact on desistance from offending, it is not to suggest that this is the only, or even the predominant, relevant factor. However, as a UK Home Office report described: '[a]ppropriate and accessible accommodation is the foundation of successful rehabilitation and management of risk of harm to others. It is crucial to sustaining employment, treatment, family support and finances.'[22] Having a job and somewhere to to live may not necessarily be sufficient in themselves to rehabilitate someone, but, without either of these, someone is likely to be really fighting an uphill battle. Probation officers have long recognised the importance of assisting homeless offenders find accommodation and access related support services.

According to Seymour, probation officers in a significant research study in Ireland[23] described how:

> ...tracking homeless offenders was problematic given their lack of a stable address. They estimated that almost half of

---

21 Mairead Seymour, 'Homeless Offenders in the Community: The Issues and Challenges for Probation Supervision' (2004) 1(1) Irish Probation Journal 3-13.

22 Home Office 'Reducing re-offending: National action plan,' (2004) cited in Rob Canton and Jane Dominey, Probation (2nd edn, Routledge 2018) 191.

23 Mairead Seymour and Liza Costello, 'A Study of the Number, Profile and Progression Routes of Homeless Persons before the Court and in Custody,' Probation & Welfare Service, (2005).

> those offenders on supervision who were of 'no fixed abode' would fail to turn up for initial appointments despite being offered three of them, or alternatively they would turn up on the wrong day. Further challenges related to tracking, ranged from homeless probationers going 'missing' for a period of time, to difficulties related to them receiving correspondence about probation appointments while staying in temporary accommodation such as hostels and B&Bs.[24]

In addition, as reported by Seymour:

> Probation Officers distinguished between the 'stable homeless' client and the 'chaotic homeless' client. They identified that the former group were able 'to manage their homelessness' and were also more likely to keep their appointments. In contrast, if an individual's lifestyle was chaotic and the homeless experience traumatic for them, officers thought that keeping probation appointments would not be a priority: 'If a client is moving from hostel to hostel, we are way down their list of priorities... homelessness flattens supervision.' The implication of these chaotic circumstances… is that the focus of [probation] work is largely on crisis intervention.[25]

In Ireland, as much as elsewhere, it is clear that the difficulties parolees similarly experience in obtaining employment is merely one of a myriad of barriers they encounter in their attempts to successfully transition from custody to life in the community. The challenge in securing appropriate accommodation may be an even greater challenge than finding a job,[26] with some American cities reporting rates of 30-50% homelessness amongst parolees.[27] Research has shown that the release process is critical to reducing the risk of recidivism and reoffending rates[28] and releasing a person from prison who has no accommodation or, at best, inadequate temporary accommodation serves neither a rehabilitative purpose nor supports reintegration. It is unquestionable that prisoners released back into homelessness or unsuitable accommodation are much more likely to reoffend.[29] Furthermore, homelessness impedes a person from maintaining contact with community

---

24 Mairead Seymour, at n 23, 7.

25 ibid.

26 Joan Petersilia, *When Prisoners Come Home* (OUP 2003) 120.

27 John K Irwin, *The Warehouse Prison – Disposal of the New Dangerous Class* (Roxbury Publishing Co 2005) 176.

28 See Irish Penal Reform Trust, *Progress in the Penal System – A framework for penal reform* (2017) 81.

29 Oireachtas Joint Committee on Justice, Defence and Equality, *Report on*

supervision or treatment programmes, where applicable.[30] In some instances, the difficulty in securing accommodation may not be as severe for prisoners released after serving a short sentence because it is not long since they left their homes and it may have been possible to maintain relationships with their families who may have continued to occupy the home but for many long-term prisoners this often presents a more significant problem.[31] This problem is magnified in the cases of those who have been sent to prison for certain specific types of offences, including sexual offences and cases of a high profile nature (see Chapter 8 for a more detailed discussion of this topic). It accordingly can be seen that a carefully managed reintegration programme is necessary to aid the transition from custody back to the community.

As well as the work done by probation officers in this regard, one of the valuable projects operated by partner NGOs is one operated by the Irish Association for Social Inclusion Opportunities (IASIO) in the Irish prison system, which is designed to assist the reintegration of offenders. This project, the IASIO Resettlement Service, is a primary needs service that develops with the person a realistic plan that includes the housing, welfare and social aspects of a stable return to their original community or a new one.[32] The Resettlement Service is all the more vital because, as noted previously, homelessness and the provision of suitable accommodation is one of the most frequent difficulties facing those leaving prison and the service providers supporting them on release.[33] The role discharged by the Resettlement Service mirrors the onus in the European rules to 'ensure that on release … prisoners are assisted in finding suitable accommodation and work.'[34]

---

*Penal Reform* (2013) Appendix 5.4, transcript of Lisa Cuthbert's evidence (23 November 2011).

30 Penal Policy Review Group (n 1) 77.

31 Oireachtas Joint Committee on Justice, Defence and Equality, *Report on Penal Reform* (n 29) Appendix 5.25 where the evidence of Judge Michael O'Reilly (1 February 2012) is reproduced.

32 See Irish Prison Service, *Examination of the Sentence Management of People Serving Life Sentences* (2017) 26.

33 See John Costello, Chairman of the Parole Board, Submission to The Oireachtas Sub-Committee on Justice (2012) 9, where a 2010 report by the Irish Penal Reform Trust is quoted. See also Irish Penal Reform Trust. *Progress in the Penal System* (n 28) 81.

34 European Prison Rules 2006, r 33.7.

## Mental Health and Mental Illness in Probation and Parole

Mental health issues, including mental disorder and mental illness can have significant impact on the assessment and case management of those impacted by such issues and who come into contact with the criminal justice system,[35] including those on or being considered for probation or parole. These areas have traditionally been under-researched in the Irish criminal justice context. In particular, studies in Ireland on prevalence of mental health issues in probation populations have been rare. In recent years, progress has been made in terms of relevant Irish research, including in the field of policing[36] and having regard to the prison population,[37] as well as in relation to young people engaging with the justice system.[38] A research report published by the Probation Service recently has been a considerable step forward in bridging that information gap.[39] An earlier article highlighted the prevalence of mental health issues among those under probation supervision and identified implications for practice.[40] More recently still, Brooker (2021) has drawn together a number of research studies — in Ireland and internationally — that have explored the subject of mental health issues among those on probation, something he describes as having been 'the poor relation in probation practice.'[41] Although identifying 'serious gaps in our research knowledge, for example, about effective interventions,' he suggests that 'the last decade has clarified the direction of travel that is required'[42] and concludes that:

> ...there is little evidence for effective interventions in

35 Her Majesty's Inspectorate of Probation, 'A joint thematic inspection of the criminal justice journey for individuals with mental health needs and disorders,' Manchester, (HMIP 2021).

36 Mental Health Commission and An Garda Síochána, 'Report of Joint Working Group on Mental Health Services and the Police 2009,' (Mental Health Commission & An Garda Síochána, 2009).

37 Susan Finnerty, 'Access to Mental Health Services for People in the Criminal Justice System,' (Mental Health Commission, November 2021).

38 Louise Rooney, Deirdre Healy and Fiona McNicholas, 'The Garda Síochána and Child Mental Health,' (Policing Authority, November 2021).

39 Christina Power, *Moving Forward Together: Mental Health Among Persons Supervised by the Probation Service* (Probation Service 2021) available at: http://www.probation.ie/EN/PB/0/0B47AF3EF3D3603D8025868D00349D68/$File/MOVING%20FORWARD%20TOGETHER%2004.03.21.pdf .

40 Christina Power, 'Engaging with Mental Health Challenges in Probation Practice' (2020) 17 Irish Probation Journal 107-127.

41 Charlie Brooker, 'Probation and Mental Health: Do We Really Need Equivalence?' (2021) 18(1) Irish Probation Journal, 7.

42 ibid, 7.

> mental health, suicide prevention or substance misuse for probationers. Clearly this group of people often have complex needs and lead disorganised lives as the prevalence studies show… The role of the Probation Officer with mentally ill people should be clarified urgently. It is clear that the research that exists is but a few faltering steps down a very long road.[43]

In terms of parole practice, the recent Supreme Court case of *M v The Parole Board and the Minister for Justice and Equality*[44] has brought focus to an under-considered area of Irish law and studies the respective roles and functions of the Parole Board and the Mental Health (Criminal Law) Review Board. The Parole Board engages with prisoners serving sentences in Irish prisons. Section 3 of the Criminal Justice Act 1960 allows for temporary release from the Central Mental Hospital (CMH) of 'criminal lunatics' held there. 'Criminal lunatics' are defined as those detained in the CMH 'by warrant, order or direction of the Government' and, if he or she is serving a sentence of imprisonment, whose sentence has not expired.

On occasion, prisoners who have been deemed fit to stand trial and been convicted of an offence have subsequently been transferred from prison to the Central Mental Hospital. These transfers are made pursuant to medical certification that the person is suffering from a mental disorder for which they cannot be afforded appropriate care or treatment within the prison. Once transferred to the Central Mental Hospital, the prisoner is entitled to have their case reviewed every six months by the Review Board, leading to an order directing that the prisoner be transferred back to prison or that the prisoner continue to be detained in the CMH. The Parole Board does not review the cases of prisoners detained in the CMH. Prisoners who are engaged in the parole process and who are subsequently transferred to the CMH have their Parole Board review(s) suspended whilst they are detained in the CMH. The Parole Act 2019 retains this position.

This situation gives rise to a number of practical considerations. The courts in *M v The Parole Board and the Minister for Justice and Equality* considered the issue of whether a person detained in the CMH, whilst serving a sentence, could compel the Interim Parole Board to consider their application for temporary release or parole in the same manner as a prisoner detained in prison. Various arguments were made, including one based on equality and that a prisoner

---

43 ibid, 25.

44 [2020] IESC 24.

detained in the CMH should be treated in the same manner as a prisoner detained in a prison. Further equality arguments were advanced setting out that the Minister and the Interim Parole Board would consider the case of a prisoner receiving medical treatment in a hospital and it was inequitable that they would then refuse to consider the application of a prisoner in the CMH for parole.

The manner in which a prisoner is detained in the CMH is an issue which also received much scrutiny before the Supreme Court in this case. It was argued that the Clinical Director of the CMH has a discretion to grant a programme of leave to a 'patient' in his care but not to a 'prisoner', whose only recourse was to the Review Board process. The Supreme Court however held on this point that there was no distinction between other patients in the CMH and 'transferred prisoners'. It was held that the clinical director of the CMH might consider temporary release to be as appropriate for a transferred prisoner as for a patient and these were matters best left to the judgment of the clinical director, subject to the consent of the Minister. It was accepted however that the powers to grant temporary release to a transferred prisoner could not go beyond limited periods of release before the question of a return to prison would arise in one of the Review Board's regular reviews. It was the view that once a person was well enough not to require in-patient treatment in the CMH then they should be transferred back to prison. Subsequent review and progress towards release should take place pursuant to the Parole Board process.

In this case, in considering the issue of parole, the Supreme Court reaffirmed that the early release of prisoners was an exercise in clemency, which was to be seen as a privilege rather than a right. This approach affords the Minister a very wide discretion. The courts had next to determine whether the Minister had a discretion to consider the applicant for parole, with the argument having been made that even if the Minister had a very wide discretion in the decision they could make, the Minister would be acting in an *ultra vires* fashion if they failed to consider the application as they obviously would not have acted within their discretion. The Supreme Court determined that the Criminal Justice Act 1960, s 2 (as amended) was never intended to apply to prisoners transferred to the CMH and accordingly the Minister did not have a discretion to consider the applicant for parole. Section 24 (7) of the Parole Act 2019 maintains the position that patients transferred to the CMH are not eligible for consideration by the Parole Board.

This will be an evolving area and there are additional factors to consider when the patient transferred to the CMH is a prisoner serving a determinate sentence. Matters likely to create further challenges include the interaction with the Mental Health Act 2001, where on the completion of a sentence a prisoner might be detained in an approved centre/psychiatric facility under the provisions of that Act. Another recent case of *AM v HSE*[45] illustrated the growing importance of this field of law. In that case a prisoner serving a determinate sentence was transferred to the CMH upon diagnosis of a mental illness. Shortly before he was due for release on the expiry of his sentence he was made a Ward of Court for the sole purpose of seeking an order for his continued detention in the CMH because, *inter alia*, there was no other psychiatric treatment facility available that could provide a sufficient level of care and supervision.

## Women Who Offend

Women and girls have always been a minority group in criminal justice systems, which as a result have been designed for men and do not necessarily address women's specific characteristics and corresponding needs.[46] Women may take different 'pathways' into offending than men do. They may also experience greater difficulties in reintegrating in their communities than men in similar contexts.[47] This different treatment has a long history internationally, but also in the Irish context. It is worth noting that the hugely progressive reforms introduced by Sir Walter Crofton applied different rules to male and female prisoners. Men, after passing through the various stages of their sentence, were entitled to release on licence. Women were not entitled to such release on licence as it was considered that they would have no employment opportunities and no prospects, save for 'vice and starvation.'[48] Instead of being given tickets of leave, these female prisoners were sent to either the Sisters of Mercy Refuge at Goldenbridge or the Protestant Refuge at Heytesbury Street, both in Dublin.[49]

---

45 [2019] IESC 3.

46 For example, see Janice Kelly and John Bogue , 'Gender Differences in Criminogenic Needs among Irish Offenders' (2014) 11 Irish Probation Journal 87-102.

47 Jean O'Neill, 'Women's Transitions from Custody in Northern Ireland: Time After Time?' (2017) 14 Irish Probation Journal 112-132.

48 See Tim Carey, *Mountjoy–The Story of a Prison* (Collins Press 2000) 85 which quotes Francis M Taylor, *Irish Homes and Irish Hearts* (UCD Press 2013) 55.

49 Wheatley Balme and others, *Observations on the Treatment of Convicts in Ireland* (Simkin Marshall & Co 1862) 14. See also Directors of Convict Prisons, Third Annual Report of the Directors of Convict Prisons in Ireland for the Year Ended 31 December 1856. (Thom & Sons 1857) 9.

Many such discriminatory practices and policies against women came under greater scrutiny, largely by the requirements of EU (then EEC) membership and judicial activism. The removal of discriminatory treatment against women has however to be balanced with a recognition of the fact that the specific needs and characteristics of women in the criminal justice system are different to the majority of men in the system. This situation was recognised internationally in 2010 when the international community adopted the United Nations Rules for the Treatment of Women Prisoners and Noncustodial Measures for Women Offenders (the Bangkok Rules).[50]

The Bangkok Rules outline the measures needed to ensure gender-sensitive treatment of women both in prison and those under supervision on community sanctions or other non-custodial measures. By encouraging the development and use of genderspecific non-custodial alternatives to imprisonment, the Bangkok Rules recognise that many women who offend do not pose a risk to society and that imprisonment has a disproportionately negative impact on their rehabilitation and their children's lives. It is worth emphasising that treating women differently from their male counterparts is not unfair or discriminatory. In fact, the reverse is true. Women offenders have distinctive needs that must be identified and addressed so that they can receive equitable treatment.

In Ireland the laws in relation to sentencing are gender neutral however the courts have a duty to pass what are appropriate sentences in each case having regard to the particular circumstances of that case – not only in regard to the circumstances of the particular crime but in regard to the particular person who has offended[51] and the relevant personal circumstances of the person being sentenced.[52] In other countries personal circumstances of female offenders that may be taken into account in the sentencing process would include caretaking obligations, pregnancy and circumstances where a woman may be breastfeeding.[53] Pre-sentence

---

[50] The UN Bangkok Rules are available at: https://www.unodc.org/documents/hiv-aids/publications/Prisons_and_other_closed_settings/P_BangkokRules_2010_EN.pdf See also: Penal Reform International's publication – *UN Bangkok Rules on Women Offenders and Prisoners: a short guide*, available at: https://www.penalreform.org/resource/united-nations-bangkok-rules-women-offenders-prisoners-short/ .

[51] Walsh J in *People (Attorney General) v O'Driscoll* (1972) 1 Frewen 351, 359.

[52] *People (DPP) v WC* [1994] 1 ILRM 321, 325.

[53] See Penal Reform International, 'Community service and probation for women: A study in Kenya' for an examination of this issue in the international context.

reports are particularly critical for women offenders, especially those who may be at risk of receiving a custodial sentence, as they reveal the woman's unique individual circumstances and are vital for determining the suitability of a particular sentence. For there to be a full consideration of proportionality in sentencing it is necessary for the sentencing judge to have the fullest possible knowledge and understanding of the personal circumstances of the offender and pre-sentence assessment reports undertaken by probation officers are vital in this regard.[54] The Probation Service and the Irish Prison Service have taken a joint strategic approach to the management of women in their care, including taking a gender-informed approach to female clients, incorporating dedicated resources and programmes.[55] In addition, a number of practitioner pieces in the Irish Probation Journal have reflected on this area of probation work.[56]

## Diversity Issues

Apart from some work by Denis Bracken (in relation to ethnicity),[57] other aspects of diversity have not been considered in any great detail in relation to Irish probation and parole practices. This is a reasonably complex area, as described by Canton and Dominey.[58] Graham and McNeill, in considering diversity issues with respect to the desistance from crime process, have called for greater exploration and understanding of issues associated with:

1. Race and ethnicity,
2. The influences of religion and faith-based groups,
3. Sexuality and gender diversity,
4. Class, power and privilege, and

54 Thomas O'Malley, *Sentencing Law and Practice* ( Thomson Round Hall 2016) 801.

55 Irish Prison Service and Probation Service, 'Joint Probation Service-Irish Prison Service Strategy 2014-2016: An Effective Response to Women Who Offend,' March 2014.

56 Eg Jean O'Neill, 'The Inspire Women's Project: Managing women offenders within the community' (2011) 8(1) Irish Probation Journal 93-108 and 'Women's Transitions from Custody in Northern Ireland – Time After Time?' (2017) 14(1) Irish Probation Journal 112-132.

57 Denis C Bracken, 'Probation Practice with Travellers in the Republic of Ireland' (2014) 11 Irish Probation Journal 44-62; Denis C Bracken, 'Ethnicity, identity and criminal justice,' in Deirdre Healy and others (eds), *The Routledge Handbook of Irish Criminology* (Routledge 2016) 575-592, and Denis Bracken, 'Interactions with the Travelling Community by Prison and Probation Staff' (2020) 17 Irish Probation Journal 238-252.

58 Canton and Dominey (n 7) 51-53.

5. Intersecting issues in health and justice, including the influences of victimisation and trauma,

as these can all impact on desistance processes.[59] Examples of some exceptions to the shortage of consideration of the above include Byrne's discussion of LGBT diversity in probation work,[60] and Alvey's reflections on the issue of ageing prisoners.[61] Nevertheless it is clear that more needs to be done in this area.

## Organised Crime Groups

It is probably safe to say that certain elements and areas of crime and criminality have always been organised, to a greater or lesser extent. The features of such organised crime as we know it in Ireland[62] appear to have developed much more serious, sinister, insidious and pervasive aspects to it in recent decades, particularly since the growth in the levels of drug-related crime, including international trafficking in various illegal substances and the activities of the organised groups or gangs that largely control that trade.[63] In some cases, the work of probation officers, as well as for those working in prisons and managing the parole processes, the aspect of gang affiliation and issues related to inter-gang violence and 'feuding,' as well as what has come to be described as drug-related intimidation, can have a far-reaching impact.[64] One aspect of this impact on probation and parole work for example is where issues of concern arise and have to be managed because probation or parole clients are under threat from rival gangs or individuals. In recent years the Probation Service for example has incorporated assessment of such threats and their implications for client engagement, and related issues, in their assessment and case

[59] Fergus McNeill and Hannah Graham, 'Diversifying desistance research,' in Pamela Ugwudike and others (eds), *The Routledge Companion to Rehabilitative Work in Criminal Justice* (Routledge 2020) 116-124.

[60] Colette Byrne, 'LGBT Diversity: Implications for Probation Practice' (2016) 13 Irish Probation Journal 225-233

[61] Jan Alvey, 'Ageing Prisoners in Ireland: Issues for Probation Practice' (2013) 10 Irish Probation Journal 203-215.

[62] Liz Campbell, 'Organised crime in Ireland,' in Deirdre Healy and others (eds), *The Routledge Handbook of Irish Criminology* (Routledge 2016) 556-574.

[63] Niamh Hourigan, 'Gangs and gang-related activity,' in Deirdre Healy and others (eds), *The Routledge Handbook of Irish Criminology* (Routledge 2016) 144-160.

[64] Brendan Marsh, *The Logic of Violence: An Ethnography of Dublin's Drug Trade* (Routledge 2020); Sarah Jane McCreery, Matthew Bowden, and Marcus Keane, *Debts, threats, distress and hope – towards understanding drug-related intimidation in Dublin's North-East Inner City* (Ana Liffey Drug Project 2020).

management standard operating procedures. Similar steps have been taken by prison and parole authorities.

## Violent Extremism, Radicalisation and Politically Motivated Offending

The issues associated with violent extremism, terrorism and politically motivated offending is far from unknown on the island of Ireland. More recently however, newer aspects or variations on violent extremism has come to preoccupy national governments in Europe and indeed across the world. The United Nations Office on Drugs and Crime (UNODC) have developed what they describe as a 'technical assistance handbook' on the subject.[65] The Council of Europe has developed practice guidelines[66] and a practice handbook[67] for probation and prison services in relation to responding to radicalisation to violent extremism among their respective populations. The challenges and dangers associated with such offending behaviour tends to be quantitatively or numerically small in terms of incidence but represents a potentially hugely significant problem for criminal justice agencies and the wider public. In the Irish context, some commentators have written about the evolution of practice in this area, concluding that while '...the limits of structured assessment approaches to dealing with radicalisation' have been identified, we must instead '...recognise the strengths of existing practice methods of dealing with prisoners and probationers within established criminal justice protocols.'[68] The Department of Justice strategic plan for the joint management of offenders identified the importance of this issue and committed to develop a joint information-sharing protocol and a joint training programme for the relevant agencies, in relation to such offenders.[69]

## Institutionalisation

This issue of institutionalisation has been long-identified in the Irish system. Prison can produce negative, long-lasting change and the more extreme, harsh, dangerous, or otherwise psychologically-

---

65 UNODC, Technical Assistance Handbook on Appropriate Use of Non-Custodial Measures for Terrorism-Related Offences (United Nations 2021)

66 The Council of Europe Guidelines document is available here: https://search.coe.int/cm/pages/result_details.aspx?objectid=09000016805c1a69 .

67 The Council of Europe Handbook is available here: https://search.coe.int/cm/Pages/result_details.aspx?ObjectID=09000016806f4fbd .

68 Orla Lynch, 'Understanding Radicalisation: Implications for Criminal Justice Practitioners' (2017) 14 Irish Probation Journal 78-91.

69 Department of Justice (n 9) 7.

taxing the nature of the confinement, the greater the number of people who will suffer and the deeper the damage that they will incur.[70] It is clear that the psychological effects of incarceration vary from individual to individual with few people being completely unchanged or unscathed by the experience of imprisonment.[71] For some prisoners incarceration is so stark and psychologically painful that it causes a form of traumatic stress reaction once released.[72] It has also been noted that owing to the lengthy and indeterminate nature of their sentence prisoners serving life sentences are the cohort of prisoners most likely to become institutionalised.[73] A major part of the problem of prisoner re-entry into society has been explained as having to cope with the disorganisation they experience when moving from the prison setting, which is highly regimented, to the disorganised outside society, with daily experiences which would be considered to be commonplace by ordinary citizens being completely alien to them.[74] It is recognised that there is a tipping point in some sentences, especially those of a long term nature, where the sentence stops being rehabilitative and starts to become detrimental to the prisoner's psychological well-being. It is important for probation officers and paroling authorities to identify this point in an offender's sentence as it is in society's interest to release a rehabilitated offender from prison rather than one who has been profoundly affected by an excessively long sentence.[75] A significant degree of institutionalisation makes proper integration into the community very difficult and if a prisoner becomes too institutionalised it may become too late to successfully reintegrate them into the community at a later date.[76] The function of the Parole Board in this regard can be identified as recommending releasing prisoners at the optimum time, when they are ready for release,[77] and at a time in their lives when these prisoners would still be capable of independent living in the

---

70 Craig Haney, 'From Prison to Home; The Effect of Incarceration and Re-entry on Children, Families and Communities' delivered at 'The Psychological Impact of Incarceration: Implications for Post-Prison Adjustment' conference, National Institutes of Health Natcher Conference Centre, Bethesda, Maryland, USA (30-31 January 2002), Office of the Assistant Secretary for Planning and Evaluation. http://aspe.hhs.gov/hsp/prison2home02/haney.htm. 15 June 2014.

71 ibid.

72 ibid.

73 Irish Prison Service (n 32) 42.

74 Irwin, *The Warehouse Prison* (n 27) 173.

75 Australian Law Reform Commission, *Same Crime, Same Time: Sentencing of Federal Offenders (ALRC Report 103)* (2006) 5.

76 See John Costello (n 33) 5.

77 Edith N Burleigh, 'The Future of Parole' (1920) 11(1) J American Institute of Crim Law & Criminology 61.

community.[78] It must however be noted that this 'optimum time' for release from the prisoner's point of view will not be the only factor considered by the Parole Board who must also concern themselves with public safety, the appropriate length of sentence to be served in custody and the other factors considered in earlier chapters of this book. In this regard it must be noted that the Parole Board must balance a number of disparate factors in this process.

Like all processes of gradual change, institutionalisation typically occurs in stages and, all other things being equal, the longer someone is incarcerated the more significant the nature of the institutional transformation.[79] The term 'institutionalisation' is used to describe the process by which inmates are shaped and transformed by the institutional environments in which they live and is the shorthand expression for the negative psychological effects of imprisonment.[80]

The process of institutionalisation can be exacerbated in cases in which persons enter institutional settings at either a particularly young or old age, with institutionalisation often proceeding more quickly and with less resistance with these inmates. Individual vulnerability factors which have been found to enhance susceptibility to the development of institutionalisation include compromised cognitive functioning, psychiatric illness, poor coping skills, low self-efficacy and an absence of supportive familial relationships[81] as have traits such as lack of education and illiteracy.[82] Problems with communicating also increase difficulty in adapting to a restrictive environment and have also been found

---

78 Gordon Holmes, 'Address to the Prison Law Seminar – The Parole Process' hosted by the Irish Penal Reform Trust (26 March 2009) 8. Dr Holmes delivered this speech as Chairperson of the Interim Parole Board.

79 Oireachtas Joint Committee on Justice, Defence and Equality (n 29) 21, which states that research recently conducted in Ireland appears to suggest the tipping point where the sentence stops being rehabilitative and starts to become detrimental to the prisoner's psychological well-being is, on average, at the 15-16 year mark in that life sentence prisoners can become institutionalised if they have served 15 or 16 years or more in prison.

80 Australian Law Reform Commission, Same Crime, Same Time: Sentencing of Federal Offenders (ALRC Report 103).

81 Irish Prison Service (n 32) 42.

82 Mark Mongan and Mary Kett, *The Prison Adult Literacy Survey; Results and Implications* (Irish Prison Service 2003) found that 52% of the Irish prison population had literacy levels of one (the lowest level of literacy) compared to 25% of the general population. See also Probation Service, Annual Report (2016) 4, where it is set out that many of the offenders under the supervision of the Probation Service have complex needs such as alcohol or drug problems, literacy issues and social skills deficits.

to place the individual at greater risk of institutionalisation.[83] Furthermore, the longer someone remains in an institution, the greater the likelihood that the process will adversely transform them anyway.[84]

It has been noted that prison life isolates the individual from family and friends and allows little or no scope for 'normal' maturation and growth through the exercise of autonomy and moral responsibility.[85] Losing contact with family, losing employment and social or community services, even for a short period, can have long lasting negative effects.[86] In addition, it has been noted that inmates in prison find their links with people in the free community weakening as the months and years pass by and studies covering a period in excess of a year have shown that as many as forty one percent of prisoners did not receive any visits during that period.[87] This is all the more regrettable as it has been shown that contact with children and families plays a key role in the rehabilitation and desistance process.[88]

It has been noted that in the course of becoming institutionalised, a gradual transformation takes place. The process of institutionalisation can be subtle and difficult to discern as it occurs. Thus, prisoners do not 'choose' to succumb to it or not, and those people who have become institutionalised may not even be aware that it has happened to them. Fewer still consciously decide that they are going to willingly allow the transformation to occur.[89] Institutionalisation in the prison setting can thus be best considered as a psychological adaptation to the unnatural environment in which the prisoner finds themselves on incarceration.[90]

Institutionalisation or 'prisonisation' renders some people so dependent on external constraints that they gradually lose the capacity to rely on internal organisation and self-imposed personal limits to guide their actions and restrain their conduct. Some inmates come to depend heavily on institutional decision-makers

---

83 See Irish Prison Service, *Examination of the Sentence Management* (n 32) 42.

84 See Haney (n 70).

85 Paul O'Mahony, *Criminal Chaos – Seven Crises in Irish Criminal Justice* (Round Hall Sweet & Maxwell 1996) 107.

86 Agnieszka Martynowicz and Martin Quigley, 'It's like stepping on a landmine...' Reintegration of Prisoners in Ireland (Irish Penal Reform Trust 2010) 2.

87 Graham M Sykes, *The Society of Captives – A Study of a Maximum Security Prison* (Princeton Univ Press 2007) 65.

88 Irish Penal Reform Trust (n 28) 6.

89 See Haney (n 70).

90 Martynowicz and Quigley (n86) 9.

to make choices for them and to rely on the structure and schedule of the institution to organise their daily routine. In extreme cases, profoundly institutionalised persons may become extremely uncomfortable when their previous freedom and autonomy is returned.[91] These difficulties in coping with the outside world may, in some instances, manifest itself in the prisoner not wanting to leave the prison.[92] This unwillingness to leave prison has been noted in an international setting where the phenomenon of 'self-sabotage' has been noted, where offenders engage in destructive behaviour, with the motivation frequently being a desire to prolong their period of detention.[93]

The psychological consequences of incarceration may represent significant impediments to post-prison adjustment and may interfere with the transition from prison to home, impede an ex-convict's successful reintegration into a social network and employment setting, and may compromise an incarcerated parent's ability to resume his or her role with family and children.[94]

Internationally, growth in institutionalisation may be connected to trends towards increasingly harsh policies and conditions of confinement in prisons as well as the much discussed de-emphasis on rehabilitation as a goal of incarceration in some jurisdictions.[95] The increase in the prison population in Ireland who are serving life sentences or very long determinate sentences has led to a significant reduction in the opportunities for prisoners to participate in education and work activities as the resources and facilities for such activity have not matched the increase in the prison population.[96] A further feature in modern prisons, including those in Ireland, is increasing degrees of constraints on prisoner movement with many subject to longer lock up times and hundreds of prisoners being kept in their cells for twenty two hours if not the whole day.[97] A

91 See Haney (n 70).

92 See Costello (n 33) 5.

93 Nigel Walker, *Sentencing Theory, Law and Practice* (Butterworths 1985) 211, where examples of such 'self-sabotage' including escapes and attempted escapes of prisoners who are close to their date of release, with the purpose of being apprehended and further detained are noted.

94 See Haney (n 70).

95 See Sykes (n 87) where he states: 'Life in the maximum security prison is depriving or frustrating in the extreme.'

96 Jesuit Centre for Faith and Justice, *The Irish Prison System – Vision, Values, Reality* (2012) 27.

97 ibid 30. It must be acknowledged however that significant progress has been made in reducing the number of prisoners in solitary confinement in Ireland. Between July 2013 and April 2017, the number of prisoners on 22-23 hour lock up fell from 211 people to 44 people – a reduction of 167 or 80%. In 2017 an amendment to the Prison Rules committed to ensuring that every prisoner

significant proportion of those on extended daily lock up are in those conditions because they have identified themselves or been identified by staff as being under threat from others in the prison.

It is also clear that some groups of people are somewhat more vulnerable to the pains of imprisonment than others and that widespread overcrowding has been found to exacerbate this problem by adversely affecting the living conditions in prisons. Notwithstanding reductions in the prison population and the efforts to reduce prison overcrowding, research has shown that the prison population needs to be considerably further reduced to maintain a safe custody limit.[98] Prison overcrowding, where it occurs, also greatly limits prisoner access to meaningful programmes.[99] An additional problem in accessing these programmes, as has been acknowledged by the Irish Prison Service, is that there have been prison school closures and suspension of these vital programmes across the prison estate as a result of prison staff shortages.[100] The availability of such programmes is one of the factors behind a very wide disparity between prisons in the rates of prisoners participating in education.[101] The Irish Prison Service has however acknowledged that prisoners should, to the greatest degree possible, be accommodated with security standards and regimes that are appropriate to their needs, and to the security risks they pose, and should not be subjected to security standards substantially and unnecessarily beyond those needs. The Irish Prison Service has expressed the hope that by applying more appropriate and less restrictive regimes that the damaging effects of institutionalisation will be prevented and normalisation will be promoted.[102]

---

had at least two hours of out of cell time involving meaningful activity. For further see Irish Penal Reform Trust, *Progress in the Penal System* (n 28) 67.

98 See Irish Penal Reform Trust (n 28) 33 where it is stated that the safe custody limit in the Irish prison system is 2,829 prisoners. The prison population around the time of the IPRT publication (on 21 July 2017) was 3,710 prisoners, or 87% of total bed capacity that day. The prison population on 1 December 2021 was 3,808, also reflecting 87% of bed capacity, as assessed by the Irish Prison Service that day.

99 See Haney (n 70).

100 See Irish Penal Reform Trust (n 28) 55.

101 See Dáil Debates Vol 957, No 3, 11 July 2017 – Written Answer of Charles Flanagan TD, Minister for Justice and Equality, to Jonathan O'Brien TD, where it was disclosed that the level of participation in education in Loughan House Prison was 79.5% and Arbour Hill Prison was 64% of the prisoners whilst it was as low as 22% in Cloverhill Prison and 23.9% in Wheatfield Place of Detention.

102 Irish Prison Service, Capital Strategy 2016 -2021 (2016) 21. This document is available at Irish Prison Service. http://www.irishprisons.ie/wp-content/uploads/documents_pdf/capital_strategy_2016.pdf. 7 November 2021.

## Offenders Who Maintain their Innocence

Those who have been convicted by a criminal court yet who deny their guilt have traditionally presented challenges when it comes to the involvement of probation or parole services. A major part of the probation system's approach in Ireland is premised on the foundation that probation officers work with those who have been convicted and who accept their guilt. A very high percentage of those appearing before the District Court, and particularly among those where the facts are proven, plead guilty anyway and so the issue of denial of guilt arises in a tiny proportion of cases coming to the Probation Service's attention. In a small number of cases, persons who may even have pleaded guilty at first subsequently decide to appeal their conviction. Either way, a probation officer attempting to engage with such a person will likely struggle to establish and maintain a 'normal' probation officer — client relationship in such circumstances. It should be noted though, that in more recent years, probation officers have begun to work with individuals who have not been referred to them following conviction for an identified offence. Such probation involvement may be in the context of specialised programmes such as the Joint Agency Response to Crime (JARC – see above), or in special individual circumstances where either 'voluntary' supervision (see Chapter 4 – Probation Work for more on this) is warranted, in the interest of public safety or having regard to significant needs of an individual service user. The situation regarding challenges posed by those who deny their guilt is probably even more pronounced when it comes to parole.

In the period 2011-2013 the Interim Parole Board reviewed the cases of 255 offenders. In the 83 cases where sentencing was at the discretion of the sentencing judge 82% pleaded guilty whereas of the 172 reviews involving a mandatory life sentence for murder a mere 24% pleaded guilty,[103] it being noted that this discrepancy may be due to the mandatory nature of the life sentence where there is no incentive for a person charged with murder to plead guilty.[104] The vast majority of those that are convicted after a 'not guilty' plea subsequently accept their guilt on conviction and engage

---

103 Parole Board, Annual Report (2013) 5. See also Diarmuid Griffin, *Killing Time: Life Imprisonment and Parole in Ireland* (Palgrave Macmillan 2018) 46, where the 2014 figures for murder convictions are quoted with there being 19 murder convictions for that year, 16 of which were following contested trial by jury with only 3 defendants pleading guilty. During the same year 92% of convictions on indictment followed a plea of guilty with only 3% of cases being a result of conviction by jury.

104 See Griffin, *Killing Time* (n 103) 47.

with the appropriate therapeutic services in prison. However, a certain number of people continue to maintain their innocence throughout their sentence. Of the 255 cases considered by the Interim Parole Board in the 2011-2013 period 145 had pleaded not guilty at their trial but a mere 16 of these offenders had not accepted responsibility for the crime of which they were convicted to the therapeutic services in prison when their case was being reviewed by the Interim Parole Board.[105]

In light of parole's roots in the rehabilitative ideal of punishment, it should come as no surprise that words and acts associated with rehabilitation — acceptance of responsibility, remorse and repentance — linger as fixtures in the contemporary parole evaluation process.[106] There is no rule or policy which automatically prevents the Parole Board recommending release in the case of a prisoner who maintains their innocence but the Board takes as their starting position the assumption that the prisoner was rightly convicted.[107] It is not the function of the Board to investigate possible miscarriages of justice or to raise any misgivings they have about the correctness of a conviction.[108] Research in England and Wales has shown that a prisoner's acceptance of responsibility is vital to their prospects for an affirmative parole decision.[109] In some jurisdictions complete acceptance of responsibility for the crime is viewed as a mitigating factor whilst denial of responsibility or minimisation is viewed as an aggravating factor in considering parole.[110] Accordingly, an incentive exists for all prisoners facing parole boards to admit guilt and apologise for the crime in order to maximise their chances for release, irrespective of their true feelings or culpability.[111] In circumstances where proclaiming innocence at a parole hearing typically harms one's case and admitting guilt can serve as a mitigating factor, there is evidence of even innocent prisoners surrendering to the lure of admitting guilt before a parole

---

105 Parole Board, *Annual Report* (2013) 5.

106 Daniel S Medwed, 'The Innocent Prisoner's Dilemma: Consequences of Failing to Admit Guilt at Parole Hearings' (2008) 93(491) Iowa Law Review 513.

107 Northern Ireland Parole Commissioners, *Parole Commissioners for Northern Ireland Handbook – A Guide for Parole Commissioners* (Undated) 71. See also ibid 115.

108 Ibid 115. See also *R (on the application of Hepworth and others) v Secretary of State for the Home Department* [1997] EWHC 324 (Admin). For a discussion on the Irish position in this regard see Griffin (n 103) 129.

109 Medwed (n 106) 514 where it is quoted in England and Wales that in twenty four per cent of cases where prisoners maintained their innocence parole was granted as compared with fifty one per cent of all applications granted.

110 ibid 515.

111 ibid 516.

board to boost the odds of obtaining a recommendation for a grant of parole.[112]

This intense pressure to comply and admit guilt is despite the fact that denial of guilt in itself does not indicate an increase in risk above that which would be present for a prisoner who admits their offence.[113] Paradoxically, denial of guilt is deemed to lead to a high risk of reoffending/harm status as these prisoners are deemed to be in denial however in relation to the specific issue of the validity of denial as a measure of risk it has been noted that this contention is based purely on clinical judgement rather than any scientifically founded measure of risk.[114] The problem posed by someone's denial is that it may be harder to form a proper assessment of the factors contributing to their offending and so there may be less certainty about the level of their risk and the extent to which it has been reduced during their sentence.[115]

Prisoners who maintain their innocence present particular problems for the criminal justice system. They frequently refuse to engage in offence-related work claiming that to do so would be admitting their guilt,[116] or are often precluded from engaging in such work due to their maintenance of innocence[117] as many such programmes depend on an offender being willing to discuss their offences.[118] Admission of guilt, however, is a prerequisite for admission to many courses addressing serious crime, such as violence or sex offending and accordingly maintaining a 'not guilty' stance frequently prohibits prisoners partaking in these courses as they are deemed unable or unwilling to give a full and frank account of the crime.[119] Such a policy stance was taken for some time in the context of programmes offered to those serving custodial sentences for sexual offences in Ireland.[120] More recently,

---

112 ibid 524. See also *State v Goodman* 763 P2d, 786, 786 (Utah 1988).

113 See Association of Prison Lawyers (APL) and Progressing Prisoners Maintaining Innocence (PPMI) conference 'The Dilemma of Maintaining Innocence' (25 January 2011). See also Griffin (n 103) 130 where it is noted that targeting the capacity for empathy has been identified as important for treatment, particularly for sex offenders.

114 See Medwed (n 106) 514.

115 Her Majesty's Prison Service, *Instruction Manual, PSI 36/2010* (2 July 2010) 199.

116 Hamish Arnott and Simon Creighton, *Parole Board Hearings – Law and Practice* (Legal Action Group 2010) 71.

117 Association of Prison Lawyers (APL) & Progressing Prisoners Maintaining Innocence (PPMI), 'The Dilemma of Maintaining Innocence', Conference (25 January 2011).

118 Her Majesty's Prison Service (n 115) 199.

119 APL & PPMI conference 'The Dilemma of Maintaining Innocence' (n 117).

120 Irish Prison Service, 'Sex Offender Management Policy: Reducing Re-offending, Enhancing Public Safety,' 22 April 2009; and Joint policy statement, 'The

there have been changes in approach, with a view to engaging those who deny responsibility for sexual offending convictions in bespoke treatment programmes.[121]

The application of this rule requiring admission of guilt made the victims of some high profile miscarriages of justice such as those involving The Birmingham Six, The Guildford Four as well as others ineligible for parole, due to their unwillingness to accept their supposed guilt for these crimes.[122] However, in England and Wales prisoners convicted of murder who consider that a manslaughter conviction was more appropriate are not inevitably precluded by the Probation Service there from attending certain offence-related courses.[123] In addition, it should be noted that not all rehabilitative courses within prisons are dependent on a prisoner admitting guilt for a particular offence, for example drug and alcohol treatment courses.[124]

The English Courts have held that their Parole Board acted unlawfully in refusing parole in cases where the denial of guilt was the primary reason for refusing parole or because of factors that flow directly from that stance such as an inability to undertake certain offence related programmes.[125] In such cases the reasons for refusal for parole must focus on the presence of risk factors and not founded solely on denial.[126] A prisoner's current level of risk must be the pre-eminent factor in determining whether that person is ready to progress to be released – protestation of innocence or denial of guilt is only one element to be taken into account in reaching the release decision.[127] The main considerations applied in such cases were summarised in the case of *R (on the application of Hepworth and others) v Secretary of State for the Home Department*[128]

---

Integrated Treatment and Management of those Convicted of Sexual Violence, Irish Prison Service, Probation Service, Department of Justice and Equality, 2016, available at: http://www.irishprisons.ie/wp-content/uploads/documents_pdf/sex_offender_management_may2016.pdf (accessed on 2 December 2021).

121 Conor Gallagher, 'Sex offenders denying guilt to be allowed on treatment programme, Irish Times, 23 September 2019, available at: https://www.irishtimes.com/news/crime-and-law/sex-offenders-denying-guilt-to-be-allowed-on-treatment-programme-1.4026509, accessed on 2 December 2021.

122 Medwed (n 106) 514.

123 Arnott and Creighton (n 116) 71.

124 ibid 71.

125 *R v Parole Board and Secretary of State for the Home Department ex parte Oyston* [1999] EWHC Admin 750; [2001] 1 PLR 45.

126 *R (Osborne) v Governor of HMP Littlehey* [2010] EWHC 1277 (Admin). See also Northern Ireland Parole Commissioners, Parole Commissioners for Northern Ireland Handbook, 71.

127 See Her Majesty's Prison Service (n 115) 200.

128 [1997] EWHC 324 (Admin).

when Laws J decided that each case should be dealt with on its own particular facts however in the majority of cases a prisoner should not be denied parole merely because of their attitude towards the offence.[129]

In cases where the applicant for parole continues to deny their guilt for the offence for which they were convicted it has been held as essential to look for evidence that risk may have been reduced for reasons other than formal programme work, such as impact of the prison sentence, genuine motivation to change, commitment to change lifestyle, positive effect of release plan etc. Other factors may also lead the Parole Board to conclude the risk to the public is acceptably small such as ill-health, incapacitation or genuine religious conversion (which may of course in itself be difficult to assess).[130] As previously stated, the Interim Parole Board have stated that the safety of the public is the essential consideration in all parole release decisions and in making these decisions all factors must be considered including any material factors in any reports which suggest that the risk to the public has been reduced.[131]

Denial of the offence appears to have an impact on a parole board's assessment of risk with a recent survey by the Parole Board of England and Wales showing that 31% of those maintaining innocence were released on parole or life licence as compared with 46% of all prisoners.[132] It is worthy of consideration to examine whether there is any logic or merit in the Parole Board of England and Wales maintaining their position of apparently treating those who deny their involvement in a crime differently from those who accept their guilt. In 2002 a study of 144 inmates convicted of sex offences in England determined that whereas offenders perceived to be 'in denial' by the Parole Board (about one third of the sample) were much more likely to be rated as 'high risk' than those who accepted responsibility for their offence, only one of those 'high risk

---

[129] ibid.

[130] See Her Majesty's Prison Service (n 115) 201.

[131] *R v Parole Board and Secretary of State for the Home Department ex parte Oyston* (n 125).

[132] Parole Board of England and Wales, 'Denial of Guilt and The Parole Board' (Press Release 17 January 2002) available at www.mojuk.org.uk/bulletins/paroleboard.html. 7 November 2021. See also Anita Bromley, 'After Stephen Downing, further questionable cases' (The Guardian 21 January 2002) https://www.theguardian.com/theguardian/2002/jan/21/guardianletters2. 7 November 2021 which states that these figures are misleading as the prisoners 'in denial' who subsequently obtain parole are mainly prisoners serving determinate sentences as opposed to prisoners serving indeterminate sentences.

deniers' was subsequently reconvicted of a sex crime, as compared with seventeen of the ninety six 'non-deniers'.[133]

In Ireland there is no rule or policy that automatically precludes the granting of parole to a prisoner who denies responsibility for the offence in respect of which they were convicted. However, similarly to the position in England and Wales, it is acknowledged that these prisoners present particular challenges in that they will often not engage in offence-related work as they feel to do so might be deemed to be admitting guilt. In addition, some prisoners who refuse to accept their guilt are simply precluded from participating in some rehabilitative courses.[134] The Interim Parole Board in Ireland has stated that prisoners in this situation may be delayed in obtaining parole as a result of failure to address risk factors as opposed to their denial of guilt.[135]

## Conclusion

The foregoing chapter serves to highlight the complex nature of the factors contributing to crime and offending, the additional challenges involved in probation and parole work, as well as the need for a 'joined-up' response to the relevant issues, if the State is to be as collectively effective as possible in reducing offending and victimisation, creating safer and more just communities, and making good — for the benefit of all stakeholders — the harm caused by crime. It also behoves those working in probation and parole to appreciate the complexity of the issues and challenges facing those with whom they work and to realise that in a context where people are individually unique, that even where they may be organisationally classified as belonging to a particular category of individual, that indeed one size does not fit all as regards how we respond to them in practice.

133 Medwed (n 106) 537.

134 *R (on the application of Hepworth and others) v Secretary of State for the Home Department* (n 128).

135 See Parole Board, *The Parole Board – Handbook for Members* (undated).

# INDEX